D0849809

Press,
Platform,
Pulpit

Press, Platform, Pulpit

Black Feminist Publics in the Era of Reform

Teresa Zackodnik

The University of Tennessee Press / Knoxville

Library of Congress Cataloging-in-Publication Data

Zackodnik, Teresa C.
Press, platform, pulpit: Black feminist publics in the era of reform / Teresa Zackodnik.
   p. cm.
Includes bibliographical references and index.

ISBN-13: 978-1-57233-826-5 (alk. paper)
ISBN-10: 1-57233-826-1 (alk. paper)

  1. Feminism—United States—History—19th century.
  2. African American feminists—History—19th century.
  3. African American social reformers—History—19th century.
  4. African American clergy—History—19th century.
  I. Title.

HQ1423.Z33 2011
305.48'896073009034—dc23
2011021560

For Ailsa Brazeau,
whose hero is Rosa Parks

Contents

Illustrations

Acknowledgments

My seven-year-old daughter recently declared, though I need no reminding, that "an important history" is represented in this book. She's right, of course. And I'm mindful that it marks, inevitably, only a partial sense of the astonishing work these women undertook, just as I'm mindful that there were so many more women laboring for black feminist causes at this time about whom we know little or nothing. Yet learning what I have been able to about the work of early black feminists and their context has been a fascinating process and a rich pleasure for which I am grateful; I can't imagine any other work being as interesting or as sustaining over a number of years as this was.

Like any book, this one owes many thanks and carries many debts, the largest of which is to those African American women who risked so much to keep "the colored woman" at the center of reform debates in the nineteenth century. Their work was essential to the well being of black communities, specifically, and of the country more generally, in ways that reach beyond their own moment and into ours. We would know little of their labors were it not for the recovery work undertaken over the past several decades, scholarship that paves the way for and enables further studies like this one that begin to question the historiographies created from that recovered material and begin to look anew at figures we have known for some time alongside those who are new to us. Without the formidable scholarship on the black church, abolition, woman's rights, suffrage, anti-lynching, and the black press, studies like this are not possible.

This book and the archival research undertaken for it were funded by a research grant from the Social Sciences and Humanities Research Council of Canada (SSHRC). SSHRC funded the research assistance of several people who made the project possible, and I am grateful as well to the Department of English and Film Studies at the University of Alberta for also providing essential research assistance for this project. For their research skills, I thank Jackie Baker, Michael Borshuk, Mridula Chakraborty, Karen Engle, Heather Kitteringham, Ross Langager, Christie Schultz, and Vivian Zenari. Finally, the University of Alberta's Faculty of Arts Undergraduate Research Scholarship enabled me to work with Sara Ghebremusse on her research interests in African American women journalists, which also benefited the project. I am grateful to several chairs of my department for their support as this project developed: Jo-Ann Wallace, Garrett Epp, and Susan Hamilton. The University of Alberta's Interlibrary Loan office was patient and diligent in tracking down many key documents. The assistance of the following libraries, museums, and societies was essential: the Ontario Black History Society, the University of Chicago's Department of Special Collections, the Peabody Essex Museum, the British Library's Newspaper Library at Colindale, the Boston Public Library's Rare Books Department, the Irish National Library in Dublin, the Schomburg Center's Rare Book and Manuscript Division and Newspaper Collection, and the Amistad Research Center at Tulane University. I am also indebted to the archives and collections, as well as their staff, that granted me permission to reproduce photographs, which include Ellen Sandberg at the Granger Collection in New York, the Library of Congress, Mike Millner at the University of North Carolina, the National Archives of Canada, and the Peabody Essex Museum.

Working with Scot Danforth, Kerry Webb, Stan Ivester at University of Tennessee Press has been a pleasure. I thank Karin Kaufman for copy editing of the manuscript. I am very grateful for the work of the anonymous reviewers the press secured, whose critique improved this book significantly. I have presented or published parts of many of these chapters as they were developing, and I am grateful for the feedback that generated. Parts of chapter 3 appeared as "'I don't know how you will feel when I get through': Racial Difference, Symbolic Value and Sojourner Truth," *Feminist Studies* 30.1 (Spring 2004): 49–73; parts of chapter 4 as "Ida B. Wells and 'American Atrocities' in Britain," *Women's Studies International Forum* 28.4 (Summer 2005): 259–73; and parts of the conclusion as "Reaching Toward a Coalitional Feminism? Anna Julia Cooper's 'Woman versus the Indian,'" *Indigenous Women and Feminism: Culture, Activism, Politics,* edited by Cheryl Suzack, Shari Hundorf, Jeanne Perreault, and Jean Barman (Vancouver: U of British Columbia P, 2010). Finally, I am grateful for the thinking prompted by my students in courses on African American women's writing and oratory over the years.

I doubt I would have finished this book without the support and unflagging energy to read and respond to my work that my writing group demonstrated time and again. My deep gratitude goes to Lesley Cormack, Sara Dorow, Judy Garber, Susan Hamilton, Lois Harder, Daphne Read, and

Susan Smith. To my good friends who cared that this left my desktop and who will help me celebrate that it has, my heartfelt thanks: Katherine Binhammer, Gail Corning, Corinne Harol, and Cheryl Suzack. If Steven Kruger had not encouraged me to apply for grant funding way back when, and if he and Glenn Burger hadn't offered me their sofa in Queens, this book wouldn't be out there in the world. They also bolstered me, in their quiet and sure ways, when I felt it might never be. I'm grateful to say their friendship continues to be a gift. To my dearest friend, Susan Hamilton, I owe so much more than is spoken, but I trust she knows my heart. She is an inspiration by example in so many ways and the kind of friend one hopes to have pass into one's life; that she has is my great fortune.

My daughter was born as I was beginning this project, and so I cannot think of this book without thinking of her. She has made many things possible and is my joy and delight all in one. My partner, Rob Brazeau, held us together when I was sick near the end of this project and brings much laughter into our house and my inbox. Together, they bring me a clarity and grounding that makes it all fall into place.

Introduction

Going Public: African American Feminism in the Era of Reform

On October 1, 1858, William Hayward wrote William Lloyd Garrison at *The Liberator* from Silver Lake, Indiana, to tell of Sojourner Truth's handling of a rather outrageous challenge at one of her antislavery meetings in the north of that state. An activist for abolition, woman's rights, universal suffrage, and the rights of freed and working-class African Americans, Truth was regarded as an electrifying speaker during a career in reform politics that spanned three decades. By the late 1850s, she was so well known that she was able to convene her own series of meetings. As Hayward makes clear, Truth was a sufficiently formidable threat to proslavery interests that they attempted to discredit her and end her tour of the area. "The border-ruffian Democracy of Indiana . . . appear to be jealous and suspicious of every anti-slavery movement. A rumor was immediately circulated that Sojourner was an impostor; that she was, indeed, a man disguised in women's clothing. It appears, too, from what has since transpired, that they suspected her to be a mercenary hireling of the Republican party," wrote Hayward. "At her third appointed meeting in this vicinity . . . a large number of democrats and other pro-slavery persons were present. At the close of the meeting, Dr. T. W. Strain, the mouthpiece of the slave Democracy . . . stated that . . . [he] believed the speaker to be a man. The doctor also . . . now demanded that Sojourner submit her breast to the inspection of some of the ladies present, that the doubt might be removed by their testimony" (Gilbert and Titus 137–38). As one might expect, an "uproar ensued," which Truth quickly calmed by asking Strain why he suspected she was a man. Strain's response registers the well-established prohibition against women speaking in public. Yet it also importantly underscores that "woman" and "slave" were mutually exclusive categories to many white Americans at mid-century, be they pro- or antislavery: "'Your voice is not the voice of a woman, it is the voice of a man, and we believe you are a man'" (Gilbert and Titus 138). Notably, in this account Truth does not simply claim to be a woman but claims an experience that denied her the mid-century hallmark of femininity: motherhood. "Sojourner told them that her breasts had suckled many a white babe, to the exclusion of her own offspring; that some of those white babies had grown to man's estate; that, although they had sucked her colored breasts, they were, in her estimation, far more manly than they (her persecutors) appeared to be; and she quietly asked them, as she disrobed her bosom, if they, too, wished to suck!" Then, in a powerful gesture, Truth "told them that she would show her breast to the whole congregation; that it was not to her shame that she uncovered her breast before them, but to their shame. . . . Sojourner exposed her naked breast to the audience" (Gilbert and Titus 139).

Yet Truth's reported presentation of herself as once having been a wet nurse while enslaved is as interesting as Strain's accusation that she was an impostor. Truth's response—both her words and actions as recalled by Hayward—raises the possibility that she recognized and had come to turn to her advantage such a moment of coerced embodiment. Indeed, Truth is arguably most famous for two speeches in which she is reported to have given a sort of "bodily testimony": her 1851 Akron, Ohio, speech and this address at Silver Lake seven years later.[1] In what has become a rather mythic incident in accounts of Sojourner Truth's life and work, one on par with her arm-baring "A'n't I a Woman?" speech, Truth gains a certain rhetorical force for her argument at Silver Lake by symbolizing a slave "type" that by 1858 was a convention with some currency on the antislavery lecture circuit. In her acclaimed biography of Truth, Nell Irvin Painter argues that it is unlikely Truth ever nursed a white child: "As a young woman she lived with the Dumonts, whose daughter was not much younger than she. Wet nursing by slaves was far more prevalent in the plantation South than Dutch New York." She goes on to contend that at this time, Truth's appearance as a former slave connoted for her northern, white reformer audience a southern rather than northern setting and set of experiences (Painter, *Sojourner* 141). Even though Painter argues that "[a]s an authentic representative of slavery, Truth . . . was refashioning herself as a Southerner," how much Truth may have played to and capitalized on such expectations is difficult to determine.[2] Yet it is significant that her "defence" against Strain's accusation, that her "voice is not the voice of a woman, it is the voice of a man, and we believe you are a man" (Gilbert and Titus 138), is not to stress her femininity but to present herself as a "type," the mammy or wet nurse of the South. At Silver Lake, Truth does not invoke notions of decorum or propriety as conventional codes of femininity to which she should, rightly, have access, though she is represented as doing so in Frances Dana Gage's version of her "A'n't I a Woman?" speech, which I will examine in chapter 3. At Akron, Gage "recalls" her as bemoaning the fact that "[n]obody eber helps me into carriages, or ober mud-puddles, or gibs me my best place" (Gage, "Reminiscences" 1: 116).

It is almost as if Truth strategically ignored Strain's challenge that she was more believable as a man and instead took up his suspicion of her as an "impostor" on the grounds of her believability as *both* a former slave and a woman. According to this report, Truth foregrounds an economy of race, gender, property, and labor in which "the breast" as bodily evidence of her identity as woman is, in fact, impossible evidence to give. Rather, she is said to expose her "colored breast" and thereby testify to the mutual exclusion of "slave" and "woman" as identities she can claim, presenting her breast as the tool of a maternal labor enforced so that the white woman, not the slave, can prove herself to be "womanly." Even as she does so, Truth chastises her audience for their lack of "shame," a shame they would only feel were they to take her as a woman forced to disrobe on the platform and not a slave. That they lack it, implies Truth, reveals their inability to conceive of her as a woman and, by extension, the impossibility of black femininity for mid-nineteenth-century white Americans. As Xiomara Santamarina has argued, one of the great challenges Sojourner Truth posed to her audiences and those who represented her in the press was her "insistent valuing of her enslaved labor and the moral agency she attributed to that labor" (37). Even as she may have retrospectively recast the parameters of her labor while a slave, she nonetheless asserted time and again the validity and moral authority of enslaved and working women's labor and the material conditions of their lived experience through strategic references to her own.

According to Hayward, Truth easily and spectacularly silenced Strain and his Democrat meddlers, managing a moment of coerced embodiment so that it served her purposes. His letter closed tongue-in-cheek: "I heard a democrat say, as we were returning home from meeting, that Dr. Strain had, previous to the examination, offered to bet forty dollars that Sojourner was a man! So much for the physiological acumen of a western physician" (Gilbert and Titus 139).

Truth's Silver Lake appearance raises a number of issues key to understanding early African American feminism. Perhaps the most obvious is what we might call a politics of embodiment facing African American women, a politics with both a history and a contemporary resonance. African American women who chose to address the public necessarily worked to create a space from which to speak between the poles of a Victorian womanhood based upon the self-effacing female body and the mythic black female body constructed as available and on display. Within the abolitionist movement that politics was further heightened by the demand for the "truth" of slavery and slave experience that the black body was believed to convey. It is significant that Truth reportedly chose to respond to the accusation that her "voice is not the voice of a woman, it is the voice of a man, and we believe you are a man" by baring her breast and presenting herself as a slave. Truth's actions highlighted a personal and collective reality for African American women at that time—their circulation in an American cultural imaginary as sexualized and hence inviolable, as denied the privacy of womanhood and so open to display, scrutiny, and ridicule. For Truth's audience, perhaps including the abolitionist William Hayward, "slave" and "woman" were mutually exclusive identities. To claim to be both and to do so as the basis of one's authority to address an audience was to be, as Strain protested, an "impostor."

That either/or position—slave or woman—exemplified in Strain's accusation and ultimately challenged even as it was enacted in Truth's reported response is as much a defining aspect of early African American feminism as Sojourner Truth has come to be herself. This study examines the ways in which early black feminists repeatedly negotiated a politics of embodiment informing public perceptions of "blackness" and womanhood in the wider U.S. imaginary as they labored in the public sphere to effect political transformation, whether it was the materiality of the black female body in a discourse of democratic citizenship premised on the priority of interiority and the soul, the violent embodiment of African Americans that was a prime driver in abolitionist politics and later central to the highly visual politics of lynching, the use of black women as a proxy to voice white women's concerns over bodily integrity in woman's rights discourse, or the disciplining of laboring black women as morally unruly in a politics of respectability serving racial uplift, black nationalism, and white philanthropy. Despite that repeated negotiation by so many early black feminists, Sojourner Truth remains, for many people, *the* African American feminist, both the most distinctive and one of the very few nineteenth-century black feminists of whom they are aware. Yet Truth was neither the first nor the only African American woman to challenge her audiences to see the interimplications of race, gender, and class. She was not unique in addressing a variety of publics ranging from those she reached as an itinerant preacher, as an antislavery lecturer, as a reformer active in the woman's rights movement, to those publics interested in temperance, in black civil rights agitation, and in the freedmen following the Civil War. Truth was neither the first nor only African American feminist to manage the competing interests of the reform networks in which she was active. She was also not the first to challenge leaders within black public politics and the roles they imagined women should fill. For some an important contemporary, for others a foremother, Sojourner Truth was one of a significant number of African American feminists who were reaching critical mass during a century that would end with the proclamation that "woman's era" was just beginning. In fact, "woman's era" was well underway and had been for some time, as African American women sought not to achieve a public voice for the first time near the end of the nineteenth century but to maintain it.[3]

Yet even as the study of "first-wave" black feminism has continued to develop and turned to examine the roots of the first wave earlier in the nineteenth century, there persists a perception that black feminism is "visible" or emerges into public politics at the century's close with the development of the national black women's club movement. Those black feminists active earlier in the nineteenth century tend then to be positioned as foremothers to black feminist organizing at the turn into the twentieth century rather than recognized as at the center of significant black feminist organizing in their own moment. Far from ignoring developments in black feminism earlier in the century, new scholarship nonetheless tends to place a particular stress upon the achievements of a "public" face for its politics come the 1890s.[4] This study argues that black feminism neither emerged into public nor reached its peak at the end of the nineteenth century, nor was early black feminism marginal to, or effectively marginalized by, the publics it addressed. Where we look for black feminist work and how we construct its relationship to a wider political culture will create very different understandings of both its aims and accomplishments, as this study shows. A number of historians and literary critics have produced groundbreaking scholarly studies of early African American feminist politics and black women's political culture focused on particular movements such as abolition, the Black Baptist Women's Convention, suffrage, the black women's club movement and organized reform, and, more broadly, the "woman question" in black political culture.[5] Scholars also have worked to draw together a variety of political organizations and discourses in which black women participated by focusing on particular regions of the country and offering us a thick reading of that context and location for black feminisms.[6] Much work that established the field, and recent work that has continued the deepening of our understanding of early black feminist politics, has offered us rich readings of its greats, such as Sojourner Truth, Frances Harper, Ida B. Wells-Barnett, Mary Church Terrell, Maria Stewart, and Mary Ann Shadd Cary.[7] We are now, thanks to such essential scholarship, able to question what narratives of black feminism we have established with the critical lenses we have thus far employed, and why these "greats" have achieved that status in the field's historiography. How might we achieve new understandings of early black feminism, of both its central figures and lesser-known women, by working to place black feminists in a complex context and examining how they actively created publics for their politics?[8] Might we shift and deepen our understanding of early black feminism—its position in reform and its varied publics—if we were to consider these activists as central rather than marginal to the politics of their day or as part of a significant critical mass of black feminists rather than preparatory to such an achievement, as they have tended to be positioned within extant historiographies of black feminism?

Press, Platform, Pulpit is not, primarily, a work of recovery but one of re-vision. This study examines anew, with detailed attention to the particular political context in which these women worked at key moments, some of early black feminism's major figures in order to further complicate existing understandings of their political work. In doing so, I pursue a thick reading of the arguments black feminists forwarded at particularly crucial moments as well as those with which they contended. That reading is necessarily grounded in a sense of what appeals are possible, where they can be forwarded, and what black feminist traditions inform them. Yet in seeking to highlight a critical mass of black feminism in the era of reform that informed the work of women largely understood as singular or "firsts" of their kind, I also examine lesser-known figures who were active in shaping that critical mass and who form, with those major figures, a black feminist political culture that was multiply located and had such impact upon its publics that, at times, it caused deep anxiety over calls for change. To do so, I have attended to women little heard of, such as preachers and evangelists Aunt Dinah, Julia Pell, Chloe Spear, and Annie Brown; or work that has received little critical attention, such as that undertaken by Ellen Craft, Sarah Parker Remond, and Ida B. Wells in the United Kingdom. I also have endeavored to shift the way in which well-known figures have been understood, considering Maria Stewart primarily as a journalist rather than an orator, Sarah Mapps Douglass as a feminist black nationalist rather than an abolitionist, or women such as Gertrude Mossell,

Virginia Earle Matthews, and Josephine Silone-Yates first as journalists rather than club women. My goal has been to focus on how black feminists worked in very different locations, particularly how they appealed to varied audiences as they shaped existing reform discourses and demanded a hearing for African Americans generally and African American women specifically. Overall, I ask how our understanding of black feminism changes if we understand black women not as absent from but as participating in the public sphere, and if we understand early black feminists as having achieved their own national, indeed, international visibility before the turn into the twentieth century.

Press, Platform, Pulpit thus is indebted to a generation of scholarship, much of which focused on the importance of the club movement to black feminism at the turn into the twentieth century, and joins a still-developing dialogue that argues for a longer historical reach for black feminism, one that understands black feminism as far from only visible in the national organizations of the club and anti-lynching movements at the turn into the twentieth century.[9] Expanding our understanding of early black feminists' participation in the various reforms of their day, as well as furthering our knowledge of the competing pressures these women negotiated, can enable new understandings of established early black feminists and the significance of lesser-known figures to emerge as we examine the building of black feminist publics. Black feminists were active in the central reform movements shaping American public politics at this time, developing from the religious fervor of the Second Great Awakening, in which black women preached and evangelized, to abolition, woman's rights and suffrage, and the struggle for black civil rights. Within what came to be interconnected publics and reforms, black feminism developed its politics and forms of address from at least as early as 1808 in the preaching of women such as Old Elizabeth. The varied manifestations of that early black feminist voice, the publics black feminists not only addressed but actively created, and the distinctive challenges they rose to time after time is the subject of this book.

Early black feminism's rich complexity in its locations, arguments, and rhetorics are evident across the chapters that follow. African American women established female benevolent and literary societies, voiced their views on emigration and colonization at public meetings and in the press, and contested intimidation tactics such as rape and lynching in their writings and in the lecture tours they mounted to draw national and international attention to such atrocities. African American women also negotiated competing and often conflicting demands within interracial reform movements like abolition, woman's rights, and temperance, as well as within organizations such as the black church. At times those competing and conflicting demands cohered around racial difference in white-dominated reform movements, but at other times they resulted from the need to make black women's concerns heard within black public politics and social institutions. At still other times black feminists pursued class-based arguments that were central to their larger politic, which held African American community concerns to be an integral element of their feminism; those arguments could produce liberatory rhetorics but they could also be exclusive and vilify working women in order to make a case for the voice of middle-class black women in the public sphere. Early black feminisms were far from monolithic, and the politics black feminists pursued were as varied as the publics who heard them. African American feminists pursued varied rhetorics, ranging from advocating a domestic and maternal feminism to arguing for ecstatic worship practices that were being banned by "reforming" churches and promoting the black nationalist principles of communal unity and economic self-sufficiency. Early black feminists were also keenly attuned to opening useful venues to black feminist voices, from the pulpit and platform to the press, and urged the women who followed them to continue this important work. The spaces of early black feminism ranged from the camp meetings of the Second Great Awakening to wagon pulpits, from the abolitionist platforms of organized antislavery lecture tours to tent gatherings and addresses in black churches, from organized reform circuits in the Northeast to dangerous and covert addresses to slaves and free people of color in the South, from local appearances to transatlantic tours, and from the pages of prestigious mainstream periodicals to those of black weeklies and monthlies.

African American feminists in the early nineteenth century established a tradition of arguing that the advancement of "the race" was directly linked to the status of African American women. Across the nineteenth century, black feminists pursued a remarkable array of politics to advance black women's interests, accessed and actively created political networks to forward those goals, and achieved national as well as international recognition for their efforts and causes. That they undertook such work despite personal risk to themselves or in the face of considerable demands on their commitments to family and community is a testament to their belief that they could make a difference in the lives of black women and in their communities. In some of this work black feminists formed their own collectives, yet they also participated in reform networks that were predominantly white, in predominantly male political networks within their communities, and within international reform networks. Early black feminism is arguably unique in the ways in which it negotiated competing claims from the publics it addressed and sought to motivate for change, publics that had class, racial, and gender interests that might differ from and at times effectively silence the politics African American women were advancing.

"Talking Back": Oratory, the Press, and Early Black Feminism

I take as my starting point the premise that early African American feminists produced a "double-voiced" discourse as a result of overlapping and conflicting demands among the various publics they negotiated.[10] Scholars of African American expression in general, and that of black women in particular, have long argued for attention to "talk[ing] out both sides" of one's mouth as a distinctly black political and creative strategy. As John Ernest has recently put it, this strategy is a defining feature of African American presence or "blackness": "What is African American about that presence is, in part, a set of performative strategies for resituating and re-reading white representation, negotiating the terms not simply of blackness but also of subjectivity and authority, with blackness understood as the historically constituted and contending frameworks within which these negotiations are moderated" ("Floating Icon" 461).

While Henry Louis Gates Jr. has documented the historical longevity of the Enlightenment belief that "blacks were reasonable, and hence 'men,' if—and only if—they demonstrated mastery of . . . writing" (*Signifying Monkey* 129) as the major framework within which African Americans negotiated a public authority and subjectivity, Philip Foner and Robert Branham have recently reminded us that during the nineteenth century "reason" was often believed to be *most* evident in oratorical skill: "For both male and female African American orators of the nineteenth century, when public speaking was prized as the highest achievement of human intellect, proficiency at the public platform was frequently used to refute notions of race and gender inferiority" (7–8). Within black political culture itself, Patrick Rael documents, "[b]lack leaders relied overwhelmingly on the power of public speech to sway their audiences" (45). Yet even more than persuasive, Molefi Kete Asante argues that "African American oratory" is also an Afrocentric form of communication, understood as "construct[ing] a discourse capable of calling forth *nommo,* the generative and productive power of the spoken word" (17). And as John Ernest importantly contends, black leaders recognized the twinned forces of oratory and publication: "[P]ublished oratory was perhaps the primary mode of African American publication before the Civil War" and "emphasized the presence of African American organizations" in the larger antebellum American political culture (*Liberation* 224). Oratory was, indeed, central to nineteenth-century American politics and culture more generally, "as instructor and propagandist among a . . . people who had limited facilities for acquiring news and knowledge" (Brigance 1: 155). However, political oratory and writing were not only modes of participation in public national life for African Americans but also, as these scholars have argued, of signal importance to the preservation of Afrocentric forms and African American agitation for equality and recognition as full citizens of the nation.

Much work on African American oratory addresses publics split along racial lines, attending to how activists spoke across the color line as they entered the public sphere.[11] Of course for African American women, race was further complicated by gender, creating publics which might make or contest a space for them as African American but which also often voiced opposition to a woman speaking in public. As Karlyn Kohrs Campbell has noted, women rhetors "were a group virtually unique in rhetorical history because a central element in women's oppression was the denial of her right to speak" (9). If, as Sidonie Smith argues, nineteenth-century white bourgeois women were "stranded between the granite core of 'metaphysical selfhood' [which sought to subordinate the body to 'reason'] and the material surfaces of 'embodied selfhood' [marking 'woman' as an 'encumbered self']" (83), African American women become doubly embodied by both their race and gender, doubly "other" to both "metaphysical" and "embodied" white selfhoods. The need, then, to prove the measure of one's humanity through a mastery of oratory and writing, as well as the pressure to prove one's womanhood through a "feminine" self-effacement, meant that early black feminists carefully walked a fine line. Class and regional differences often further complicated the demands of negotiating the publics that early black feminists sought to address. Consequently, these women effectively found themselves in the position of "talking back" to more than one public simultaneously, employing a double-voiced discourse in order to be heard. As black feminist critics like bell hooks point out, "[F]or black women, our struggle has not been to emerge from silence into speech but to change the nature and direction of our speech, to make a speech that compels listeners, one that is heard. . . . To make the liberated voice, one must confront the issue of audience—we must know to whom we speak" (6, 15).

Making Black Feminism Public

In raising the issue of what is heard and by whom, bell hooks proceeds from an underlying assumption of a pluralized public for black feminist politics and address, enunciative situations for which contest rather than an ideal of consensus may be a defining feature. Ultimately, this study of early black feminism also contends that how we critically understand "the public," or publics, and their location is integral to the narratives of early black feminism we will produce. The call of scholars, such as Nancy Fraser, for an exploration of competing publics and a pluralization of the public sphere in order to account for groups that may be opposed or may overlap according to class, gender, and racial differences has made public sphere theory an important lens through which to consider early African American feminism, even though that theory has also been criticized for a lack of attention to race and ethnicity.[12] Fraser argues for an understanding of the public as conflictual and contested, of "competing counterpublics" arising "virtually contemporaneous with the bourgeois public" and "elaborating alternative styles of political behavior and alternative norms of public speech" (Fraser, "Rethinking" 116).[13] As important as shifting what is understood as "the public sphere" to an understanding of multiple and competing publics is the development of a "critical model of public space and public discourse," forged in part through interrogating the process of *"making public,* in the sense of making accessible to debate, reflection, action, and moral-political transformation" (Benhabib 94; emphasis added). As Fraser has put it, "[R]elations among differentially empowered publics in stratified societies are more likely to be *contestatory* than deliberative" ("Politics" 292). Consequently, pluralizing the public sphere has also meant questioning deliberation as its privileged mode of interaction.

This work to press on participation in the public sphere importantly opens to our scrutiny not just modes of interaction but also what bodies are deemed capable of what forms of speech communication, a central concern for understanding how black feminists negotiated the publics in which they worked. Michael Warner's point that merely adopting acceptable speech norms will not guarantee one access to an arena of public debate is an important reminder of what women like Sojourner Truth faced when they addressed an American middle-class and white reform public:

> The rhetorical strategy of personal abstraction is both the utopian mo-
> ment of the public sphere and a major source of domination. For the abil-
> ity to abstract oneself in public discussion has always been an unequally
> available resource. . . . The bourgeois public sphere claimed to have no
> relation to the body image at all. Public issues were de-personalized so
> that any person would, in theory, have the ability to offer an opinion
> about them . . . [in] public debate without personal hazard. Yet the bour-
> geois public sphere continued to rely on features of certain bodies. Access
> to the public came in the whiteness and maleness that were then denied
> as forms of positivity, since the white male qua public person was only
> abstract rather than white and male. ("Mass Public" 239)

Far from accessing disembodied abstraction, African American women were
often further embodied by their daring to take the public platform, to "expose" themselves to "promiscuous" audiences in a culture that saw public
speaking as risking a woman's femininity and black women undertaking
such work as oddities. What is more, the ways in which some black feminists
spoke or preached to their audiences also contributed to their embodiment in
an era in which, as Christopher Castiglia has recently argued, "vigilant self-
scrutiny" aimed at rigorous "self-management" were seen, in and of themselves, as forms of valid and "effective democratic action" (2). To behave
otherwise marked one as outside viable democratic citizenship. As Castiglia
contends, the "discordant human interior, . . with its battles between appetite
and restraint, desire and deferral . . . became . . . a microcosm of the equally
riven sociality of nineteenth-century America" (2). Access to the public sphere
depended upon the degree to which one could claim, but also demonstrate,
disembodied rationality. Yet an African American tradition of public address,
and that of African American women in particular, values a "speech culture"
that Iris Marion Young describes as "more excited and embodied, more valuing the expression of emotions, the use of figurative language, modulation in
tone of voice, and wide gesture."[14] Conversely, the speech of white bourgeois
men, she argues, tends to be "more controlled, without significant gesture
and expression of emotion" (qtd. in Dahlberg 114). Not coincidently, that
"more controlled" speech culture is aligned with the democratic and rational
debate which is the hallmark of the public sphere.

Work in public sphere theory, then, to emphasize a pluralized public
and counterpublics, as well as contestatory, conflictual, and embodied debate rather than "rational" deliberation, has substantially altered the ways

in which we can work with a notion of the public. Yet that current stress on the public sphere as pluralized and contestatory can tend to focus "critical attention only to those movements from margin to center," as Robert Asen and Daniel Brouwer have argued, and situate counterpublics on the margins speaking back to the center (9). Ironically, then, a focus on a pluralized and contestatory public sphere can make the center the center of attention, even while undertaking to consider how counterpublics might work to disrupt that hegemony. Scholars such as Catherine Squires further contend that the pluralizing of the public sphere has also resulted in an overreliance upon identity markers to differentiate between those multiple publics, which can have a homogenizing effect by bringing into view "the" black counterpublic even as "other important issues" are obscured, "such as how constituents of these publics interact and intersect" (447).[15] Instead, Squires maintains, attention to "periods of 'fragmentation'" in the black public sphere "reveals that multiple, simultaneous Black publics emerge in different historical periods . . . constituted by groups that share a common racial makeup but perhaps do not share the same class, gender, ethnic, or ideological standpoints" (452).

Yet even with a more recent focus on gender and the contemporary black public sphere complicating notions of a monolithic black counterpublic,[16] "the" black public sphere is often understood as a masculine and a largely twentieth-century phenomenon, according to prominent scholars in African American studies. Writings in *The Black Public Sphere,* a landmark publication, take up the broader notion of a black public sphere and include important feminist work but nonetheless gender that sphere and limit its historical reach. From Houston Baker's contention that Martin Luther King Jr. single-handedly "made the black public sphere visible and expanded the black public's expression, experience and influence" (16) to Michael Dawson's assertion that the "black counterpublic has been multi-class with a male and patriarchal leadership, due in no small part to the importance of male religious leaders in the Black community" (201), the contributions of many black feminists working well before King and the civil rights era and those challenging the very hierarchy of leadership Dawson affirms are written out of the black public sphere. Indeed, that occlusion is underscored in Thomas Holt's closing remarks. Insisting that "historically a black public could only come into existence after slavery emancipation or in communities of freed slaves," Holt claims that "the conditions of slavery precluded the existence of institutions which could sustain politically viable speech communities." He continues, "The exponential growth of churches, newspapers, mutual aid associations, political organizations, literary societies, and other elements of organizational life after the Civil War underscores the vital difference between the speech and informational networks that could be sustained by slaves, and the complex institutional infrastructure of the freedpeople's public sphere" (327). Whether that "vital difference" also marks the distinction between "viable" and presumably unviable speech community as Holt suggests is highly debatable, as is the assumption that a black counterpublic came into existence only after chattel slavery ended.[17]

All the organizations and tools central to Holt's postbellum black public sphere were established and grew alongside, and in many ways because of, slavery, intersecting with, participating in, and benefiting from "the speech and informational networks" of slaves in varied ways. Freedpeople involved in antebellum black publics saw neither their political institutions nor their political future as separate from the condition of enslaved African Americans, and we would be mistaken to so separate them now. Rather, highly visible institutions within the black public, like the black convention movement and the newspapers it fostered, took as their starting point the linked conditions and possibilities of freed and enslaved African Americans. While black women's participation in organized public politics like the convention movement were limited, as was white women's at the time, this does not mean they were absent from black publics or from reform networks and publics in larger American society.[18] This study answers calls like Patrick Rael's to "privilege" gender in subsequent studies of early black political culture (7) and works to counter assertions that women were "generally absen[t]" from a "masculinized public sphere" (Rael 6–7). Placing early black feminist work as participating in multiple publics, and seeing this as political strategy, not simply a result of political necessity, has much to offer what continues to be a gendered and historically limited understanding of the black public sphere and can elaborate existing understandings of American "publicness," suggesting an additional complexity to assertions like Mary Ryan's that "the most robust expressions of American publicness date from the 1820s and 1830s" ("Gender" 264) with a fuller consideration of how race, gender, and class shaped publics in the nineteenth-century United States.

African American oratory in general, and black feminist double-voiced oratory and writing in particular, "are acts of rhetorical criticism designed to transform the context in which they are understood and interpreted" (Foner and Branham 11). In an important sense, that transformative work must continue in the way in which we take up early black feminism. What scholars regard as early black feminism's publics will expand and complicate our sense of counterpublics, their formation and political styles, as well as our understanding of the black public sphere. Considering early black feminism as "making public" will also transform a prevailing understanding of what constitutes black feminism itself. Such attention to competing and intersecting publics, in turn, necessitates the interrogation of binaries—public/private, marginal/central—that have come to produce a significant critical lens through which black feminism of this era is understood.

Contemporary black feminist theorists have argued for an attention to the historical, racial, and class specificity of gender that results in a breakdown of public/private distinctions in the lived experiences of black women.[19] Their work marks the material and ideological ways in which the very *lack* of such a distinction in black women's lives enabled the assertion of a public/private dichotomy in the lives of bourgeois white women. Yet a public/private binary risks resurfacing if we limit black feminism to certain locations or spaces. If we focus largely on the autonomous or the national organization as either the primary or the most significant form of public black feminist politics, or if we attend only to the voice of the "marginalized" seeking to motivate the will of the "dominant" in reform organizations, we risk invoking a public/private binary. Choosing to focus on one public may mean marginalizing what was often quite central to another, so that African American women preachers who commanded a hearing during the Second Great Awakening—a "central" movement of its time given the vast numbers of people it drew together and its influence upon social reform—risk becoming marginal figures if we focus on women's positions in organized denominations like the nineteenth-century African Methodist Episcopal (AME) Church.[20] Yet black feminist styles of communication can be understood as more complex when we consider them to be not merely contestatory but cannily double-voiced, appearing to adopt a politics and rhetoric that they, in fact, simultaneously critique as they move between and within established publics and create their own. Attending to that complexity will help us to resituate early black feminists "from positions of marginality . . . that were peripheral to the dominant culture and . . . to their own" (Peterson 6–7)[21] to more fluid positions, as Carla Peterson's groundbreaking work has called for. Paying attention to intersections and overlaps helps us to see one public's margin as another's center and consensus as well as contest as viable and sometimes simultaneous rhetorical positions. Overall, we would do well to heed Xiomara Santamarina's caution to not limit our examination of black feminist activism to organized reform, and instead attend to the possibilities that other kinds of discourses, beyond those affiliated with reform, allowed African American writers to claim social and civic authority from a wide range of backgrounds and statuses. Such an approach may not offer the neat consolidation of racial identity embedded in our received notions of "black reform" or "protest," but . . . does offer us a broader, more historical sense of the multiple traditions African Americans shaped and participated in as they quested for racial justice and equality. (167)

In many ways Elsa Barkley Brown's call to shift our critical focus in the study of black women's politics continues to have resonance for the field. Arguing that scholarly studies of black women's political activity have tended to center on the turn into the twentieth century,[22] Barkley Brown contends they have created two central misconceptions of early black feminism: first, that the turn of the century was "the height of black women's participation in politics," and second, that black women's emergence in politics is "tied to external factors" like the disenfranchisement of black men, or "vitriolic attacks" on black female morality (137). Through her attention to black women's political practice, Barkley Brown amplifies Susan Lebsock's earlier contention that existing studies of nineteenth-century women and American politics have established a "consensus . . . that for women the standard form of political participation was the voluntary association" (36), thereby emphasizing autonomous, and often national, women's organizations. That focus on the turn into the twentieth century and the autonomous, if not national, federation is notably predicated upon a public/private distinction that we should consider carefully and critically. As You-Me Park and Gayle Wald note, the "illusion of separate 'public' and 'private' spheres is reinforced through the fact that the entrance of women of color into the public sphere is often predicated upon the maintenance of the public/private divide" (234). To see African American feminism as reaching its height when it assumes a particular form of publicness, one notably opposed to "the private" of communal rather than the "public" of national politics and organizations, not only discounts earlier and very different modes of political culture in which black women engaged but also assumes a divide that does not accurately speak to black women's experiences. Moreover, as Park and Wald further contend, we must understand that when African American women participated in some publics their "racial-ethnic . . . identity [was] compromised by the demand that they maintain their 'private' (i.e. degraded) identities even in the 'public' sphere"

(234). This compromise is clear in Sojourner Truth's appearance at Silver Lake and in those of other black feminists as related in their own writings and in press coverage of their lectures.

In addition to considering how the places or locations of early black feminism might be understood, we must also attend to what we understand as political and feminist. I would argue that some early black feminist activism has been occluded by misperceptions that it is apolitical or part of a depoliticizing trend; this has been argued not only of nineteenth-century black women's spiritual writing but also of the domestic fiction so prevalent near the century's close that shares affinity with the domestic feminism many African American activists forwarded in their work.[23] Similarly, we will render invisible important black feminist work if we take the term "feminist" to mean politics concerned only with woman's rights and roles. Early black feminism is marked by a sustained concern with more than a single, or singular understanding of, oppression. Early black feminists went beyond an exclusive focus on "the woman question" to pursue critical challenges to linked or interdependent oppressions. For these political activists the concerns of women could not be separated from those of the larger black community; concerns for enslaved African Americans necessarily entailed those for free blacks, and concerns for "the slave" at home were linked with those for "the white slave" abroad, both of whom suffered under the international effects of a slave economy. Embedded in this larger view of oppression, its sites and victims, was black feminists' persistent attention to black women's material realities, particularly under the exploitations of slavery and the so-called free labor market, which flew in the face of the very reform discourses in which they participated. This is no less true for black preaching women than it was for black feminists active in abolition, anti-lynching, woman's rights, or black nationalism and racial uplift. Taking the places of early black feminism and its politics together, we can see clearly that these activists were not only working with "local" rhetorics and politics at "home" but also taking black feminism public in an international frame that highlighted interlocking oppressions and their particular affect upon women.

Despite, or perhaps because of, their complicated association with established organizations, these women frequently reached larger audiences than any one organization could provide by choosing to affiliate with different organizations and by traveling throughout the North and South, and outside the country. By moving outside existing publics to create their own, most notably through religion and the press, black feminists pursued a multifaceted and self-transforming politics. Indeed, in many ways early black feminism can be understood through Lauren Berlant's notion of the "juxtapolitical," operating in political spaces that "flourish . . . in proximity to [what is recognized as] the political because the political is deemed an elsewhere managed by elites who are interested in reproducing the conditions of their objective superiority" (*Female* 2). Through a thick reading of black feminist oratorical and written texts produced in a variety of locations, and in association with varied movements and organizations both within the United States and the British Isles and Ireland, this study seeks to expand existing critical paradigms that have shaped what we conceive of as early black feminist political culture. Arguably this is the foundational period of black feminism, which would lay the groundwork for what historians such as Dorothy Salem and Paula Giddings have identified as the "second stage" or "new era" in black feminism after World War I,[24] and we see much in the way of a developing and sustained politics that comes to inform that turn toward the "second stage" and the twentieth century.

This book moves not only historically from considering black feminist work in the church early in the nineteenth century toward a black feminism in the press at its close but also, necessarily, with attention to contiguity so that we see connections between black feminist politics across the century and across specific reforms. With what I would mark as an ironic emphasis upon "critical recall," Houston Baker rightly contends that the black public sphere is structured through contiguity: "Black intellectual and political self-interest, therefore, demands emphasis on an integrity of critical recalls. . . a historically verifiable emphasis on how the black public sphere has always been restructured through contiguity" (35). That critical recall must, of course, include those many black women who helped create and define a nineteenth-century black public sphere.

Whether it be found within Methodist, Shaker, or Baptist denominations or the clearings of the Second Great Awakening, the religious fervor of the early nineteenth century was the seedbed of reform. As Jean Humez has noted, "Historians of the great social reform movements of the nineteenth century have shown that ultimately political liberationist movements like abolitionism and feminism were deeply rooted in the successive layers of religious enthusiasm that spread out over the northeastern United States in the first four decades of the century" ("Introduction" 2). Beginning, then, with black women who answered the "call" to preach and evangelize in the North, the South, and outside the country, this book opens by considering attempts to control the black female body, varied claims to authority and a public voice black women made through their spiritual beliefs, and prevailing sanctions upon excited and embodied speech in religious discourse and testimony. Chapter 1, then, takes up the central issues of which bodies and speech acts were acceptable in a central black political institution like the church, how African American women sought to intervene in and circumvent those sanctions in order to continue to preach, and how black women worked to create their own religious communities and publics, often through travel and itinerancy.

We see those issues of embodied speech and debate continuing to be central to African American women's participation in abolition and their careful negotiation of what some scholars have coined "feminist abolitionism."[25] Much work has been done on black female abolition in the United States as it negotiated a nascent woman's rights movement which began in abolition. In chapter 2 I move beyond that predominant focus in the study of black women in abolition to consider the ways in which class, the market, and national feeling shaped the work Ellen Craft and Sarah Parker Remond would undertake as they took black feminism public internationally through the transatlantic abolition movement. Central to this chapter are considerations of the ways in which Craft and Remond were negotiating discourses of labor reform that argued the interests of the "white slaves of England" and managing national feeling, whether in the British Isles or in a newly post-Famine Ireland where nationalism and abolition had become uneasy bedfellows. Craft's and Remond's appearances reveal their awareness of the mobility of "the white slave" as both political trope and a powerful lens through which they, themselves, and their appeals were viewed by audiences on the other side of the Atlantic. Together, Craft and Remond make us aware that early black feminism was not only working with "local" rhetorics and politics but also going public internationally.

Like Craft and Remond, Sojourner Truth also worked with complex appeals to manage her participation in abolition and woman's rights networks. Truth is an important figure for this book, and the focus of chapter 3, since her successful career, including preaching, abolition, and woman's rights agitation, enables us to see both the connections and fractures between African American rights and a developing white American feminist movement. Yet placing Truth's woman's rights and black civil rights work within the larger context of other black women's labors in organized religious denominations and revivals, as well as abolition, enables us to see her less as a black feminist "first" and more as part of a critical mass of black feminists at mid-century.

This chapter also takes up the question of Truth's persistence as "the" early black feminist in historical memories of American feminism and her complicated position in contemporary critical negotiations of "difference" within white feminism. I argue we need to reconsider not only Truth's place in a canon of U.S. feminism that has made gestures toward racial inclusivity but also the rituals which she continues to be made to serve in feminist discourse, rituals that echo in uncanny ways the first wave's representation of Truth to serve its purposes.

Tracing black women's varied speaking styles and appeals across these first three chapters illuminates audience and location as mediating factors in public address and politics, as well as black feminists' methods of negotiating and sometimes capitalizing upon a public "embodiment" created by their "blackness" and femaleness. Consequently, this book considers both the advantages and risks of addressing competing and overlapping publics as well as marks the importance of critically understanding communication and its styles in varied publics. While women like Ellen Craft and Sarah Remond were often represented as decidedly "feminine" in their lectures to abolition's predominantly white "promiscuous" audiences, many African American women preachers were seen as "bodied" threats to the black church's transition to an organized denominational structure. Such judgments are a matter of acceptable oratorical style or expression, as well as self-presentation, that varied according to these publics but were also disciplined in service of that larger notion of what constituted democratic citizenship and rational debate. While Craft and Remond were praised by British audiences for "earnest" appeals and ladylike demeanors, a different form of earnestness, particularly an unqualified belief in sanctification and the practice of ecstatic worship, made women such as Julia Pell threatening to the AME Church. Addressing yet other publics, Sojourner Truth's vernacular style, though often taken as incomprehensible by reporters and amusing by her audiences, marked her as "primitive" oddity yet also enabled her to sharply critique the woman's rights movement even as she seemed to support its goals and means to achieve them. While black feminists employed a range of communicative styles to reach their audiences, those styles themselves were deeply political as were the ways in which they were represented by others to a wider public.

Black women in the church, and in abolition and woman's rights networks, forged paths for future black feminist activism by opening new public arenas like the press and a transatlantic reform network to the voices of black women. Chapter 4 focuses on Ida B. Wells, part owner and full-time editor of *Memphis Free Speech,* a southern black Baptist weekly through which she launched her militant anti-lynching crusade of the 1890s. Wells's astute analysis of the economic roots of white mob violence and lynching, and the attention she drew to the rape of black women and girls, were central to nineteenth-century black feminist activism. Yet later in her career Wells was marginalized by the very organizations she helped make possible—the National Association for the Advancement of Colored People and the black women's club movement—for her political style. She has come to us largely as a lone militant figure. However, by concentrating on her anti-lynching lecture tours of Britain, this chapter examines her self-positioning at the center of reform networks forged by earlier movements such as transatlantic abolition. In these British lectures and her interviews with the British press, Wells proves herself an astute and savvy reader of political discourses likes eugenics and the "new abolitionism" that she used to her own, very different, ends. And while concerns over embodiment are rather different for Wells in the 1890s than they were for Craft and Remond in the 1850s, they remain important to understanding Wells's effect upon the publics she addressed and the appeals she chose to use. Wells risked a great deal in speeches that "graphically" detailed the rape and lynching of African Americans, and at times such violently embodied content clearly also meant that Wells herself was subject to scrutiny of her person and background. Finally, this chapter considers the ways in which Wells's knowledge of the press as a southern journalist makes her an important figure for considering how this tool not only influenced and often schooled its readers but also could be used to actively create a public.

Press, Platform, Public moves from Wells's pedagogy of the press to a consideration of feminist black nationalism as it develops in the periodical press. In chapter 5, I return to the 1830s via Maria Stewart's and Sarah Mapps Douglass's contributions to *The Liberator* in the Northeast, move to Canada in the 1850s and Mary Shadd Cary's work to establish her paper, *The Provincial Freeman,* and then go on to the writings of prominent African American women journalists with southern roots at the end of the century. This chapter aims, in different ways, to shift the way we have understood these women. Maria Stewart was not only the first woman orator in the United States but also, importantly, one of the early contributors of feminist black nationalist appeals to the press along with Sarah Mapps Douglass. Mary Shadd Cary was not only a staunch abolitionist, emigrationist, and woman's rightist, but she actively built a black public supporting those causes with the remarkable independent run of her paper. And women prominent in the black club movement, such as Gertrude Mossell, Victoria Earle Matthews, Josephine Silone-Yates, and Addie Hunton, were also journalists who could be critical of its discourse of racial respectability for configuring southern black working women and black women migrating to the North as social "contagion." Together these women pursue a feminist black nationalism in the press that directly takes on the ways in which black women's work was not only undervalued but also actively denigrated as embodied in discourses of uplift, with that embodiment of labor often sliding into presumptions of promiscuity and immorality against which working women had to defend themselves.

While this chapter's temporal scope is generous, and takes up black feminist journalism in the North, the South, and in Canada, it shows us an evolving feminist black nationalism responding to the central political concerns of its time through what was, and continues to be, regarded as *the* political venue second only to the church in the nineteenth century—the press. Whether writing for the black press or for white weeklies and nationally circulating periodicals, these black women journalists negotiated gendered and raced publics in different regions of the country and outside its boundaries but with a shared political focus—arguing that working-class and migrant women were central agents in, not the feared or pitied objects of, a racial politics of uplift. This final chapter also returns to and carries forward the interconnections traced by the study as a whole among the black church, nineteenth-century reform movements, the press, and black feminism by examining Maria Stewart's social and feminist gospel, which placed the working black woman at its center; Mary Shadd Cary's insistence that abolition, emigration, and woman suffrage were important and linked political concerns for a black public; and late-nineteenth-century black feminist journalism as championing the achievements, rather than stressing the failings, of working and migrant black women, contrary to the rhetoric of racial respectability that runs throughout the century.

I conclude by focusing on a crucial moment for American feminism, the 1891 National Council of Women in Washington, D.C., which also marks an important generational shift in black feminism and black suffrage. I inquire into the positions Frances Harper and Anna Julia Cooper have come to occupy in historiographies of black feminism; though Cooper has not often been positioned as one of its "greats," as Harper is, she was central to what Rosalyn Terborg-Penn identifies as the "third generation" of black feminists agitating for black rights and the vote for women. Reading Anna Julia Cooper's response in "Woman versus the Indian" to Anna Shaw's and Frances

Harper's speeches at the National Council, I briefly explore the possibilities and limitations of taking black feminism public in yet another way, through forging feminist coalitions between women of color.

* * *

If contemporary scholarship on the black public sphere can be said to forget its history both by excluding women and by delimiting certain forms of publicness to the postbellum era, this study attends to the way in which a feminist black public politics carries its history with it, elaborating its utility and validity in new contexts, styles, and venues. That sense of continuity not only enabled early black feminism to achieve critical mass but also was actively mobilized as black feminists developed their modes and sites of address. Looking beyond black feminism's "greats," such as Sojourner Truth, to lesser-known activists, such as Julia Pell, Sarah Mapps Douglass, and Aunt Dinah, and seeing "great" black feminists afresh in new contexts, such as orators or club women primarily as journalists, opens the black feminism we have known to a more complex understanding. Examining the ways in which black feminists negotiated existing publics and political discourses also, importantly, helps us to recognize that black feminism was neither marginal nor always marginalized in this period but played a very active part in the central reforms of its day. Finally, and perhaps most important, considering the ways in which black feminism actually created its own publics helps us to see this politics as neither derivative of nor dependent upon the white feminist or black masculine public politics it both participated in and critiqued. Early black feminists transformed existing reforms, generated new publics, and challenged dominant conceptions of democratic citizenship and rational disembodied debate in their shared effort to make the black woman central to "woman's era" and the era of reform.

Chapter 1

Soul Winners and Sanctified Sisters: Nineteenth-Century African American Preaching Women

Despite institutional sanctions against their licensing or ordination, African American women were active in the nineteenth century as preachers, exhorters, evangelists, and missionaries. From Rebecca Cox Jackson's Shaker mission among African Americans in Philadelphia to the itinerant preaching of women such as Jarena Lee and Sojourner Truth and the revivalist and evangelical work of Amanda Smith and Annie Brown, African American women defied open hostility and attempts to limit if not prevent their work. Often taking their messages to whoever would receive them, they addressed men and women, whites and blacks, at camp meetings, in churches, in streets and alleyways, and in private homes. Indeed, these women should be understood as participating in the center of nascent American "liberationist movements like abolitionism and feminism" that, as Jean Humez documents, "were deeply rooted in the successive layers of religious enthusiasm that spread out over the northeastern United States in the first four decades of the century" ("Introduction" 2).

Much historical scholarship on evangelical religion in nineteenth-century America has documented its importance in "open[ing] up a whole new world for northern women discontented with their roles," offering them "a new field in which they could become active, assertive, and relatively free agents responsible for nothing short of the redemption of the world" (Grammer 6).[1] As Elizabeth Grammer notes, religion was regarded at the time as belonging to "a world somehow between the public sphere of men and politics and the private, domestic sphere, which was considered by many Americans the proper one for women" (6). For African Americans, however, religion was central to the public sphere and the church was the locus of black politics. This difference may, in part, account for not only the fierce contest over women's right to preach but also a historical record that has actively marginalized women and their role. Even though Methodism was, as Catherine Brekus characterizes it, open to "the poor, the unlearned, the slave, or the female [who] felt qualified to preach the gospel" (145), this was not the case in reforming African Methodism.

Studies of nineteenth-century African American preaching women tend to characterize their position as marginalized, given that institutional positions were denied them for much of the century. Certainly, many of these women labored outside religious institutional structure, yet to take this as indicative of their position among those they worked to convert and to minister to, both the churched and the unchurched, is to underestimate and misunderstand their position and influence. Rather, Evelyn Brooks Higginbotham's understanding of the black church as "a discursive, critical arena—a public sphere in which values and issues were aired, debated, and disseminated through the larger black community" (7), should be extended to religious gatherings in general. In what we might then call these "small publics" we can better recognize the important ways in which black preaching women contributed to, even as they challenged, the church as public sphere. As Gary Fine and Brooke Harrington argue, small or "tiny" publics "permit individuals to collaborate flexibly for common interests without the infrastructure and resources that organizations entail" (349). That flexibility meant that preaching women arguably reached more potential converts outside the church's formal structure than they would have had they been licensed by a denomination or given a pastorate. Invited to preach in churches by sympathetic ministers, both black and white, of varying denominations, and sought after to participate in interdenominational camp meetings or to address large gatherings in urban areas, African American women often worked at the center of nineteenth-century religious life rather than at its margins.

Both the Second Great Awakening and the Holiness revival movement defined nineteenth-century American religious life, converting thousands of people organized denominations did not reach and reclaiming "backsliders" who had strayed from the church. Erica Armstrong Dunbar has recently documented that the "North, in particular, saw a tremendous rise in the number of African Americans who belonged to a Methodist denomination, in particular the African Methodist Episcopal Church" during the Second Great Awakening because "emotional conversion" was more attractive to people who "had been uncomfortable with other denominations that relied heavily on literacy" (99). These movements provided numerous opportunities for African American women to preach, exhort, and evangelize. Where opportunities were not readily available, these women made their own, traveling to reach their audiences, even into the dangerous southern slave states. It should be stressed that the church was, and continues to be, regarded as central to African American political life, if not the center of "the" black public sphere. Noting that nineteenth-century African Americans were drawn to revivals and camp meetings for their sense of social solidarity, E. Franklin Frazier also cites their ability to vote within churches to elect church officers, and the church as one of the only arenas in which individuals might "achieve distinction and status" (49), as markers of the church's centrality to African American political life. C. Eric Lincoln and Lawrence Mamiya add that the black church has been key to social cohesion among African Americans (92). Indeed, the church-affiliated press was "a major site of print production in black communities," making it "instrumental" in the "dissemination of a black oppositional discourse" and the development of a viable counterpublic (Higginbotham 11). Particularly in the late nineteenth century, with rising literacy rates among African Americans, churches led the virtual explosion of the black periodical press.

While the black church, itself, has for some time been the center of political life for its communities, it is also important to understand that constructions of the spiritual in nineteenth-century America were foundational for participation in the public sphere. As Russ Castronovo has argued, the soul and spiritual inner life, far from depoliticized or prepolitical at that time, were central to constructions of the democratic citizen subject and the public sphere. "The question is not whether the spiritual is political," writes Castronovo; rather, "we need to ask what sort of politics are deployed (and delayed) by invocations of the spirit" (138). Consequently, African American preaching women undertook highly political struggles to mark and contest the social hierarchies enabled by, indeed established through, appeals to "spirit," whether they sought to improve women's and blacks' access to both black and mixed churches or raised questions regarding freedom of religious worship. We risk taking as "marginal" and depoliticized what was quite central political work undertaken by women who, while socially subordinate, were deeply convicted in their beliefs and hopes for religious community.

Characterizing these women and their work as marginal has consequences for our understanding of early black feminism, its politics and its publics, to which we must attend, for doing so contributes to the prevailing sense that black feminism gained a "voice" largely in the late nineteenth century with the advent of the black women's club movement. Yet as Elsa Barkley Brown has argued, black feminists "were seeking in the late-nineteenth century not a new authority but rather a lost authority" (112), one that was built, I would argue, through the work of nineteenth-century African American preaching women. Martha Jones's work on the woman question in nineteenth-century African American political culture makes a strong case for black women's work in the church and religion in general as a sort of training ground for black women's activism late in the century, noting that "before they were club women, temperance organizers, anti-lynching crusaders, or suffragists, most female activists learned to navigate issues of gender and power in churches and fraternal orders" (171). It is this work to recenter women in the black church, and that of Joycelyn Moody, Katherine Clay Bassard, Evelyn Brooks Higginbotham, and Jualynne Dodson before Jones, upon which this chapter builds. Preaching women are of significant importance to a revised understanding of African American feminism as rooted in the early years of the century and in the work of women who challenged the authority of religious institutions, popular views of women's place, and abstract notions of ideal citizenship that were premised on the denial of material inequities. A more productive understanding of African American preaching women as feminists can be reached by conceiving of their position as liminal, not marginal, and of their work as occupying a "threshold," though no less significant, position in American religious life as it found expression in the nineteenth century. Recognizing the potential of a "betwixt and between" state, neither marginalized nor institutionally approved, helps us to reconsider the religious and political work of women who left family and home to participate in the larger spiritual community.

William Andrews's *Sisters of the Spirit* (1986), the publication that brought nineteenth-century African American preaching women Jarena Lee, Zilpha Elaw, and Julia Foote to the wider attention of scholars, positioned their spiritual autobiographies as important precursors to the slave narratives and marked their need to "prov[e] that black people were as much chosen by God for eternal salvation as whites" (1). These women addressed the position of blacks in antebellum and postbellum American society and argued for the right of women to preach, whether explicitly or implicitly through the example of their own spiritual labors. Consequently, Andrews contended that their spiritual autobiographies "celebrate" a "radical spiritual individualism" (17) and explore "the possibilities of a deliberately chosen marginal identity that morally and spiritually engaged the world without being socially engulfed by it" (12). To what degree the marginalization of these women was "deliberately chosen" is questionable, yet it does not follow that social marginalization due to one's race, class, and gender resulted in a marginal position or influence within the religious movements of the day. However, scholarship on black women's spiritual autobiographies has tended to follow this line of argument, contending that these women "worked and wrote from positions of marginality, from social, psychological, and geographic sites that were peripheral to the dominant culture and, very often, to their own" (Peterson 6–7). Scholars also follow Andrews's lead in stressing that these narratives detail the self-empowerment and authority preaching women lacked in their daily lives but located in their divine calling.[2]

Far from isolating themselves or choosing marginal positions, however, African American preaching women believed deeply in community and in direct connection with the divine and with their fellow believers and potential converts. It was also this profound faith in the possibility and power of direct connection that saw these women claim an experience of divine presence, in the forms of conversion and sanctification, that inspired them to preach and testify to God's power rather than to their experience of self-empowerment. Their feminist politics was more complex, stressing the spiritual as an end in itself even as, in their writings and preaching, they frequently addressed social inequities that African Americans, particularly black women, faced. These women clearly believed in society's capacity for change and in the contribution of their own work toward realizing that potential. Yet to see black preaching women locating self-empowerment in spirit and in contrast to their more limiting material realities is to reinscribe the very hierarchy of disembodiment/embodiment upon which democratic citizenship and access to the public sphere was based, a hierarchy these women challenged.

As Castronovo notes, that hierarchy and the exclusions it enabled were repeatedly elided in the utopian fantasy of a democratic public sphere, even as they were constitutive of it. "Democratic fantasies of commonality and equality have hinged on the disappearance of material differences" (Castronovo 118), even as those differences enable some subjects to claim a privileged interiority and "abstract universality" admitting them to the public sphere (Habermas 54). If the "spiritual functions as a political apparatus" that is, itself, constituted by the distinctions between material realities or differences and abstract universality (Castronovo 120), bringing together the spiritual (as abstract) and the material matters a great deal to contesting the powers and boundaries of the democratic public sphere. African American preaching women underscored the politics of the soul in nineteenth-century America with their refusal to elide the material realities of black Americans and their struggles to challenge the gender hierarchy of institutionalized denominations, even as they claimed an inner life and the attainment of spiritual redemption for African Americans.

Abolition, Civil Rights, Woman's Rights

African American preaching women consistently foregrounded the politics of "soul winning," contesting the inequities of a democratic public sphere that depended upon the exclusion of "uniquely embodied" persons in its production of the liberal subject (Castronovo 124). Advocating the right of a woman to preach and speaking against slavery, despite the danger of doing so, preaching women effectively drew attention to the politicization of the soul. Some, such as Old Elizabeth, Jarena Lee, Zilpha Elaw, and Julia Foote, took their religious messages into the southern slave states at great personal risk.

Born a slave in Maryland in 1766 and separated from her parents at eleven years of age, Old Elizabeth "betook" herself "to prayer" and was converted during a vision before she was thirteen (7). Seeing with her "spiritual eye" a man "in white raiment," Elizabeth was "*taught* to pray" and taken on "a long journey to a fiery gulf" where she "was sustained by some invisible power" and eventually saw "the Savior" and "heaven's door [at] which . . . I saw millions of glorified spirits in white robes" (5–6). Elizabeth affirmed her willingness "to be saved," was converted, and was "told I must . . . call the people to repentance" (6–7). She did not begin to preach until she was forty-two, however.[3] Though she mentions African Methodist Episcopal opposition to her ministry at least five times in her short spiritual autobiography of nineteen pages, Elizabeth held meetings for "coloured sisters" (10) even in the face of a formal complaint against her for "being a woman" and leading religious gatherings (15).[4] Elizabeth wrote of this censure: "I often felt that I was despised on account of this gracious calling, and was looked upon as a speckled bird by the ministers to whom I looked for instruction" (13). In Elizabeth's experience, then, spiritual calling and its validity was intimately bound up with the gender politics of her religious community. "The ministers" could claim the interior life of the soul and its communication with the divine, not Elizabeth or her "coloured sisters."

Elizabeth's narrative is also, itself, a protest against slavery, that "peculiar institution" that separated her from her parents yet kept them within "twenty miles" of one another. As Frances Smith Foster documents, "in spiritual autobiography, details such as family history, physical descriptions, education, occupations, the names and circumstances of siblings, spouses, or children and even the dates and places of crucial incidents in the narrator's life are minimized." Instead, such autobiographies "were narratives of religious testimony, the spiritual and ministerial experiences of those who heeded God's call" (*Written* 60).[5] Unusual for a spiritual autobiography, Elizabeth's text offers details of her childhood and family as they form a protest against the "peculiar institution" and its violence to familial ties. As we shall see, Elizabeth's text and those of other African American preaching women formed a tradition of spiritual autobiography that attended to the ways in which the material realities of slavery, racism, and sexism complicated and could not be separated from the spiritual quest.[6] As a child, Elizabeth risked and received a severe lashing for visiting her mother against her overseer's prohibition (3–4). She was sold at least twice and did not attend "religious meetings" until she was free, despite being owned by a Presbyterian whom she characterizes as sympathetic for having manumitted her. Elizabeth's narrative testifies to the effective silencing of her call under slavery and her reluctance to speak at religious meetings she attends when free, undoubtedly due to her awareness of woman's subordinate status within the AME Church. Yet she came not only to preach but to oppose slavery openly in her ministry, risking imprisonment while on a daring preaching tour in the slave state of Virginia "because I spoke against slavery" (17).

Jarena Lee, born free on February 11, 1783, in Cape May, New Jersey, was converted at the age of twenty-one (Lee, *Life* 27–28), a process that included her contemplation of suicide on several occasions. Supported by its founder and first bishop, Richard Allen, Lee was permitted by the AME Church to exhort and hold prayer meetings "in my own hired house" (*Life* 42), but she was never licensed as a preacher.[7] Her "eye of faith" revealed a man in white who said, "'Thou shalt never return from the cross'" (*Life* 37), and Lee found herself persevering in her spiritual labors in the midst of AME opposition to women preaching, a subject to which I will return. Like several women who followed her, Jarena Lee offered explicit arguments for women as preachers in her spiritual autobiography and personified that position through her labors. Basing her contentions that a woman may preach in the fact that "the Saviour died for the woman as well as the man," Lee cited Mary as "first preach[ing] the risen Savior" and noted that divine inspiration to preach was not limited to men alone (Lee, *Life* 36–37).

In a text "tolerated and even supported by church leaders" (F. Foster, *Written* 57), Lee daringly took the AME Church to task for enacting "by-laws" that prohibited women's ministry. "O how careful ought we to be, lest through our by-laws of church government and discipline, we bring into disrepute even the word of life," wrote Lee. "For as unseemly as it may appear now-a-days for a woman to preach, it should be remembered that nothing is impossible with God" (*Life* 36). And in her 1849 text, *Religious Experience and Journal of Mrs. Jarena Lee,* Lee boldly concluded by declaring herself a preacher of the AME Church, a position she was officially denied her entire career: "Thus ends the Narrative of JARENA LEE, the first female preacher of the First African Methodist Episcopal Church" (97). Rather than displacing the political inequities of appeals to the privilege of an interior spiritual life and calling from which women were explicitly excluded onto a fantasy of transcendent universality in which "the Savior died" for *all our* sins, Lee challenges the AME Church to recognize the hierarchies that make such a fantasy possible.

In 1824 Lee's itinerant ministry saw her deciding to travel to the slave states to preach.[8] While in North Carolina, Lee "preached in the Old Methodist Church" of Snow Hill "to an immense congregation of both the slaves and the holders" (*Journal* 37). On this tour, Lee even preached in the houses of "slave-holders" and saw "poor slaves come happy in the Lord," walking "from 20 to 30, and from that to seventy miles" to hear her (*Journal* 39). Lee does not comment upon what surely must have been an unusual circumstance of a black woman preaching to southern slaveholders, particularly so given that religious men and folk preachers Gabriel Prosser and Denmark Vesey had planned slave insurrections that were discovered and prevented in 1800 (Richmond) and 1822 (Charleston), respectively. Perhaps she was not perceived as a threatening figure and merely as an oddity. This was certainly the case even in the North, where Lee described preaching at her uncle's house near Cape May, New Jersey, as reaching people "who had come from curiosity to hear the woman preacher" (*Journal* 19). In other words, perhaps it was Lee's liminal position as black but not a slave, an itinerant preacher from the North, a woman, and so "betwixt and between" black southern slaves, male insurrectionaries, and their white slave owners that enabled Lee to preach safely in slaveholding states and to speak before audiences we might not expect her to address.

Consequently, it is important in understanding the reach and influence of African American preaching women to consider physical spaces, as well as ideological location or positioning, as liminal. Liminality can enable one to access sites and listeners that would ordinarily be off limits if not physically imperiling. While the AME Church refused to sanction Lee's labors, she was penetrating states and reaching both white and black communities where the church had very little presence or influence. Even by the late 1890s, the AME Church counted relatively few stations in the South, as these numbers indicate: Georgia (8), Tennessee (10), Alabama (2), Mississippi (2), Louisiana (1), and Arkansas (1) (Waller 13). And while Lee does not offer details of what she preached while in the slave states, it is clear from her reception by slave owners that she did not preach the insurrection of a Prosser or a Vesey, nor did she likely take a strong antislavery stance. Instead, perhaps Lee chose when to offer that message depending upon whom she addressed, negotiating proslavery interests in order to be able to preach to southern slaves without interference or physical threat. Remarkably, Lee's opposition to slavery seems not to have endangered her in the south and yet her preaching did not temper her antislavery politics: Lee joined the American Anti-Slavery Society at its New York convention in 1840.

Zilpha Elaw (born c. 1790) and Rebecca Cox Jackson (born 1795), both born free near Philadelphia, shared a common concern with the welfare and condition of enslaved and free African Americans in ways that directed their ministry. Elaw was a Methodist who pursued her ministry even though her black Methodist prayer band rejected her: "[A]fter I commenced the work of the ministry, I was a person of no account . . . and I became so unpopular, that all of our coloured class abandoned me excepting three" (Elaw 83). Undoubtedly, Elaw's "abandonment" was a result of choosing to follow her call despite being a woman, a decision she staunchly defends in her spiritual autobiography, saying that Paul's injunction against women speaking in church was, judging from "Scriptures[,] . . . not intended to limit the extraordinary directions of the Holy Ghost in reference to female Evangelists or oracular sisters; nor to be rigidly observed in peculiar circumstances" (Elaw 124).[9] While African American preaching women's prayer bands often gave them their first opportunities to preach in a supportive environment, such was not the case for Elaw. Instead, she seems to have had better success with a more liminal position, as she preached to intersecting and competing publics, sometimes a racial "insider" to the communities in which she labored and sometimes an outsider, but always that unusual phenomenon of a woman undertaking public ministry.

Undaunted by the prohibitions and reactions of her first religious community, Elaw preached to whites and blacks alike in an itinerant ministry that led her to the southern slave states in the spring of 1828, just four years after

Jarena Lee had done the same. Despite her "fear of being arrested and sold for a slave, which their laws would have warranted, on account of my complexion and features" (Elaw 91), Elaw preached to crowds of slaves, drawing the interest of whites "collecting from every quarter to gaze at the unexampled prodigy of a coloured female preacher" (Elaw 91). That interest may have been at the root of Elaw's ability to impress "many of the elite in Washington, D.C., and nearby Virginia." Such was Elaw's reputation that "General Lee's wife invited her to their home to preach" during this first of her two trips to the South (Horton and Horton 136). While in Maryland, Elaw would have been constrained by both the Black Code and the 1793 Fugitive Slave Act. The code, as Joycelyn Moody documents, forbade "African Americans' public assembly . . . racially integrated worship services . . . [and] any colored minister, as well as any colored people belonging to another state, from entrance there" unless they were slaves or servants ("Road" 42). Elaw, like Elizabeth, who preached in both Maryland and Virginia, defied such sanctions and risked imprisonment to reach African Americans who had, in many cases, fugitive access to religion. In her *Memoirs,* self-published in London in 1846 just before her return from a preaching tour of England, Elaw castigated slave owners and the institution as "a wrong, the deepest in wickedness" (98), taking an antislavery stand during a period of intense abolitionism in the United States. "[E]very case of slavery, however lenient in its inflictions and mitigated its atrocities, indicates an oppressor, the oppressed, and the oppression," Elaw wrote (98).

Rebecca Cox Jackson, initially a Methodist like Elaw, faced opposition to her preaching from her husband and her AME preacher brother. She was eventually drawn to the ascetic lifestyle and beliefs of the Shakers, who advocated a triple Godhead that included Holy Mother Wisdom and held strong abolitionist sympathies (Humez, "Introduction" 26–27). The Shakers believed that Christ had been resurrected as a woman and "integrated black members on an apparently equal basis. . . . [T]he northern Shaker communities may have acted as stations on the Underground Railroad" (Humez, "Introduction" 26). Jackson's personal religious views were, in the main, in accord with Shaker doctrine: they viewed celibacy positively, encouraged ecstatic worship, believed human beings could be instruments of the divine through spiritual visions, and saw institutionalized churches as usurping divine authority (Humez, "Introduction" 26). Jackson lived at the Watervliet Shaker community near Albany, New York, in the late 1840s but left in the summer of 1851 because she "was brought into deep tribulation of soul about my people, and their present condition" (Jackson 213).

Despite their shared spiritual outlook, Jackson had come to see the Shakers as too insular: "Believers seemed to be gathered to themselves, in praying for themselves and not for the world. . . . [T]hey seemed to be busy in their own concerns, which were mostly temporal" (220). In contrast to that inwardness, Jackson's concerns were for African Americans, like herself, who often experienced either the threat or reality of racialized violence. Jackson attended to and sought to address the material conditions of African Americans rather than adopting that Shaker world view. In doing so, she refused to elevate a spiritual interiority over the often brute realities of the "earthly" world. Her writings detail visions that attend to the violence that invaded and could structure her world. That violence is frequently one directed against both her race and gender and from which she seeks God's protection.

One notable vision, "A Dream of Slaughter," depicts Jackson's disembowelment by an intruder who Jackson recognizes as a Methodist preacher opposing her ministry (94–96). As Dianne Sasson notes, Jackson's visions do not express "confidence in the protection offered by the community. When houses appear in her visions, they are often prisons instead of havens" (172), registering Jackson's concern for her own welfare and that of other African American women in communities like Philadelphia, where labor markets limited their employment prospects largely to domestic work in which the home was a site of their exploitation. As Jean Humez notes in her introduction to Jackson's writings, Jackson would have been well aware of "the growing tensions that produced the explosions of white mob violence [in Philadelphia] . . . beginning in 1829 and reoccurring in 1834, 1835, 1842, and 1849" caused by "the simultaneous influx of freedmen, fugitives, and foreigners into a large city" (14). Often black neighborhoods sustained days of destruction of property and physical violence, and the mob attacks of 1835, in particular, saw black women flee the city with their children (Humez, "Introduction" 14). By 1848 Jackson felt she had been called to undertake a Shaker mission to African Americans—"I dreamed that I was going south to feed the people" (213)—and left Watervliet for Philadelphia in 1851, despite the opposition of Shaker elders who regarded her as apostatized. Jackson's vision of "feeding the people" in "The Dream of the Cakes" boldly appropriates to herself Shaker imagery of sustenance that is "granted by Mother Ann [Mother Wisdom] and the Community of Believers" (Sasson 168).

Rebecca Cox Jackson so firmly believed that she must preach to Philadelphia blacks and those in the surrounding area that she returned to Watervliet in September 1857, reached a compromise with Shaker elders, who sanctioned her ministry the following year, and eventually formed the first black Shaker community, the Philadelphia Shaker Family. Predominantly female, Jackson's community combined "elements from Shakerism and others from the female praying band traditions" of Methodism, Jackson's first faith and ministry (Humez, "Introduction" 40). Notably, then, Jackson's ministry was improvisatory and syncretic, adapting Shaker beliefs and practices to suit the particular needs of Philadelphia area blacks she believed were in need of support and religious guidance come the 1840s and 1850s and integrating those Methodist practices that gave prominent roles to women in religious meetings. Jackson's work reveals the ways in which liminal religious practices, out of which "new models . . . [and] paradigms arise" (Turner 28), could be devised to empower women and forge community among African Americans marginalized and threatened by whites at midcentury in northern urban centers. Jackson's ministry importantly integrated the material and spiritual, refusing a hierarchy that would see the material as needing to be transcended, and so ultimately elided, through the interiority of spirit or soul. Leaving what she once thought was her spiritual home, Jackson chose African American community over the predominantly white Shaker communities of upstate New York. That choice gave her a leadership role and the opportunity to combine her "radical" spiritual beliefs and practices, like celibacy and asceticism, with those elements of black Methodism that, as we shall see, were regarded by the majority of African Americans as essential forms of worship.

Undoubtedly the most famous early African American feminist, Sojourner Truth, began her public career as a preacher. Even though Truth continued to combine the spiritual and the political throughout her reform career—she was well known by the 1870s for laboring "in the cause of Christ and humanity" (qtd. in Gilbert and Titus 263)—Truth has circulated in scholarship on black women's political culture primarily as a reformer with passing attention to her work as a preacher.[10] Yet Truth was known by her contemporaries as a "miraculous" preacher of extraordinary skill (Mabee 27) who "out-prayed and -preached her compeers" (Vale 126). Initially affiliated with Methodism and a member in the 1830s of what would become the mother church of AME Zion in Church Street, New York City, Truth was a "zealous" Methodist (Fitch and Mandziuk 14) who was drawn to the social gospel and Holiness inflected "free meetings" of New York perfectionism while living with James Latourette and his wife (Painter, *Sojourner* 40).

From 1829 to 1831, Truth, born Isabella Baumfree and later known as Isabella Van Wangenen, became "established . . . as a powerful and moving preacher," largely through camp meetings around New York City and appeared with some of the century's most "charismatic" preachers (Painter, *Sojourner* 43–44). Early in her career, Truth's preaching was focused on women's material condition as she evangelized prostitutes and undertook moral reform with the Magdalene Asylum in New York City (Stetson and David 79). However, Truth, like Elaw, was not welcomed by African Americans she sought to minister to and convert. She later spoke of that rejection experienced in New York while at the height of her reform work. In a lecture advocating black civil rights at the First Congregational Church in New York City on September 6, 1853, Truth reportedly said "she wanted to get among her own colored people and teach them . . . but they repulsed and shoved her off; yet she felt she wanted to be doing." This transcript of her speech published in the *New York Tribune* continued, "She used to go and hold prayer meetings at the houses of the people in Five Points, then Chapel st., but she found they were always more inclined to hear great people, and she instanced the case of one colored woman who declining her prayers, said she had two or three ministers about!" ("Address" 146).

Taking the name Sojourner Truth, she left New York in the summer of 1843 to undertake an itinerancy in "the east" (Gilbert and Titus 99) and preached throughout Long Island and Connecticut, primarily at camp meetings of Second-Day Adventists or Millerites.[11] In 1879, Truth would be quoted by a Chicago newspaper as saying that during this itinerant period from 1843 to 1844 she preached "religion and abolition all the way" until she settled at the Northampton Association, where she would remain until it broke up in 1846 (qtd. in Mabee 47).[12] Truth undertook a second itinerancy after her stay at Northampton and continued to preach during a career that has been documented as primarily reform focused, testifying to her conversion well into her eighties and describing her reform work as "inspired by the Almighty" (Gilbert and Titus 204, 238). Indeed, in the 1870s Truth was being introduced as "the venerable preacher and missionary" at reform speaking engagements and was known by some as "Mother in Israel" (Gilbert and Titus 249, 265), having become established as a nationally recognized speaker for abolition, woman's rights, temperance, and the civil rights of African Americans.

At least since Jarena Lee's time, then, preaching women argued for women's and African Americans' rights and contended with fierce opposition to their work, placing them and their ministries in a liminal position within the various communities they reached. Julia Foote (b. 1823), a freeborn woman who grew up in the Burned-over District of New York[13] and joined the AME

Zion Church of Boston after moving there, had always "opposed . . . the preaching of women, and had spoken against it" (Foote 201). Yet she felt herself called to preach around the age of eighteen and did so in her Boston home in the early 1840s, when her AME Zion minister denied her access to the church (Foote 205). Eventually excommunicated from the AME Church for refusing to heed their sanctions against her work, Foote included a chapter titled "Women in the Gospel" in her spiritual autobiography. There she argued against the necessity of a woman "work[ing] a miracle" to "prove [her] right to preach" and cited Philip's four preaching daughters, Paul's "helpers" Priscilla and Aquila, and Phoebe's ministry. In a sharp turn of phrase Foote quipped, "When Paul said, 'Help those women who labor with me in the Gospel,' he certainly meant that they did more than to pour out tea" (Foote 209).

Foote also labored in the slave states at personal risk. In the summer of 1849, Daniel Payne, who would be elected bishop in 1852, invited Foote to work with him in Baltimore. While it had been dangerous for Elizabeth and Zilpha Elaw decades earlier, preaching in Maryland was even more of a risk in the volatile late 1840s, when abolition had clearly emerged as a reform with which to be reckoned. Foote was examined as a potential runaway slave on more than one occasion: "Upon our arrival there we were closely questioned as to our freedom and carefully examined for marks on our person by which to identify us if we should prove to be runaways. While there . . . [t]hey often came to our bed and held the light in our faces, to see if the one for whom they were looking was not with us" (219–20).[14] Foote uses these incidents to indict slavery as "the monster" and recounts further itinerant labors in which she took a stand against white racism and advocated racial equality: "The white Methodists [of Chillicothe, Ohio] invited me to speak for them [in April 1851], but did not want the colored people to attend the meeting. I would not agree to any such arrangement, and, therefore, I did not speak for them. Prejudice had closed the door of their sanctuary against the colored people of the place, virtually saying, 'The Gospel shall not be free to all'" (222). Foote refused to abstract religion from the social inequities it could be used to enable and secure, marking Chillicothe's notion of spiritual transcendence as produced through its inaccessibility "to all."

Later in the century, nationally renowned evangelists Amanda Berry Smith and Annie E. Brown were still denouncing racial prejudice, advocating black civil rights, and agitating for woman's right to preach. Yet the focus for those political arguments had shifted: black civil rights and the realization of freedom's promise, rather than abolition itself, became the goal, and the issue of women in the pulpit in the 1880s and 1890s, part of earlier woman's rights discourse, would by then be heard as connected to a primarily suffragist-oriented woman's rights movement. Amanda Smith, born a slave in Long Green, Maryland, January 23, 1837, pursued a Methodist Episcopal evangelizing mission from 1878 to 1890 in which she spoke against racism. Growing up in a home that was a main station on the Underground Railroad in New Market, Pennsylvania, Smith saw her mother publicly shame slave catchers "in front of the largest Tavern" and effectively drive them from the town (A. Smith 31, 34).

Amanda Smith followed that preaching women's tradition of speaking out at personal risk and with considerable personal experience of the need to do so: she was born a slave and in September 1862 her sister, freeborn in Pennsylvania, was kidnapped and sold into slavery (A. Smith 51). Experiencing racism in the white Free Methodist church she wished to join for its antislavery position, Smith testified in her spiritual autobiography to the racial inequities she experienced, suggesting that "people would understand the quintessence of sanctifying grace if they could be black about twenty-four hours. . . . [W]e who are the royal black are very well satisfied with His gift to us in this substantial color" (A. Smith 116–17). Yet Smith was also often called "a 'white folks' nigger'" by "some of my own people" (A. Smith 232) for her successful missions among white Americans and their financial support of her work, even though she saw her work at predominantly white camp meetings in the 1870s as "curing" whites of racism (A. Smith 184, 223, 477–78). Smith's experience of white racism and her belief that she was instrumental in eradicating it among the whites she encountered and preached to are hardly incidental, given the time period in which she labored. Reconstruction was clearly failing African Americans, with President Johnson instituting Black Codes and opposing the Freedmen's Bureau and its work while white mob violence was on the rise. By 1877, newly elected President Hayes would bargain away federal authority to the interest of southern states, leaving African American civil rights unprotected and black men and women quite literally in fear for their lives. In the midst of such national regression in the securing of African American civil rights and protections, Smith was recognized across the country for her work and the conversions she brought about. A "trailblazer for black female evangelists of the nineteenth century," she was "the most visible black preaching woman of the period" (Dodson, "Introduction" xxvii, xxxii).

Smith's religious career, then, saw her positioned in complex ways. A national figure, yet one who experienced racism at predominantly white camp meetings where she was, nonetheless, a sought-after figure of spiritual inspiration, Smith also was treated as an outsider, as one who had betrayed "the race" despite battling against racism during the volatile 1870s because her ministry reached these different communities rather than remained focused on African Americans. As a woman, Smith could not preach within black Methodism, and her decision to preach to those who would have her became further grounds for her rejection by some African Americans. Taking her mission even further afield in 1882, Amanda Smith began missionary work in Liberia among blacks who had emigrated from the United States during the colonization movement. She would continue that work for eight years, though in no less a contested position, agitating for temperance despite opposition to her efforts. While on tour in India in the early 1880s, opposition to Smith's preaching was so strong among her "Plymouth brethren" that it was registered in the press, causing Smith to directly address it in a sermon at Bangalore. She gave her "version" of Paul's prohibition against women speaking in church, titled "Let your 'men' keep silence in the church," and "the newspaper articles . . . and the letters stopped, and I went on till I got through" (A. Smith 321).

Annie Brown, itinerant evangelist famous for her Gospel Wagon and successful revivals, advocated both black civil rights and woman's right to preach during a ministry active while lynching was on the rise and the woman suffrage movement was gaining additional strength through its reunification. Born in Washington, D.C., in 1862, Brown began evangelizing in 1893 at the age of thirty-one. She preached to and converted whites and blacks throughout the 1890s, earning the attention of the religious and mainstream press alike, who referred to her as "perhaps the most remarkable and successful soul winner of color in America" (A. Brown 55). Brown was a licensed Methodist Episcopal evangelist who preached to thousands in urban revivals that often began with her preaching from her wagon in alleyways and streets. Using her traveling pulpit to speak "on the 'Negro Problem,'" Brown argued against seeing whites as the "enemies of blacks" and for African Americans to get "God on your side" before entering politics. Founder of the Light House Rescue Mission for "fallen women" in New York City (A. Brown ii), she was also a strong advocate of women's rights, noting that "the colored race" had been "hindered" by "not respect[ing] the women" (A. Brown 46–47). By the early 1900s, Brown had become famous for "her celebrated lecture, 'Should a woman preach'" (A. Brown 55).

Spiritual Publics: Recognizing the Political and Its Locations

Yet while Brown's late-nineteenth- and early-twentieth-century feminist sermons on woman's right to access the pulpit and her declarations that African American racial advancement depended upon according greater respect and roles to women would arguably link her work to feminist agitation at that time, she is no more regarded an important feminist political figure than those preaching women who made similar arguments early in the nineteenth century and onward. Brown's significance seems limited to her singularity as a successful itinerant black female evangelist, even though *what* and *how* she preached extends the feminism of black preaching women into the early twentieth century. Brown's absence from narratives of nineteenth-century black feminism is instructive for understanding why African American preaching women as a whole tend not to be taken up as central to that history, despite their antislavery and feminist political stances recorded in their spiritual autobiographies. At a time when black women were forming regional, state, and national associations primarily through the black women's club movement and extending the suffrage movement through black women's suffrage associations, a nationally recognized figure like Brown, and the press coverage her feminist sermons garnered, should have been quite important for taking the message of women's rights to both white and black communities and the nation at large. Yet because the critical tendency has been to understand "first wave" black feminism as reaching its apex with the development of national organizations and federations at the century's close, the work of black women in other arenas has been overlooked or under examined. How we focus our critical lens, how we define political and/or feminist work, will determine to what extent we recognize the labors of African American preaching women.[15]

As we have seen from African American preaching women's spiritual autobiographies, the emphasis on the late nineteenth century as the flowering of black feminism does not reflect available documents, but rather reflects, as Elsa Barkley Brown has argued of histories of black women's political culture in general, "the conceptual paradigms . . . guid[ing] the investigation of black women's politics" (141, n. 52). Yet even if we ignore the significant history of African American preaching women throughout the nineteenth century and concentrate only on the 1890s, we should at the very least give full hearing to Emilie Townes's contention that "the primary responses of the late-nineteenth-century African American woman to her struggle with the narrow space and dark enclosure of racial and economic subordination were expressed through her commitments to *religious and social organizations*" (156; emphasis added). Undoubtedly, we scratch only the surface with the African American preaching women we do know of, and yet even this incomplete view of their political and spiritual labors shows us a vital black feminism in the face of significant opposition and harsh material conditions. Brown was part of that tradition and one of the few, along with the likes of Sojourner Truth and Amanda Berry Smith, whose work was nationally respected and admired.

However, the central place black preaching women gave their spirituality has meant that their labors are not always immediately recognized as political. Political associations were not their foremost form of community, even in the case of someone like Jarena Lee who was a member of an antislavery association.[16] As Katherine Clay Bassard notes, unlike slave narrators, black women spiritual autobiographers wrote and "published outside of any 'political' movement" ("Gender" 122), self-publishing and distributing their own manuscripts at religious gatherings. The spiritual was central to their lives and work and must be understood as such, making recognizing the political in their labors a more complicated matter than we might expect. This may explain why scholars like Nellie McKay and William Hunter have argued that African American preaching women's writing pursued little in the way of feminism or the political. McKay has contended that while spiritual narratives give us insight into "Afro-American intellectual thought," they lack "the immediate overt political value of the slave narratives (i.e., they seldom clamored for abolition)" (141). As we have seen, however, African American preaching women did preach abolition in addition to woman's and black civil rights. Yet William Hunter argues that though preaching women "made great strides in gaining their own independence, their importance as feminist voices is limited" (85). Such assessments both misstate and underestimate the work of black preaching women of the nineteenth century and leave unexamined the conceptions of "feminist" and "political" upon which they rest.

In contrast, when scholars studying the spiritual autobiographies and careers of African American preaching women have contended that their labors were political, they take a rather straightforward view of the political and assert that preaching women argued for a woman's right to preach as an issue of gender equity.[17] Claiming that their authority to speak came with their divine call, and referring to themselves as instruments of God, African American preaching women have been understood to advocate the political position they did by *disavowing* their personal or political motivations in what they represented as divinely led and determined spiritual labors.[18] Consequently, one could neither fault nor persecute these women for risking unfavorable positions on gender and racial equity when they claimed such positions came from God. However, the religious and divine were not rhetorical tools, as such scholarship has tended to imply, but were always uppermost for these women, and their call for a woman's right to preach was based not in gender equity in and of itself but in their belief that an individual must fulfill her call regardless of her gender or role, status, and power. To not do so would be to willfully reject the role God had determined for her and to fail to attain her most holy relationship with the divine and the human community. Similarly, all are seen as equal before the divine power in which they believed, and to preach against inequities of condition based in racial and gender prejudice was not simply a matter of politics but was part of fulfilling one's call and mission. Preaching women thus politicized the soul by insisting upon the connection between material realities and a spiritual life; the spiritual was not understood as transcending the material or social, nor was it seen as a rhetorical tool.

Understanding these preaching women as motivated to fulfill a "divine" call as they pursued a "secular" politics does not, however, diminish the political efficacy of what they did preach or write. But it does necessitate that we understand it on its own terms, rather than attempt to conform their spiritual work to contemporary notions of what is political and feminist. I would urge those who argue these texts are part of a "depoliticizing trend common in black spiritual life-writing of the nineteenth century" (Douglass-Chin 36) to reconsider what they define as political and from where those definitions derive. To preach the spiritual is not to sacrifice the political; rather, the spiritual was highly politicized at the time these women actively preached. Importantly, as Katherine Clay Bassard asserts, refusing such a split has been a basic tenet of black religious culture: "The African American church was the primary institutional vehicle to register collective consciousness in formation, serving not only as a spiritual center but as schoolhouse, [and] meeting place for political gatherings. . . . The refusal of a split between religious and social, sacred and secular, is fundamental to African American religious culture" (*Spiritual* 93).

Rather than depoliticizing their messages by delivering them in spiritual autobiographies, African American preaching women were effectively taking them to the heart of collective African American politics, the church and religious culture itself. Yet even scholars who note that "the few discussions of black women preachers present them as being concerned primarily with religious and spiritual matters, leaving little space to consider them as the very active agents for social change that they actually were" (Haywood 92), persist in asserting that "though prior to [the late 1800s] black women had always played active roles in shaping and defining black life and culture, at the turn of the century they were more actively and vocally questioning the status quo" (Haywood 90). Yet the status quo, whether racialized, gendered or classed, was vigorously questioned by these women as they undertook the work of God well before the turn into the twentieth century.

Although these abolitionist, civil rights, and feminist agitations from the itinerant pulpit and revival meeting might strike some as less political or less politically effective forms of protest because they were part of religious practice with a stress on the spiritual, and because they took place in what appear at first glance to be "marginal" spaces, it is imperative that we understand the political differently and understand appeals to the spiritual or the soul as, themselves, political. An inability to recognize the political in the spiritual is to hold to the notion that the spiritual is somehow prepolitical rather than constitutive of a public sphere "of supposedly open and equal access" (Castronovo 139). Participation and leadership in organized societies, institutionalized denominations, and state and national organizations are also far from the only recognizable forms of early black feminist politics despite a longstanding tendency to center black feminism and its "defining moment" in these forms.[19] What Carol George argues of male itinerant preachers advocating abolition is true of preaching women agitating against slavery and for woman's and black civil rights: politicized leadership "was as likely to be found among men in small parishes and on the itinerant circuit who, despite their less favorable circumstances, were able to stoke the fires of antislavery sentiment by suggesting new options to the black folks who heard them from day to day. The church was as close to a grass roots movement as the free black community could sustain at that stage in its development" (157).

Even though African American preaching women may not have always seen themselves as part of a grass-roots political movement, their labors were political nonetheless. One might argue that feminist sermons defending a woman's right to preach, like Annie Brown's "Should a woman preach," were highly effective for the people they reached. Indeed, Brown routinely preached at revivals numbering several thousand of both races. And in the case of preaching women addressing much smaller audiences and congregations, such politicized preaching, exhorting, and evangelizing reached people who otherwise would have limited access to such messages. This is particularly true of the South under slavery, where, as Albert Raboteau argues, "the great majority of rural slaves remained outside the reach of the institutional church" (152). Finally, the importance of the church, and religious meetings in general, as political sites should not be underestimated. As Evelyn Brooks Higginbotham reminds us, the "black church . . . [is] a social space for discussion of public concerns" (10). A revised understanding of what counts as political and feminist, a strong sense of the black church as central to African American political life, and a recognition of the spiritual and political as intimately linked are necessary to appreciating the import of preaching women's work.

Institutional Opposition: The Example of the AME Church

We have a more extensive record of AME preaching women actively agitating for a woman's right to preach than of any other denomination. That record includes not only Jarena Lee's request to be licensed in 1809 and renewed in 1817, a year after the AME Church was officially organized, but also references to women who followed her, such as Sarah Ann Hughes, licensed in 1882; Margaret Wilson, appointed a pastorate in 1883; and Florence Randolph, licensed as a local preacher in 1897 and one of the first women elders in the AME Church.[20] Yet as Jualynne Dodson notes, despite "a record-keeping tradition" that predates its formal organization in 1816, the AME Church "has yet to reclaim women" in its history ("Introduction" xxvii–xxviii), even though "women were the numerical majority of the AME Church throughout the 19th century" ("Power" 38). The largest black denomination in America and the first to be independent of white denominations, its position on the licensing of women as preachers is an instructive example for our understanding of black preaching women in the nineteenth-century northern and southern United States.[21] But more important, as Cheryl Townsend Gilkes contends, "the origins of black *biblical* feminism probably lie in the African Methodist Episcopal (AME) Church" (99; emphasis added) and the arguments it heard on woman's right to preach. We need to extend Gilkes's assertion, however, so that African American preaching women, within the AME Church and without, are acknowledged as central figures to early black feminism. Their spiritual labors took up social concerns and was responsible, in its very pursuit, for challenging social norms and hierarchies within the church and the wider society.

Founded in 1794, the AME Church began with Richard Allen establishing AME Bethel Church in Philadelphia in response to the treatment of

African American congregants at St. George's Methodist Episcopal Church in that city.[22] Dunbar notes that "mother Bethel had a congregation comprising, for the most part, poor, working African Americans. . . . [A]nd although Mother Bethel advocated formal education for its congregants, the church remained sensitive to the limitations and barriers to literacy faced by many black men and women" (99). The black Methodists' main branches are the AME, AME Zion, and Christian Methodist Episcopal Church (CME), first known as the Colored Methodist Episcopal Church. The CME Church, which wished to remain distinct from the AME and AME Zion churches of the North, was founded by former slaves in the South in 1866 and formally organized in 1870 (Lincoln and Mamiya 62). The AME Zion, founded in New York City in 1796, broke with the Philadelphia AME in 1824 and became known as the "Freedom Church," claiming famous members such as Sojourner Truth, Harriet Tubman, and Frederick Douglass. Living up to its name, AME Zion was the first to ordain women (Lincoln and Mamiya 58). Women were ordained deacons in Zion in 1894 (Julia Foote) and elders in 1898 (Mrs. Mary J. Small) (Lincoln and Mamiya 74, 285).[23] In contrast, full ordination for women in the AME Church was not achieved until 1948, and in the CME Church not until 1954 (Lincoln and Mamiya 286).

Jean Humez notes that "early pioneer Methodism had allowed women a prominent role as lay and licensed preachers" as early as the 1770s ("Female Preaching" 313), yet when the subject of women preaching began to be considered at the AME general conferences in the 1840s, the church was undergoing significant changes. In the 1830s the AME Church was already "becoming more heterogeneous, and more class-conscious, than it had been at the turn of the century." One result of its changing demographic was the leadership's desire to alter the public image of African Americans by weeding out an "uneducated ministry" through "educational requirements for the ministry at all levels—lay, 'licensed,' and ordained" (Humez, "Female Preaching" 311–12). These education requirements were presented and passed as resolutions at the Baltimore Annual Conference in 1845 (Payne 17). Viewed as part of these "improvements," AME attempts to contain the preaching activities of women included defeating the initial petition for the general conference to "make provisions for females to preach and exhort" in 1844 and the Daughters of Zion's subsequent petition to license women in 1848 (Dodson, "Nineteenth-Century A.M.E." 280). Through much of the 1850s and 1860s, AME general conferences either defeated similar petitions or refused to discuss them. In 1852, for example, the general conference held in New York was attended by many of its 139 members, who heard Rev. William Paul Quinn request that "something distinct may be done that will be satisfactory to all, and the question [of licensing women] be put to rest" (Payne 271). While the conference discussed the issue "with a great deal of judgment and spirit," rather than ignored it, "the motion was . . . lost by a large majority" (Payne 273).

The pressure to acknowledge the work preaching women undertook on the church's behalf remained strong, however, and AME leadership responded by creating the official position of stewardess and the Board of Stewardesses in an attempt to officially limit women's roles within the church. As Dodson documents, the "position of stewardess did not entail ordination[,] . . . existed under the strict control of churchmen[, and] . . . formalized the subordinate, serving role of women in the AME church" ("Nineteenth-Century A.M.E." 282). At this 1858 General Conference of the AME Church, roles women were already permitted were reaffirmed—exhorter, missionary, evangelist—as arguably an empty gesture of appeasement designed to stem the demands that preaching women be allowed the same status and position as preaching men within the church. The resolution of the 1858 conference was also an attempt to bring preaching women from liminal and clearly powerful positions beyond church structure into subordinate positions under its control. The church not only delimited the work preaching women could undertake in the late 1850s but also felt the need to repeat this maneuver some twenty-five years later.[24]

In 1884 the general conference again heard a resolution that proposed licensing preaching women. Even though "it was evident that a majority of the convention were in favor of the resolution," it was referred for amendment and substantially diminished. The resolution returned simply authorized women "as stewards, trustees and class-leaders" and was passed ("General Conference"). Several preaching women were in attendance, including Sarah Ann Hughes (North Carolina), Margaret Wilson (New Jersey), Mrs. Williams (South Carolina), Mrs. Cooper (Baltimore), Mrs. Mary Palmer, Mrs. Hall, and Mrs. Askins (Angell 100). Dodson notes that this conference seemed particularly nervous about appeals to license women as preachers and saw a subsequent resolution introduced and adopted which sought "to clarify the boundaries of women's authority": "'Whereas, We have in church some female ministers who have been holding pastoral charges much to the detriment of church, Therefore be it Resolved, that they are hereby prohibited from assignments to any special work, and hereafter shall labor simply as evangelists'" (qtd. in Dodson, "Nineteenth-Century A.M.E." 286).

During the 1880s, the majority of men in the AME ministry supported women in the role of evangelist, or "evangelist of conference," an unsalaried position that entailed "conducting regular or special worship on a one-time-only or limited-time basis" (Angell 95). Clearly this kept preaching women, even nationally renowned and charismatic figures such as Amanda Berry Smith, in a secondary position and ensured that women would not compete with men for pastorates or higher positions like that of deacon. Far from marginal in a church that refused to ordain them, the very fact that they were repeatedly refused ordination, and positions were devised in the hopes of quelling their agitation for further access within the church, registers just how powerfully central preaching women's labors and politicizing of the ministry actually were to the church.[25] And while the AME Church sought to silence them in the pulpits of their day and in the history it wrote thereafter, we know of women who continued to preach despite significant attempts to limit their work.[26] Early black feminism as it was enacted within the black church was itself central, a politics from within the church and its preaching ranks responding to the inequities its own community faced and promulgated. Some of these inequities were produced in response to shifting class dynamics within the church, making it necessary for black feminism to take up a complex position and politics that addressed more than gender and more than the larger American society and its racism. Yet black feminism as preaching women pursued it also responded to the loss of position for women within the church. Women had enjoyed greater access to the church and positions within it under early Methodism than they were being permitted under the institutionalizing AME Church.

Praying Bands, Holiness, and Ecstatic Worship

Women not only threatened the AME Church with their agitations to be licensed, ordained, and permitted access to leadership roles but also created anxiety among a leadership interested in "sanitizing" the image of African Americans by banning ecstatic or "extravagant" ministry. Sanctions against the ecstatic style of their worship, perhaps more so than the denial of status and position to women in the church, caused some AME preaching women to leave the church during the height of midcentury struggles over their role. Daniel Payne had singled out as "heathenish" and "disgraceful" the "extravagant" worship styles and practices of largely female "praying and singing bands" in 1841 and again in the 1870s after he had become bishop (qtd. in

C. Smith 126). While preaching women left AME churches to join the Holiness revival (Humez, "Female Preaching" 315), many stayed and continued an ecstatic form of preaching and worship. Importantly, Payne remarks that he "usually succeeded in making the [praying and singing] 'band' disgusting" among "[t]he most thoughtful and intelligent . . . but by the ignorant masses . . . it was regarded as the essence of religion" (qtd. in C. Smith 126).

Women such as Old Elizabeth, Jarena Lee, Rebecca Cox Jackson, Amanda Smith, and Harriet Baker associated with Methodist and Holiness praying bands that were clearly instrumental in their faith and their own coming to preach. And as Jean Humez notes, the predominantly female praying bands provided women both support and a route to preaching from the early days of black Methodism onward: "Predominantly or entirely female 'praying bands' were an early and continuing phenomenon of black Methodism in America and were the original unit of the Holiness movement. . . . [T]estifying to spiritual experience in these small groups, meeting weekly at the homes of their members, encouraged substantial numbers of devout black Methodist women to think of preaching to larger audiences. In these relatively intimate, highly participatory, democratic religious gatherings, in the familiar private world of women friends, spiritual talents and speaking skills were developed and protected" ("Introduction" 6). Humez effectively describes female praying bands as what Catherine Squires would call an "enclaved public." In her call to attend to "the public struggles and political innovations of . . . groups outside traditional or state-sanctioned public spaces and mainstream discourse" (446), Squires stresses the importance of multiple publics, including counterpublics, enclave publics, and satellite publics. In the separate spaces or institutions of enclaved publics, she asserts, individuals can "foster their public speaking skills, create campaigns, and facilitate resistance . . . hidden from the view of the dominant public" (458). As we will see in chapter 2, enclaved publics such as mutual benevolent associations and literary societies proved the entryway for black women into abolition politics.

The importance of praying bands is registered in several preaching women's spiritual autobiographies. Old Elizabeth persevered through both self-doubt and opposition in order to preach first at the gathering of a praying band of African American women: "[T]he Spirit directed me to go to a poor widow and ask her if I might have a meeting at her house, which was situated in one of the lowest and worst streets in Baltimore. . . . I appeared there among a few coloured sisters . . . and while I was speaking, the house seemed filled with light" (10). Jarena Lee writes of the difficulty of "leav[ing] . . .

those who composed the *band* of which I was one" in Philadelphia in order to move to Snow Hill with her husband, six miles away, in 1811 (*Life* 39). Lacking such "agreement and closeness in communion and fellowship [as] I had in Philadelphia," Lee fell "into a state of general debility, and in an ill state of health, so much so, that I could not sit up" (*Life* 39–40). Prayer meetings were also her first preaching opportunities. Even though Lee felt called to "speak to the people in a public manner," she felt she could only do so in "the house of a sister belonging to the same society with myself" where she first addressed "but five persons" (*Life* 45).

Harriet Baker's and Amanda Smith's experiences reveal Daniel Payne's inability to rid black Methodism of the praying band. Prayer bands were so instrumental to Harriet Baker's faith and call to preach that she may have never labored spiritually without them. John Acornley's 1892 biography of Baker relates her conversion in "1842, when about twelve or thirteen years of age" at a band meeting some five miles from her home: "[T]he women began to come in, two or three at a time, until there was about sixteen of them. Then they got up and locked the door, . . . put a great bar across . . . [and] commenced the meeting. . . . [T]hat night, praise God! He saved my soul. . . . He taught me by his spirit to read his holy Word, and . . . to understand it also" (Acornley 30–32). Baker's conversion experience at this female prayer band meeting "inspired" her to become literate and led her to her calling as a famous evangelist and an itinerancy that began in 1872 when she was 43 (Acornley 41).[27] Amanda Smith's spiritual autobiography closes with her admiration of the "many . . . Christian sisters among all the colored churches in Philadelphia, New York, and Baltimore . . . generally called Band Sisters and . . . noted for their deep piety and Christian character. I loved them for this" (493–94). Smith's reference to African American praying band sisters dates from the 1890s, evidence that, despite Daniel Payne's attempts decades earlier to eradicate them, they were alive and flourishing in the eastern states just as Harriet Baker's spiritual autobiography indicates they were in the 1840s, when he first began trying to convince AME Church members to abandon them.

The centrality of female praying bands in the experiences of these particular women and others, as evidenced by their existence and longevity, should not be underestimated simply because such groups lacked institutional endorsement and were not part of formal black Methodist Church structure. Their role in the everyday religious life of black female Methodists was a central one, for they provided a place for female-led worship while operating outside institutional structure. To women who experienced hostility and opposition to both their call and their very persons, the space praying bands afforded them was surely sustaining. And according to Daniel Payne's own account of his attempts to rid black Methodism of the prayer band, it was far from a marginal phenomenon. Rather, as we recall Payne saying, it was "regarded as the essence of religion" by "the masses." Because prayer bands were a form of liminal religious practice located between church structure and what the majority of nineteenth-century African Americans regarded as religion, they were threatening to the AME Church's desire to consolidate its role and influence with its public. This threat is clearly evident in Daniel Payne's and the AME Church's attempts to contain and eradicate the predominantly female praying bands.

Payne's anxiety also extended, we recall, to "bad customs of worship." Particularly in need of "correction" were "extravagant" worship styles, even though these had been part of black Methodism from its inception. AME services before institutionalization at midcentury seem to have resembled Holiness meetings as Jarena Lee describes them in her spiritual autobiography. Lee relates interrupting sermons at Philadelphia's Bethel AME with exhortations that were not only permitted but also referred to by a presiding minister as a "witness of the power of Christ" (*Life* 29), incorporated in a call-and-response fashion. Later, Bishop Allen would call Lee's intervening exhortations evidence of her call to preach (*Life* 45). While undertaking her itinerant ministry, Lee conducted services that enabled worship of an expressive and participatory nature, in which "much weeping was heard among the people" (*Life* 47) and the "wonderful shock of God's power" was evidenced "everywhere by groans, by sighs, and loud and happy amens. I felt aided from above. My tongue was cut loose" (*Life* 48). Indeed, AME founder Richard Allen believed that Methodism initially attracted African Americans because of its style of "'spiritual extempore preaching'" (qtd. in Humez, "Female Preaching" 311).

Katherine Clay Bassard documents the characteristics of AME services before Payne became bishop in 1841, including "spirituals, spontaneous and antiphonal singing, and the ring shout, a holy dance adapted from African sacred dance ritual" (*Spiritual* 94). Yet despite Daniel Payne's attempts to have it otherwise, to the vast majority of AME members, ecstatic preaching, like the prayer band, was religion as they knew it, making preaching women and their style central to "the masses" whatever Payne thought of them. In this way, then, nineteenth-century preaching women in the AME Church worked at the center of what most African Americans identified as religious worship, not at its margins where, in fact, a more "educated" ministry labored in a restrained style. Payne may have sought to make that kind of spiritual work the norm, but he could not overcome a long-lived and widely accepted style of preaching and worshiping, nor could he contain the effect of the Holiness revival movement gaining hold outside his churches.

As Melvin Easterday Dieter notes, "[F]rom the time of the Great Awakening until the close of the nineteenth century revivalism was the dominant force in the shaping of American Protestantism."[28] The Holiness movement or Holiness revival was "at the center of . . . Christian tradition . . . bringing thousands of new converts into the Christian faith and churches . . . [and] reform[ing] the church itself" (1, 6). Significantly, women led the Holiness movement, beginning, as it did, with Sarah Lankford's "house church" in 1835, or the "Tuesday Meetings for the Promotion of Holiness," and extending with Lankford's sister Phoebe Worrall Palmer's Tuesday meetings that became the Palmer movement (Dieter 26–27).

Holiness stressed the importance of a public testimony of one's attainment of grace and held that after conversion the second experience of grace, spiritual perfection or sanctification, was necessary for salvation. As Jean Humez defines it, conversion or justification was the "conviction that [one's] sins were forgiven and [one] was 'made just' through Christ's love." Sanctification, the second state of grace or blessedness, was the experience of "full freedom from 'intentional sin,'" a "second, higher, heartfelt experience of divine grace" ("Introduction" 5). Holiness attracted women because it so highly valued personal testimony, which "gave many a . . . woman the authority and power to speak out 'as the Holy Spirit led her'" (Dieter 42), and Holiness "had a particularly strong appeal for black women," likely because, Humez speculates, attaining sanctification, a feeling of "complete personal security[,] . . . could be of great psychological value for a woman who had to deal daily with white racism" ("Introduction" 5).

Even though Holiness was Methodist in origin, it was an interdenominational revivalist movement that spread through the private and domestic Tuesday meetings held in homes as well as through public revivals and camp meetings. By the mid-nineteenth century, Tuesday meetings were common in "the major cities of the east and west," camp meeting reporters were giving accounts of sanctifications as well as "the more usual conversions" as "increasingly common" experiences at revivals, and Holiness had moved to a more public arena through "inter-denominational evangelism" (Dieter 45, 48). The Second Great Awakening of the nineteenth century, which reached beyond the United States to Canada and Great Britain, was rooted in the Holiness revival begun in the 1830s.

Holiness was *the* mass religious movement of the nineteenth century in America, reaching believers both within and beyond institutionalized denominations and empowering both black and white women in ways they had been denied. For preaching black women, regardless of denomination, the experience of sanctification was paramount and drew many to Holiness revivals and camp meetings. In current scholarship, much has been made of sanctification as an experience of direct contact with the divine that gave African American preaching women the authority to preach. Such scholarship contends that these women claimed a self-empowerment ensuing from that experience of "perfection" or from the earlier experience of conversion itself.[29] Many preaching women wrote of receiving the call to preach after they received the blessing of sanctification, yet their narration of the experience of sanctification does not seem to serve the purpose of claiming authority or self-empowerment to undertake those spiritual labors but stresses the liminal qualities of sanctification as a step toward the religious community that their ministries both sought and helped to foster.

Women such as Jarena Lee, Rebecca Cox Jackson, and Julia Foote tell of physical phenomena accompanying their sanctification, often an unusual bodily experience that signaled the direct contact of the divine and a merging of spiritual and material worlds. Lee writes of being on her knees praying for sanctification when, "that very instant, as if lightning had darted through me, I sprang to my feet and cried, 'The Lord has sanctified my soul!' . . . The first I knew of myself after that, I was standing in the yard with my hands spread out, and looking with my face toward heaven. . . . So great was the joy, that it is past description" (*Life* 34). Julia Foote found herself "prostrate . . . to the floor" during her experience of sanctification, and like Lee, she felt the physical sensation of a divine presence: "There was, indeed, a weight of glory resting upon me" (Foote 186).

Rebecca Cox Jackson was converted during a summer storm in July 1830, when she "was wakened by thunder and lightening at the break of day" (Jackson 71).[30] Her later sanctification was unusual for the powers of self-preservation it seemed to give Jackson, powers so strange she frightened her husband. Having been ill for at least three weeks, Jackson attended a revival meeting in a neighbor's home and, like Foote, became prostrate for several hours praying for sanctification.[31] At midnight she received it, and "at that hour my burden rolled off. I felt as light as air. I sprang upon my feet, shouting and leaping the high praises of God" (76). Jackson continued for a full hour and then returned home, where she marched "from the [open] cellar door to the [hot] stove and when I would get to the stove I would lay my hands on the stove and then turn to the cellar with my eyes shut all the while. . . . He [Jackson's husband] expected every time I laid my hands on the stove to see the skin come off . . . and when I went to the cellar door, to see me fall down the cellar. . . . He got up as if he was afraid of me and set me down on a chair" (77). A controlling man who was violent with her because he opposed her religious views and celibate lifestyle, Jackson's husband was so affected by her travels between the dangers of cellar and stove that he could do little but watch her until finally her state shifted and he could persuade her to sit while he got her a glass of water.[32]

For Jackson, sanctification unsettled her husband's position of power in their relationship and, subsequently, shifted her role so that her beliefs and ascetic practices steered their relationship, despite his opposition, until they parted in 1836. Jackson insisted on a celibate lifestyle and on spiritual labors in the face of her husband's, the AME Church's, and her own brother's op-position, who was a preacher with that denomination. Significantly, then, Jackson was determined to integrate Shaker (celibacy), Methodist (the pray-ing band), and Holiness (sanctification) beliefs in what would become her in-dependent spiritual ministry, causing her work to be regarded as controversial and to be opposed by black Methodists and Shakers.[33]

Many of these women's experiences of sanctification were characterized by liminal states of consciousness. Jarena Lee lost sense of where she was, dis-covering she "was standing in the yard" after having "retired to a secret place to pray" (*Life* 35, 34). Rebecca Cox Jackson was not aware that she was at turns risking falling down her cellar steps and burning her hands on her hot stove. Receiving sanctification in a liminal experience while attending a camp meeting, Zilpha Elaw could not say "whether I was in the body, or whether I was out of the body . . . but this I do know, that at the conclusion of a most powerful sermon . . . I became so overpowered with the presence of God, that I sank down upon the ground, and laid there for a considerable time." Elaw continues: "[W]hile I was thus prostrate . . . my spirit seemed to ascend up into the clear circle of the sun's disc; and . . . I distinctly heard a voice speak unto me, which said, 'Now thou art sanctified; and I will show thee what thou must do'" (66). Elaw describes her experience as a "trance or ecstasy" during which she was unaware "that hundreds of persons were standing around me weeping" (67). Repeatedly, for these women, sanctification entailed falling prostrate before God, a position that signaled the willingness to give oneself over to the divine and to this direct experience of grace. Self-control was lost to such a degree that these women were neither fully aware of where they were nor of what they were doing and, instead, fell into a liminal state both in and out of the body. Indeed, as Amanda Smith testified, sanctification is a bodily sensation of direct, unmediated contact with the divine. Smith wrote of feeling "a hand, the touch of which I cannot describe. It seemed to press me gently on the top of my head, and I felt something part and roll down and cover me like a great cloak! I felt it distinctly . . . and O what a mighty peace and power took possession of me!" (79). Smith stressed she felt taken possession of, not that she felt she was now in possession of the ability and confidence to preach to others.

Despite scholars' investment in reading self-empowerment in these narratives, for women like Lee, Foote, Jackson, Elaw, and Smith, neither personal authority nor individual empowerment were uppermost in their attainment of sanctification. Indeed, as Douglas Strong points out, Julia Foote "was much more likely to write about the 'light' or 'illumination' received by sanctified Christians" than she was to use "the terminology of 'empowerment.'" When Foote "did use 'power' terminology . . . she always spoke about God's power—never her own" (24). Rather, direct contact with the divine was sought through sanctification, which then led preaching women to reach out to other individuals creating community through their spiritual labors and working toward the possibility of social and spiritual change.

However, narratives of feminism, and I would argue this is true of narratives of black feminism also, often reflect the value placed on transgression of social convention as women "demand . . . political rights and . . . exercise . . . a public voice" (Scott, "Fantasy" 294). Joan Scott has called this image the fantasy of the female orator, what she calls an "iconic figure" in the "annals of . . . feminism" ("Fantasy" 293). While these transgressive acts may find company, across time, with those of other feminists, they are frequently part of narratives that highlight the lone militant who transgresses, in part, the social order of her community or society. This narrative is present in histories of black feminism that single out exceptional figures such as Maria Stewart, Sojourner Truth, Ida B. Wells, and Frances Harper, all of whom were orators transgressing that injunction against woman taking the platform or podium and many of whom are understood as alienated within their communities or reform publics. Sanctified nineteenth-century African American preaching women could be included in such a narrative of black feminism as well, for in the case of many of these preaching women, sanctification unsettled the positions accorded them within society as a whole and their religious groups and families in particular.

Defying gender norms and risking humiliation and physical danger in the face of racial prejudice, these preaching women stepped out of the place their society deemed appropriate for them and, in the process, challenged the hierarchies governing social relations in their day. Perhaps nowhere is the risk of such a challenge more evident than in Rebecca Cox Jackson's case. Her beliefs and the course she chose in her life meant she risked not only social ostracization—even by fellow preaching women like Jarena Lee—but her very safety in her home until her unwavering commitment to those beliefs triumphed.[34] Yet social transgression and self-empowerment, powerful images of feminism though they may be, are not necessarily the goals of African American preaching women. Even though they might pursue courses of action that transgress the dictates of certain communities, like the AME Church, black preaching women sought connection to community and the divine. Sanctification, far from an experience whose primary meaning was self-empowerment, enabled that connection through states of consciousness or awareness in which these women gave themselves wholly over to the experience of divine grace or this second blessing.

Sanctification was so essential and powerful an experience that these preaching women sought to reach others and testify to conversion, sanctification, and divine power at the risk of strong opposition. Their spiritual autobiographies are not only testaments to their experiences and beliefs but instances of preaching itself, making the recounting of their experiences of sanctification a call to others to receive the "second blessing" and, as they experienced it, that blessing's attendant experience of submission and connection to a divine power directly experienced. In this sense, then, their texts are calls for social change one reader at a time just as they preached it to one congregation or camp gathering at a time.

Offering narratives of their conversion and sanctification importantly gave African American preaching women access to community and the opportunity to build publics. Conversion was understood by African Americans as "founded on a religion of spiritual resistance where women and men ask not for God's forgiveness but for God's recognition," argues Kimberly Connor (13). But perhaps more important is Anthony Wallace's understanding of conversion as "a deliberate intent by members of a society to effect . . . revitalization" in which " a deliberate, organized, conscious effort by members of a society to construct a more satisfying culture" is undertaken (qtd. in Connor 29). In this respect, then, conversion was far from an individual or insular experience but was understood to be a central element of and concrete step toward social change within the community. However, that community for black preaching women was not the black church, as it often was for the convert, given its opposition to the religious practices that were inextricably linked to what they believed to be the second stage of attaining grace, sanctification. Although conversion "placed an individual in a group of people [a 'black church community'] with similar goals and views of the racial conditions in nineteenth-century America at the same time that it provided access into a unique organization able to fight for these goals" (Hunter 81), sanctification was another matter.

Many African Americans did see sanctification as central to religion, particularly "old-time" religion, but the institutionalizing church did not. Consequently, preaching sanctification, African American women accessed a segment of black religious community and more often than not *created* community through their preaching and conversion of souls. In doing so, preaching women made equal access to the pulpit regardless of gender or class and the freedom of religious practice central concerns in their religious communities in addition to a focus on racial issues. In effect, black preaching women made concerns we can identify as feminist central to religious communities they were necessarily active in forming. They not only challenged the black church to consider their labors and concerns from within its ranks but also formed publics outside the church in which such concerns could become central. They preached the community they needed; they could not rely on extant religious community that would "fight for" goals they shared.

Advocating sanctification was hardly a neutral position for these women to undertake. The "second blessing" was a Wesleyan teaching within early Methodism and, like the praying bands that "had sprung up within Methodism with the explicit purpose of encouraging members to seek this . . . experience of divine grace" (Humez, "Introduction" 5), sanctification challenged the institutionalizing AME Church and its hierarchy, particularly under Bishop Daniel Payne. In his view, sanctification went hand in hand with the "disgusting" praying band and the so-called heathenish and disgraceful extravagant or enthusiastic worship styles that many nineteenth-century preaching women were accused of practicing. While an early Methodist teaching, sanctification, or "perfection," became popularized through the camp meetings and revivals of the Second Great Awakening and the interdenominational Holiness movement. Significantly, sanctification was seen as a class-inflected spiritual belief and practice within the AME Church, as Lincoln and Mamiya document: "[I]f anyone said that they were 'sanctified,' it was immediately assumed that they were lower class" (268). A growing middle-class institution, the AME Church at midcentury sought to promote a "respectable" image of African Americans, one that rose above the "lower class" at the expense of some long-lived elements of religious worship. For example, replacing the spirituals that "worshippers sing, or to which they can clap, sway, and respond verbally" (Lincoln and Mamiya 367), the "cornfield ditties," as Daniel Payne called them (qtd. in C. Smith 126), with arranged hymns was designed to regulate AME services and remove "remaining African remnants of religious antistructure" (Lincoln and Mamiya 367).

To advocate and narrate one's experiences of sanctification immediately placed one beyond the pale of the changing AME Church at midcentury, even though most AME congregants were sympathetic to if not believers in sanctification. Women like Jarena Lee, Rebecca Cox Jackson, Zilpha Elaw, Amanda Smith, and Julia Foote risked what little support for their work they may have mustered within the black Methodist Church by testifying to an experience that, ironically, was an established tenet of Methodism. Sanctification may have placed them firmly within a Methodist tradition and at the center of Holiness beliefs and the camp meeting revival movement, but it put them in a precarious position within black Methodism as it was being "reformed." The black Baptists also rejected sanctification. Among Baptists at midcentury, ministers who preached sanctification were dismissed from their churches and excluded from their state associations (Lincoln and Mamiya 80), and as southerner Virginia Broughton's spiritual autobiography attests, debates regarding the status of sanctification preoccupied the Baptist church at the century's close. Broughton believed that "both [Baptist] ministers and laity" were in "grave need of greater consecration and loyalty to Christ's cause" in the form of sanctification, and she "contend[ed] for this truth" though "persecutions . . . follow[ed] so aggressive a movement" for sanctification underway among the Baptists in the 1890s (79). Broughton writes of "bearing up bravely under her persecution," though she offers no details, and of advocating sanctification "in the ranks of our Bible women" (79, 80).

Sanctification was not only linked to the praying band, which we must remember was a feminized religious practice, but also directly associated with enthusiastic worship that included "shouting," a descendant of the ring shout practiced by enslaved African Americans. Condemned in the early nineteenth century by Methodist, Presbyterian, and Baptist revivalists as "sinful," the ring shout was described by one of its detractors, John Watson, in his 1819 attack on extravagant worship practices in Methodism: "In the *blacks'* quarter, the coloured people get together, and sing for hours together, short scraps of disjointed affirmations, pledges, or prayers, lengthened out with long repetitious *choruses*. . . . With every word so sung, they have a sinking of one or other leg of the body alternately; producing an audible sound of the feet at every step. . . . If some, in the meantime sit, they strike the sounds alternately on each thigh. . . . [T]he evil is only occasionally condemned and the example has already visibly affected the religious manners of some whites" (qtd. in Raboteau 67). In addition to condemning the ring shout as evil and revealing his anxiety that it appeals to whites and well as blacks, Watson's chief complaint is that the practice is to sing "the original religious songs of blacks—as distinguished from the standard Protestant hymns," songs that "are actually composed as sung and are almost endless" (qtd. in Raboteau 67). The ring shout's extempore and participatory quality most affects and worries Watson, as there is no predictability and, hence, no control of it.

Black Methodist leaders also condemned the ring shout. Bishop Richard Allen was "critical of what he recognized as African carryovers in Christian worship . . . [and] rejected groaning, shouting, clapping, ring-dancing, and all such activity" (Sobel 143), ecstatic worship elements that would have been popular among Mother Bethel's working-class and poor congregants. Bishop Daniel Payne described people participating in a ring shout as "clapp[ing] their hands and stamp[ing] their feet in a most ridiculous and heathenish way." Payne, dismayed that "some of our most popular and powerful preachers labor systematically to perpetuate this fanaticism," seemed anxious that observers "called it the 'Voodoo Dance,'" hardly an image of black Methodism he would want to circulate (qtd. in C. Smith 126–27). Payne favored excommunication, if necessary, and "an intelligent ministry" to both eradicate the ring shout, "evil practices . . . [that] disgrace the Christian name and corrupt others," and safeguard "the intelligent, refined, and practical Christians . . . in the bosom" of the AME Church (qtd. in C. Smith 127).

The ring shout did not disappear, however, and developed into the shout, or holy dance, which has been described by Lincoln and Mamiya as a "spiritual possession experience in which the worshiper 'gets happy' or is 'anointed by the spirit' and praises God in paroxysmal dance. . . . [T]he shout serves as a testimony to the shouter's felt sense of Spirit Baptism or sanctification. The shouter is, therefore, someone . . . who possesses that much-approved 'good old-time religion'" (365). No longer a dance to extempore singing, the shout nevertheless retained the ring shout's spontaneity. While Holiness believers might approve of shouting and getting happy, and while the black Baptists kept it in their tradition, despite its link to sanctification (Sobel 142), the "good old-time religion" was being much maligned within the AME Church as it attempted to weed out enthusiastic or extravagant preachers and congregants in its midst.

To practice "enthusiastic" preaching and encourage ecstatic worship, including the shout, was to do more than fly in the face of the AME hierarchy and its reforming impulses. Rather, to undertake and encourage such religious practices was arguably a feminist act. Although the AME Church used educational qualifications to eradicate these practices among its male clergy, making class central to this way of "reforming" the church, it targeted women preachers with a complete ban on their preaching activities, limiting them to supporting roles like those of exhorter or evangelist. Women, then, also faced the educational qualifications men did, qualifications the church well knew they would find nearly impossible to meet because of both class and gender concerns.[35] But women also labored under open hostility to their work, denial of the pulpit, and excommunication as the AME Church sought to remove women from the ministry. Since women were banned from preaching at all, taking up the ministry, preaching sanctification, and pursuing religious practices that were forbidden, like worshipping in prayer bands and conducting ecstatic services that encouraged participation and "shouting," were all highly political undertakings that refused the intimidation and control exercised by the AME hierarchy.

Moreover, preaching women undertook cooperative ministries, thereby fostering women's religious culture. Jarena Lee "enjoyed good seasons together" with Zilpha Elaw (*Journal* 88) in the late 1830s and early 1840s, until Elaw took her ministry to Great Britain. In the mid-1840s, Julia Foote "hired a large place in Canal street," Philadelphia, and preached for "eleven nights, and over one Sabbath" with "three sisters" she had met at an AME conference held in that city (211). Foote goes on to note that "some of the dear sisters accompanied me to Flatbush," where they preached together at a camp meeting (212). And Foote also writes of traveling with "Sister Ann M. Johnson" from the summer of 1849 until 1856, when Johnson died (219–25). Together, Foote and Johnson labored in the Northeast, Maryland, Ohio, Michigan, and Canada. Rebecca Cox Jackson also lived and labored with Rebecca Perot during the 1850s.

African American preaching women clearly saw their place in a feminist line of descent as central to their labors and writing, as is evident in the place they gave arguments for woman's right to preach in their spiritual autobiographies and in the asides they wrote directly to women who would follow them. Jarena Lee's spiritual autobiography opened with a biblical refrain to "your *daughters* [who] shall prophecy" (*Life* 27). And Julia Foote directly addressed her preaching sisters in her spiritual autobiography: "Dear sisters, who are in the evangelistic work now, you may think you have had times; but let me tell you, I feel that the lion and the lamb are lying down together, as compared with the state of things twenty-five or thirty years ago. Yes, yes; our God is marching on. Glory to his name!" (214). Yet in addition to their feminist spiritual labors that challenged gender and class inequities, preaching women's practice of ecstatic worship, the prayer band, the shout, and calling converts to sanctification arguably preserved African retentions within syncretic religious practices and so preserved a distinctly African American culture that was being threatened by the AME Church's middle-class, reformist interests. These religious practices were arguably a form of "subjugated knowledge," and Patricia Hill Collins has marked such forms of knowledge as "essential to the survival of African-Americans" in both "the rural south and northern urban" centers (12).

Preaching women upheld African Americanisms in their ministries in the face of opposition within the AME Church and ridicule by whites who did not understand their work and the form it took. Indeed, responses to and representations of preaching women's ecstatic worship styles mark the ways in which they were regarded as embodied speech acts and thus implicitly a challenge to notions of a democratic public sphere and its abstract citizen subject. In politicizing the soul and soul winning, preaching women were drawing attention to the body as the unacknowledged site of the public sphere's domination even as it promised a utopian abstraction to "all." "The bourgeois public sphere claimed to have no relation to the body image at all. . . . Yet the bourgeois public sphere continued to rely on features of certain bodies," writes Michael Warner. "Access to the public came in the whiteness and maleness that were then denied forms of positivity, since . . . [the citizen subject] was only abstract rather than white and male" ("Mass Public" 382–83).

Allen's and Payne's concerns that ecstatic worship would be regarded as ridiculous, fanatic, and unrefined mark a larger concern that such embodied speech acts serve to exclude black Americans from the public sphere and mark them as unable to "master" its rhetoric. Such concerns and fears are, in fact, borne out in Lydia Child's *Letters from New York,* where we learn of Julia Pell. Child's descriptions of Pell's preaching are rife with stereotypes, as Child encounters a person she clearly finds unusual. Child describes Pell's preaching in a Methodist church on Elizabeth Street in New York late in 1841 as "such loud and earnest noises" (61). She finds Pell "remarkable . . . intelligent . . . uncultivated, yet highly poetic" (61, 62) and likens Pell's voice to that of "a sailor at mast-head" and her gestures to a "muscular action like Garrick in Mad Tom" (64). Child clearly makes little attempt to follow much less understand Pell's extempore preaching, which she calls "an odd jumbling together of all sorts of things in Scripture, such wild fancies . . . such vehemence of gesture, such dramatic attitudes . . . I verily thought she would have leaped over the pulpit" (64). In sharp contrast to the citizen subject regarded as able to participate in depersonalized, reasoned debate within the public sphere, Pell is depicted as a being beyond control, one "strangely fantastic, and even supernatural," delivering her sermon at a "shouting pitch" (65). Yet Child unknowingly reveals just how deliberate Julia Pell's services were, as she worked to rouse her congregants' emotions and channel them into song, prayer, and worship.

While Child notes Pell's "rude eloquence" stirred both her African American audience and Child herself, she presents as happenstance Pell's skilled management of that enthusiasm. "Luckily for the excited feelings of her audience, she changed the scene, and brought before us the gospel ship, laden with saints. . . . Her audience were wrought up to the highest pitch of enthusiasm," writes Child. "Emotion vented itself in murmuring, stamping, shouting, . . . and wailing. . . . [T]he audience . . . [sought] rest in music, for their panting spirits and quivering nerves. All joined spontaneously in singing an old familiar tune. . . . [T]he tones were soft and melodious" (67–68). While Child dwells on the "universal" African "gift of song" (68), she mistakes Pell's skillful orchestration and management of religious enthusiasm as the "spontaneous" outbursts of "an audience so ignorant, and so keenly susceptible to outward impressions" (68) and seems to know little of ecstatic worship as a long-lived tradition within black Methodism. Far from beyond control, Pell was managing, even as she solicited, the religious enthusiasm of her following.

Child also was unaware of black Methodism's attempts to reform the church by eradicating such practices and believed that Pell's ministry was opposed solely because she was once "led astray by temptations, which peculiarly infest the path of coloured women in large cities . . . [and] to this prejudice was added another, against women's preaching" (69). Child was correct to assume that Pell's past and her gender were threatening to black Methodism, but Pell was also preaching in an ecstatic manner at precisely the time Daniel Payne began his campaign to educate and "refine" the black Methodist ministry. We must recognize the political stakes of denouncing certain forms of soul win- ning and institutionalizing others as part of the church's operation as, itself, a public. In fact, critiques of the Habermasian bourgeois public sphere have focused on its reification of rational communication, a privileging that echoes markedly with Payne's attempt to "refine" black Methodism. As John Brooke notes, such critiques "challenged [Habermas's] claim that the only significant public discourse was rational communication arguing that both hegemonic and counterhegemonic forces deploy a spectrum of emotional and emotive performances in public to achieve their ends" (94).[36] While Payne may have been motivated, in part, to reconstruct black Methodism in ways that saw its styles of worship seem less embodied and consequently, we might argue, less "other" to the democratic citizen-subject ideal, he did so by accepting the very grounds of African Americans' exclusion from a dominant public sphere. That preaching women recognized the potential costs of outlawing ecstatic worship—a loss of cultural practices and the world view informing them— underscores the importance of their political work.

Allen's and Payne's positions on ecstatic worship explain much of the forceful opposition women like Zilpha Elaw, Old Elizabeth, and Julia Foote experienced. These women labored under the dual hazard of their gender and their belief in sanctification with its inextricable links to praying bands and ecstatic worship. Old Elizabeth's spiritual autobiography clearly marks this double sanction. "Our meeting gave great offence, and we were forbid holding any more assemblies. Even the elders of our meetings joined with the wicked people, and said such meetings must be stopped," writes Elizabeth. "But I . . . continued to go, and burnt with a zeal not my own. The old sisters were zealous sometimes. . . . I felt at times that I must exercise in the minis- try, but . . . I felt that I was despised on account of this gracious calling. . . . [S]ome would cry out 'You are an enthusiast'; and others said, 'the Discipline did not allow any such division of the work'" (12–13). Zilpha Elaw describes her ecstatic worship services during her preaching tour of southern slave states in her *Memoirs*. "The gallery of the chapel was occupied by the slaves, and the body of the building with proprietors; and all were alike affected. . . . [T]he powerful operation of the Holy Spirit disdained the limits prescribed by man's reason, and bore down all the guards of human propriety and or- der," relates Elaw. "[T]he coloured people in the gallery wept aloud and raised vehement cries to heaven; the people below were also unable to restrain their emotions. . . . I was obliged to stop in my discourse, and give vent to my own feelings, and leave it to God to preach in His own more effectual way"

(101). And while Elaw defends the right of women to preach, she also finds it necessary to defend ecstatic worship in her text: "Order in divine worship and in the house of God is graceful and appropriate; but the life and power of religion is not identified with, nor in proportion to, the polish of the minister, the respectability of the congregation, or the regularity and method of its services." Elaw continues, "Our duty is humbly to submit to, rather than attempt to limit, the Holy One of Israel; and when God is at work, though the ark may seem to rock with irregular motion, let not men pretend to more wisdom than their Creator" (107).

Revivals and Camp Meetings

While women such as Elizabeth and Zilpha Elaw labored under opposition to their preaching styles or embodied speech acts within black Methodism, others, such as Amanda Smith and Julia Foote, were drawn to the Holiness revivals of the midcentury. Foote does not speak to an ecstatic worship style in her spiritual autobiography, but she did become one of the earliest female Holiness preachers. Amanda Smith refers repeatedly in her spiritual autobiography to "feeling liberty" in her preaching and to "getting the blessing" at a Love Feast, "when it seemed a finger touched my tongue, and the power of God came upon me in such a wonderful manner that I talked, it seemed to me, about ten minutes. . . . And the fire seemed to fall on all the people" (112).[37] Importantly, neither woman was driven out of black Methodism by the opposition to her gender and extravagant ministry, despite attempts to "clean up" the church. Their decision to join both the interdenominational Holiness movement and to continue their affiliation with black Methodism was likely regarded as threatening, for far from ceasing "extravagant" worship such women were linking black Methodism to a religious movement that practiced it wholeheartedly. Smith's success at revivals and camp meetings would have underscored the Holiness movement's momentum, the role "old-time religion" played in drawing African Americans to its revivals, and the powerful role women played in the conversion of souls despite black Methodism's opposition to such women and their preaching styles. Indeed, Smith's assertion that Holiness "is the only hope for Methodism all over the land" must have raised some hackles (146), given that she reached thousands at camp meetings where she also converted Methodist preachers to the Holiness doctrine (210–11).

Annie Brown's ecstatic services garnered coverage in the *New York Times* in early 1907: "Her meetings are always marked by surprising fervor and enthusiasm. She sweeps her audience from its feet and sets it singing and shouting in a sort of religious ecstasy. The manner in which the services are conducted is impressive. . . . In a moment her hearers are worked up to a high pitch of excitement" (qtd. in A. Brown 91). Defiant in her defense of ecstatic worship, Brown's comments to the *Times* reporter indicate that vilification of "extravagant" ministry continued throughout the nineteenth and into the early twentieth century. At Bethel AME Church in New York, Brown declared: "'You are getting so high-toned that you talk about old-fashioned religion and revival meetings making you nervous. Well, I'll make you so nervous that you'll die of prostration'" (A. Brown 91).

While Holiness revivals and camp meetings offered women central roles to play in the conversion of souls and welcomed enthusiastic worship, Holiness also "contributed significantly by the end of the century to the rise of the social gospel," which saw a "turning outward of the concept of individual freedom from sin to the creation of a society free from evil as well" (Dieter 24). Such a shift marks quite clearly the spiritual as a social and political phenomenon that can be reconceived when a politics of interiority comes to be critiqued for neglecting those social inequalities upon which it, in fact, rests. In the rise of social gospel we see another form of what Castronovo calls "the spiritual . . . as political apparatus" (120). This emphasis upon social change would have been an important factor in drawing African American preaching women to Holiness, for it affirmed their already established spiritualistic feminist interests in the abolition of slavery, and the securing of black civil rights and woman's rights. Holiness made good on its roots in women's home churches with new Holiness churches at century's end granting "full ministerial rights to women" (Dieter 43). The centrality of Holiness as a major religious movement among nineteenth-century Americans, promoted most effectively through camp meetings, dovetailed with the popularity of camp meetings among African Americans, making revivals a crucial place for African American women to preach. It was the camp meeting, not the church itself, that seems to have been central to African Americans in the north at midcentury, and this had been true in the South as well, where Dickson Bruce documents it was "a major social and religious institution" (3).

At camp meetings, believers made their lodgings in tents in an area cleared for the purpose. The larger trees remaining formed "a natural canopy . . . creat[ing] a cathedral in the wilderness." The preacher's pulpit was "elevated from 5 to 6 1/2 feet above the ground. Immediately in front of the stand was an area variously known as the altar, mourners' bench . . . anxious seat . . . [or] 'the glory pen.'" This area was "separated from the congregation and the pulpit" and was where sinners were converted. Those who attended and preached at camp meetings saw the religious enthusiasm that dominated them as manifestations of God, not the workings of preachers favoring ec-static worship, thereby defending meetings against charges of extravagance and explaining why African Americans were so drawn to them.

Camp meetings preserved what many black Americans saw as "old-time" and essential religion and provided what was rapidly declining in the black church. Conversions themselves were particularly ecstatic, with "enthusiastic physical and emotional displays" (Bruce 6), and conversions were the raison d'être of the camp meeting. It is significant, then, that women were often convert exhorters, new converts who offered testimonials of their own con-versions "during morning services" whose "chief duty was inviting sinners to enter the [glory] pen" and be converted during main services (Bruce 76, 75). The "professional" leaders of camp meetings were preachers and exhorters, both white and black, with preachers leading services and exhorters working to convert sinners. While Bruce suggests these activities were racially segre-gated, Frances Smith Foster notes that accommodations were segregated yet "certain activities or services were dominated by whites and others by blacks" (*Written* 67). The accounts of African American preaching women bear out Foster's assertion and indicate their central roles even as they also testify to the racism they encountered at camp meetings.

Amanda Smith was a much sought after figure at camp meetings, receiv-ing invitations to meetings she could not afford to travel to, but she set out with a firm belief that God would provide for her journey and her accom-modations and meals while there. At a camp meeting in June 1871 Smith was "introduced . . . to the people as the 'Fifteenth Amendment'" and clearly functioned as a professional exhorter calling people into what she called "the fountain of cleansing": "The most of the time I stood on my feet and ex-horted, and sang, and talked, and prayed" (A. Smith 187). Exhorting was evidently demanding work, for Smith exhorted without pause at this meeting "from half past two till six o'clock, and we could hardly close then. . . . When I got out . . . I could scarcely walk. I was thoroughly exhausted" (A. Smith 187). Smith was also, at times, regarded as an oddity at camp meetings, and "everywhere I would go a crowd would follow me" (A. Smith 183).

Despite experiencing racism at meetings, African American preaching women were drawn to revivals and most of the women we know something of labored at them. Rebecca Cox Jackson and Sojourner Truth attended camp meetings even though they could be dangerous as opposers and ruffians sought to break them up. Jackson wrote of one such experience at a New Jersey camp meeting in 1823: "It was said that there was five hundred men had surrounded the camp. 'And soon as it is dark, they are going to set the camp on fire'" (113). Jackson testifies to praying for protection and receiving it, while Truth herself protected a camp meeting in 1844 from "a party of wild young men" who became mesmerized by her singing, praying, and preaching (*Narrative* 115). Julia Foote preached at revivals numbering some "five thousand" in the 1870s (164–65) and wrote that during that decade "the glorious wave of holiness, which has been rolling through Ohio, . . . has swept every hindrance out of my way, and sent me to sea once more with chart and compass" (226).

Well before Jackson's camp-meeting experiences in the 1840s and the rise of Holiness revivals, Chloe Spear was active as a revivalist in and around Boston, where, as Santamarina notes, she was also a laundress (8). Spear's 1832 biography, written "by a Lady of Boston," is unique in detailing her capture in Africa about 1762 and her purchase at about twelve years old by a Mr. B. of Boston (*Memoir* 2–18). Spear became literate through covert lessons with a local schoolteacher, who taught her the alphabet through a psalter the young Chloe had purchased for twenty-five cents (24–25). Baptized a Baptist in November, 1788 (49–50), Spear "was ardently attached to the people of God, of whatever denomination" (50) and eventually dissolved her connection to the Baptist Church, choosing instead to hold religious meetings in her home (59–60). Chloe Spear's interdenominational leanings lead her to the revival movement: "[I]n seasons of revival . . . she was frequently invited . . . and was instrumental of good" (77). Through both her home church and revivals Spear reached blacks and whites. She was said to be "useful . . . especially among those of her own colour" (76), yet "pious ladies, of the first respectability" also attended her meetings (72). Spear must have been a figure of some note around Boston, for "a short memoir of her . . . was published in the *Massachusetts Baptist Missionary Magazine* by its editor, Dr. Baldwin" (86) in 1815, and her biography was later published in 1832 by James Loring printers of Boston. Her biography was not only advertised in William Lloyd Garrison's *Liberator* in its Ladies Department of May 12, 1832, but the paper promised extracts from it would appear in a future number.

Another little-known preaching woman, Aunt Dinah, preached at revivals in the Northeast. Born into slavery a decade after Chloe Spear, in 1722, Aunt Dinah eventually purchased her freedom from her owner in Duchess County, New York ("Aunt Dinah" 370). Dinah was converted "in a Methodist revival," and like Spear she learned to read in order to "read the Bible. . . . [S]he became so much a scholar as to have accumulated quite a library of standard theological works, the writings of Jonathan Edwards being her favorites" ("Aunt Dinah" 370). "Identify[ing] herself . . . as a revival preacher" (Fowler 40), Dinah attended revival meetings with Edward Norris Kirk, a powerful evangelist and Presbyterian preacher who was also a "radical" reformer and abolitionist ("Life"). She traveled within New York as a revivalist and was known as "a woman of remarkable native vigor of mind, intuitive knowledge of character, rare discrimination in . . . preaching, and [possessing] . . . a thorough study of the Bible . . . which often surpassed the skill of doctors in divinity" (Fowler 41). Henry Fowler, whose *American Pulpit* briefly documents Dinah's work, reveals the curiosity African American preaching women could be to whites who encountered them at revivals and camp meetings: "Her person was not attractive. She was much bent . . . by an injury to her back, caused by a blow from her master; her features were strongly marked; her color that of the full-blooded African, strikingly contrasting with the snow-white headdress she usually wore; and her manner heartily affectionate, blunt, earnest, and decided" (Fowler 41). Dinah, as oddity, was accommodated to that image of female blackness with which white Americans seemed most familiar and comfortable at the time, the black mammy. She is represented as marked by slavery yet benignly "affectionate," a woman who offered "pathetic appeals" to religious conversion (Fowler 41). Dinah died "March 20, 1846, aged 74 years," having occupied "a room in the basement of one of the New York churches" during the last few years of her life (Fowler 41).

While Chloe Spear and Aunt Dinah indicate the importance of revivals to African American preaching women in the Northeast early in the nineteenth century, Harriet Baker and Annie Brown register their continuing importance in that area, farther west, and into the upper South at the turn into the twentieth. Baker's preaching, like that of other African American women, was strongly opposed, but she claimed she was "called and chosen . . . to this work" and asked God to "'let the people know it here and now.' And the Lord did manifest himself in such power that the opposition was disarmed" (Acornley 38). First accepted as an evangelist in white evangelical churches (Acornley 43), Baker came to be renowned for her work at camp meetings and was invited to preach in "Pennsylvania, Ohio, Virginia, Maryland, Delaware, New Jersey, New York and Connecticut, in connection with the Methodist Episcopal, Primitive Methodist, Methodist Protestant, United Brethren, Evangelical, Baptist, African Methodist Episcopal, and African

M.E. Zion churches" (Acornley 45). Baker was so popular that she preached to camp meetings numbering fifteen thousand at times and was such a draw that camp goers would pay for the privilege of hearing her: "At Belfor, Ohio, at the camp-meeting they took seven hundred and ninety dollars at the gate, at ten cents per head . . . [and] scarcely half . . . payed as they entered the grounds" (Acornley 46). Baker approached her labors seasonally, preaching at camp meetings in the summer and at church-based revivals in the winter (Acornley 51).

Annie Brown preached mainly in the upper South from her Gospel Wagon and at camp revivals where she converted thousands. Like Baker, Brown reached potential converts of all denominations and both races (A. Brown 28–30). And like Amanda Smith, she worked determinedly to convert souls often at the expense of her health, suffering nervous collapses and refusing to cease preaching in order to take the bed rest her doctors recommended (A. Brown 39). Brown not only attended camp meetings but also seems to have made her own, traveling with a "tent which seated five thousand people" (A. Brown 39). Favoring ecstatic worship, Brown was particularly popular among African Americans, though whites were also among her converts: "[T]he older Negroes are awaiting [Brown's meetings] with such thrills of pleasure as they have not experienced since the old camp meeting days in the South. . . . While Sister Brown sings revival songs the older negroes pray and shout out loud" (A. Brown 90–91). Brown effectively continued the camp meeting tradition in the upper South after camp meetings virtually disappeared in the South in the 1840s with greater institutionalization and a growing reputation for being a less respectable form of worship (Bruce 56, 59). In fact, her preaching routinely drew upward of fifteen thousand people in places like Baltimore (A. Brown 43). So popular was Brown that she was able to charge admission and transcriptions were made of her sermons (A. Brown 46–47, 50).

Camp meetings and revivals were clearly significant sites for preaching women throughout the century, places where they could reach substantial numbers of potential converts and established believers, places where their roles as preachers and exhorters were not questioned or undermined. Whether they labored at revivals independently or along with other notable revivalists and reformists, as did Dinah, their abilities were respected and admired and their ecstatic preaching styles welcomed. Taking on central roles in revivals and camp meetings, African American preaching women were hardly marginal figures in these locations. With the rise of the Holiness movement and the increase of camp meetings and revivals that came with it, African American preaching women could be found participating in the major religious movement of the nineteenth century. Their race, gender, class, or denominational affiliation, or lack of it, did not affect their participation or position within this movement. Even when they were seen as oddities, as Amanda Berry Smith narrates, that liminal position could often be turned to advantage as curious whites sought out their prayer and testimony. Camp meetings and revivals not only gave preaching women a "home" for the religious practices they pursued despite the interdict of a reforming black Methodism, a public that believed in the power of liminal experiences like sanctification, but preaching within those publics also brought black preaching women to the center of American religious life. Rather than working at the margins, most of the African American preaching women we know of labored in those revivals and camp meetings that could draw thousands to hear them. Consequently, their spiritual teachings and positions on slavery, gender equity, and black civil rights were part of that nascent liberationist seedbed for abolition and woman's rights that was the religious enthusiasm of the early to mid-nineteenth century. Moreover, preaching women who followed them continued that tradition into the late nineteenth and early twentieth century, fostering later forms of black feminism.

Mistaken as "depoliticized," less vocal and active than their late-century feminist sisters, and as producing writing that is less "overtly" political than the slave narratives we have tended to privilege over their spiritual autobiographies, nineteenth-century African American preaching women have been diminished in narratives of black feminism and have not been given their due in histories of the black church. Yet they were far from marginal figures working on the periphery of the dominant culture and their own. Rather, nineteenth-century African American preaching women took their ministries to the center of American and African American religious life as revivalists and evangelists often in great demand during the Holiness movement. Reaching competing and intersecting publics, African American preaching women entered into dialogues on abolition, civil rights and woman's rights, agitating for change among both the white and black audiences they reached. Indeed, we see preaching women creating their own publics, reminding us that the public sphere is "a contested participatory site in which . . . a public body . . . emerge[s] in negotiations and contestations over political and social life" (Crossley and Roberts 16).

Rather than a monolithic black public sphere based in "the" church, the work of these women helps us to see competing and pluralized counterpublics in which very different work to politicize the soul or the spiritual was taking place, from the refinement of black Methodism to the persistence of ecstatic worship in revivals and camp meetings. Although those political positions were sometimes explicitly stated in their sermons or writings, we often have to consider less immediately apparent elements of their lives and work as feminist, being careful not to separate the spiritual from the secular or social as we consider the politics they pursued and the beliefs they held. A fuller understanding of preaching women's feminism not only promises to extend the historical reach of narratives of black feminism but also asks us to reconsider what we define or recognize as feminist and political. Soul winners and workers for social change, African American preaching women challenge us to shift our critical focus, examine our investments in particular understandings and images of feminism, and take their work on its own complex terms.

Chapter 2

Internationalizing Black Feminisms: Ellen Craft, Sarah Parker Remond, and American Slavery in the British Isles and Ireland

The work African American preaching women undertook to politicize soul winning, particularly their attention to the elision of material realities in the abstraction of the spirit or soul, is linked to the abolitionist work of black women at midcentury. Black female abolitionists, whether working in the United States or within the transatlantic network, also challenged a politics of (dis)embodiment that enabled some bodies to all but disappear while others bore the burden of an extreme and often violent embodiment. Their use of rather particular strategies of address was necessitated by the complex position from which they worked. Whether they were fugitive slaves themselves, as was Ellen Craft, or free born, as were Frances Harper, Sarah Parker Remond, and Mary Ann Shadd Cary, or emancipated slaves, as was Sojourner Truth, when black female abolitionists addressed predominately white antislavery audiences, they were frequently negotiating the politics of who was recognized as a "victim" of slavery and what slavery was understood to be.

In order to examine the demands of making a black feminist politics public in the context of mid-nineteenth-century organized reform and to argue that black feminism was developing a significant international reach upon which it would later build, this chapter briefly sketches the antislavery context in the United States from which black female abolitionists Ellen Craft and Sarah Parker Remond emerged and then considers in more depth the work that established them as public figures in the transatlantic abolition network. The tendency is to read black female abolition as part of a developing black feminism within the United States and as managing the politics of antislavery and the woman's rights movement there, while the transatlantic work of women such as Craft and Remond comes to be isolated from that tradition because it addressed foreign audiences with rather different political concerns. When their work in the UK is brought into scholarly focus, it tends to be read through the lens of political concerns prominent in the United States—developing woman's rights agitation and its use of black women as proxy figures for white women's concerns—without attention to the political scene Craft and Remond entered when they crossed the Atlantic. Consequently, we come to recognize figures such as Frances Harper, Sojourner Truth, and Mary Ann Shadd Cary as the women who "sowed the seeds of black feminism"[1] through their work with antislavery and woman's rights reform at "home" and accommodate Craft and Remond to that script rather than understanding that black feminism had arguably achieved a critical mass by midcentury and through Craft and Remond's work reached beyond the United States (and North America) to pursue its politics in an international frame. In order to understand that black feminists were doing much more than capitalizing upon existing reform interests and networks in the United States but were quite savvy in their work to create and manage publics for their political interest, we need to adopt a more expansive view of early black feminism.

Craft and Remond's abolitionist lecture tours were both more sustained and more successful in the British Isles and Ireland, where they appeared at midcentury, than their work in the United States. Their success resulted from the timing of their appearances and their intelligent use of appeals that roused UK and Irish publics to the cause of American abolition after a period of relative inaction in British and Irish antislavery following the British West Indies Emancipation and the Slavery Abolition Act of 1833. In the British Isles the context for their appearances and appeals was complicated by the state of abolition, the centrality of class to public politics, and the market. "Slavery" for British audiences had come to connote not only the experience of white women politically disenfranchised, as it had in the United States by midcentury, but also that of the working classes. Slavery resonated differently in Britain due to labor and market concerns which could collide with national "feeling." Although the felt moral superiority of Britain over the United States might be appealed to, British markets were nonetheless dependant upon American cotton and, by extension, American slavery, thereby limiting the "moral suasion" that the Crafts or Remond could muster.

It would be difficult to indict the British for their effective perpetuation of American slavery through the cotton market, even as one tried to enlist their felt moral superiority in a campaign to censure the United States, internationally, for American slavery. In Ireland, the appeals Remond forwarded were shaped by her awareness of that country's emerging nationalism, its recovery from the Great Famine, and its perception of and investments in the United States as a destination for many Irish emigrants. Consequently, when Ellen Craft and Sarah Parker Remond appeared before audiences in the UK and Ireland in the 1850s, they solicited and managed competing and complex political sympathies, economic interests, and national feeling. Yet their ability to manage those competing political sympathies makes them key figures in an internationalizing of early black feminism at midcentury. What transatlantic publics could these women access and how did they do so? What strategies could gain them a hearing outside the United States? What risks must they manage in "going public" across the Atlantic?

Black Feminist Abolition in the United States

Early black feminist organizing in the United States resulted in societies such as the African Dorcas Association, literary societies in major cities in the northeastern United States, and in female and mutual-benefit, charitable, or benevolent societies that then fostered both all-black and racially mixed female antislavery societies. As Martha Jones has observed, "[S]ome of black public culture's most seasoned female activists turned their efforts toward female associations" (83). In this work, black feminists were actively building what Catherine Squires has called enclaved publics, which fostered the development of a politics and its tools outside dominant publics and their spaces. They extended and built upon the work black preaching women undertook in enclaved publics like the praying bands examined in chapter 1. Philadelphia was home to what is thought to be the earliest female benevolent society, "the Female Benevolent Society of St. Thomas, formed in 1793" (Dunbar 60). By 1830 Philadelphia claimed some eighty mutual-benefit societies, over sixty of which had been established by African American women (Dunbar 60). Dunbar has unearthed society records that tell us "organizations such as the Daughters for the County Angola Beneficial Association, founded in 1808, grew in size and wealth; its forty members and annual income of one hundred dollars went to support black women and men" (60). The size of such Philadelphia associations varied, from "240 women in the Female Shipley Association" to 200 in the Daughters of Africa and "thirty-four members" in the Daughters of Jerusalem (Dunbar 60–61).

These societies were venues for black women to continue their active support for their communities, but they were also sources of sustained mutual support for themselves. The African Dorcas Association supported the Free African Schools network in Boston and New York and provided care for black children. Other female or mutual benevolent societies effectively provided a form of insurance for working African American women through their membership fees, thereby creating a fund upon which members could draw when in need. But these working women's associations also pooled what resources they could to support the sick and others in their communities. Given Maria Stewart's important feminist black nationalist work in the early 1830s to link the labor of working black women to the political advancement of "the race," which I will examine in chapter 5, these benevolent societies must be regarded as offering both immediate material assistance and political promise to their communities.

African American female literary societies worked in related ways, offering outlets for black women's creative and political writing, acceptable venues to discuss concerns affecting the community and women within it, and an important sense of women's collectivity. The Female Literary Association of Philadelphia, founded in 1831, and the Afric-American Female Intelligence Society of Boston (1832), which gave Maria Stewart one of her earliest public speaking opportunities, are significant in this regard. From Philadelphia and Boston, black women's literary societies spread to New York, Baltimore, Albany and Rochester, Cincinnati, and Pittsburgh in the 1830s and 1840s (Dunbar 102). Elizabeth McHenry argues that such societies provided free African Americans "with opportunities to practice and perform literacy and allowed them to experiment with voice and self-representation in ways that approximated the ideals of civic participation" (56). Indeed, the Female Literary Association of Philadelphia first drew William Lloyd Garrison's attention to the writing skills and political views of African American women in the early 1830s, influencing him to establish *The Liberator*'s Ladies' Department in order to share the addresses read at the "mental feasts" of black women's literary societies with his readers. That link between Garrisonian abolition and black women's literary societies has been marked as central to the emergence of black female abolition: "In the 1830s the generation of politically charged African American women who would play such an important role in abolition had indeed emerged from the arena of the literary society" (Dunbar 97).

Finally, African American female associations established for mutual support also proved to be effective sites in which women tried on leadership roles, taking what they learned and practiced into reform politics, particularly abolition. Such was the case for Clarissa Lawrence, who once led the Colored Female Religious and Moral Society of Salem, founded in 1818 with a mandate to write about and discuss the conditions of enslaved African American women. Lawrence also held a leadership role in the Salem Female Anti-Slavery Society, a racially mixed organization founded on June 4, 1834. It had formed from the reorganization of the Female Anti-Slavery Society of Salem, a black female organization founded in February 1832 to promote the general welfare of African Americans. In important ways, benevolent associations and literary societies fostered the all-black female antislavery societies that were clearly foundational and sustaining for black female abolitionists who also worked in interracial abolition efforts.

African American women had been active in organized abolitionist networks since at least the early 1830s, when the first female antislavery societies were founded. In addition to the racially mixed Salem Female Anti-Slavery Society (1834), the mixed Philadelphia Female Anti-Slavery Society (PFASS) was founded in December 1833,[2] and the Boston Female Anti-Slavery Society was founded just two months earlier.[3] Although the establishment of racially mixed antislavery societies facilitated black women's participation in the movement and their use of its networks, and Erica Armstrong Dunbar has argued associations like the "PFASS provided black women with the first opportunity for recognition and leadership in a political arena separate from the black church" (79), many also felt these societies compromised their politics. Shirley Yee has noted that some white women's "narrow view of abolitionism" meant that they wanted finances and energy "channeled toward antislavery newspapers and lecturers," while many black women "wanted to direct much of their society's resources to the free black community" (89) in the tradition of those benevolent and mutual-aid societies in which they also held memberships.

In still other cases, white members of antislavery societies, such as the Ladies' New York City Anti-Slavery Society, opposed racial mixing and sought to exclude black women from membership (Yee 90). And Dunbar documents that black women left the PFASS in the 1840s[4] when its goals shifted to an exclusive focus on immediate emancipation, leaving "little room for the betterment of free blacks' lives" (95). Sarah Mapps Douglass, who was a key player in the founding of the PFASS, helped establish the all-black Women's Association of Philadelphia in 1848, which "supported Frederick Douglass's call for black nationalism" (Dunbar 95). Identifying as antislavery did not guarantee one was antiracist, nor that one supported black civil rights in the North. Charlotte Forten wrote Angelina Grimké in 1837 of the racism within the American abolition movement: "To some of them it clings like a dark mantle obscuring their many virtues and choking up the avenues to higher and nobler sentiments" (qtd. in Dunbar 92). Some African American women clearly valued the spaces all-black female societies offered them for their politics and others maintained memberships in both racially mixed and all-black female antislavery societies.[5]

Transatlantic Female Abolition

If race complicated the ways in which African American women participated in abolition, so too did antislavery's increasing appeal as a medium for forwarding the politics of a nascent white woman's rights movement. In *Women and Sisters,* Jean Fagan Yellin documents the rise of the "slave woman as sister" image circulating in Britain as early as 1826 and officially adopted as abolitionist emblem by British and American women by 1836: "The female version of the supplicant slave emblem . . . came from England. . . . Members of the Ladies Negro's Friend Society of Birmingham, England, chose this emblem to decorate the cover of their *First Report,* published in 1826. . . . The female slave image also appeared in American print in 1830. It was reproduced by editor Benjamin Lundy in the May issue of *The Genius of Universal Emancipation,* facing 'The Ladies' Repository,' a new feature designed to attract female readers. . . . By 1836, the female supplicant had become the unofficial emblem of the antislavery women" (10–17).

White southerner Angelina Grimké's address to the 1837 convention of American Women Against Slavery (New York City, 9–12 May 1837), published as *An Appeal to the Women of the Nominally Free States* (1837), contains a groundbreaking use of the "sister slave" metaphor in feminist abolitionist rhetoric. Using moral suasion, Grimké invokes the slave as proxy for woman, silenced and "fettered" in ways that extend well beyond public disapprobation for their participation in politics such as abolition: "All moral beings have essentially the same rights and duties, whether they be male or female. . . . The denial of our duty to act, is a bold denial of our right to act; and if we have no right to act, then may we well be termed 'the white slaves of the North'—for, like our brethren in bonds, we must seal our lips in silence and despair" (qtd. in Yellin 35).[6] The affect of Grimké's analogy was registered in Britain, as Claire Midgley notes:

> News of these American developments [including Grimké's address to the Massachusetts legislature and Sarah Grimké's publication of *Letters*

on the Equality of the Sexes, and the Condition of Women (1838)] reached leading British women abolitionists through their American contacts, through reports in periodicals, and through Harriet Martineau's descriptions in "The Martyr Age," in which she praised American women activists for both fulfilling their duties and exercising their rights. Martineau's *Society in America* (1837) contained her first explicitly feminist statements. . . . Breaking with the dominant tendency among British women abolitionists to contrast their own position with that of enslaved women, Martineau likened the position of "free" women in North American society to that of slaves. (*Women* 156)

In turn, Martineau's writings would become Britain's "first stirring of agitation for women's rights among women and men of all classes" (Midgley, *Women* 156), but Midgley also notes that the analogy that became "woman as slave" was emerging in Owenite socialist feminist writings and lectures in Britain between 1835 and 1839 (Midgley, *Women* 156). The "woman as slave" metaphor has had considerable attention in scholarship on white and black female abolition in the United States for at least forty years since the work of Gerda Lerner and others on the Grimké sisters first brought it to our attention.[7] Certainly, its appeal to some British feminists makes it relevant to understanding the work of black female abolitionists in the transatlantic network, as we do see activists such as Remond and Craft drawing on the popularity of the tragic mulatta and slave woman as proxy for their own purposes.[8] Yet exclusive attention to this rhetorical appeal in their work risks aligning the British reform scene too closely to its American counterpart without attending to important differences that can highlight unique appeals black female abolitionists made in the British Isles as well as Ireland. Moreover, reading primarily for black feminist abolition work with the "woman as slave" trope also risks tying the internationalizing of black feminism solely to those developing transatlantic networks of white feminism.

Even as influential British antislavery women were in correspondence, and often agreement, with their abolitionist sisters across the Atlantic,[9] most distinguished themselves from their sisters in the American struggle by clearly defining their role as "auxiliary and supportive" and articulating their desire to remain within their "appropriate sphere" (qtd. in Midgley, *Women* 158). However much women like Martineau and the Owenites may have coupled "woman" and "slave" in their understanding of woman's condition and in their politics, the vast majority of British women abolitionists did not, nor did they see antislavery as a vehicle for woman's rights appeals. Consequently, though it may be tempting to take the World Anti-Slavery Convention in London in 1840 as a turning point for the place the "woman question" would hold in British antislavery discourse, we must attend instead to the differences between female abolition it highlights on both sides of the Atlantic.[10] The appointment of American women delegates to the convention by Garrisonian abolitionists forced the question of women's role in antislavery, and the British and Foreign Anti-Slavery Society (BFASS) committee's refusal to accept these women's credentials put the debate squarely in focus.[11] There were British women abolitionists who emerged from the discord of the convention as Garrisonian supporters,[12] with strengthened convictions in their work for woman's rights and other radical reforms such as the Anti-Corn Law League, universal suffrage, and the married women's property act (Midgley, *Women* 162–164). Yet most British female abolitionists opposed the growing use of antislavery rhetoric to forward woman's rights politics, and, as Kathryn Kish Sklar has argued, "in crucial instances their women's rights activism can be traced to other movements" than abolition (460 n. 9).

Indeed, women did not begin to participate equally in British abolition until the 1850s. In 1853, the Leeds Antislavery Association was formed, which broke with the tradition of single- sex abolition societies and adopted the "Am I not a woman and a sister" emblem alongside the more popular "Am I not a man and a brother" figure. In 1854 the BFASS accepted two women from the Manchester Ladies' Anti-Slavery Society as delegates to their national conference and in 1855 "female delegates [were] received 'as a matter of course' to the World's Anti-Slavery Convention in London" (Midgley, *Women* 170). Co-incident with these developments in British abolition were advances in woman's rights agitation, which included the Married Woman's Property Committee and petitioning campaign (1855), *The Englishwoman's Journal* (1857), and the Association for the Promotion of the Employment of Women (1858). Yet as Midgley and Sklar have documented, though there was much intellectual and political traffic across the Atlantic in antislavery circles, and though an American abolitionist-feminism influenced a developing woman's rights political culture in the UK, there are important differences between an American abolitionist-feminism and British female abolitionism "reluctant" to raise woman's rights within the movement.[13]

One important difference was the relevance of the "woman as slave" analogy in the UK, which Midgley argues was affected by the UK sense of slavery as "a colonial problem" happening somewhere out there ("Transatlantic Perspective" 126), as well as by British female abolitionists' established rhetoric of extending the "privilege" of their own position to women they variously viewed as "enslaved," ranging from black women under colonial slavery to Indian women's oppression by Indian men under *sati*. In such rhetoric, British women did not recognize or mark their own condition as oppressed but likened themselves to liberators. Though that analogy was used by British feminists, it was by no means a central rhetorical tool in UK female-abolitionist circles as it was among American feminist-abolitionists. Instead, Midgley documents the development of British female abolitionist discourse as following a separate trajectory to a discourse of woman's rights in Britain.

A further difference was the role class played in British public politics as well as abolition. By the 1840s, the British antislavery movement was "concerned that working-class men might hijack for their own ends the continuing campaign in support of American abolitionists" and Chartists had begun disrupting antislavery meetings "seeking to promote the rights of 'white slaves'" (Midgley, "Transatlantic Perspective" 126). While in the United States, race proved the significant impediment to full and equal participation in women's auxiliaries, despite the exceptions of some integrated societies, in the UK class divided the movement into middle-class run auxiliaries in which working-class women were "encouraged to support the movement through donations, signatures to petitions, and participation in the boycott of slave produce" even as they were excluded from committees (Midgley, "Transatlantic Perspective" 135). British women activists were highly attuned to the ways class structured English public politics as well as antislavery politics and knew very well that this affected the degree to which woman's rights could be forwarded as an appeal through the movement. Elizabeth Pease wrote Maria Weston Chapman after the 1840 convention, noting, "I find very few people who are aware that with you all *white men* are on a legal equality and that consequently our class restrictions, religious disabilities, landed propertied monopolies, etc, etc, all the host of oppressions under which we groan resolve themselves with you into distinctions of *sex* or of color" (qtd. in Sklar 482–83).[14] Pease's letter stresses that the achievement of universal white male suffrage in the United States meant that neither woman's rights nor antislavery appeals vied with those of working-class white men as they did in the British Isles. Her letter also reminds us that in a political culture in which a "host of oppressions" clamored for a hearing, "slavery" could be a useful metaphor that, for some, was far too mobile. This mobility, and the readiness of slavery to be equated with class oppression in particular, alongside the sense that slavery was another nation's concern, together make the work women like Ellen Craft and

Sarah Parker Remond undertook across the Atlantic rather different from their labors in the United States.

When Ellen Craft and Sarah Parker Remond left the United States, the "woman as slave" analogy had been making it difficult to register crucial differences between the material conditions of the enslaved and women for a decade, and it was this tendency toward identification and occluding analogy that African American female abolitionists had been managing for some time in their own rhetoric. The analogy, and its use within a developing woman's rights discourse in the United States, made it possible to reach audiences already predisposed to hear of the female slave's suffering, but to wrench that image from distorting abstraction and an all-too developed circulation as proxy for the white woman's condition was challenging to say the least. Yet when black female abolitionists like Craft and Remond entered the transatlantic network, they also had to negotiate the analogy between the white working classes and "the slave" in Britain and Ireland, as well as a very different situation for abolition and women's place within it.

The "Sister Slave" and the Transatlantic Antislavery Network

While African American female abolitionists participated in both all-black and integrated antislavery societies in the United States and with their white colleagues had begun to enter into roles previously closed to women such as antislavery lecturing, black women such as Remond and Craft were effectively internationalizing black feminism through the transatlantic network. Less attention has been paid, however, to the work black female abolitionists accomplished in an international frame and perhaps understandably so because very few women undertook this kind of work. Of the nine women listed by the *Black Abolitionist Papers* as having visited the British Isles, only Craft and Remond undertook lecture tours.[15] That they did and were extraordinarily successful in their endeavors is highly significant. Black men dominated the transatlantic scene. As we see in introductions to Remond's speeches, it was not at all common for women—white or black—to take to the platform, yet there was a well-established practice of black male abolitionists touring the British Isles. Attending to Ellen Craft's and Sarah Parker Remond's work is vitally important, not simply because it was rare but because it alters a received understanding of early black feminism as more local than is actually the case.

Taking Ellen Craft as a trailblazer, we see that the ability to read an existing set of rhetorical appeals and political interests in order to access existing reform publics and interests for one's own ends was absolutely central to the success of an internationalizing early black feminism. Appeals that might not at first appear to be feminist actually kept that established black feminist politic of concern for the viability of a larger oppressed community, and attention to the links between various forms of oppression, firmly at the fore. In this way, we can understand the black feminist principles of the Woman's Association of Philadelphia—"the elevation of the colored people"—and not exclusively the pursuit of woman's rights as formative of the politics Craft and Remond would pursue in the British Isles and Ireland. There, these women further developed an attention to oppression in different locales and based in different material realities as linked: the oppression of the enslaved in America was not simply similar to that of the British working classes; rather, these must be understood as intimately linked oppressions under the global cotton market which demanded a collective, not competing, politics.

Craft clearly understood the importance of class to the appeals she, her husband, and William Wells Brown could forward, and the way in which her gender and ensuing sympathies for her, far from circumscribing her politics, made her the drawing card for the trio's appearances.[16] Remond, appearing after Craft effectively opened up Scotland, the north and west of England, and reform strongholds in the southwest such as Bristol and Clifton to black female abolitionist work, benefited from Ellen Craft's complicated circulation and the techniques she had employed to negotiate the vexed terrain of British antislavery and labor politics. Indeed, the Crafts were at the heart of British antislavery by that time: when Remond arrived in 1859 to begin her highly successful lecture tour, they became members of the London Emancipation Committee. Examining the work of both Ellen Craft and Sarah Parker Remond through the dual lenses of transatlantic reform and early black feminisms enables us to reconsider questions earlier scholarship seemed to have pronounced upon in ways that accorded Remond and Craft very little, if any, agency or control over their work:[17] Were these women managed by others or did they skillfully manipulate the interest they generated? Were they able to be more than sensation, more than the latest entertainment at the hotels and music halls at which they appeared? And are their transatlantic appearances oddities or can they shift what we understand early black feminism to be?

The transatlantic abolition network expanded early in the 1850s due to the participation of black abolitionists within it and in response to the Fugitive Slave Law. So popular were black lecturers, particularly fugitive slaves, that "the transition from fugitive-on-the-run to anti-slavery practitioner could be swift" (Ripley et al. 1: 5). To a degree unheard of in the United States, "black Americans had real authority in the British Isles . . . [where] professional black abolitionists could produce results as few others could, if left to their own efforts." In fact, greats like Frederick Douglass were recognized as international political forces. Black abolitionists clearly understood that Britain had come to enjoy, and continued to actively cultivate, a position as global moral leader, and they worked to exploit that national feeling and international influence for their own ends at midcentury. As Elisa Tamarkin has documented, widespread anglophilia in the United States at this time was reflected in a distinctly black anglophilia in which Britain was lauded as that "wider field within which African Americans could operate in ways *not* circumscribed by the project of abolition" (447). Historical scholarship on the transatlantic network has similarly argued that black abolitionists enjoyed a greater independence in the British Isles, where they were able to attend and speak before meetings of rival antislavery organizations unlike in the United States (Ripley et al. 1: 8, 18).[18] In fact, that independence has been cited as enabling black abolitionists to appear to the British reform public as a "third alternative" to rival abolition groups (Blackett, *Building* x) then roughly divided between the BFASS and its associations and pro-Garrisonian societies such as those based in Glasgow, Edinburgh, Dublin, Bristol, and Clifton.

In the writings of such greats as Frederick Douglass, Britain emerges as an ideal, a place where "(racial) caste proves no hindrance to blacks . . . who may then enjoy distinctions only (social) class provides" (Tamarkin 456). As Van Gosse argues, British solidarity with black abolitionists "peaked in the early 1850s" (1018) under the influence of the Fugitive Slave act and the enormous success of Harriet Beecher Stowe's *Uncle Tom's Cabin,* which sold "a million copies in eight months [and] brought anti-slavery feeling to such a pitch that 562,448 Englishwomen led by the Duchess of Sutherland signed the 'Stafford House Address,' asking their American sister to abjure slavery as unchristian" (1016). Yet what of those black abolitionists whose solidarity seemed to lie with the working classes who attended their lectures in high numbers? Was social class simply a distinction to be enjoyed by the unfettered African American on tour, or does black anglophilia such as Douglass's mask the far more vexed and central role class played in black abolition in the UK?

Far from capitalizing on straightforward support, black abolitionists appearing in the British Isles in the 1850s entered a transitional moment in black abolition politics, following a period when the demand for African American appearances and lectures far exceeded the number of black abolitionists available and just preceding the Civil War period when so many African Americans found their way to England that "they were often the object of English relief organizations whose sole purpose was to aid them" (Ripley et al. 1: 33). By the time Ellen Craft and Sarah Parker Remond were captivating audiences, the black abolitionist fad meant that the exploits of a few had cast suspicion on the lot. R. J. M. Blackett notes that "blacks [on the antislavery lecture circuit] were aware that their color had become an asset" (*Building* 40). In fact, the success of fugitive slave abolitionists in Britain was reported in New York's *Express* in 1847 as a fad of no small proportions: "'[N]othing goes down . . . so well as the genuine black.' . . . They were seen in every public place in London and were so much in vogue that white men and women were 'coloring their faces and hands, and going about London, imitating their sable visitors,' who were reaping a harvest 'bringing off their pockets full of money'" (Blackett, *Building* 39).

The American Fugitive Slave Law of 1850 had turned "the trickle of fugitives" lecturing in Britain into "a flood" (Blackett, *Building* 5). British abolitionists and the public at large knew of cases in which black antislavery lecturers claiming to be affiliated with an abolitionist society for which they were raising funds were lecturing independently for personal profit. The phenomenon continued into the mid-1860s, at that time fueled by interest in the Civil War. In the summer of 1865, BFASS secretary Louis Chamerovzow wrote his colleagues in the United States of William Howard Day's accumulation of "a considerable sum" of "contributions," yet when "doubts [were] raised as to their appropriation, he left the country" (qtd. in Blackett, "African Americans" 56). The previous fall, Rev. W. Mitchell, on a mission to raise funds for fugitives in Canada, was "brought up before the mayor of Cardiff for trying to slip away without paying his hotel bill. He had evidently done the same in Newport, Penmark and Llancarven" (Blackett, "African Americans" 56). Add these recognized figures in black abolition to the countless anonymous men appearing as "itinerant lecturers" in what Chamerovzow referred to as "the remoter provinces" (Blackett, "African Americans" 56), and it is understandable that the British public was often warned to be wary of imposters, warnings that must have affected their interest in and potential commitment to the antislavery efforts of black Americans.

While the authenticity and reliability of black abolitionists was a public concern in the 1850s and 1860s, complicating the work that Craft and Remond would undertake, so too was the focus on the so-called white slave. Scholars such as Jennifer DeVere Brody have documented that a "marked concern with 'white slaves'" had become established in England by the mid-to late 1850s (17). That preoccupation was sufficient to make abolition a vehicle for the concerns of the working classes, even as working- and middle-class whites critiqued "upper-class English sympathy for and involvement in abolitionism" (Brody 79). The "slave" could be simply mapped onto the white worker in abolitionist discourse, "which often analogized class and race, . . . ma[king] 'blacks' stand-ins for the more pressing national concern of *white slavery*" (Brody 80). Certainly, Ellen Craft's "whiteness" was frequently said to move her audiences: : "He [Rev. R. L. Carpenter] made the remark from observing that many persons, when they heard that his friend, Mrs Craft, was nearly white, expressed more horror than before" ("American Slavery" a). And her appearances with her husband, William, and William Wells Brown were advertised as "Views of American Slavery" with a special appearance by the "White Slave," Ellen Craft.

Sarah Parker Remond's audiences were sufficiently taken with the image of a slave woman with "whitened" features sold at auction into concubinage that she raised this "story" in nearly every speech she gave in the UK. Yet exactly what fascinated their audiences remains a complex question. Appeals to the sympathies and alliances of class were of significant potential use to them, as Blackett notes: "[T]he British working class had been active participants in the struggle for abolition in the British West Indies and had taken a keen interest in the cause in the United States in the years after 1834" ("African Americans" 52). However, appeals resting on analogies of class, labor, and enslavement were troubling for black abolitionists, given a vested working-class British interest in American cotton and the obvious differences between waged labor and enslavement that any antislavery African American would be loathe to dismiss. Yet time and again, Ellen Craft was taken to be the "White Slave" incarnate, appearing on the platform as William Wells Brown played on his audiences' class sympathies.

The White Slave

Ellen Craft arrived in Liverpool in early December 1850. The Crafts were well known in the United States, and their "daring escape . . . [was] widely reported in British newspapers" as well as American periodicals (Blackett, *Beating* 97). Ellen and her husband William had run from Macon, Georgia, in December 1848: William posed as her slave and Ellen disguised herself as a rheumatic southern gentleman en route to Philadelphia for treatment. They traveled by train and steamer in full view and in contact with other passengers, arriving in Philadelphia only four days after they left Macon. The Fugitive Slave Law, passed in September 1850, forced them to leave the United States in early November for England, where they lived for nineteen years until they returned to Georgia to establish a vocational school for freedmen and freedwomen near Savannah. Soon after they arrived in Liverpool, the Crafts got up a lecture tour with William Wells Brown[19] of the north and west of England, as well as Scotland, from January to May 1851. Together the trio appeared at numerous antislavery meetings, and by 1854 they were acknowledged as a force in UK abolitionist circles. Brown and the Crafts sought to manage their audiences' class sympathies as well as their political investments and national feeling in their work to forward an antislavery appeal.

Addressing an audience of three thousand at the Glasgow Emancipation Society on January 6, 1851, Brown plays on a British national feeling of moral superiority to America, which still practiced the barbarisms of slavery, and when Ellen Craft takes the platform, she confronts the audience with its inconsistencies. In 1850, the Austrian general Julius Jacob von Haynau, infamous for his brutality against Hungarian revolutionaries and sympathizers—including the public flogging of women—was attacked by draymen while touring the Anchor Brewery in Southpark. Although the Austrian ambassador demanded an apology, Foreign Secretary Lord Palmerston refused, and only with Queen Victoria's intervention was an apology sent to Vienna. "Public feeling in England was completely on the side of the draymen, who became the heroes of many a street ballad" ("Anchor Brewery"). Raising a national incident with which his audience would be very familiar, Brown carefully indicts those who would make the Anchor draymen folk heroes yet remain silent on the violences African American women endure under slavery. Brown begins by noting that the British denounce slavery yet say nothing to American slave owners they may happen to meet: "He sometimes thought that the people of this country acted very inconsistently in denouncing the institution of slavery, which separated the husband from his wife, and the mother from her child; while at the same time, the American slave owner was received into European society."

While Brown opens with "this country," Britain, as the target, he ends by indicting "European society," cannily letting his audience off the hook at the same time he accuses them of moral failing. Brown then immediately turns to laud the British people for their scourging of Haynau and the oppression for which he stood: "He knew of no code of morality by which the slave owner would be received with open arms by the very same individuals who applauded the draymen of Barclay and Perkins, for driving General Haynau out of the country." The audience cheers in response, yet he immediately tempers those self-congratulatory cheers with the reminder that the American slave owner is no different from the Austrian tyrant by marshaling Ellen Craft as the embodied representative of all American bondswomen: "For was not the individual who could enslave Ellen Craft, and who after she had made her escape, in a manner unparalleled by any man or woman,—could claim her as his property, pursue her to Boston, and then drive her from the land of her birth—was that individual not as mean and contemptible as the man who caused females to be flogged on the soil of Hungary?" ("American Fugitive Slave Bill"). At the close of Brown's address, "Mr. Wm. Craft was then introduced by the Chairman. His wife, in whom the negro blood is scarcely perceptible, accompanied him to the front of the platform. Their appearance was greeted with the utmost enthusiasm" ("American Fugitive Slave Bill"). In what would become an established pattern on this tour, William narrated their escape while Ellen stood by silently.

Unlike the way in which midcentury abolition, white or black, is said to have "trade[d] on a discourse of intellectualism and cultural advancement that is teleologically Anglophilic, that says that Great Britain is simply further along in ways America has yet to manage for itself" (Tamarkin 458), Brown and the Crafts refuse to let "advanced" Britain off the hook, charging that society with its selective approach to public censure of moral wrongs. However, there is a slipperiness to this charge that makes Ellen Craft's whiteness key to its success, for Brown is able to rouse his listeners to cheers even as he indicts them with political and moral inconsistency. Just as his British audience is not quite those Europeans who would socially receive the American slave owner, Ellen Craft is "not quite white," for she is an escaped slave reputed to be the daughter of her master. Yet Ellen is "white enough" to remind her audience of the Hungarian women upon whose behalf they were collectively outraged. It is never said that Ellen was "flogged" herself, yet she stands as a proxy her audience can imagine had suffered that violence and the countless other abuses endured by the American slave woman. In this way, Craft can be said to stand as a strategically ambivalent reminder of her audience's moral failings *and* moral superiority, much as Brown has reminded them of both. Brown's address and Ellen Craft's appearance on the platform together demand that the moral authority Britain once brought to bear on American slavery must be reawakened, that their moral authority in rousting

Haynau must be realized in their support for the American slave if it is not to count as simply another instance of "European" hypocrisy.

Ellen Craft's appearances were part of a well-practiced routine honed in the United States during a lecture tour of the Northeast in 1849 first documented by Benjamin Quarles: "During the first six months of 1849, Brown toured the antislavery circuit exhibiting William and Ellen Craft. . . . Brown took the couple in his charge and gave them maximum exposure. He arranged meetings for them throughout New England, sometimes charging an admission fee, an almost unprecedented practice in abolitionist circles. But the Crafts were drawing cards. They said little, but Ellen's appearance created an instant sympathy in a white audience" (62–63).[20] William Farrison describes the lectures on this 1849 tour as consisting of Brown's lengthy introduction of William Craft, William's recounting of the Crafts' escape, a persuasive speech by Brown, followed by Ellen's introduction. Ellen "sometimes added a few words to what her husband had said" (136–37). Even though Brown introduced the Crafts to the antislavery lecture circuit, some scholars speculate that William and Ellen were well aware of the attention her appearance garnered, courting and manipulating it to advance their cause. Blackett writes of Ellen's silent displays at the close of these lectures as a "pattern" the Crafts had "refined," a "careful orchestration . . . guaranteed to provoke strong antislavery sentiments" in both New England and, later, Britain. During the 1849 American tour, William would heighten Brown's sentimental and domestic appeals by personalizing them: "Using his own experiences, he told how easily families were broken up and sold separately" (*Beating* 98, 99). Ellen would then appear, embodying her audiences' worst fears that slavery would not spare even the most womanly and white.[21]

Benjamin Quarles's early insight that William and Ellen Craft were William Wells Brown's "drawing cards," enabling him to charge admission to his lectures for the privilege of seeing them, is borne out in their UK appearances. Yet I would argue that in the UK, distanced from American slavery but in the thick of labor reform, the Crafts' escape read for many of their audiences rather differently. That abolitionist staple of broken families would read in that context as a narrative of family ties threatened by the market; one's ability to find work meant keeping family together, yet labor separated parents from children, and the meager earnings it could afford made dependants either a liability or laborers, themselves, necessary for the family's survival. Brown and the Crafts' appearances deliberately appealed to their British audiences' familiarity with representations of slavery as an inhuman system violating domestic bonds: the "slavery" of the white working classes, whether child or adult, and the inhumanity of the factory owner and, ultimately, the market. Judging from Joseph Limpton's letter to Samuel May Jr. dated May 3, 1851, the Crafts and William Wells Brown had established a strong draw with working-class audiences. And since the trio's success is clearly due to Ellen Craft's notoriety, judging from the prominence of invitations to see "'The White Slave' Ellen Craft" in advertisements for their lectures, it was Ellen Craft herself who was a figure of fascination for the working-class English men and women who came to see them. Their meetings at Bradford and Leeds were "packed almost entirely by working class" (Limpton to May). Indeed, their appeal to working-class audiences may well be behind the worry that the "tone" of their shows had become a liability for those British abolitionists who supported them.

In his May 1851 letter to Eliza Wigham, Scottish abolitionist and suffragist British reformer John B. Estlin worries about Brown's and the Crafts' respectability given the spectacular nature of their appearances. "We have been endeavoring to improve the tone of Brown and Crafts [*sic*] Exhibition," writes Estlin, "altering their *showman like* handbills, and securing a higher position for Ellen. She fully feels the propriety of all we have said and done and is very thankful to us" (qtd. in Farrison 186). Brown toured with his enormous panorama of American slavery, "painted on 2000 feet of canvas" as one advertisement for a Brown and Crafts lecture boasted, and their appearances were often a mix of entertainment and argument: "The Lecture will be enlivened by the Recital of ANTI-SLAVERY MELODIES; and Wm. CRAFT will relate some of the most interesting circumstances connected with the Escape of himself and his Wife from Slavery" ("Views of American Slavery"). Their appearances, in other words, were far from simple lectures or addresses, and they seem to be fashioned to appeal to a particular market. Indeed, Brown was experienced in appearances that went well beyond the standard lecture. John Ernest has argued that, in the United States, Brown "challenged his audience's expectations concerning what a black anti-slavery lecturer might present," even performing "plays written for performance on the anti-slavery lecture circuit" rather than confining himself to the presentation of slavery's "facts" (*Liberation* 334).

The Pauper

The domestic appeals William Craft forwarded and Ellen Craft underscored with her silent appearances closing meeting after meeting read at first glance as examples of abolition's use of melodrama to play on the sympathies of its supporters.[22] Yet in the UK, before working-class audiences, the domestic had an arguably different connotation. John Ernest has called the Crafts' narrative, *Running a Thousand Miles for Freedom,* "unusually domestic" for a slave narrative, a genre "often associated with individual struggle" ("Chaos" 479). Particularly suggestive is Ernest's observation that this narrative "presents domestic relations primarily in stories of violation, separation, *restriction,* and *alienation*" ("Chaos" 479; emphasis added). William Craft is said to have written the narrative in England while he and Ellen became settled, were educated and briefly worked at the Ockham School outside London, began their family, and worked on the London Emancipation Committee (McCaskill, "Introduction" xiv). Yet their narrative was originally published and since reprinted as authored by both William and Ellen.[23]

The Crafts' appearances drew the attention of William Tweedie, a London publisher who also distributed the *Anti-Slavery Advocate;* Tweedie published the narrative in 1860 (McCaskill, "Introduction" xv). It seems reasonable to suppose that the narrative was influenced by the Crafts' appearances with Brown, that as their role in those appearances—including William's narration of their escape at their lectures—was shaped over the course of their tour, so too was the narrative's depiction of the domestic shaped. I would argue that we must consider that depiction as, at least in part, Ellen's creation. Ernest's assertion that the domestic is presented as not only violated, a stock depiction in slave narratives, but as alienated and restricted in addition to his observation that the domestic is stressed to an "unusual" degree is telling. I would argue that the Crafts' awareness of the market—as they came to know it in the UK—and of the privileges it restricts to the middle and upper classes at the expense of the working classes, informs its uniqueness within the slave narrative genre. But the additional referent we must bear in mind to understand the success of the Crafts' appeal both through *Running* and their public appearances is the pauper. Particularly, Ellen stood as the pauperized mother when the fear she shared with William for her children's safety and freedom was invoked in both *Running* and in his narration of their escape preceding her appearances on the platform.

The Crafts appeared in the British Isles with the New Poor Law of 1834 fully entrenched, mandating that the poor could receive relief only in the workhouse, itself designed and operated with the goal of deterring the poor from seeking social assistance. In the workhouse, paupers were barely sustained and families were divided. Wives were separated from husbands and children from parents, denying the poor any right to a family so as to prevent the rise of "infant paupers," as Anna Clark has carefully documented (*Breeches* 188). The New Poor Law's infamous bastardy clauses freed men from common-law relationships and the obligation to support children within them, casting mothers on the questionable mercy of the workhouse. These clauses spurred violent protests by working people in London in the mid-1830s through the early 1840s, and in 1837 in the North, where poor rates were much lower.

The bastardy clauses also instigated mass protests of women in 1838 against their effect, which ultimately was to separate mothers from children (Clark, *Breeches* 189, 191). By the 1850s, reformers were drawing attention to the ways in which the New Poor Law, given the 1844 Poor Law Amendment Act making married women responsible for the maintenance of their children, had come to mean far more women and children were being forced to seek social relief than men. Clark documents that in 1850, "out of 878,944 receiving outdoor relief, only 178,068 were adult males" ("New Poor Law" 269). Workhouse conditions were so dire and the specter of divided families so powerful that local poor law guardians repeatedly sought to give un- or underemployed men outdoor relief (relief outside the workhouse) rather than force a family to sell their possessions, enter the workhouse, and essentially become permanently pauperized (Clark, "New Poor Law" 265). Yet despite such efforts, poor families were separated even before they faced the last resort of the workhouse, and with the 1844 Amendment Act, men were taking the difficult decision to abandon their families rather than seek outdoor relief or enter the workhouse with them.

The Crafts' narrative locates the possibility of family, of domestic relations, as the impetus to their decision to flee slavery in its opening paragraph: "[T]he mere idea that we were . . . deprived of all legal rights—the thought that we had to give up our hard earnings to a tyrant, to enable him to live in idleness and luxury . . . but above all, the fact that another man had the power to tear from our cradle the new-born babe and sell it in the shambles like a brute . . . haunted us for years" (3). But it is also here that we see the Crafts likening slavery to wage labor (what slave has "earnings" to give up?), the political position of the slave as akin to the disenfranchised working-class man and the pauper confined to the workhouse (both "deprived" of legal rights), and through these now-established analogies the worker/pauper-slave as alienated from not only his or her labor but also the domestic, which can be violated on the whim of "a tyrant" or guardians implementing the New Poor Law and its version of relief. Ultimately the tyrant was the market itself.

To prioritize family as something to safeguard when one is a slave is a daring claim, a claim that, for both the working classes and "the slave," asserts one's right to a privilege from which one is restricted, a "privilege" reserved for those in a higher social position. That privilege, the distinctions of position upon which it rests, and the very market that underwrites them, is enabled by the alienation of the worker-slave from his or her labor and from the domestic. Family, like "earnings," becomes a fictive and daring claim to assert, and the Crafts' claim to a life free of restriction, violation, and alienation would have made their story—in either public speech or written narrative—riveting to the working-class audiences who thronged to see them.

The Crafts appear to have been well aware that they were reaching audiences motivated by the specter of the workhouse and the pauper and attuned to working-class factory reformers' rhetoric, which stressed the right of all peoples, rich or poor, to domesticity. But more than this, the New Poor Law amplified reform rhetoric that positioned the working classes as slaves. Factory operatives were frequently styled the "white slaves" or "Christian slaves" of England (Clark, *Breeches* 216, 218), and Chartists referred to women workers as "sisters in bondage" (Clark, *Breeches* 234) in ways that echoed the abolitionist tendency to depict slaves, particularly bondswomen, as victims in need of chivalrous protection because they were incapable of resistance or political organization themselves. However much protests against the New Poor Law may be said to have given women a political voice, particularly in their defense of the domestic against the bastardy clauses, working women were often marshaled as the silent sufferers of the factory's "enslavement" in reform rhetoric. In what Lauren Berlant has identified as indicative of "the poverty of a mass politics," both abolition and labor reform built their political "coalitions via grandiose public dramatic performances of injured subjectivity" (*Queen* 228).

Audiences' great excitement at seeing the "White Slave" take to the platform signaled their thrill at seeing slavery's zero limit, be it women under American bondage or British wage slavery. Ellen Craft strategically stood as a symbol for both—the American slave and the pauperized British mother, both pressed to extremes to hold their families together yet defeated in their very attempts by a power that could wrench wife from husband, child from parent, with no possibility for redress. Both the American slave code, which had long held the child followed the condition of the mother,[24] and the New Poor Law held the mother finally, and impossibly, responsible for her child's welfare. Ellen stood as a silent reminder of such violations of womanhood and domesticity on both sides of the Atlantic, and her silence was arguably key to facilitating that dual imagining. While William spoke of the threats to domesticity under American slavery cast in terms that further enabled audience empathy given their parallels to the effects of the New Poor Law, Ellen took the stage only after that empathy was already well at work. She did not speak of her particular experiences, a specificity that could disrupt that empathy, but rather in her silence facilitated that final circuit in which American slave and white slave of England came to be united. With such carefully orchestrated appearances, the Crafts clearly worked with an already established comparison between working-class or pauperized women and the slave that had been forwarded by women activists in the Owenite, Anti-Poor Law, and Chartist movements (Midgley, *Women* 204).

While scholars have tended to read Ellen's silence as disempowering,[25] we simply cannot know what role she took in determining the nature of her appearances, just as we cannot know where we see her hand in the narrative some credit her as coauthoring with her husband. I believe it safe to assume that she knew very well the disapprobation women generally faced if they spoke in public on political matters, for she was quite familiar with American antislavery in the late 1840s and part of the inner circles of British antislavery upon her arrival in Liverpool. To imagine she would have lectured alongside her husband and Brown, and to bemoan the fact that she did not as evidence of her "handling" or management by Brown and/or their British supporters, is to ignore or underestimate the gender politics under which she worked. That she played an active and key role in facilitating the trio's successful appeals to reform and working-class audiences, and did so through a symbolic critique, however silent, of social and economic conditions that were particularly damaging to women marks the feminist politics of her work. The New Poor Law and the ways in which women and children suffered under its implementation is essential to understanding how Ellen's symbolization of the slave-mother risking all to keep family together resonated with working-class and reform audiences. Ellen Craft was active in cultivating the following that the trio enjoyed, a success they achieved together because they had become attuned to the ways in which existing political sympathies could be managed and redirected.

The way in which her onstage appearance as the slave/pauper mother may have played on her highly popular engraved portrait is of further interest, for it suggests that she circulated as both victim and hero in her audiences' imaginations. Identical to the one first published in the *London Illus-*

trated News on April 19, 1851 (Weinauer 49), engravings of "Ellen Craft, The Fugitive Slave" in the disguise in which she escaped slavery were offered for sale at the trio's lectures. They were also advertised for sale in British antislavery publications; in 1857 the Leeds Anti-Slavery Association advertised both a "youth edition of *Uncle Tom's Cabin* . . . [and] a shilling portrait of Ellen wearing masculine garments" for sale (McCaskill, "Introduction" xvii). This coupling is highly suggestive, since it indicates Ellen Craft held her own with the likes of Harriet Beecher Stowe's novel in the midcentury British popular imaginary, a novel that is credited with "set[ting] the terms of debate for abolitionism in England in . . . the 1850s" (Fisch 6).[26]

These engravings of Ellen Craft dressed as a man, a reminder of her heroic escape from slavery with her husband William who posed as her slave, were central to the Crafts' self-promotion only a few months after they began touring the UK, and the popularity of Ellen's engraving had clearly reached a pitch some six years later. Well after the heyday of her public appearances in 1851, Ellen's engraving continued to satisfy some desire in the public for a hero figure that I would argue goes beyond the stereotypical interest in fugitive slaves and their escapes. The context in which the Crafts appeared and their deliberate design to appeal to the working-class audiences that formed the bulk of their following, throws the desire for the heroic escaped slave into relief somewhat differently. Ellen's platform appearances called up the effects of British wage slavery upon women and mothers, positioning them as helpless victims, yet her engravings presented these same audiences with the image of woman as heroic, as able to throw off the chains of slavery and risk everything to be free. But since Ellen is dressed as a man in them, they seem to have titillated without offending her audiences' sensibilities and gender politics. Clearly her engraving sold well if it was offered not only at the trio's appearances but was also available for order through antislavery societies and publications, thereby registering a desire for an image and a shared imagining of the triumph of the oppressed worker over the market and its ruthlessness.

Working-Class Solidarity

If we continue to place class at the center of how we read Ellen Craft's work, we can see that in cases such as their Great Exhibition promenade, she, her husband, and William Wells Brown were not only courting empathy and solidarity with the working classes but at times targeting the British upper classes as well as the American slaveholder for critique. American abolitionist

Henry Wright wrote to abolitionist James Haughton of Dublin in early February 1851, suggesting that the Crafts and William Wells Brown be part of London's Great Exhibition at Crystal Palace: "Above all, an American slave-auction block must be there, with William and Ellen Craft on the block, Henry Clay as auctioneer, and the American flag floating over it. . . . Or, if they cannot be admitted *into* the Fair, with other specimens of American ingenuity and skill, they must be exhibited in some place *outside,* but near it, so that they can be seen and examined with convenience" ("American Slavery in the World's Fair"). In a letter dated June 26, 1851, William Farmer wrote William Lloyd Garrison of the Crafts' and Brown's appearance at the Great Exhibition; the letter was published in the July 18, 1851, edition of *The Liberator.* In his letter, Farmer notes the British bested the Americans "in the illustrations of their manufactures. Along with the self-acting mules, jennys, and other machinery they have brought in, in *propria persone,* specimens of that alleged proletarian class in this country, factory men, women and children, who are to be seen daily in their common dress, engaged in their ordinary employments . . . the degraded and miserable condition of 'the white slaves of England.'" ("Fugitive Slaves"). But he also takes much of the letter to express relief that American slaveholders refrained from exhibiting similar specimens of American slavery in the attempt to present the peculiar institution as superior to British wage slavery, which Farmer fears would have swayed public opinion and damaged the abolitionist cause.

Yet Farmer is decidedly in favor of exhibiting Brown and the Crafts themselves as American slavery specimens, and in a self-satisfied tone recounts their attendance at the fair, promenading for "between six and seven hours . . . arm in arm" ("Fugitive Slaves") with British abolitionists "George and Jenny Thompson [and their daughter Amelia], Richard and Maria Webb, and William Farmer" himself (Blackett, *Building* 32). With flourish, Farmer claims that no one they encountered "dreamed of any impropriety in a gentleman of character and standing, like Mr. McDonnell,[27] walking arm-in-arm with a colored woman; or an elegant and accomplished young lady, like Miss Thompson, becoming the promenading companion of a colored man? Did the English peers and peeresses? Not the most aristocratic among them" ("Fugitive Slaves"). Yet what is unspoken though quite clear in Farmer's letter is the challenge to class prejudices that Brown and the Crafts must have posed to those they encountered, not to mention the undertone of miscegenation that their promenade may have raised,[28] since in addition to Ellen's "whiteness" Brown would also have drawn attention for being "a light Mulatto," as

John Ernest has documented of his American appearances (qtd. in *Liberation* 60). The group deliberately chose to appear at the fair on "Saturday . . . a day upon which the largest number of the aristocracy and wealthier classes attend the Crystal Palace. . . . Some 15,000, mostly of the upper classes, were there congregated, including the Queen, Prince Albert, and the royal children, the anti-slavery Duchess of Sutherland . . . the Duke of Wellington . . . a large number of peers, peeresses, members of Parliament, merchants and bankers" ("Fugitive Slaves").

Though Farmer asserts that the promenade was arranged to indict American slaveholders, who were also in numerous attendance, we must remember the parallel live exhibit for Crystal Palace visitors was the "white slaves of England" in their daily toil and attire. Elite English and elite slaveholding Americans become equated in Farmer's letter, despite what appears to be his intention: the former exploits the "white slaves" on display, the latter exploits the "American slave" now walking among them. While Farmer may claim no English elite noted any impropriety in upper-class white reformers keeping company with fugitive slaves, what goes unspoken is the certain impropriety that would be seen in a similar pairing of the English elite and working classes. Surely Ellen Craft's whiteness, her public renown as the "White Slave," created just such an uncomfortable shock of recognition, but one that could be safely contained by her "foreignness" as both American and fugitive. Yet that comfortable containment only raised, in turn, the specter of racial mixing. Similarly, the responsibility a British market hungry for American cotton bears in the "horrors" of slavery is occluded by Farmer's indictment of the North: "The North may for a time be content to be dragged through the mire in its copartnership with the South in the guilt of slavery; but its entire loss of religious and social caste in the world will be too heavy a price for it to pay, even from the lucrative gains of cotton merchandise" ("Fugitive Slaves"). Unspoken is Britain's lucrative gains in the cotton industry, not only at the cost of American slaves but also at the expense of those factory operatives exhibited at the Crystal Palace.

Much as they confronted their Glasgow audience with their moral inconsistency in lauding the Anchor Brewery draymen for rousting Haynau while falling silent on American slavery, the Crafts and Brown would have confronted the British elite for some six hours with their moral inconsistency in profiting from one form of "slavery," evidenced by the live exhibit of English workers in the Palace, while having outlawed another, in congratulating themselves for a social congress with African Americans that nonetheless had its limits. Ellen's and Brown's very skin marked those limits and their transgression quite clearly. I would argue that given Ellen's presence and the confrontation she couldn't help but present to slaveholder and British elite alike, the Crafts' and Brown's solidarity arguably comes to be with the British working classes rather than with the abolitionists with whom they strolled in Crystal Palace. They had clearly come, by this point, to recognize that both class politics and reform created spaces for their own political aims and, even more, offered them ready audiences and a degree of public notoriety. An appearance such as this shows them using such opportunities to cultivate empathy or discomfit as it best served their aims. Such a canny reading of opportunity is further indicated in their acquiescence to a silent promenade through the exhibits on this first visit, only to return on several occasions to verbally confront slaveholding Americans. William Still documents one such visit in *The Underground Railroad:* "Brown and the Crafts have paid several other visits to the Great Exhibition, in one of which, Wm. Craft succeeded in getting some Southerners 'out' upon the Fugitive Slave Bill, respecting which a discussion was held between them in the American department. Finding themselves [the Southerners] worsted at every point, they were compelled to have recourse to lying" (372). However much Farmer claimed he and his fellow white abolitionists "regarded them as our equals," the Crafts and Brown were evidently more at liberty to express their views when they returned to the Great Exhibition on their own. Indeed, it is their very inequality with which the trio confronted American slaveholder and British elite alike; one might say both were "worsted" at every point whether on promenade or in heated debate.

Historians of midcentury labor have debated for some time the political consciousness of British workers, the effects of a transatlantic network and movement of labor activists between Britain, Ireland, and America, as well as slavery's impact on labor rhetoric and thought. Yet current scholarship contends that British labor maintained a "long-standing commitment both to anti-slavery and anti-capitalism" (Toole 162).[29] This commitment is often measured by the decision of Lancashire cotton workers to oppose calls to politically recognize the American South in order to restore the supply of American cotton to English mills during the Cotton Famine.[30] Rhetorically, such a stance is evident earlier in Chartist writings, such as those of Peter McDouall's in *White Slaves of Great Britain* (1841). McDouall cast white workers as "'white slaves,' whose suffering must be laid at 'the door of the white slaveowner of the British capitalist'" (qtd. in Toole 165). That suffering increased in the late 1850s, when employers, seeking to extricate themselves from the effects of overproduction brought on by high cotton yields in the United States and demands for textiles in India, instituted a "7.5 percent wage cut and a three-day week, first in the weaving districts and then in the spinning towns of South Lancashire, Cheshire and Derbyshire" (Toole 167).[31] In the weaving districts, the employment of the 1852 Outdoor Relief Regulation Order stipulating that male paupers work in return for outdoor relief may have kept more factory operatives out of the workhouse but did so at the cost of making them unfit for future mill work with mandatory hard labor such as "stone-breaking on the roads and oakum picking," which blistered their hands (R. Hall 230 n. 22). The late 1850s saw rising poor rates in Lancashire, with the workhouse peopled mainly by the elderly, the ill, and children, meaning that even with outdoor relief families could not remain together. Yet despite these conditions, by and large Lancashire cotton operatives refused to bend in their solidarity with enslaved African Americans or their support of U.S. president Abraham Lincoln and the North.

Ellen Craft was in Lancashire only briefly, arriving in Liverpool in early December 1850 and then traveling to Edinburgh for a January 3, 1851, appearance with her husband and Brown. Though she spent much of her time at antislavery meetings in Scotland, northern England, London, and the southwest, she nonetheless prepared the way for Sarah Parker Remond to move audiences in Lancashire in the late 1850s through the force of widespread coverage of her appearances with her husband and William Wells Brown. Ellen Craft's feminist work to link the plight of American bondswomen with that of the working poor and pauperized women of Britain, and thereby to elicit sympathy and support from her audiences, is an essential precursor to the further international attention Remond would draw to American slavery. Remond and those with whom she was connected in transatlantic abolition understood the importance of Lancashire and its working-class support for abolition in the late 1850s, for her earliest lectures in the UK were in Lancashire with multi-day speaking engagements in Warrington as well as appearances in Manchester and Liverpool. Remond would return to Lancashire from public addresses in Ireland, Scotland, and the southwest of England during a remarkably sustained lecture tour that ran from January 1859 to January 1861.[32]

Irish Nationalism, the Famine, and American Slavery

By this point in her reform career, Remond was an accomplished orator comfortable on the platform: she had been appointed a lecturing agent for the

American Anti-Slavery Society in 1856, which took her through the northeastern United States from 1856 to August 1858, and she had become involved in woman's rights reform, attending the New York Woman's Rights Convention May 13–14, 1858, before sailing that December for Britain. Remond's skills at appealing to British audiences were honed in the weaving and spinning districts hardest hit by the Cotton Famine, and like the Crafts her British lectures repeatedly turn on images of families torn apart by slavery and the "horrors" of cases such as Margaret Garner's infanticide. Yet it is her appearances in Ireland to which I now wish to turn in order to consider how class, sectarianism, nationalism, and the none-too-distant horrors of the Great Famine shaped her work. Remond's appearances in Ireland show us the degree to which her rhetorical strategies and their effects differed according to the particularities of place, not only as she entered a transatlantic context but even as she moved within Ireland.

Remond appeared in Dublin in March 1859 and then traveled to Waterford, Clonmel in County Tipperary, and Cork in April of that year, lecturing at mechanics' institutes, town halls, and hotels. Like Ellen Craft before her, Sarah Parker Remond appeared before audiences familiar with not only the specter of the pauper but also an even more strict version of the New Poor Law imposed on the country in 1838 by the British Parliament, despite Irish politicians and social investigators protesting that it was an unsuitable model for an unindustrialized Ireland. Ireland, they argued, "had few jobs for poor people to take" when they fell upon the questionable mercy of outdoor relief. The British response to this critique was to "blanket" Ireland "with regimented workhouses," to which "few able-bodied adult men could gain entrance, so most workhouse inhabitants were women, children and the aged" (Clark, "Wild" 389).

R. F. Foster documents the rapid rise of workhouse inmates during the famine, noting that "the Irish poor-houses had 135,000 inmates by February 1848, 215,000 by June 1849. . . . Irish Poor Law Unions were already far larger units than those in Britain, containing 63,000 people on average instead of 27,000: overcrowding was horrific" (328). While workhouses were pushed beyond their limits, the country lost 2.25 million people to disease, starvation, and emigration under the famine, with "the labourer class . . . hardest hit, followed by the smallest farmers" (R. Foster 323). Clark notes that Irish Poor Law guardians were largely Protestant, the workhouses were "divided into sectarian territories," and the "vast majority of paupers were Catholic" ("Wild" 390). In addition to this distinctly Irish political cast to the workhouse, its gendering echoed that of the English workhouse with women and children comprising the majority of its inmates.[33] When Remond was lecturing in Ireland, riots led by workhouse girls were not uncommon with the most notorious being in South Dublin and Cork. She could hardly have been unaware of both the politics of the famine and the Irish workhouse, particularly since her speaking tours in Lancashire would have attuned her to the effects of the New Poor Law there upon factory operatives impoverished by the Cotton Famine. Indeed, in Ireland the workhouse and the New Poor Law had become a "nationalist and class issue" in the periodical press. Papers such as *The Nation* decried both as "tools of the plutocracy and landed gentry" and nationalists cited their effects as cause to "repeal the union with Britain" (Clark, "Wild" 395). The rioting workhouse girls themselves became a cause célèbre with the press and some of the same papers that covered their uprisings and New Poor Law debates also covered Remond's appearances.

Remond also would travel to Ireland with a knowledge of Irish abolition, Irish nationalism, and their key figures gained from her brother, the black abolitionist Charles Lenox Remond, who knew the Irish nationalist Daniel O'Connell, the "Liberator." They first met at the 1840 World Anti-Slavery Convention in London: "For thirteen years have I thought myself an abolitionist but I had been in a measure mistaken, until I listened to the scorching rebukes of the fearless O'Connell" (qtd. in Nelson 58). O'Connell was the main attraction at this convention and the first delegate to address those assembled. He had been drawn to abolition as early as 1824, when a Quaker merchant from Liverpool visited Ireland to propose a "network of cotton manufactories . . . that would sell Irish textiles to India in return for the sale of East Indian sugar to Ireland," the twinned effects of which would be blows to Irish poverty and slavery in the West Indies (Nelson 64). The plan did not develop,[34] but O'Connell's sympathies for the slave arose in conjunction with his continued commitment to ameliorate the condition of the Irish worker. His labors for Catholic emancipation introduced abolition to "a mass movement whose backbone was formed from illiterate, Catholic peasants," thereby shifting Irish abolition from its middle-class Protestant associations established with the Hibernian Anti-Slavery Society founded in 1837 by Richard and Davis Webb (Quakers) and James Haughton (Unitarian) (Kinealy 51). Throughout his work with the Loyal National Repeal Association (LNRA), which he founded in 1840, O'Connell used Repeal meetings to give a platform to antislavery; at the Dublin Repeal Association meetings weekly antislavery reports were routinely read out to those gathered. O'Connell's antislavery politics were so well known and respected that when Frederick Douglass visited Ireland in 1845 to lecture, O'Connell dubbed him "the Black O'Connell," which Douglass took as the highest compliment. What is more, O'Connell would argue for equal participation for women in antislavery, which Sarah Parker Remond would obviously value having come from the United States where she could be and was commissioned as a traveling antislavery agent just as a man might be. As early as 1832, O'Connell called for female petitions at the Anti-Slavery Society annual meeting in London, and in 1833 he "defended women's right to petition during an antislavery debate in the House of Commons" (Midgley, *Women* 64).

Yet throughout the life of the LNRA, O'Connell's nationalist and antislavery politics were uneasy bedfellows, particularly when it came to Irish American nationalism. Irish American Repeal associations, especially those in the South, criticized O'Connell for his antislavery views, arguing that they threatened Irish American citizenship in the face of rising nativist sympathies that questioned Irish immigrants' loyalty to their new country. O'Connell's pursuit of Irish nationalism and an antislavery politics was ambivalent. He was an important signatory of "An Address of the People of Ireland to their countrymen and countrywomen in America" in 1841 with sixty thousand Irish signatures obtained in a door-to-door campaign, an address that appealed to Irish Americans to support abolition. Yet until 1843 O'Connell was also accepting financial donations to Repeal from southern slave owners, making him as uneasy a figure for antislavery as he was for Irish American Repeal associations.[35] When the Pennsylvania Anti-Slavery Society wrote the LNRA in 1843 critiquing the apologias for slavery that were becoming mainstays of Irish American papers and Repeal associations, O'Connell recognized the damage being done in the name of Repeal. Yet that very recognition led ultimately to the LNRA's downfall, when O'Connell's famous 1845 address at a Dublin Repeal Association meeting threatened "the American eagle" with the aligned force of Ireland and Britain should the U.S. government persist in its intent to annex Texas and wrest the Oregon Territory from partial British occupation. Both were seen as part of a "slave power conspiracy" which Britain would oppose as an "abolitionist empire" (Murphy 5). When O'Connell pledged Irish support of British foreign affairs in return for legislative independence, American Repeal associations rang the alarm arguing such a position would be seen as a dangerous test of their American loyalty during a period of anti-Irish sentiment in the United States (Murphy 6–7).[36] The crisis in Irish nationalism on both sides of the Atlantic that this speech provoked coincided with the onset of the Great Famine; O'Connell died in 1847, and the LNRA essentially with him. With the LNRA's demise, the Young Irelanders[37] rose in popularity. The Young Irelanders was a nationalist organization that sought repeal of the Union but opposed the parliamentary reform O'Connell had fought for as well as abolition in favor of "transatlantic unity on behalf of Irish independence" (Murphy 19). Consequently, its members tended to characterize American slavery as a "minor and external subject," favoring instead the "abolition of *white* slavery" in Ireland (qtd. in Nelson 79); some members, most notably John B. Mitchell, were even apologists for slavery.[38]

When Sarah Parker Remond toured Ireland to speak against American slavery, then, she did so at a complex and less than sympathetic time. Ireland in the late 1850s was recovering from the Great Famine; nationalist interests saw abolition as a foreign concern at best, a hypocritical and self-congratulatory interest of British empire at worst; and, as in Britain, organized abolition was largely regarded as defunct.[39] Consequently, much like the Crafts in Britain, Remond would see her initial opportunities in Ireland with ladies' auxiliaries, the effective outposts of a dwindling abolition; these early appearances created a draw for further stops on her tour. On March 11 and 18, 1859, Remond appeared at the Dublin Rotundo under the auspices of the Dublin Ladies' Anti-Slavery Society, with an intervening March 14 lecture at the Dublin Mechanics' Institute. Her lectures quickly drew attention in the southeast of Ireland, for she was much anticipated by the people of Waterford, where she appeared at the Town Hall the evenings of April 5 and 7. In that city, Remond was hailed as "the well known and highly gifted lecturer on American Slavery" whose ability to draw "members of all creeds" to her lectures was praised in advertisements for her upcoming appearances ("Miss Remand's [*sic*] Lectures"). On April 12 and 13 she lectured at the Mechanics' Institute in Clonmel, County Tipperary, going on to the west to address audiences at the Imperial Hotel in Cork City on April 15 and 16. Remond's appeals in Clonmel and Cork did not have the same impact they did in Dublin and Waterford, the result, I will argue, of a very different material and political situation in the uplands and the west of Ireland during and following the famine. Overall, that complexity of context into which Remond entered meant that her work moved well outside that standard reading of black women's abolitionist appeals as carefully managing the empathy elicited through moral suasion and identificatory appeals. Rather, Remond confronted the degree to which eliciting empathy was limited at best and, in many cases, perhaps impossible.

We might gauge Remond's popularity by the fact that at every lecture she gave in Ireland, save her first at the Dublin Rotundo, admission was charged with a range of tickets offered, from one shilling for a seat near the platform to sixpence at the back of a venue and three pence for a gallery seat. Charging admission was a common response in Britain to the crowding of her lectures and was used to guarantee that the "better class" of townspeople could attend rather than being crowded out by the working classes as papers noted. It was unlikely that Remond was heard in Ireland by many poor or even working-class audiences given that country was still recovering from the famine, and we can surmise from the content of her speeches that she appeared before audiences that were Protestant, perhaps predominantly so.[40] As we shall see, Remond needed exactly that predominantly Protestant audience, since a major goal of this tour was to elicit international censure on American Protestant churches that took proslavery stances, whether overtly or by welcoming proslavery and slave-owner parishioners to their congregations. Remond made that appeal time and again in Ireland. And because that audience was key for her, she also would need to take care that antislavery as she presented it was not seen to be in firm alliance with a nationalist politics, even as she worked with nationalist feeling and sympathies in her lectures.

Remond's lectures in Ireland are distinctive, in many ways utterly unlike the lectures she gave in Britain that effectively bookend her Irish tour. In Britain, Remond stressed repeatedly the unique material conditions enslaved American women faced, particularly their sexual vulnerability, as she offered three key images in lecture after lecture: Margaret Garner's infanticide, the auction of mulattas sold as concubines, and bondswomen unprotected from their masters' sexual appetites.[41] These points of emphasis, repeated across coverage of her British lectures, indicate the ways in which she was successfully appealing to a developing woman's rights and feminist political culture in that nation and was using her frequent appearances before "promiscuous" and "ladies" meetings to reach women in particular.[42] Remond's references to the sexual violation of bondswomen appealed to an as-yet-unspoken but growing feminist concern for woman's bodily integrity in her British speeches as well as her first Irish address to the Dublin Ladies' Anti-Slavery Society on March 11, 1859.[43] In Dublin she stressed, more than once, "womanhood defenseless, exposed to the very wantonness of insult, and without protection from the licentiousness of a brutal master" ("Miss Remond's First Lecture" 222). Yet this image of defenseless womanhood occurs in coverage of her Irish speeches on only one other occasion, despite the fact that Remond continued to appear before audiences of men and women, and largely female audiences, throughout her tour. In coverage of her first Waterford lecture on April 7, 1859, Remond described Margaret Garner's case before her Irish audience, raising also the figure of those enslaved black women who "could not protect themselves from the licentiousness which met them on every hand—they could not protect their honour from the tyrant. . . . There were no morals there; no genuine regard for womanhood or manhood" ("Lecture on American Slavery" b). We cannot know whether Remond did, in fact, continue to work with her audiences' anxieties over woman's bodily integrity in these ways through her Irish tour because we are limited to coverage of her speeches, and this coverage becomes quite thin on her Clonmel and Cork appearances, a point to which I will later return. Perhaps she did, and other appeals that ran alongside these in her addresses simply registered more strongly with her audiences or with the individuals covering her speeches; even this last distinction between effect on audience and individual is impossible to know.

Nonetheless, in coverage of her Irish lectures several recurring themes mark her awareness that she had entered a unique political situation which she must carefully manage by balancing the following: an Irish view of the United States as a land of freedom and opportunity with her indictments of American slavery, a call to reactivate Great Britain's mission against slavery with an awareness of that nation's history of class- and ethnic-based oppression in Ireland that roused many Irish citizens to a growing nationalism, and a moral indictment of Protestant churches in America for their proslavery stance with an awareness that antislavery associations in Ireland remained dominated by Protestants and that power in Ireland was largely divided along Catholic and Protestant lines. Overall, the coverage of her lectures indicates that she particularly challenged a Protestant audience, since Irish Protestants were effectively using the British middle class, including Britain's lauded moral reputation on international issues such as slavery, as their model while indenturing Catholics at home. Repeatedly Remond can be seen to demonstrate that African Americans, slave or free, were deserving of full freedom and capable of self-government, while she repeatedly raised the question of liberty in a broader sense; together these appeals would implicitly raise the question of Irish (read Irish Catholic) self-government. Yet the Protestant middle class delayed the cause of sovereignty at this time with precisely this argument—the incapacity of Irish self-rule. Remond's references to the slave and appeals to Irish civilization as "lovers of freedom" are deliberate though indirect appeals to audiences well aware of, and largely rankled by, the fight for Catholic emancipation and ultimately Irish nationalism.

That the Dublin *Freeman's Journal*[44] covered Remond's appearances in that city gives us a sense of how Remond circulated from the beginning of her Irish tour. The *Freeman* covered parliamentary reform meetings and debates of the Irish poor laws, expressing concern over "Catholic paupers" in the workhouse (*Freeman* 25 March 1859) at the same time it covered Remond's speeches. Remond's Dublin speeches stressed a shared concern with freedom in a broad sense: "She said she stood before that enlightened assemblage the representative of four millions of men and women, robbed of every right, deprived of every privilege—a race of outraged and injured fellow-beings, whose wrongs should command the deepest sympathy, and the redress of whose grievance should of right obtain the heartiest co-operation and the most energetic aide from all lovers of freedom in every civilized country (cheers)" ("Miss Remond's Anti-Slavery Lecture"). With such an opening, Remond quickly roused her audience to cheers, and she consolidated that supportive outburst by immediately sketching the power imbalance in American politics that could not help but be seen to echo the state of Irish politics under the Union with Britain: "She showed that over thirty millions of people, *who ought to desire, not only to be free themselves, but that mankind should be free,* were held in subjection by the influence of about one hundred and thirty-four thousand tyrants who uphold this vile system (hear, hear)" ("Miss Remond's Anti-Slavery Lecture"; emphasis added).

In this sleight of hand, Remond positions her audience as proxy slaves who are encouraged to imagine an American slave's desire to be free as not unlike a more familiar desire for freedom from the tyranny of an Anglo-Irish or British absentee landholding class, which Remond marks as kith and kin to the American slaveholder. Yet their position as slaves to the Union far from relieves the Irish of a moral duty to which Remond holds them to account, as those who "desire . . . to be free themselves" must also "desire . . . that mankind should be free." All concern for Irish American citizenship and Irish nationalism considered, the Irish in America and at home cannot be excused for their silence on American slavery or, worse yet, for supporting it in exchange for their own political gain. Given her brother's acquaintance with Daniel O'Connell and her own involvement in American antislavery politics, Remond arguably knew quite well that Irish American Repeal associations had done just that in the mid-1840s and that the new face of Irish nationalism, the Young Irelanders, preferred to ignore American slavery or to argue for the priority of the white slave of Ireland in the political sympathies of Irish nationalists. Yet Remond mitigated her critique of Irish and Irish American positions on American slavery with her implicit praise of Ireland as freedom loving and civilized.

We can immediately see how successful Remond's careful management of her audience's loyalties and empathy was in Dublin, for Rev. Dr. Abelthashauser, a professor at Trinity, moved the following as soon as Remond had "resumed her seat amidst enthusiastic plaudits." He urged the audience to "take this opportunity of renewing the expression of our sympathy with the American abolitionists . . . that we are confident that all *true hearted Irishmen* will range themselves on the side of freedom for all men, irrespective of colour or clime; and that we deeply regret that some of our countrymen in the United States have disgraced themselves and their native land by a base truckling to the slaveholders in the trans-Atlantic republic" ("Miss Remond's First Lecture" 223; emphasis added).

The chair of this lecture, respected abolitionist James Haughton, also "wished to say that he had often experienced a sinking of heart when he came to consider the conduct of Irishmen who had made America their home (hear, hear). He had asked himself, how it was that they had become in America so inconsistent and so false to the principles of freedom which they so earnestly advocated at home (hear, hear)?" Haughton went so far as to say that if Irish emigrants could not "adhere to the cause of Freedom" in America, "they had better remain at home" ("Miss Remond's First Lecture" 224). In these invocations of "true Irishmen" as those uncorrupted by American slavery, Remond's supporters in Dublin reveal an O'Connell style nationalist politics. Haughton, an abolitionist since the early 1830s, worked alongside O'Connell for a nonviolent repeal of the Union and was active in temperance and in debate on the poor law and its effect upon families. To have his stamp of approval at the outset of her tour indicates that Remond arrived with both a sound reputation and the credentials transatlantic Garrisonianism offered. But she was also well aware from the outset that whatever hearing she could gain would mean a careful managing of nationalist sympathies.

Remond's stress upon Irish civility, as proven by their love of freedom, would appear again and again in her Irish lectures. In Waterford, Remond opened by referencing the *Dred Scott*[45] case as an affront to the civilized world: "She was there as the representative of a race, which, in the estimation of American law, had *no rights which the white man was bound to respect.* . . . And this infamous doctrine had the sanction of the established courts of law in that country . . . a law that would disgrace any country in any age—a law which would receive, and deserved to receive, the execration of the civilized world. (Applause.)" ("Lecture on American Slavery" a; emphasis added). And in Clonmel, Remond's lecture at the Mechanic's Institute saw her rouse her audience with a similar appeal to "the lovers of LIBERTY" that quite clearly marks her awareness that she had a fine line to walk when invoking an Irish love of freedom between nationalist and Unionist sympathies, a rhetorical deftness to which I will return ("Lecture on American Slavery" b).

Yet what began to change as Remond's tour progressed from Waterford to Clonmel and on to Cork was the way in which she hailed and managed an empathic sentiment in her audiences for the American slave. In Waterford, Remond began to work with the image of white liberty and unfreedom in highly untypical ways. Even as she was raising the specter of "the white man" enfranchised as citizen with the full power of the American Supreme Court behind him as he refused to respect the rights of African Americans, Remond was also conjuring for her audiences the image of "White" rights under threat. Rather than have her appeals turn predictably upon an equivalency of "the American slave" with "the white slaves" of Ireland—be they Catholic paupers or exploited laborers and tenant farmers—Remond played on a fear of imperiled white rights. Given her audiences would have been largely Protestant and at times directly responsible for having created those "white slaves," this is a canny appeal designed to keep her audiences with her by raising their shared concern about their own rights and privileges rather than risk alienating them. This appeal is entirely unique to her Irish addresses, and though white abolitionists in the United States had long been arguing that a nation that denied rights to African Americans could not help but erode the rights of whites in turn, we must not underestimate how surprising this is as an appeal used by a black abolitionist.

Remond, like other black abolitionists before her, spent a good deal of effort carefully demarcating the distinctiveness of American slavery and the enslaved's suffering. In many speeches she is recorded as having argued that "no tongue could tell" of these wrongs, no words could adequately represent the violences and material conditions enslaved African American men and women endured. Jacqueline Bacon, following Kenneth Burke, has called this rhetorical appeal the "mystery of race," in which black abolitionists turned racial distinctions, "what Burke calls 'mystery'—the ineffable cultural force of differences," to rhetorical advantage, "highlight[ing] the very aspects of racial difference that are used against them" (70). Black abolitionists tended to draw attention to the distinctiveness of their positions as people of color in a white supremacist society, challenging the arbitrariness of racial divisions, as Frederick Douglass did, for example, in this 1853 speech at the American and Foreign Anti-Slavery Society (AFASS) convention in New York: "I am a colored man, and this is a white audience. No colored man, with any nervous sensibility, can stand before an American audience without an intense and painful sense of the immense disadvantage under which he labors" (qtd. in Bacon 75). Far from appealing to the specter of threatened white rights, Douglass is here underscoring the hegemony of whiteness in America as he challenges his audience with their inability to establish a "complete identification with him," as Bacon argues (75). While Remond spent much of her career, judging from the record left us, at pains to underscore the very different material conditions of enslaved and free African Americans from the lives her white listeners enjoyed, she undertakes a marked shift in her Irish addresses to an unprecedented rhetorical appeal best understood as an intelligent reading of and response to the distinctive political context in which she was working.

Significantly, this turn in her appeals to the endangerment of "White" rights earned her approbation, as indicated by this piece in *The Waterford Mail*. "The views which she takes of the real nature of the struggle that is going on in America are broad and very correct. She says there is now enrolled in the contest the rights of the White, the liberty of speech and of action, the liberty of the press, all of which are menaced by the slavery party," notes the writer. "She showed that the war in Florida with the Seminole Indians and the war with Texas, were the consequences of the grasping, overbearing policy of the slave-owners, who wished to acquire greater powers, and if they did so, the rights not only of the free Blacks, but also of the Whites, would be menaced" ("Lecture on American Slavery" b). It would seem no accident that Remond chose here to echo arguments of the "Liberator," Daniel O'Connell, in his "American Eagle" address of 1845, which caused nativist anti-Irish sentiment in the United States to rise against his suggestion that the Irish would side with Britain in stemming the slave power by preventing the annexation of Texas. In doing so, she could nod to concern for the rights of Irish immigrants in the United States as a way of carefully raising the rights of all Irish in Ireland under the Union with Britain, the latter a concern much more difficult to plainly speak in lecturing venues where she shared the platform with Protestant clergy and in a country where her lectures were made possible by predominantly Protestant antislavery associations.

Remond's strategy had exactly the desired effect; she was followed by a Dr. Elliott who gave a "very appropriate speech, in which he shewed how the encroaching spirit of the slaveowners was menacing the rights of the Irish emigrants" ("Lecture on Slavery"). The meeting's resolution that Remond's views be "approve[ed]" and that she be "recommend[ed] to the sympathy of Christian friends in these countries" was then "carried unanimously" ("Lecture on Slavery"). That Remond managed to bring her audience to this unanimous support for abolition of American slavery is remarkable given that she was also indicting Protestant churches in the United States as "debased" while "prais[ing] the conduct of Roman Catholics in admitting the coloured race to their chapels" there ("Lecture on American Slavery" b).

In Clonmel, Remond was promoted as offering at the Mechanics' Institute a *"viva voce"* follow up to the impression made by Harriet Beecher Stowe's *Uncle Tom's Cabin* ("American Slavery" b). As Elizabeth Neswald documents, "Mechanics' institutes [in Ireland] fulfilled a variety of social functions in addition to their stated goal of providing artisan education" (506), and their value and impact lay most with the opportunity they created for "forms of civil interaction" across sectarian divides, even when these were not always successful (507). Irish mechanics' institutes were largely middle class in their constituency and were often the result of connections their memberships recognized and forged "between science, temperance and Irish nationalism" (Neswald 530). Sobriety was regarded as enabling one to recognize the value of education, and education occupied body and mind distracting from the temptations of drink, but in Ireland the link between temperance and education also served a larger nationalist politics: "[A] prosperous, sober, industrious and educationally enlightened Ireland was an Ireland that would be capable of ruling itself, free from British domination. As one contemporary proclaimed, 'A sober people are eminently entitled to political freedom'" (Neswald 531). To what would have been, then, a largely nationalist and middle-class audience, Remond stressed an appeal based again on love of freedom: "[T]oo sensibly have the lovers of LIBERTY, living under the glorious Constitution of England;—too sensibly have they felt the privileges they enjoy not to lend a willing ear" to the plight of American slaves ("Lecture on American Slavery" a).

Yet we must remember that nationalist sympathies did not translate easily into abolitionist sympathies by the late 1850s, and encouraging an audience to recognize the particularities of American slavery and the need for their collective action opposing that system remained a challenge for Remond in Ireland. In this short coverage of her speech we see that her stress upon privileges enjoyed and denied obviously reached her audience without risking an offense that would result from indicting self-examination, for they did see freeing

American slaves, not the whites slaves of Ireland, as their object: "Resolved— That this meeting . . . do further desire to express their detestation of a system which would level a large portion of our fellow creatures with beasts of bur- then—debarring them of their privileges as rational beings and Christians, and depriving them not only of liberty but of all those familiar and endear- ing ties which would tend to render their bondage more supportable, though not less to be condemned and deplored" ("Lecture on American Slavery" a). Indeed, a second resolution proposed by Gerald Fitzgerald, the subsherriff of Clonmel, "contrasted the position of the 'hereditary bondsmen' of England and Ireland with that of the unhappy millions who had the *privilege* of liv- ing beneath the 'merciful *freedom*' of 'American Independence!'" ("Lecture on American Slavery" a). Remond managed to get her listeners to recognize the hypocrisy of the American Constitution while remaining blind to the hypocrisy of her praise for "the glorious Constitution of England," despite the nationalist sympathies that would have been shared by some of her listeners. In an impromptu speech immediately following her lecture, a local MP, Mr. Bagwell, declared "he had just been reading that evening the Declaration of American Independence, and what a contrast, the Charter upon which they then based their liberties, and the course now pursued" ("Lecture on Ameri- can Slavery" a).

That Remond's appearances in Clonmel were quite successful in making her audiences appreciate the differences between American slavery and the so-called white slavery of Ireland is remarkable to be sure. But this is also a very powerful rhetorical move that we should not mistake as Remond casting about for what current political issue might serve her best. Rather, in refusing a sentimentalist rhetoric and choosing to highlight privilege and the hierar- chies it creates, Remond was taking a radical step beyond typical abolitionist strategies and implicitly critiquing them as she did so. In her recent work on intimate publics, Lauren Berlant has argued that "sentimentality from the top down softens risks to the conditions of privilege by making obligations to action mainly ameliorative, a matter not of changing the fundamental terms that organize power, but of following the elevated claims of vigilant sensitiv- ity, virtue, and conscience" (*Complaint* 35). Yet Remond refused that abstrac- tion enabled by sentiment in her decision to forgo the more conventional route of rendering equivalent "the American slave" and "the white slaves" of Ireland. In refusing that equivalency and the sentiment or feeling that would accompany it readymade, Remond also refused the "traffic in cliché . . . [that] provid[es] the privileged with heroic occasions of recognition, rescue, and inclusion" (Berlant, *Female* 35). Drawing attention to white rights and privilege as imperiled, Remond denied her audience the position of hero rescuing the slave, a position whose corollary is always the slave as dehumanized and incapable of resistant agency herself.

Yet I also would argue that coverage of her appearances raises the larger question of exactly what her audiences were prepared to hear and to recognize. This issue, always shaping what Remond argued whether in Britain or in Ireland, becomes further complicated by the question of how prepared her audiences were, in the late 1850s, to contemplate in any sustained way the trauma from which they were emerging. The Great Famine and emigration would forever change the country, cutting its population in half from 8.2 million in the early 1840s to 4.4 million by 1911 (R. Foster 323). Remond was lecturing just eight years after emigration from Ireland reached a peak; in 1851 alone 250,000 people left the country, with overall emigration from 1841–51 at a staggering 1.5 million. Between 1845 and 1870 at least 3 million Irish left the country (R. Foster 345). Remond's appearances in Clonmel, as well as those that immediately followed in Cork, were advertised as lectures "on NEGRO SLAVERY in the UNITED STATES, which is rapidly becoming *White* Slavery" ("Miss S. Remond"), a fact that is quite interesting if read in the light of the famine's effects in those parts of the country.

Unlike Ellen Craft, who was advertised as living spectacle—the "White Slave"—and along with her husband and William Wells Brown presented a mix of entertainment and political appeal, Remond is entering a rather different territory in which white slavery circulates as a muted concern. The uplands of County Tipperary along with western and southwestern Ireland were the areas hardest hit by the famine, reflecting "the prevalence of subsistence farming on tiny holdings" (R. Foster 322). Yet Remond's appearances in Cork, billed as ones that would strike a chord with audiences concerned with "white slavery" in all its resonances in a blighted area, are hardly covered at all in local papers. In fact her lectures were given sparse advance advertisement creating "very small" audiences ("Anti-Slavery Meeting"), and what little coverage exists of her "very thinly attended" speeches makes them seem as though they were delivered to the void. In Cork, coverage of her April 15 address is limited to a few lines, the reporter casting her most rousing appeal as her usual one for "moral influence not political interference" and finding only statistics useful to note: "Four hundred and fifty-seven slave owners were the oppressors of four millions of slaves; but the end must come, for the latter were increasing at the rate of 150,000 a year, and in time they would be eight million, when it would be impossible for their masters to retain them" ("Anti-Slavery Meeting").

In Britain, rather than appearing to reduce the human cost of slavery to numbers, Remond's attention to figures and facts would be seen as building a reality effect to her appeal, in the tradition of humanitarian narratives such as industrial novels and inquests, where Thomas Laqueur argues "the statistical body becomes the lived body" (195). Certainly, these figures could have registered in similar ways in Ireland with audiences well versed in the same genres, but this coverage also gives us pause around the question of identification and empathy, hallmarks of abolitionist appeal. Could a region seeing such staggering poverty and death alongside incredible rates of emigration possibly identify with an image of the oppressed growing at such an unstoppable rate they would soon overthrow their masters? Could they identify with the oppressor as master when it was not the specter of the absentee landlord they had to blame? In Cork, it was not the English absentee landlord of the large estate who profited from the sufferings of the poor, that standard image of the Great Famine and the oppression of the Irish poor, but local farmers who had holdings of sufficient size they "escaped" not only "almost unscathed" from the famine but were able to add to their holdings and strengthen their position because subsistence farmers failed, depressing land prices in 1850 to between .2 and .5 sterling pounds per acre (R. Foster 336). These are not narratives of external oppressive forces, imperial or otherwise, that make for the cultivation of sympathy and identification in typical abolitionist ways. In a very real sense, Remond reached a public undertaking the unspeakable challenge of accepting their own survival, raising the question of how much this muted coverage of her appearances in the southwest even as it seems to have dampened interest in them.

This muting was at work throughout her tour if we pause to consider that she would have retained elements in her speeches as she proceeded from Dublin to Cork, giving nine lectures and traveling some 250 kilometers by coach in the span of a month.[46] To give very similar speeches was certainly Remond's practice in Britain both before and after her Irish tour. In her first addresses in Dublin she was raising that standard empathic appeal for families torn apart by slavery that she offered again and again in Britain: "It might be enough to state that at the beck of a cruel master, husband and wife are continually separated and sold, never again to meet in this world; children are torn from their parents, and mothers bereaved of their beloved little ones" ("Miss Remond's First Lecture" 222). These moments in her speeches would have resonated with her audiences much like Ellen Craft herself did, calling upon their knowledge of the workhouse and its severing of families as women and children came to be the brunt of its inmates but with the additional referent of death and emigration in postfamine Ireland. The main resolution that followed Remond's first speech in Clonmel allows us to infer that she must have raised the specter of the workhouse again, given that resolution's attention to deprived privileges "not only of liberty but of all those familiar and endearing ties which would tend to render their bondage more supportable" ("Lecture on American Slavery" a).

It would be difficult in this case to argue that the shadow of the famine, the workhouse, and their shared effects result from spotty coverage, since coverage of this speech took up a full column on page 2 of the *Clonmel Chronicle.* Coverage of her speech was given prominence in that paper as it was in Waterford's papers and in Dublin's *Freeman,* yet throughout this tour that standard abolitionist appeal to broken families seems largely silenced. The unspeakable horrors of the overcrowded Irish workhouse, the failure of outdoor relief in an unindustrialized country, mass death and the mass flight on what were known to be "coffin ships" were perhaps all too present for Remond's audiences to be much discussed. Finding them at all gives us another way to understand Remond's insistence that American slavery was both unknowable and unspeakable. Although she presented her audiences with "sickening and soul-harrowing scenes," she also firmly maintained that "people here do not and cannot fathom the terrible depth and darkness of the abyss of 'American slavery' (hear.) There was no use in concealing or glossing over the fact" ("Miss Remond's First Lecture").

To call Remond's Irish lectures unique, then, is also to recognize that the all-too-familiar abolitionist trade in empathy, in which slavery's violences were offered up for an audience's identification so that they might be moved to act, presented different challenges in different political and social contexts. In her consideration of the risks of empathy in antislavery discourse, Saidiya Hartman has argued that "the endeavor to bring pain close exploits the spectacle of the body in pain and oddly confirms the spectral character of suffering and the inability to witness the captive's pain" (20). The result of imagining oneself into the body and experiences of another is the obliteration of that other and the installation of the self in her stead. The other, the enslaved, simply disappears as that pleasure of imagining, of confirming one's moral superiority through one's empathy with her, is exercised in what Lauren Berlant has dubbed a "soft supremacy" (*Female* 6). Yet Remond's Irish tour reveals that suffering may circulate as spectral even when it is not that of another, that the "ghostly presence of pain," rather than resulting from the evacuation of the enslaved other from the affective scene in which one installs oneself, might register instead an overwhelming level of "feeling," the haunting pain of one's own losses and the inexplicability of one's own survival when so many others died. Remond did not risk the obliteration of slavery's particular violences or the enslaved herself in the empathy she might elicit from her Irish audiences, but she risked an appeal that would fail because it required far more than simply imagining oneself into the body of the enslaved; rather, it asked that the Irish consider their own suffering and loss.

In many ways we might consider the muting of those calls to empathy in coverage of Remond's Irish lectures alongside those vexing questions of why Ellen Craft said nothing on platform after platform. Silence may facilitate an imagining, but at what costs and for whom? When might silence also register empathy's impossibility? Can empathy only be hailed in people whose lived experience is nothing like that of the slave, in which case empathy's success rests on the very obliteration it risks and must manage? This is what Berlant would call the terms of the "sentimental bargain," in which pain and suffering are replaced by imaginings of the "sublime overcoming" of violence and its effects, a replacement that produces "pleasure both as a distraction from suffering and also as a figure for the better life that sufferers under the regime of nation, patriarchy, capital, and racism ought to be able to imagine themselves having" (*Female* 66). But what if, as Remond encountered, one's audience could imagine neither that "sublime overcoming" nor that "better life," could find no pleasure in the bargain? Remond, I would argue, met with far more than the empathy she was accustomed to working to win in her audiences; she stood before audiences who together claimed such a recent experience of starvation, death, and unimaginable loss that perhaps they could not face identifying with yet more. And so what might appear to be dispassionate appeals far afield from the concerns of the slave—appeals to an Irish love of liberty, to white rights, to civility—register the very national "feeling" that shaped the appeals Remond could forward.

Craft and Remond's appeals, then, were shaped by their reading of the political and socioeconomic context into which they entered on their transatlantic tours, but they were also informed by the black feminist principles of the benevolent associations that provided an entryway into abolition for black women. Black feminism had established a concern for addressing linked or interdependent oppressions. Attending to the ways in which their appeals were shaped and the effects they had requires us to reconsider early black feminism as an "American" phenomenon, very local in its concerns and in the publics it sought to form or to reach. Far from being limited and defined by the existing reform publics they accessed and the rhetorical appeals that had proven successful with those publics, early black feminists were aware of and sought to mobilize complex and multiply located concern for the politics and causes they themselves defined, causes that often ranged further than the condition of black women, enslaved or free, in the United States.

Ellen Craft and Sarah Parker Remond clearly understood that the abuses and sufferings of American slavery implicated a market that would also dispossess British and Irish workers, a shared view of the oppressed that could see "care" as a worsening rather than amelioration of their condition, and a discourse and exercise of power that sought its sanction and justification in the so-called inherent inferiorities of color, caste, and ethnicity. While we have access to their work because they were subjects of newspaper coverage, it is quite clear that they were savvy readers, not only of their audiences in the moment, but also of the same newspapers that covered their appearances and offered them a knowledge of local politics and their implication for a black feminist rhetoric and appeal. They knew how to reach their audiences because they were reading coverage of the same issues and concerns.[47] Taking black feminism international was far more than seeing additional opportunities to exert political pressure on the slave power at home; it involved taking up the role of reader and politicized citizen in order to enter into existing publics but also create and marshal publics of one's own both at home and in a larger political context. Remond and Craft found more than additional venues across the Atlantic, they found that larger international context that affirmed what they had always known, that the unfreedom of some will always imperil the freedom of all. Moreover, in taking black feminism to transatlantic publics, Craft and Remond would make it possible for women like Ida B. Wells to do the same some thirty years later.

Chapter 3

"I don't know how you will feel when I get through": Racial Difference, Symbolic Value, and Sojourner Truth

> My friends, I am rejoiced that you are glad, but I
> don't know how you will feel when I get through. I
> come from another field—the country of the slave.
>
> —Sojourner Truth, May 9, 1867, First Annual
> Meeting of the American Equal Rights Associ-
> ation, Church of the Puritans, New York City

At the 1867 convention of the American Equal Rights Association (AERA), Sojourner Truth readied her audience to hear her speak on a subject she believed they had begun to ignore—the rights and material conditions of formerly enslaved African Americans, including "the colored woman." During a career of political agitation and public speaking that spanned three decades, Truth spoke at woman's rights meetings and antislavery societies, demanding her audiences' attention to slavery and its abolition, the freed people and working-class African Americans, universal suffrage, and the rights of African American women. Truth, though singular in style, was not unlike other early black feminists who often maintained multiple political associations and negotiated the conflicting demands of competing and intersecting publics. Much like Ellen Craft and Sarah Parker Remond, feminists like Truth also worked in ways that demand we consider the location of their speeches and writings and the ways in which they have been represented. Such considerations, however, are not only salient to understanding how nineteenth-century black feminists circulated in their own moment but also bear significantly on how they circulate in the histories of woman's rights and feminism we have inherited and continue to perpetuate.

Why and how certain black feminists acquire representative status and come to "embody" early black feminism in our historical memory is a central focus for this chapter. Despite the ever-growing body of work on early black feminism, many people recognize a single name, Sojourner Truth, as "the" black feminist of the nineteenth century.[1] Remaining in our memories and imaginations for longer than any of her contemporaries, Truth has become a highly transportable symbol of black feminist "difference." Yet like her black feminist contemporaries, be they preachers as she was or reformers like Craft and Remond, Truth challenged her listeners to see interdependent oppressions and insisted upon a politics that addressed not only black women's rights but also those of workers, the freedmen, and the black community at large.

Recently, two biographies—Nell Irvin Painter's *Sojourner Truth: A Life, a Symbol* (1996) and Carleton Mabee's *Sojourner Truth: Slave, Prophet, Legend* (1993)—have fostered a debate over the authenticity and mediation of Truth's most famous address, the "A'n't I a woman?" speech. Delivered at the 1851 woman's rights convention held in Akron, Ohio, this speech was first reported in the *Anti-Slavery Bugle* and later "recalled" in Frances Dana Gage's "Reminiscences" published in 1863 and included in *The History of Woman Suffrage*. Painter's work in particular has fueled two larger scholarly trends: the belief that the "A'n't I a woman" speech is largely Gage's fabrication and the search for the "real" Truth, which entails choosing either the *Anti-Slavery Bugle* version or Gage's account as the more authentic.[2] The *Bugle*'s report neither presents Truth's speech in dialect nor includes the question that became etched in popular memory. Instead, Marius Robinson quoted Truth as proclaiming, "I am a woman's rights. I have as much muscle as any man, and can do as much work as any man" (Robinson). In contrast, Gage's account employs a plantation-style dialect through which Truth invokes notions of decorum as well as strength: "Nobody eber helps me into carriages, or ober mud-puddles, or gibs me my best place. . . . And a'n't I a woman? Look at Me! Look at my arm. . . . I have ploughed, and planted, and gathered into barns, and no man could head me! And a'n't I a woman?" (Gage, "Reminiscences" 1: 116).

This focus on the "authentic" Truth begs the question of exactly how particular representations of her may have served interests within the nineteenth-century woman's rights movement and shaped the image of Truth we have inherited through the narrative of that struggle. Even though we may never know with any certainty exactly what she said, we can know something of

Truth's politics and how she circulated by attending to a wider body of her work and listening for more than that signal refrain "A'n't I a woman?" A fuller understanding of elements in the speeches that have come to define Truth, as well as a critical interrogation of how she was represented at the time, will tell us more about Truth's moment and begin to suggestively complicate the place she occupies in historical memories of U.S. feminism. The influential *History of Woman Suffrage* was particularly concerned to represent Truth as unproblematically advocating woman's rights. Yet these speeches encode biblical precept, references to "the colored woman" and the labor of both slaves and free blacks, and African Americanisms in ways that suggest Truth was working to keep African American concerns part of reform meetings that elided them in favor of a focus on woman's rights.

"We" are not all invested in Gage's Truth for the same reasons, yet many African American and white feminist scholars are reluctant to interrogate representations of Truth's speeches too closely, perhaps for fear that we will be left with even less of Truth and what we believe she uttered. Partly this is because representations are largely what we have to work with, as is the case for most black feminists who were orators as Truth was.[3] But for many scholars and activists, Truth's value also remains largely symbolic; as Painter herself has argued, "The symbol we require in our public life still triumphs over scholarship" (*Sojourner* 287). While investments in Truth as symbol vary, there persists the significant legacy of Gage's "Reminiscences" of Akron and accounts of other speeches published in *The History of Woman Suffrage*—reducing Truth's complex work and positioning to an unproblematic advocacy of woman's rights. In part, this is the result of taking *The History of Woman Suffrage* as both artifact and *the* record of that struggle. In addition, to manage the "difference" race makes to feminist inquiry, contemporary white feminists have frequently invoked Truth in ways that echo her representation by woman's rights advocates. Truth's difference, and the differences she called her audiences to recognize, continue to be collapsed in strategic negotiations of identification and disavowal and in attempts to ground abstract arguments or theories.[4] Yet when the investments that structured particular nineteenth-century representations of Truth and their contemporary repetition are examined, and the ways in which her speeches might be understood differently are considered, she emerges as a more challenging historical figure whose work tells us much about the complex positioning of black feminists in the reform publics they accessed.

Embodiment and the Platform: Remembering "A'n't I a woman?" in 1863

Critics continue to argue that Truth embodied what she spoke for, the rights of "the slave" and "woman." To embody or stand as physical "testimony" (Terry 426) for these causes, however, is hardly unproblematic.[5] Although both Painter and Mabee have argued convincingly that the most cited version of Truth's Akron speech, Gage's "Reminiscences," is heavily mediated, neither pursues the specific implications of embodiment for nineteenth-century American women speaking in public. This concern is central to understanding Gage's account. Nineteenth-century opponents to women taking the platform, a "disorderly" act that exposed the female body to public scrutiny and "unsexed" the speaker, often argued against women's involvement in public politics by isolating the body as a site of obsessive concern. Woman's body was configured not only as unruly but also as sexually disorderly; indeed, Caroline Levander notes that "with increasing frequency, nineteenth-century linguists and social philosophers invoked the precarious sexual purity of the speaking female body in order to control women's public utterances" (473). Rational debate within the public sphere, we are reminded, was very much conceived as, and secured through notions of, disembodiment.

Within this context black feminists who publicly voiced their political concerns faced heightened notions of their embodiment, doubly embodied by their race and gender. Their "unseemly" embodiment on the platform risked further compromising a womanhood that black American women were often denied on the basis of their "race." From the popular mythology of black female "licentiousness" to their exclusion from notions of "womanhood" promoted by discourses of domesticity and true womanhood, black women were violently embodied, be that violence epistemic or material, and materialized as the limit of acceptable or intelligible subjectivity.[6] African American women understood, as Sandra Gunning points out, that "the black woman's struggle for ownership of her body was closely tied to the historical struggle to maintain a voice within an American public arena" (78). Within reform associations, particularly, their ability to be heard often depended upon their skill at appealing to a sense of "sisterhood" with white women. Yet in the process their "womanliness" was necessarily risked by their acts of public speech, as their representative status as "black" was further reinforced. Qualities such as the speaker's manner or gestures, her evident emotion or feeling, her tone, and her appearance inevitably noted for scrutiny in nineteenth-century press accounts of both black and white women's speeches,[7] tended to demarcate the

African American speaker as an exemplum of "blackness," heightening the embodied character of these speech acts and positioning her as the embodiment of the blackness and black womanhood she was taken to represent.

Sojourner Truth has circulated as just such an exemplum making it hardly accidental that she is most famous for her "A'n't I a Woman?" speech as "recalled" by Frances Dana Gage, in which she is reported to have given what we might call "bodily testimony."[8] In Gage's account, Truth is reported to have "[b]ared her right arm to the shoulder, showing her tremendous muscular power" and to have asked at several points, "A'n't I a woman?" (Gage, "Reminiscences" 1: 116). This moment has been lauded as exemplary of the black woman's insistence upon the intersection of race and gender, a first of its kind. Through this account Truth has come to embody black feminism's attention to the "dual" oppression of sex and gender. Nell Irvin Painter notes that Gage's version of this speech first appeared in New York's *Independent* newspaper on April 23, 1863, shortly after Harriet Beecher Stowe's popular article on Truth, titled "The Libyan Sibyl," was published in the April 1863 edition of the prestigious *Atlantic Monthly* (*Sojourner* 164).[9] The timing of Gage's publication and its adoption within a historical narrative of woman's rights marked by its inclusion in the ambitious *History of Woman Suffrage* are critical to understanding Truth's circulation within both mid-nineteenth-century reform culture and later narratives of American woman's rights agitation consolidated through the *History*.

Gage turned to Truth as symbol at a rather crucial moment when woman's rights agitation had been suspended because of the Civil War. Carleton Mabee argues this was perhaps the most "inopportune time" for a piece on woman's rights, even though Gage may have deliberately sought to remind a reform audience that "black and women's causes should be tied together . . . [a] tie . . . personified in Truth" (79). At the time, the report was "scarcely noticed," but it began to gain more attention when it was reprinted in Truth's 1875 *Narrative* and again in 1881 in *The History of Woman Suffrage*.[10] The greater notice it received as part of the Stanton and Anthony *History* is significant. Here we see Gage's account accorded institutional standing within the woman's rights movement as part of a document with a self-declared aim to amass "an arsenal of facts . . . [for] a faithful history . . . written by its actors . . . [and so] nearer the soul of the subject" (*HWS* 1: 7–8). The *History of Woman Suffrage*, as feminist artifact and "an archive in itself" (Hersch 72), continues to shape historical record of the American woman suffrage campaign. Studies such as Eleanor Flexner's *Century of Struggle* (1959, 1975,

1996), still considered a "classic and essential text on the 'first wave' of American feminism" (Lasser 344), follow and thereby perpetuate Gage's account of the Akron convention.

Gage's "Reminiscences" begins by creating an atmosphere hostile to a formidable Truth and the coupling of woman's rights with abolitionist politics: "The leaders of the movement trembled on seeing [Truth,] a tall, gaunt black woman in a gray dress . . . march deliberately into the church. . . . A buzz of disapprobation was heard all over the house, and there fell on the listening ear, 'An abolition affair!' 'Woman's rights and niggers!'" (Gage, "Reminiscences" 1: 115). Gage does not mention that the convention had been advertised as inviting "[a]ll the friends of Reform, in whatever department engaged" (qtd. in Painter, "Difference" 151), explicitly naming reform concerns like "slavery, war, intemperance and sensuality" (Painter, *Sojourner* 120). Nor does Gage "recall" any of the twenty-seven contemporary reports of the convention published in 1851, appearing in antislavery journals, religious papers, and dailies, praising Akron for its "generous hospitality" (Mabee 70). The convention was described as a "pleasant social gathering," lacking in even "one discordant note" or "the sly jeer, the half uttered jest, that you might imagine" a woman's rights convention to elicit (Mabee 70–71). None of these contemporary reports notes a "mobbish" spirit about to overwhelm the proceedings. Interestingly, Gage herself wrote in the Pittsburgh *Saturday Visiter* of July 26, 1851, that "'the great press . . . have noticed' the convention,' and few have sneered at or abused it'" (qtd. in Mabee 70). Moreover, since white American feminists gained the public platform in greater numbers than ever before through their participation in the abolitionist cause, and since the Akron convention attracted women and men involved in both abolition and woman's rights, Gage's representation of herself as one of the few white women present who did not fear having woman's rights "mixed up with abolition" is quite unlikely.[11] Rather, this is a gesture at which much more is at work, one through which Gage is managing her own "unseemly" embodiment.

Gage recalls Akron as a meeting of "timorous and trembling" women, "very few [of whom] in those days dared to 'speak in meeting,'" and she has Truth take the platform when "some of the tender-skinned friends were on the point of losing dignity" (Gage, "Reminiscences" 1: 115):[12]

> The tumult subsided at once, and every eye was fixed on this almost Amazon form, which stood nearly six feet high. . . ."Dat man ober dar

say dat womin needs to be helped into carriages, and lifted ober ditches, and to hab de best place everywhar. Nobody eber helps me into carriages, or ober mud-puddles, or gibs me any best place!" And raising herself to her full height, and her voice to a pitch like rolling thunder, she asked, "And a'n't I a woman? Look at me! Look at my arm! (and she bared her right arm to the shoulder, showing her tremendous muscular power). I have ploughed, and planted, and gathered into bars, and no man could head me! And a'n't I a woman? I could work as much and eat as much as a man—when I could get it—and bear de lash as well! And a'n't I a woman? I have borne thirteen chilern, and seen 'em mos' all sold off to slavery, and when I cried out with my mother's grief, none but Jesus heard me! And a'n't I a woman?" (Gage, "Reminiscences" 116)

The dramatic culmination of Truth's highly bodied intervention, complete with a voice "like rolling thunder" and an arm bared to show her "tremendous muscular power," was an audience roaring in applause and brought to tears. Gage concludes by expressing "gratitude" to Truth, who "had taken us up in her strong arms and carried us safely over the slough of difficulty turning the whole tide in our favor" (Gage, "Reminiscences" 116–17). In stark contrast, neither *The Liberator* nor the *Anti-Slavery Bugle* reports published in 1851 describe Truth as baring her arm. In the *Bugle*, Robinson records her as simply requesting to "say a few words" (Robinson). In fact, no press accounts of this address note her raising the rhetorical question for which she is now famous—"a'n't I a woman?"—and which Gage remembers her asking no less than four times.[13] Gage's Truth repeatedly demands to be recognized as a woman[14] but never actually voices a desire to take the platform. Instead, she mutely "turn[s] her great speaking eyes to" Gage and ascends (Gage, "Reminiscences" *HWS* 116).

This deliberate embodiment of Truth in her "Reminiscences"—an Amazonian form, thundering voice, bared muscular arm—is designed to give Gage a different access to her own embodied, and therefore encumbered, selfhood. Gage was a well-known reformer in temperance, antislavery and feminist circles, whose writing "had appeared regularly in [Jane Swisshelm's] *Saturday Visiter* since 1849" (*Sojourner* 121) and in "a number of feminist and agricultural newspapers in the 1850s and 1860s" under the pen name "Aunt Fanny" (*Sojourner* 175). Painter notes that "[t]hroughout her career, Gage focused her women's rights rhetoric on strong, working-class women," but she does not further explore how this might have structured Gage's representation of Truth (*Sojourner* 177). Gage's frequent references to the labor of working-class and poor women throughout her essays for the *Saturday Visiter* indicate she attended to, rather than avoided, women's laboring bodies, however "unwomanly" they might seem. Still, such images were not wielded unproblematically. Gage criticized her fellow woman's rights activists, like Swisshelm, for ignoring black and working-class women.[15] Yet even as Gage "wrapped her critique of conventional society in the commonplaces of her role as wife and mother," she tended to displace her own bodily labor as a farm wife and mother of eight onto images of poor and working women (Painter, "Representing" 477). Indeed, the working-class woman is presented in extreme forms in Gage's writing, "half bent to the earth with a burden that few men could have carried," or walking miles "with a child six months old . . . on her left shoulder, while on her head she is holding some thirty, forty, or fifty pounds of flour" (qtd. in *Sojourner* 177).

In sharp contrast, Gage's reference to her own physical labor marks her awareness that such personal revelations risk her public reputation and reception. At the 1867 AERA convention, she claimed: "My strong hands have tilled the fields . . . harnessed the horse, and brought wood to the door. . . . These are things I do not often tell in public. I have braved public opinion; I have tilled my garden . . . [and] I find my womanhood not one bit degraded" ("American Equal," *HWS* 2: 199).[16] Xiomara Santamarina's important intervention in Truth scholarship has been to argue that Truth was a challenging figure for reform precisely because she stressed the value of her labor, particularly while enslaved, as the basis of her claim to citizenship and equal rights. Truth spoke "the value of antebellum labor and freedom during a period in which both labor and freedom were being commodified, . . and in which freedom and democracy became unequivocally identified with, and rendered legitimate only in relation to, capitalist forms of . . . self-expression and production" (37). Gage recognized that being publicly identified as an "agriculture and domestic worker" was not only a gendered problem but also one of class and race, and she manages that risked embodiment by deflecting it in her Akron account onto Truth. This is a useful and relatively easy move because Truth, by this time, was circulating as an "exotic" in reform, in part because she refused to temper her references to labor in her speeches in order that her work could be more easily accommodated to an abolition and racial uplift rhetoric that rendered "suspect . . . all women's public labor" (Santamarina 14).

Gage is well aware, then, that forms of embodiment like the working body risk "degrading" one's womanhood and, as a public speaker, she would be all too aware that the embodiment effected by the platform was also regarded as degrading to women. Although Gage may have advocated the rights of working-class women, and was one herself, she nonetheless sought to deflect the embodiment that her class and her platform speaking created onto other bodies. Those rhetorical gestures included positioning "blackness" as a physiological extreme beyond the working-class white body. Much as she worked to displace the risks of embodiment onto other women, in her "Reminiscences" she drew the reader's attention to Truth's body as a sort of proxy for her own. By representing Truth as a masculinized black body demanding to be recognized as a female subject, a working black female body denied gestures of decorum and civility accorded to "true women," and an abused slave's body that bore the lash and a "mother's grief" as her thirteen children are sold (Truth, in fact, had five), Gage works to sediment rather than efface racial difference. As Karen Sanchez-Eppler has argued, for both "women and slaves" the "human body was seen to function as the foundation not only of a general subjection but also a specific exclusion from political discourse. For women and slaves the ability to speak was predicated upon the reinterpretation of their flesh. . . . Transformed from a silent site of oppression into a symbol of that oppression, the body becomes within both feminist and abolitionist discourses a means of gaining rhetorical force" (30).

One might ask where the black woman was in this effort to gain rhetorical force through symbolizing oppression. In Gage's "Reminiscences" we find her in the figure of Truth at the very heart of the project. Through Truth's heightened embodiment and initial mute appeal, Gage asserts not only her own right to speak and to grant that right to "the other," thereby gaining access to a version of personhood relatively unencumbered in comparison to Truth. Although Gage as a speaker in the cause for woman's rights would be a woman unsexed, she is able to regain her womanliness by asserting Truth's difference: "Nobody eber helps me into carriages, or ober mud-puddles, or gibs me my best place" (Gage, "Reminiscences" 1: 116).[17] Notably, Gage invoked notions of propriety and images of womanhood that were raced and classed through discourses of domesticity. Moreover, she arguably gained access to some form of disembodied selfhood through positioning herself as the recorder of Truth's "unruly" and impassioned speech, which she represented in plantation-style dialect in contrast to her own standard English.[18]

Gage needed Truth at this moment in order to present a more sensational account of Akron that might interest a public whose attention had been drawn to the Civil War. She gave them an exceptional "slave" who symbolically linked the forgotten cause of woman's rights to one much more visible in 1863, the emancipation of enslaved blacks. But she also materialized Truth's racial difference in ways that discursively deflected attention from her own unruly and encumbered presence on the platform. Gage assumed a seemingly "objective" position—watching Truth, detailing her gestures, "recording" her speech and "reporting" the occasion—that enabled her to all but disappear in the attention she drew to the acts, exposure, and excess of Sojourner Truth's body. Gage's very attempt to transcend the situation and impartially report Truth's intervention in the proceedings shows us most clearly her investment in overdetermining Truth's difference in order to secure her womanliness with a public that has come to see her as radical, an "extremist in American reform" (Painter, *Sojourner* 176). Moreover, Gage distanced herself from these events by claiming simply to "transcribe" events drawn from memory and "faint[ly] sketched" (qtd. in Mabee 68). While the *History*'s editors sought to "restore" immediacy to Gage's account by omitting this admission, Gage took the time to stress her temporal remove from Akron in the *Independent* version of her "Reminiscences." In the spring of 1863, then, Gage needed Truth to draw attention to woman's rights and to help her mitigate against her own "unwomanly" reputation as a radical, a reputation that may well have caused readers to dismiss her work.

It is important to note, however, that in this speech Truth may be read as challenging rather than shoring up the dialectical relationship between white womanhood and the mythic black female body. Robinson's account of the "A'n't I a woman?" speech shares with Gage's version repeated references to labor through which Truth has been read as asserting female equality and arguing "the right of equal pay for equal work" (Painter, *Sojourner* 171). According to Robinson, Truth proclaimed, "I have plowed and reaped and husked and chopped and mowed, and can any man do more than that? I have heard much about the sexes being equal; I can carry as much as any man, and can eat as much too *if I can get it*" (Robinson; emphasis added). Far from stressing an uncomplicated equality, Truth foregrounds one of the material consequences of her perceived difference as a black woman. By Robinson's account, Truth opened her speech with the assertion "I am a woman's rights" (Robinson)— and then proceeded to argue her claim to such a position and rights on the grounds of her past labor as a slave and now as a working-class woman, neither of these experiences "equal" to those of her largely middle-class, reform audience.[19] Truth points out that although she "can do as much work as any man," this in itself does not ensure she will earn a living wage. Instead, Truth insists upon differences between her abilities, her remuneration, and who she is perceived to be, differences that expose inequities rather than assert equality. What Santamarina has said of sections of Truth's *Narrative* is also applicable to this speech: Truth asserts that "she fails to prosper . . . because she, as a northern worker, is not free enough" (6). In other words, while Truth asserts that she can work "as much as any man" and deserves as much remuneration, she is not assured equal treatment or pay: "I . . . can eat as much too if I can get it." That Gage handles this challenge by representing her as "the slave" is certainly ironic and reveals that "emancipatory rhetorics" could reproduce "a different form of subjugation" for African Americans (Santamarina 18).

Yet if we also read Truth's closing alongside her assertion that she "is a woman's rights" and has labored as slave and working-class woman, her references to work become even more clearly an assertion of difference and inequities within the woman's rights movement. Gage's "Reminiscences" has Truth opening with the following: "Wall, chilern, whar dar is so much racket dar must be somethin' out o' kilter. I tink dat 'twixt de niggers of de Souf and de womin at de Norf, all talkin 'bout rights, de white men will be in a fix pretty soon" (Gage, "Reminiscences" 1: 116). Robinson's *Anti-Slavery Bugle* account, however, has Truth conclude with a different version of this claim: "But man is in a tight place, the poor slave is on him, woman is coming on him, and he is surely between a hawk and a buzzard" (Robinson). At first reading, Truth appears to link the causes of abolition and woman's rights against an image of beset white manhood that will surely become carrion. Gage's representation makes such a reading all the more available with its omission of man "between a hawk and a buzzard." However, we see that this omission is a rather telling one, for in this turn of phrase Truth is encoding an African Americanism as Carla Peterson argues in *Doers of the Word*: "'[H]awk' and 'buzzard' are . . . figures from an African American folktale in which the two vultures are seen as oppositional and come into conflict in a struggle for survival, the buzzard, a descendant of the powerful African 'King Buzzard,' always gains the ascendancy. To an African-American audience this colloquialism . . . makes it possible to see the position of 'slave' and 'woman' not as symmetrical but as divergent and possibly hostile" (54).[20] In Robinson's account, even while Truth is perceived to be arguing for the equality of all women she is asserting the "difference" race makes within the woman's rights movement. She thereby employs a double-voiced strategy of address to argue that the interests of "the slave" and "woman" are often opposed, with the interests of African Americans frequently subordinated to woman's rights.

This closing becomes all the more important when we consider the larger context of addresses to the Akron convention preceding Truth's speech and the way in which Gage's "Reminiscences" is presented within *The History of Woman Suffrage*. While the *History*'s account of the convention includes only Gage's opening remarks to those gathered and her "Reminiscences," *The Liberator* notes that during Wednesday's evening session Emma Coe "addressed the legal condition of woman. She ran the analogy between the condition of woman and that of the slave. . . . She read many of the slave laws and the laws pertaining to woman, producing a powerful effect on the audience" ("Woman's Convention"). Significantly, then, the evening before Truth addressed the convention the "woman as slave" trope was used, an analogy that risked the collapse of material differences between "the slave" and "woman." As we saw in chapter 2, as early as the 1830s and 1840s the "woman as slave" analogy had become a rather graphic identification for white abolitionist feminists. Abby Kelley Foster is just one example: "When I . . . become myself the slave, . . I feel the naked cords of my neck shrinking away from the rough edge of the iron collar, when my flesh quivers beneath the lash, till in anguish I feel portions of it cut from my back. . . . We must resort to the expedients of barbarous nations and express ourselves by significant signs, speaking through eloquent gesticulations. . . . We must do this until we can invent a language that is equal to the subject" (qtd. in Yellin 50).

As Foster put it in this 1841 letter, "the slave" worked as significant sign for a feminism seeking language "equal" to the subject of woman's rights, though it did so by deliberately positioning the slave as inferior to "woman" who, in order to rise to the role of the slave's rescuer, must liberate herself. Indeed, white women like Foster came to understand their own position through their identification with "the slave" and their abolitionist work: "'In striving to strike his irons off, we found most surely that *we* were manacled *ourselves*" (Kelley Foster qtd. in Hersch 34). Given this context, we must question the all too common reading of Truth's speech as arguing solely for gender equality and woman's rights.[21] To do so positions Truth as the embodiment of the very analogy that worked to elide differences of material condition between "woman" and "slave" in order to gain greater rhetorical force for woman's rights appeals through the image of the prostrate and suffering slave. This positioning frames the *History*'s presentation of Gage's "Reminiscences": "Sojourner Truth, Mrs. Stowe's 'Lybian Sibyl,' was present at this Convention. Some of our younger readers may not know that Sojourner Truth was once a slave in the State of New York, and carries to-day as many marks of the diabolism of slavery, as ever scarred the back of a victim in Mississippi. . . . Although the exalted character and personal appearance of this noble woman have been often portrayed, and her brave deeds and words many times rehearsed, yet we give the following graphic picture of Sojourner's appearances in one of the most stormy sessions of the Convention, from 'Reminiscences' by Frances D. Gage" (*HWS* 1: 114–15).

Here Truth is violently embodied as the "scarred" victim of slavery, equivalent to a southern slave, in order to create an image of the "peculiar institution" more in accordance with its circulation in the popular imagination. At Akron and later with the *History's* publication, Truth as "slave" is recuperated as symbol, rendered victim in order for the white woman to claim agency as her liberator. Paradoxically, even though Truth is represented as the towering advocate of woman's rights who carries the fearful leaders of the movement to safety, she does so only by embodying the sister slave whom her white counterparts must ultimately rescue from the borderlands of womanhood where she is said to ask repeatedly, "A'n't I a woman?" For most white woman's rights agitators, Sojourner Truth could not be both "woman" and "slave."

The Proxy and Analogical Verification: Contemporary Recollections of Sojourner Truth

In twentieth-century white and black feminist texts, Truth and her speech are most often invoked as symbols of race and gender's intersection. Significantly, contemporary white feminists often position Truth in distinctive ways that replicate elements in those much earlier discourses as exemplified in Gage's "Reminiscences." Truth serves as a "proxy" who will distance and deflect attention from an embodiment white women would disavow; and the "woman as slave" trope makes white woman's and the slave's condition analogous, verifying "woman's" need for emancipation. Phyllis Marynick Palmer and Deborah McDowell interrogate such invocations and expose a recurring tendency to capitalize on Sojourner Truth's symbolic currency, although they do not pursue the particular echoes that we must attend to here.

In "White Women/Black Women: The Dualism of Female Identity and Experience in the United States," Palmer calls Truth " a standard exhibit in modern liberal historiography. White feminists who may know almost nothing else of black women's history are moved by Truth's famous query 'A'n't I a woman?' . . . Women such as Sojourner Truth *embody* and *display* strength, directness, integrity, fire" (152–53; emphasis added). Initially, it appears that

Palmer is arguing Truth represents what white feminists would like to be themselves; however, contending that our current image of Truth "builds upon her role for white women at the 1851 convention," Palmer goes on to suggest that Truth as "black woman" symbolizes what many white feminists admire in an "other" and would disavow in themselves: "The characterization of Sojourner in this account [Frances Gage's] is fierce and yet maternal, a leader and yet a servant and 'mammy.' The image has . . . exerted a lasting appeal . . . to a more modern audience that still sees black women as those who, laboring in hospitals and laundries, challenge the stereotypes of female incapacity. It is black women rather than white who popularly symbolize courageous, industrious womanhood. In both centuries, too, . . black women [have been] for many white women the quintessential victims of sexist oppression" (153). These twentieth-century echoes reenact the tendency of nineteenth-century white woman's rights agitators to position Truth as symbolizing the very material conditions they would argue must be overcome without acknowledging that these conditions were not only very different from their own but, in fact, sustained their own racialized class positions and gender identities. Admiring Truth's "fierceness" yet disavowing their complicity in the struggles that marked her life, representing her as strong "mammy" to their own incapacitated womanliness, white woman's rights agitators used Truth as proxy for what they might desire yet not claim for themselves, an "unwomanly" strength. In these ways, Truth absorbed what her white contemporaries would disavow, becoming a proxy through which they were able to speak their political desires without risking their social position.

The proxy has two specific uses in nineteenth-century discourses of abolition and woman's rights that are pertinent here: to facilitate empathic identification and disavowal. As Saidiya Hartman suggests in *Scenes of Subjection*, the slave's suffering was believed to be best understood through empathy or empathic identification, which would "disrupt the comfortable remove of the reader/spectator" who might work to change the slave's condition (17–18). However, empathy came with significant risks to recognizing and fully acknowledging the enslaved's suffering: "Properly speaking, empathy is a projection of oneself into another in order to better understand the other. . . . Yet empathy in important respects confounds [one's] efforts to identify with the enslaved because in making the slave's suffering [one's] own, [one] begins to feel for [oneself] rather than for those whom this exercise in imagination is presumably designed to reach" (Hartman 18–19). These moments of "facile intimacy" open onto what Hartman calls the "precariousness of empathy" or its "ambivalent character" (19).[22] Empathy, as facilitated by the proxy, might even reduce suffering to a titillating spectacle—we know such sensation often fueled the consumption of slave narratives—but its risks are also realized in the "woman as slave" trope circulating in white women's abolitionist discourse. While such a trope clearly obscured if not elided the specificities of bondswomen's lived experience and material conditions through an appeal to the analogic experience of the slave and the white woman, a point I will return to, we need also to attend to what Jean Fagin Yellin documents as the paradoxical identification and disavowal encoded in the trope and white women's abolitionist strategies: "[A]ntislavery women . . . created multiple strategies, alternately addressing and avoiding issues of race, sexual conformity, and patriarchal definitions of true womanhood. . . . Enacting these complex patterns of address and avoidance, they recoded and re-recoded the emblem ['Am I Not a Woman and a Sister?'], . . picturing themselves as chain-breaking liberators and as enchained slaves pleading for their own liberty, then asserting it and freeing themselves" (25).

The proxy, then, was seen as the most forceful way to bring an "alien" suffering near, making it known and empathically "felt" and thereby moving individuals to advocate for the enslaved. Yet it was also a "useful" strategy by which antislavery women not only came to "recognize" their own condition as like that of the enslaved but also to distance themselves from particular aspects of that condition they would prefer to leave unspoken or to disavow. Karen Sanchez-Eppler has outlined the ways in which "feminist abolitionists" used "the bound and silent figure of the slave metaphorically" in order to gain "rhetorical force" for their arguments (31). Particularly, she notes the sexually exploited female slave's use as proxy: through her, white women were able to voice and simultaneously disavow or deflect their own "sexual anxieties onto the sexualized body of the female slave" (33). The proxy was part of carefully negotiated strategies of identification and disavowal from which the particularity of black women's material conditions often disappeared, as they became either analogous to white women's condition or extremes beyond the pale.

While Palmer does not name it as such, I would argue the proxy is clearly still operative in a twentieth-century white feminist desire to champion "the" black woman's strength under oppressive and victimizing extremes that can be disavowed as alien to their own experience however intimately linked to their social positions. That notion of simultaneous attraction and disavowal extends to the symbols "the women's movement" would mobilize: "[B]lack women are used as symbols at the same time as they are criticized for their failure to support the movement [as evident in 'their unwillingness to talk about sexism in black society']. . . . [This is] a symbolization that *does not* entail political coalition" (Palmer 155). Sojourner Truth specifically, and black women in general, symbolize the intersection of race and gender as two of contemporary feminism's concerns. Yet merely invoking the symbol without considering the complexities and possible limits of the political coalition it is believed to signal suggests a powerful blind spot in the current moment: many white feminists have yet to really hear Truth or what their own black female contemporaries might have to say. In fact, the desire for political coalition is often secondary, at best, to the desire for some symbol or embodiment of an "inclusive" gesture. Are white feminists interested in a form of "difference," then, that challenges feminist inquiry to make very little difference or change at all?

In "Transferences—Black Feminist Discourse: The 'Practice' of 'Theory'" (1995), Deborah McDowell also argues that merely uttering Truth's name or that rhetorical question suffices, calling up Truth as symbol without necessitating one consider to what extent she participated in or had access to a "political coalition" with the white women reformers of her day. However, McDowell reads such invocations as not only gesturing toward those qualities white feminists believe Truth embodies, qualities they paradoxically would admire in others and disavow in themselves, but sees them as deliberate attempts "to rematerialize [feminist theory's] signs of omission around race" (98). Truth becomes, in effect, unmoored from history and the particularities of her political and rhetorical situation and sent traveling as symbol, or "metonym for black women . . . in an era with at least nominal pretensions to interrogating race and the difference it makes in critical discussion" (McDowell 98–99). To invoke Truth, McDowell argues, is enough to satisfy the demand that feminist critical discourse include an interrogation of racial difference within its conceptualizations of gender difference.[23] "As a figure in remove, summoned from the seemingly safe and comfortable distance of a historical past," she writes, "'Sojourner Truth' can thus act symbolically to absorb, defuse, and deflect a variety of conflicts and anxieties over race in present academic contexts. . . . [T]he repeated invocation of 'Sojourner Truth' functions not to document a moment in a developing discourse but to freeze that moment in time. Such a chronopolitics operates not so much as history but as an interruption of history" (98–99).

Ann duCille has contended that black women more generally hold a symbolic value in a contemporary academic concern with difference: "It is not news that by virtue of our race and gender, black women are . . . the quintessential site of difference. . . . [W]here gender and racial difference meet in the bodies of black women, the result is . . . a hyperstatic alterity" (592). Preceding duCille and McDowell, Valerie Smith has argued that black women's "quintessential difference" appears when white feminists seek to "rematerialize the subject of their theoretical position": "[I]t is striking that at precisely the moment when Anglo-American feminists . . . begin to reconsider the material ground of their enterprise, they demonstrate their return to earth, as it were, by invoking the specific experiences of black women and [their] . . . writings" (45).[24] We must attend to the way Sojourner Truth is invoked as a proxy who symbolically acts to "manage" an academic anxiety regarding race and the difference it makes. But we must also hear the point that repeats across McDowell's, duCille's, and Smith's work as they argue variously that black women stand for "quintessential difference" when white feminists seek to materially ground their theorizing or "rematerialize" its omissions. If we consider such instances as akin to much earlier uses of analogical verification in abolitionist and woman's rights discourses, we will see that McDowell's notion of time frozen or history interrupted is very much to the point.

The proxy can be understood as part of the reformer's empathic identification with the slave, but it is also a tool within the larger project of anchoring or substantiating woman's rights rhetoric and an abolitionist sense of "moral right." Elaine Scarry elaborates an understanding of what she terms "analogical verification" or "analogical substantiation" in *The Body in Pain:* "The extreme fact of . . . the body itself . . . is laid edge to edge with . . . a wholly verbal and disembodied assertion. . . . What is striking about such unmediated juxtapositions . . . is that in most instances the verbal assertion has no source of substantiation other than the body. . . . The body tends to be brought forward in its most extreme and absolute form only on behalf of a [discourse] . . . that is without any other basis in material reality: that is, it is only brought forward when there is a crisis of substantiation" (126–27).[25] Through the process of analogical substantiation, a disembodied discourse evokes and enlists the suffering body in order to appeal to a basis in material reality. Scarry marks such an invocation of the body as a juxtaposition between extreme, absolute embodiment and disembodied assertion, while the resolution of such a "crisis of substantiation" is achieved through the elision of this very juxtaposition. The enslaved is not merely *spoken for* by another but is articulated *as* that other's experience or sensibility. The slave, then, was often invoked as symbolic of material conditions that white women sought to articulate as their own; how better to understand "woman's" condition in the midst of the nineteenth century than to liken it to the known—enslavement—a set of experiences that a reform public had been schooled to regard as the result of slavery's immorality and hence necessary to overcome. In a very real sense, the bondswoman functioned symbolically for all that white women found restrictive in their own condition, never matter that they were free while their "sister slave" was bound for life; as symbol, she provided an undeniably "real" material grounding for white women's understanding of and appeals to better their condition.

For her nineteenth-century white contemporaries, Truth as former slave stood as material proof of that rather abstract trope of white woman's condition, "woman as slave." However, that symbolic use value is far from limited to her historical time and place. Rather, Truth specifically, and the image of "the" black woman in general, are put to work in twentieth-century white feminist critical work in strikingly similar ways: in both the nineteenth and twentieth centuries "the" black woman symbolically bridges a gap between abstract discourse and the material. She bodies forth in her person an extreme of victimization or oppression that gives feminist appeal the rhetorical force of the violently "real" yet simultaneously makes the material manageably distant. As proxy, "the" black woman allows for a deferred or deflected acknowledgment of just how far that oppression reaches and exactly who bears responsibility for it. White women need not confront the parameters of their own victimization, nor their role in the racial oppression experienced by others when the proxy keeps these distant and the work of analogical substantiation only brings them near for particular purposes. That McDowell's and Palmer's articles are separated by a decade yet raise similar questions should give us pause, as should arguments like Smith's and duCille's that join them from the mid-1980s through the 1990s. We are, clearly, far from an adequate response to the issues they raise, or a possible resolution of the disavowals and deflections they speak of. Perhaps, instead, we are perpetuating a safe and comfortable distance at which, as duCille contends, "the black woman" and black culture continue to circulate as symbolic currency: "[B]lack culture is more easily intellectualized when transferred from the danger of black lived experience to the safety of . . . metaphor, when you can have that 'signifying black difference' without the difference of significant blackness" (600). Yet as Lauren Berlant argues, such rhetorical maneuvers have been, and continue to be, foundational to white women's access to the public sphere: "As long as they have had a public sphere, bourgeois white women . . . have mobilized fantasies of what black and working-class interiority based on suffering must feel like in order to find a language for their own more privileged suffering at the hands of other women, men, and callous institutions" (*Female* 6).

Such repetitions might be productively forestalled by refusing Sojourner Truth the symbol and taking up the complexities of her speeches, speeches that seem to conform to the reform aims and discourses they can also be read as challenging. To historicize Truth necessarily means we must grapple with the uncertainty of distinctions between representation and "the real," distinctions Truth seems to have played to and on in rather astute ways. But it also necessitates that we not isolate Truth as "the" lone black feminist working within and outside reform circles at this time; rather, her context includes the company of prominent women like Maria Stewart and Frances Harper, whose work can situate Truth's somewhat differently.

Queen Esther and Hanged Haman: The Mob Convention

Just how far nineteenth-century white woman's rights advocates were willing to go to acknowledge "difference" resurfaces in the "Mob Convention," held September 6–7, 1853, at the Broadway Tabernacle in New York City.[26] *The History of Woman Suffrage* introduces Truth's address as "the Lybian Sybil['s] . . . appearance on the platform"; Truth is said to symbolize "the two most hated elements of humanity . . . black and . . . woman," yet amid "a fresh outburst from the mob" she stands "calm and dignified," capable of a "deep insight [that] could penetrate the very soul of the universe" ("Mob Convention," *HWS* 1:567). While *The History of Woman Suffrage,* then, again deliberately represents Truth encountering formidable and mass hostility, the *New York Times* records not opposition but rather eagerness to hear her speak: "SOJOURNER TRUTH, a negro woman asked permission to speak in the afternoon. . . . Cries of "We'll be here to hear SOJOURNER—Hurrah." ("Woman's Rights Convention"). Across these varying reports of Truth's opening speech at this convention, her invocation of Queen Esther serves as the pivot for a double-voiced statement on enslavement, rights and retribution that attends to racial difference.

As a strong figure who petitioned for her rights and those of others, Queen Esther was invoked in feminist-abolitionist discourse as early as Angelina Grimké's *Appeal to the Christian Women of the South* (1836), encouraging southern women to risk censure and work to end slavery: "Is there no Esther among you who will plead for the poor devoted slave?" (qtd. in

Yellin 33). However, just two years later in her 1838 address before the Legislative Committee of the Massachusetts legislature, Grimké invoked Esther not to characterize her as a strong woman to be emulated but as a submissive slave without rights and status as citizen. "Now choosing to interpret supplication as powerlessness and implying that Esther was not actually a ruler but a sexual slave, 'the mistress of her voluptuous lord,'" writes Jean Fagan Yellin, Grimké argued that woman "'should be a citizen'" (40–41). Focusing entirely on either woman risking a petition under interdict, or woman as sexually subjugated, in order to forge an analogous identification between Esther and white American women agitating for their rights, Grimké elides Esther's signal "difference"—she is a Jew passing as Gentile in a kingdom that has enslaved and rules over Jews, exacting and condoning violence against them. Esther risks her life not to speak for woman's rights but to secure the protection of the Jews imperiled by the whim of Haman, a prince who places his political aspirations above human life. Moreover, the book of Esther ends with a narrative of retributive justice in which Mordecai (Esther's adoptive father) gains the position and political power Haman enjoyed, Haman is hanged from a gallows "fifty cubits high" (Esther 7:9), and the Jews are encouraged to slaughter their enemies in retribution.[27] Grimké and white woman's rights agitators who followed her tended to reconfigure Esther's petition to the King as one for her rights, and the rights of those held in bondage as women.

The History of Woman Suffrage account of Truth's speech is marked by the continued circulation of Esther as a biblical foremother of woman's rights reform. In this account, Truth names Esther, makes her petition analogous to American women asking for their rights, and alludes to the narrative's violent retribution only as an extreme to be avoided:

> [I]n the old times the kings of the earth would hear a woman. There was a king in the Scriptures; and then it was the kings of the earth would kill a woman if she come into their presence; but Queen Esther come forth, for *she was oppressed,* and felt there was a great wrong, and she said I will die or I will bring my complaint before the king. Should the king of the United States be greater, or more crueler, or more harder? But the king, he raised up his scepter and said: "Thy request shall be granted unto thee—to the half of my kingdom will I grant it to thee!" Then he said he would hang Haman on the gallows he had made up high. But that is not what women come forward to contend. The women want *their* rights as Esther. She only wanted to explain *her rights*. . . . Now women do not ask

half of a kingdom, but *their* rights, and *they* don't get 'em. . . . The king ordered Haman to be hung on the gallows which he prepared to hang others; but I do not want any man to be killed, but I am sorry to see them so short-minded. ("Mob Convention," *HWS* 1: 567–68; emphasis added)

In the *History's* version, Queen Esther herself, not her people the Jews, is oppressed and seeks to bring her petition before the king because she is a woman without rights as a citizen; Esther "explains" her own rights and does not request that the king end the slaughter of the Jews, sanction the destruction of their enemies, or grant her request to hang "Haman's ten sons . . . upon the gallows" (Esther 9:13). The *History's* version lacks any allusion to dispossession based on racial or religious difference, coalescing instead around gender difference—"what women come forward to contend" before "short-minded" men.

The *New York Times* report of Truth's speech differs little from *The History of Woman Suffrage* account except, rather significantly, in that middle section that alludes to the Book of Esther. Esther herself is not named and, instead, the focus is on Haman hanged from the gallows:

I know it feels funny, kinder funny and tickling, to see *a colored woman* get up and tell you about things and woman's rights, when *we've* all been trampled down so't nobody thought *we'd* ever git up agin. But *we* have come up, and I'm here. There was a king in old times in the Scripiters that said he'd give away half of his kingdom and hang some body as Haman. Now he was more liberaler than the present King of the United States, 'cause he wouldn't do that for the women. . . . But *we* don't want him to kill the men nor *we* don't want half of his kingdom; *we* only want half of our rights, and *we* don't get them neither. But *we'll* have them, see 'f *we* don't, and you can't stop *us* neither; see 'f you can! . . . Woman's sphere ought to rise—rise as high as hanged Haman, and spread out all over. ("Woman's Rights Convention"; emphasis added)

In this account, Truth speaks not of "women want[ing] *their* rights," a distanced collective in which Truth does not appear to include herself, but rather of a "we" who demand yet do not receive "our rights." While the *History's* report effectively marks Truth off as other to "woman" and so outside the cause for which she speaks, the *Times* version opens Truth's invocation of the book of Esther with her foregrounding "the colored woman" and racial oppression: African Americans, not "woman," have been "trampled down" and have "come up" again. Truth's focus in the *Times* report is also, significantly, on Haman rather than Esther which arguably works to underscore the violences Haman exacted, all of which were visited on the Jews as a people "scattered . . . and dispersed . . . destroyed . . . [and] sold for bondmen and bondwomen" (Esther 3:8, 7:4). Truth, in her use of "we," is identifying with the Jews of Esther, and thereby participating in a long history of African American syncretic reinterpretation of the Bible, particularly the books of the Old Testament, as detailing experiences akin to their own. Lawrence Levine documents the evidence of such syncretisms in African American texts and practices from slave spirituals to insurrections: "[T]he compelling sense of identification with the Children of Israel, and the tendency to dwell incessantly upon and relive the stories of the Old Testament . . . characterized the religious songs of the slaves. . . . In [slave] revolts sacred elements were . . . prominent. . . . The religious element in [Denmark] Vesey's [1822 revolt] was made evident in the testimony of his fellow slaves and rebels during his trial. . . . [H]e 'read to us from the Bible, how the Children of Israel were delivered out of Egypt from bondage'" (23, 75–76).

Indeed, Truth's most well-known precursor within a tradition of black feminist oratory is Maria Stewart, who preceded Angelina Grimké as the first American woman to take the public platform before "promiscuous" audiences, and delivered four lectures in Boston from 1832 to 1833. Stewart endured opposition to her political outspokenness until the early fall of 1833, when on September 21 she delivered her "Farewell Address"; in it Stewart defended her right to speak in public by reminding her audience of prominent women in the Old and New Testament, from Deborah of Judges to Mary Magdalene. Esther was part of this appeal, not because she was a woman asking for her rights but because she intervened to speak on behalf of her people: "What if I am a woman; is not the God of ancient times the God of these modern days? . . . Did not queen Esther save the lives of the Jews?" (Richardson, *Maria W. Stewart* 68). Stewart's most frequently used rhetorical appeal was the black jeremiad. Heavily influenced by David Walker's *Appeal* (1829), which indicted American racism and encouraged southern slaves to rise up and overthrow their white masters, Stewart followed the black jeremiad's focus on warning "whites . . . [of] the judgement that was to come for the sin of slavery" (Moses 30–31). Wilson Moses describes the black jeremiad as a "mainly pre–Civil War phenomenon . . . often directed at a white audience. . . . Sometimes its warnings were militant and direct. . . . At other times . . . the tone was that of a friendly warning, couched in the rhetoric of Christian conciliation" (31,

37). Truth's invocation of "hanged Haman," then, is firmly rooted in the black jeremidic tradition and in the black feminist rhetoric of women like Maria Stewart who came before her: she warns whites of the dispossession and violent death that they may meet, as did Haman, in answer for their attempts to render submissive, enslave, and dehumanize the African Americans in their midst. That warning is underscored by Truth's caution to her audience that she is "round watching things," repeated throughout her speech at least three times ("Woman's Rights Convention") and perhaps as many as five times ("Mob Convention," *HWS* 1: 567–68).

Finally, however, I would argue that Truth's caution is not limited to white Americans in general but specifically targeted the woman's rights movement. Truth ends her allusion to the book of Esther with a reference to woman's sphere, expanding her focus on African American identification with the Children of Israel to include the question of woman's place and role in society: "Woman's sphere ought to rise—rise as high as hanged Haman, and spread out all over" ("Woman's Rights Convention"). Initially, it appears that Truth has in mind Haman's political rise, in which he comes to occupy the highest office "above all the princes" and enjoy a "glory of . . . riches" (Esther 3:1, 5:11). Haman's power does come to "spread out all over" as King Ahasuerus agrees to all he proposes. This line is, however, ambiguous, and we must remember that Haman also rose to a height of "fifty cubits" on the gallows from which he was hanged. Truth may well be warning white woman's rights agitators that the pursuit of their political course, sidelining and later sacrificing African American rights to its own aims by opposing the Fifteenth Amendment enfranchising black men, could meet with a retributive justice not unlike that exacted in the Book of Esther or invoked in the black jeremiads. We potentially miss a great deal in the speech Truth delivered to the Mob Convention if we rely only on the *History*'s version, for it does not contain that ambiguous and double-edged line that arguably indicts not only "short-minded" men but also a short-sighted movement to alter "woman's" sphere.

While Sojourner Truth has circulated as straightforwardly advocating woman's rights reform, perhaps in large measure because Gage's "Reminiscences" continues to circulate as the standard text of her 1851 Akron speech and her best-known public appearance, Carleton Mabee's examination of Truth's speeches and venues from 1850 onward shows us that agitating for woman's rights took far less of her time and interest than her status as a symbol for that cause would lead us to believe: "[I]n those years available records indicate that when she spoke, she included appeals for slaves' rights in 63 speeches, but for woman's rights in only 9. . . . During all the years she spoke publicly as a reformer, she advocated improving the condition of blacks in 136 speeches, but advocated improving the condition of women in only 28" (182). While Mabee's figures suggest that distinct speeches addressed increasingly disparate concerns, Truth's work on the platform, according to accounts like that in the *Times,* can be seen to insist that the slave and freed African Americans are very much at the center of woman's rights rhetoric, however much that movement may have wanted their audiences to see woman's rights and "the field of the slave" as separate issues.

"I could make it answer for both": The 1867 AERA Convention

Truth's work to draw attention to "the field of the slave" in complex public appearances continued after slavery was abolished. Increasingly, she seems to have manipulated, rather than countered, her already growing mythical status and symbolic currency, using others' attempts to represent her as the paradigmatic slave and Libyan Sibyl in ways that could be read as furthering her own interests. Nell Painter contends that by the late 1850s, Truth's appearance on the lecture circuit as a former slave connoted for her audiences a southern rather than northern setting and set of experiences (*Sojourner* 141). Even though Painter argues that "[a]s an authentic representative of slavery, Truth . . . was refashioning herself as a Southerner" (*Sojourner* 141), how much Truth may have played to and capitalized on such expectations is difficult to determine. We do know that Truth exaggerated her period of enslavement as forty rather than thirty years. And it is tempting to argue that Truth knew how to appeal to her audiences' preconceptions, offering them a version of the black woman they would most readily recognize.

While it may seem a chronological leap to move from Truth's speeches in the 1850s to the first annual American Equal Rights Association meeting at the Church of the Puritans in New York City, May 9–10, 1867, these addresses give us an insight into how those threads running through her speeches a decade earlier coalesced at a key moment in African American politics—the debates over black male suffrage and the proposed Fifteenth Amendment. In three speeches over these two days, Truth returned to a focus on African American rights, especially those of "the colored women"; the menial labor of African Americans, working women, and equal pay; the "woman as slave" analogy; woman's rights; and the violent struggles to liberate the slave who was yet not entirely free.

In accounts of two of these speeches, Truth either represented herself as the slave arguing for equal rights or was presented by others as embodying the slave experience. Her first address the morning of May 9 opened, "My friends, I am rejoiced that you are glad, but I don't know how you will feel when I get through. I come from another field—the country of the slave. They have got their liberty—so much good luck to have slavery partly destroyed; not entirely. I want it root and branch destroyed" ("American Equal," *HWS* 2: 193). Truth went on to exaggerate her enslavement as part of claiming the authority to speak at these meetings: "I am above eighty years old. . . . I have been forty years a slave and forty years free, and would be here forty years more to have equal rights for all. I suppose I am kept here because something remains for me to do" ("American Equal," *HWS* 2: 193).[28] The *New York World* report of this address picks up Truth's self-presentation as slave and gives it a southern twist, noting, "She dresses much as she used to on the plantation, and wears a white 'kerchief around her head, *a la* mammas all over the South" ("Female").

Truth, now some curious amalgam of the peculiar institution both North and South, was introduced by Susan B. Anthony at her final speech on May 10 as a slave maimed by her cruel master: "Miss ANTHONY announced that they would have another opportunity to hear Sojourner Truth, and, for the information of those who did not know, she would say that Sojourner was for forty years a slave in this State. She is not a product of the barbarism of South Carolina, but of the barbarism of New York, and one of her fingers was chopped off by her cruel master in a moment of anger" ("American Equal," *HWS* 2: 224).[29] Truth's right index finger was indeed cut off, but not by her master John Dumont; rather, Truth damaged it in an accident while working with a scythe shortly after she and Dumont had settled on July 4, 1826, as the date of her emancipation (Painter, *Sojourner* 21–23).[30] Interestingly, however, Truth is not reported as countering Anthony's claim, but immediately begins her address. I would hesitate to say that Truth positioned herself as slave, and allowed others like Anthony to reconfigure that symbolization as they would, simply in order to appeal as the well-worn "sister slave" to this predominantly white and female audience of reformers.[31] Rather, we must note that throughout the convention Truth finds it necessary to remind her listeners that slavery is "not entirely . . . destroyed" despite emancipation coming "through blood" ("American Equal," *HWS* 2: 193, 225), which suggests she believed her audience had begun to assume that calls for African Americans' and workers' rights and freedoms were answered by the Civil War, the abolition of slavery,[32] and a "capitalizing work order" underwritten by "the ideology of economic individualism" (Santamarina 61, 62). Painter suggests just such an atmosphere when she contends that "[Elizabeth Cady] Stanton and [Susan B.] Anthony . . . saw emancipation as over and done with," even though the Black Codes of southern states had created neoslave conditions for African Americans and terrorism was sweeping the South (*Sojourner* 222–30).

Truth's address, as I have noted, opens with her journey from the "field of the slave" still awaiting slavery's destruction, then turns to an appeal for "colored" woman's rights: "I feel that I've got to answer for the sins done in my body just as much as a man has. I have a right to have just as much as a man. (Laughter and applause.) . . . You see, the colored man has got his rights; but has the colored woman? (Laughter.) The colored man has got his rights, but nobody makes [cries] about de colored woman's rights. (Applause.) Why, de colored man will be massa ober de woman, an' it will be jus as bad as before" ("Female"). Truth's speeches at the AERA convention have often been taken as an indictment of African American men's patriarchal privilege and a register of her concern that black men, as men, not achieve the suffrage before women.[33] To be sure, this speech does express the concern that black male suffrage may result in inequities, but Truth is not speaking of "woman" here; unlike Anthony, her concern is not that white women will be further disadvantaged by black male suffrage. Instead, Truth subtly reminds her audience of the enslavement from which African Americans have only recently been liberated—"as bad as before"—registering an indirect counter to Anthony's argument that African American men are now in a position not only to wield power over women but to imperil "the safety of the nation" should they be enfranchised ("American Equal," *HWS* 2: 215). Rather than further the black male versus "woman" suffrage debate in which black women's concerns are diminished if noted at all, Truth argues that black women will not only be oppressed by whites—both white men and women—but possibly also by black men should attention not be paid to their rights.[34] While the AERA debates gather momentum, Truth confronts those gathered with their silence on "the colored woman's rights," and goes on to mark differences of experience and material condition between black and white women:

> *The white woman knows a good deal; the colored woman don't know it*—that is, those that are lately 'mancipated. . . . *I want the colored woman to understand* that if she earns anything it is her own. But if a colored wife goes out to do a little washing—*that is about as high as black folks get*—(laughter), when she comes back with a little money the husband comes in. . . . The man claims her money, body, and everything for himself.

(Laughter and applause.). . . . I have done as much work as the biggest part of men. If I do as much work as a man, why can't I be paid so? (Applause.) . . . They don't do more than I, why should they get more pay? ("Female"; emphasis added)

While the *New York World's* account moves from this argument for working-class women's equal pay and control over their finances to Truth's optimism that "woman's rights" will be won just as she said slavery would be abolished in her lifetime, *The History of Woman Suffrage, New York Post,* and *New York Daily Tribune* all have Truth immediately following this appeal with "I suppose I am about the only colored woman that goes about to speak for the rights of the colored woman. I want to keep the thing stirring, now that the ice is broke" ("AERA," *Tribune*). According to these accounts, then, Truth did not claim to "come from the field of the slave" in order to offer her audience a well-worn vision of the black woman as "sister slave." Instead, she invoked slavery to remind her audience that though recently emancipated, black men and women had yet to achieve "freedom"; woman and the (former) slave were not one and the same. Moreover, Truth drew attention to the figure these categories did not acknowledge or accommodate, the black woman who as neither the freed men who might gain the suffrage nor the white woman who might find herself further "oppressed" as a result, was rapidly disappearing from the AERA debate.

Attending to these turns in her argument is central to understanding the careful work Truth appears to have undertaken at the convention. It is her closing, however, that is key to a full understanding of the larger context in which Truth worked to keep the freed people and their concerns part of a discussion that was increasingly focused on woman suffrage. Nearing the end of her speech, Truth's argument that working women deserve control of their earnings, earnings that should be equal to their male counterparts, comes to be of far greater concern than the suffrage. Indeed, it stands in her speech *as* woman's rights: "When woman's rights come we will have it in our own pockets. [Laughter.] We won't run to men for money. [Laughter.] . . . Women will have money as well as men" ("Female"). Of no small interest, Susan B. Anthony, who would argue the following day that "the colored man" will degrade the suffrage and that "the wisest order of enfranchisement was to take the educated classes first" ("American Equal," *HWS* 2: 214–15), stepped forward at this point to collect funds for the AERA finance committee ("Female"). The effect was to use Truth's argument to raise financial support for what Anthony, through the course of this convention, identified as white women's rights. In Anthony's opinion, black women are no more deserving of the suffrage than black men, for she speaks of their "degradation" as equaling that of "the colored man" ("American Equal," *HWS* 2: 214–15). Truth, following Anthony's collection, rather tellingly resumed her speech with the woman as slave analogy: "[T]he men had held the woman in slavery so long that they thought they owned them." Yet what initially seems to be the standard image used by white women's rights agitators immediately becomes Truth's reference to the important work she had been undertaking with the freedmen: "She had been in Washington three years. She felt that the colored woman in Washington had a right to vote as well as the colored men" ("Female").[35] Truth deftly turns the analogy back to the particular conditions of the formerly enslaved, specifically African American women.

During the morning session of May 10, Anthony went on record advocating the suffrage for "the educated," the "highest type of manhood," and "the virtu[ous], wealth[y], and educat[ed] . . . women of the country" over "this incoming tide of ignorance, poverty, and vice" heralded by black male suffrage ("American Equal," *HWS* 2: 215–16). Anthony's qualifications differ little, in some respects, from those already in effect, despite their expressed attention to a "new force in government" that could be achieved by extending the suffrage to white women. Anthony continues to advocate a suffrage that remains tied to literacy and property qualifications; Truth, in contrast, argues for another sense of ownership as the goal of equal rights reform. We can read her insistence on May 9 that "the colored woman" be able to keep her earnings as advocating self-ownership and the value and dignity of paid labor; as bondswomen, African American women could claim neither their labor, children, nor person as their own.

Truth would return to this line of argument in her final speech the evening of May 10: "Well, Sojourner has lived on through all the scenes that have taken place these forty years in the anti-slavery cause, and I have plead with all the force I had that the day might come that the colored people might own their soul and body" ("Woman Suffrage").[36] She goes on to speak of the taxes she pays for the house she owns in Battle Creek, Michigan, and of other women homeowners who, she says, worked digging stumps rather than pay road tax, concluding that since "it is easier to vote than dig stumps" women should have the vote ("American Equal," *HWS* 2: 225). It would appear that in arguing for woman suffrage Truth is favoring property qualifications: owning a house and paying "[r]oad tax, school tax, and all these things" should qualify women to vote as it does men ("American Equal," *HWS* 2: 225). However, in a letter Elizabeth Cady Stanton wrote the *New York World* on Truth's behalf shortly after the AERA convention, Truth decries both property and literacy requirements for the suffrage: "You know children I don't read such small stuff as letters. I read men and nations. . . . What a narrow idea a reading qualification is for a voter! . . . And there's that property qualification! just as bad" ("Sojourner").[37] Moreover, Stanton writes Truth as clarifying her position on suffrage: "My speeches in the Convention read well. I should like to have the substance put together, improved a little, and polished in tract form. . . . 'Sojourner Truth on Suffrage'; for if these timid men . . . knew Sojourner was out for 'universal suffrage,' they would not be so afraid to handle the question. Yes, children, I am going to rouse the people on equality. I must sojourn once to the ballot-box before I die" ("Sojourner"). It would seem that Truth, seeing the property qualification as "narrow" and exclusive, was promoting a different sense of ownership and equality at the AERA convention: self-ownership of the "soul and body." Indeed, Truth saw property qualifications as indicating that those "men and women themselves, who made money, were not of more value than the thing they made" ("Sojourner"). Owning the self should form the basis of political rights thereby enfranchising all regardless of race, gender, or class.

"A Double-Edged Song"

Tracing out Truth's lines of argument has proven difficult for some time and for a number of reasons that coalesce around a very particular and long-lived understanding of who she was. Critics who have studied Truth's life and work stress that one of her signal rhetorical techniques was to extemporize in her speeches, incorporating the addresses she heard being made around her in a kind of antiphonal, or call-and-response, text that responded to and countered those arguments with which she disagreed.[38] This skill made her speeches appear rambling to white reporters: "Her speaking is disjointed, and her 'lectures,' as she calls them, quite variable. . . . she just drifts along" (qtd. in Painter, *Sojourner* 241). Truth seems to have been well aware of how she was represented by the press, making their inability to follow both the style of her speeches and their double-voiced arguments part of her final address on the evening of May 10. The *World* described her style as marked by "all the *eccentricities of colored women.* . . . She dwells at length on some words, and then again lumps a whole sentence into a breath. She abounds in asides and parentheses" ("Woman Suffrage"; emphasis added). Ironically, the *World* went on to report Truth's evening speech as ending with a critique of her representation in the local papers:

> [T]hey can't put things down on paper as we speak, though *I speak in an unknown tongue.* (Laughter.) Now, what I sing *they A'n't got in de right way—not in de way I meant it. I am a kind of poet.* I can't read, but I can make it. A DOUBLE-EDGED SONG[.] You see I have sung in the anti-slavery meeting and in the religious meetings. Well, they didn't call anti-slavery religious, and so I didn't call my song an anti-slavery song—called it religious, so *I could make it answer for both.* (Great laughter.) Now I want the editors to put it down right. I heard it read from the paper, but it don't sound as if they had it right. ("Woman Suffrage"; emphasis added)

We might say Truth made answering for both an art, crafting addresses that were taken up as advocating the very cause she was challenging as she pushed her fellow reformers to consider the issues they were eliding.

Even though Truth's speeches were clearly complex, as were the contexts in which she made them, her addresses have descended to us in images like bared arms or in fragments taken out of context. The most frequently quoted line from her three AERA appearances, and often the only line quoted as indicative of her stance on woman suffrage and her contribution to the convention, is drawn from her opening speech in which she is understood as opposing black male suffrage: "[T]he colored men will be masters over the women, and it will be just as bad as it was before" ("American Equal," *HWS* 2: 193). Truth persists in our memories as a figure distinctly different from her black feminist contemporaries like Frances Harper, who at the 1869 AERA convention at Steinway Hall in New York City is reported to have chosen black male suffrage and support of the Fifteenth Amendment over woman suffrage: "When it was a question of race, she let the lesser question of sex go. But the white women all go for sex, letting race occupy a minor position. . . . If the nation could only handle one question, she would not have the black women put a single straw in the way, if only the men of the race could obtain what they wanted" (*HWS* 2: 391–92). In contrast, Truth has circulated as choosing gender over racial solidarity, yet both Harper and Truth were members of the American Woman Suffrage Association (AWSA), which pursued universal suffrage. Harper was a founding member, while Truth attended both AWSA meetings and NWSA (National Woman Suffrage Association) meetings.

Yet if we continue to choose a Sojourner Truth who advocated "woman's rights" over those of African Americans, we grossly oversimplify both her work and the context in which it emerged. Indeed, Painter argues that from that contentious 1867 AERA convention through to the split of 1869, "Truth sought a middle road, avoiding NWSA/AWSA politics while speaking for women's political rights in generalities. . . . But a choice was unavoidable. . . . Truth came finally to rest with the AWSA," speaking at their meetings in New York in 1870 and in Boston in 1871 (*Sojourner* 232).[39] Continuing to choose an uncomplicated Truth will also mean that like the editors of *The History of Woman Suffrage,* we are interested only in a particular version of the early black feminist, one that we can construe as less challenging in several ways. Critics such as Painter and Rosalyn Terborg-Penn have argued that the *History*'s editors deliberately chose to include Truth's speeches while they excluded those of other black feminists like Frances Harper because Truth's illiteracy made her less likely to question the ways her speeches and person were represented (Terborg-Penn 31) and made her more of a spectacle than a figure with which to contend: "As an uneducated, dark-skinned ex-slave, Truth embodied a black female authenticity that white audiences could not find in Harper. . . . Truth's style was not barbed like Harper's; she disagreed indirectly, without attacking white women straight on" (Painter, *Sojourner* 224–25).[40] Are we, then, continuing to choose an exotic, illiterate former slave as our version of "the" nineteenth-century black feminist? And are we continuing to read Truth's double-voiced rhetorical strategies as uncomplicated and straightforward expressions of agreement, rather than grappling with the possible indictments and warnings they register? Historicizing Sojourner Truth's work, rather than relying on fragments taken out of context and representations we have left unexamined, may not only complicate the position she occupies in our historical memories of American woman suffrage but also make her a less convenient symbol with which to continue some rather well-worn strategies of elision, deferral, and disavowal. More than that, seeing Sojourner Truth as one rather than *the* nineteenth-century black feminist will open us to hearing a range of political positions and strategies of appeal from those women who constituted a varied and hardly marginal black woman's political culture preceding, contemporaneous with, and following her. Sojourner Truth was a preacher, an abolition, woman's rights, suffrage, and labor activist, and in her work she pursued many of the principles early black feminists before her and working alongside her in these fields pursued.

Jarena Lee (1783–?). Library of
Congress, Washington, D.C.

Amanda Berry Smith (1837–1915).
University of North Carolina.

Sarah Parker Remond (1826–
1892). Peabody Essex Museum.

Sojourner Truth (ca. 1797–1883).
Carte-de-visite photograph, 1864.
The Granger Collection, New York.

Ida B. Wells (1862–1931). The Granger Collection, New York.

Mary Church Terrell (1863–1954). Library of Congress, Washington, D.C.

Mary Ann Shadd Cary (1823–1893). Photographer unknown. Library and Archives Canada.

Victoria Earle Mathews (1861–1907). University of North Carolina.

Fannie Barrier Williams (1855–1944). The Granger Collection, New York.

Josephine Silone Yates (1859–1912). Library of Congress, Washington, D.C.

Frances Harper (1825–1911). The
Granger Collection, New York.

Anna Julia Cooper (1858–1964). The
Granger Collection, New York.

Chapter 4

The Platform, the Pamphlet, and the Press: Ida B. Wells' Pedagogy of American Lynching

From a consideration of black feminist labors within woman's rights reform circles through a particular focus on Sojourner Truth, I wish now to turn again to black feminism as it takes the international stage and thereby keep firmly in sight the way in which early black feminism reached beyond "local" concerns, rhetorics, and politics. The transatlantic links and focus black feminism built through abolition would become an approach to activism that informed late-nineteenth-century agitation for black women's and black civil rights. Though the antebellum work of midcentury abolition seems rather removed from late-nineteenth-century anti-lynching activism, African American women faced strikingly similar issues while pursuing both reforms. Abolition and anti-lynching together saw African American women reaching across the color line and gender divide as well as crossing the Atlantic to reach British audiences, thereby creating greater pressure on Americans to abolish slavery and, later, outlaw lynching. While their work in the United States and their subsequent lecture tours in the UK were separated by over forty years and aimed to advance different causes, the abolitionist work of Ellen Craft and Sarah Parker Remond and the anti-lynching crusade of Ida B. Wells raise similar issues for our consideration.[1] As was the case for Craft and Remond, reports of Wells's lectures in British papers focused on her appearance and manner. Frequently praising her for her "womanly" and earnest appeals, the British press distinguished Wells not only as an exemplary individual but also as an oddity, the attractive though unusual product of American "miscegenation." In the United States, Wells's womanhood was frequently cast as suspect by both a white southern press "defending" that section of the nation against her "attacks" and African Americans who believed Wells's tactics risked too much for "the race" as a whole. Yet as Craft and Remond did at midcentury, Wells was able to manage and effectively channel British interest in her person into transatlantic support for anti-lynching near the century's close. And like Craft and Remond before her, Wells studied the British reform scene, strategically pitching her appeals so that they would gain the greatest rhetorical force. What is more, Wells's extensive experience as a newspaper editor and journalist meant that she was savvy in how she used the British press to bring the moral authority of international outrage to bear upon a United States blithely condoning lynching.

Historians and scholars agree that Wells's anti-lynching work would not have had the effect it did in the United States had she not created an international audience for it on her British lecture tours of 1893 and 1894, yet that work commands little scholarly attention in criticism that isolates Wells in reform rather than considers her connections within a developing black feminism. The connection between Craft and Remond's abolition work and Wells's British anti-lynching crusade is more than convenient. Not only are the stakes of embodiment significant in these women's work—both its risks and management—but Wells also called her audiences to connect abolition with anti-lynching across the decades that separated their appeals. Wells undertook what I would call a pedagogy of American lynching, carefully schooling her audiences and readers to reconsider the common justification for such violence. Drawing on the codes of domesticity, alluding to eugenics, invoking debates in both the United States and Britain on the age of consent, and directly quoting "facts" from white southern newspapers, Wells drew attention to the realities of lynching and rape, its victims, and the work of a press actively inciting mob violence rather than merely reporting it.

Ida B. Wells's entrance into anti-lynching agitation is by now infamous, thanks in no small part to the incendiary editorial she published in the May 21, 1892, issue of the Memphis paper she co-owned with J. L. Fleming, the *Free Speech*. In early March 1892, Calvin McDowell, Will Stewart, and Thomas Moss were lynched by a white mob said to be as small as ten men. Prominent black Memphians who were members of the People's Grocery Company cooperative, a black-owned store competing with a white-owned grocery in Memphis' racially mixed neighborhood known as the Curve, these men were accused of injuring three deputies in an armed standoff incited by rumors of an impending mob raid on their store. Despite two weeks of hearings, no one was indicted or tried for their murder (McMurray 135). Wells was close friends with Thomas Moss and his widow, and the *Free Speech* covered the lynchings and hearings extensively. Yet it was not until Wells ran an editorial in the May 21 edition, questioning the well-worn claim that rape motivated lynching, that her own life was threatened by the specter of a white mob.

Wells wrote: "Nobody in this section of the country believes the old thread-bare lie that Negro men rape white women. If Southern white men are not careful, they will over-reach themselves and public sentiment will have a reaction; a conclusion will then be reached which will be very damaging to the moral reputation of their women" (*Southern Horrors* 17).

The editorial ran while Wells was visiting Philadelphia and New York. News soon reached her that Memphis' *Evening Scimitar,* assuming Fleming had written the editorial, had called for his lynching: "If the negroes themselves do not apply the remedy without delay it will be the duty of those he has attacked to tie the wretch who utters these calumnies to a stake at the intersection of Main and Madison Sts., brand him on the forehead with a hot iron and perform upon him a surgical operation with a pair of tailor's shears" (qtd. in McMurray 148). Wells did not return to Memphis, Fleming fled the city, and a mob destroyed the *Free Speech* office. Wells would later write in her autobiography that the Memphis lynching challenged her own understanding of such violence: "Like many another person who had read of lynching in the South, I had accepted the idea meant to be conveyed—that although lynching was irregular and contrary to law and order, unreasoning anger over the terrible crime of rape led to the lynching; that perhaps the brute deserved death anyhow and the mob was justified in taking his life" (Duster 64). The Memphis lynching and the destruction of the *Free Speech* taught Wells that lynching was economically and politically motivated and rarely fueled by its frequent "justification," the alleged rape of a white woman.[2] Rather, lynching was a violent act intended to intimidate and control African Americans, a spectacle reminding them that they were not the equals of southern whites nor were they citizens who could expect their nation's protection.

Far from silenced by this intimidation, Wells turned the threats against her into an attention-grabbing pseudonym, accepted T. Thomas Fortune's offer to join his New York paper, the *Age,* and garnered the support of black feminists and club women, all of which enabled her to launch a national and international anti-lynching crusade. Fortune was one of the "best-known African American editors" in the late nineteenth century, was supportive of women journalists, and edited one of the few black papers "that had subscribers from all across the United States" (McMurray 90). She "purchased a one-fourth interest in the *Age* in exchange for her *Free Speech* subscription list" (Giddings 30). It was a profitable partnership for both parties, and Wells's "exile" from Memphis gave her a much wider readership in the *Age* than she ever would have achieved with her own paper. Her opening foray with

Fortune's paper was to tell of the Memphis lynchings and the threats against her life in the June 25, 1892, edition. Titling her article "Exiled," Wells would refer to herself by this name in subsequent lectures and anti-lynching pamphlets, calling herself not only an exile from the South but from the nation, a "land of liberty" as she sarcastically put it (Schechter 23). "Exiled," covering the front page of the *Age,* "sold ten thousand copies . . . far more than any other publication in the history of the African-American press" (Streitmatter, "Maria" 54). Fortune would later tout it as a "'sensation . . . referred to and discussed in hundreds of newspapers and thousands of homes'" (qtd. in Streitmatter, "Maria" 85). Requests for its publication as a pamphlet soon followed (Thompson 30), in a year when lynching reached a peak with "some 241 people, 66 percent of whom were African American," dead at the hands of the mob (Schechter 81).

Close on the heels of her article, Wells's speech to over two hundred elite black women of New York, Boston, and Philadelphia at the Lyric Hall in New York on October 5, 1892, further solidified her reputation among African Americans as a "heroine" ("Distinguished"). Organized by Victoria Earle Matthews, Sarah Garnett, and Maritcha Lyons, the event raised over six hundred dollars, much of which was given to Wells to fund her anti-lynching efforts. Attended by highly visible and respected African American women like Josephine St. Pierre Ruffin and Gertrude Mossell, Wells's address was given the stamp of respectability at a time when white southern,[3] and occasionally white northern,[4] papers were impugning her and the black press was not always solidly behind her.[5] Wells was subsequently invited to speak elsewhere and began what would be a "frantic tour of eastern cities" (McMurray 174).[6] The text of her Lyric Hall address closely followed her *Age* article, and Wells promptly published these in a pamphlet, selling for fifteen cents, as *Southern Horrors: Lynch Law in All Its Phases* in late October 1892.[7] Shortly after the highly publicized lynching of Henry Smith in Paris, Texas, by a mob numbering roughly ten thousand for his alleged assault of a four-year-old white girl (McMurray 184), Wells's work drew the attention of Isabelle Fyvie Mayo and Catherine Impey, Scottish and English activists, who invited Wells to speak in Britain, expenses paid.[8] Wells accepted and left the United States on April 5, 1893, to lecture to Scottish and English audiences. Her tour gained such attention from English journalists and, subsequently, their African American counterparts that a recent Wells biography has dubbed her "the most discussed individual in the black press—aside from Frederick Douglass" (McMurray 189).

Though Ida B. Wells would not take to British platforms until the spring of 1893, during the first of her two anti-lynching lecture tours, several of the issues Ellen Craft and Sarah Parker Remond faced are echoed in her work. Wells saw these addresses as an opportunity to reach white audiences and the white British press, and to encourage the largest importer of American cotton to censure the disenfranchisement, segregation, and lynching of African Americans in the South. She arrived in Liverpool on April 13 and by the twenty-first had begun lecturing in Aberdeen. Press accounts of her work on this 1893 tour and her subsequent tour from March to July 1894 indicate a fascination with both her manner and her person, much like Craft and Remond encountered. Wells more than managed the sensation her subject and she herself caused, deliberately drawing analogies between slavery and lynching as she negotiated highly bodied lectures with the use of quotation and a stress on "the facts" and proof. These echoes with Remond's work in particular are far from coincidental. Wells asked her audiences to recall their earlier reform impulses and invoked elements of abolitionist discourse in order to help them understand the magnitude and effects of lynching so that they might exert their influence with an American pulpit, press, and public.

As Craft and Remond did, Wells also managed particular risks that accompanied her public lectures, both the risk of embodiment and the risk that her audiences would simply conflate her appeals with those of other reform causes of the day. In contrast to the situation Craft and Remond faced, by the late nineteenth century it was Wells's subject, more than her mere appearance upon the platform, that raised the risk of embodiment.[9] Wells spoke to British audiences about the lynching of black men, the rape and lynching of black women and girls, and white women as sexual subjects. This was a public who had read of or engaged in debates over the age of consent in the 1880s and had been incensed by W. T. Stead's "The Maiden Tribute of Modern Babylon" newspaper series (1885), which exposed London brothels and their traffic in working-class white girls. Speaking of the rape of African American women and girls, and of white women in consensual interracial relationships, Wells challenged her listeners who had become accustomed to narratives of the seduction and entrapment of white women and girls. For Wells's audiences, white working-class women and girls were the victims of older, privileged (middle- and upper-class) men in the trade of "white slavery." Their understanding of sexual danger included neither a concern for the welfare of African American women and girls nor an awareness that black men could be endangered by white women's desire and the violent attempt to deny it.

While Craft and Remond confronted their listeners with the material differences between white workers "as slaves" and enslaved black women in the United States, they also built sound support with the working class and labor as they understood oppressions of class, gender, and race to be interdependent. Wells's appeals also had to account for the centrality of class in the British political landscape, as she demanded her audiences acknowledge that not all men were privileged and that class was not the primary difference in power in the scenes she sketched. Challenging her audiences' understanding of sexual danger as "white slavery," Wells also had to contend with the way in which white women were identified as either the victims of this moral panic or their potential saviors. While working-class white women and girls could be spirited away into the "trade" at any moment, white middle-class British feminists "capitalize[d] upon ["white slavery" and] the volatile political conditions of the 1880s . . . to gain access to a redefined public sphere" (Walkowitz 7) by participating in purity campaigns.[10] Wells risked losing a hearing, if not alienating much of her audience, by speaking openly of white women's attraction to black men and by insisting upon the very different "sexual danger" lynching and rape represented for black men, women and children. In order to ensure that her listeners did not simply accommodate accounts of lynching in the United States to their existing understanding of imperiled white womanhood, thereby seeing black men as potential threats to white American womanhood, Wells offered a frank analysis of lynching that could risk the dismissal of her appeals altogether.

Managing the Risks of "Harrowing Accounts"

Wells was aware that the subject of her addresses, articles, and pamphlets, and not simply her presence on a platform, could call her womanhood into question, given what her listeners described as the "graphic picture she gave of the brutal tyranny to which the colored people of the Southern States are subjected" (qtd. in Hopkins 280). Her outspokenness and her nonconformity to dictates of womanhood, whether by necessity or by choice, had drawn criticism in America well before her anti-lynching agitation drew international attention. Critics like Sandra Gunning note the false rumors the white southern press circulated "about her sexual liaisons" with her male colleagues at the *Free Speech* (82). Simply being the solitary caretaker of her siblings after their parents' death of yellow fever brought Wells under suspicion of being her youngest sister's mother (Schechter 16). Wells's autobiography documents that her work raised suspicions and censure after her British tours as well.

Shortly following her return to the United States in 1894, after her second tour, an AME clergyman opposed a resolution endorsing Wells and her work and warned that the church ought to "be careful about endorsing young women of whom they knew nothing" (qtd. in Duster 222). When it became known that Wells would be interviewed by the *New York Sun* in early August 1894, she "was waited upon by a delegation of the men of my own race who asked me to put the soft pedal on charges against white women and their relations with black men" (Duster 220). And in an uncanny echo of Sojourner Truth's experience at Silver Lake, Indiana, in 1858, white Memphis papers assumed Wells to be male after reading her *Free Speech* May 1892 editorial. Even T. Thomas Fortune characterized Wells's political style as masculine: "If [she] was a man she would be a humming independent in politics. She has plenty of nerve; she is as smart as a steel trap, and she has no sympathy with humbug" (qtd. in Thompson 18).

If not her womanliness, at times it was Wells's own humanity that was questioned. In the black press, she was depicted as a dog in political cartoons,[11] while a letter to the editor of the *Kansas City American Citizen* in December 1893 called for someone to "put a muzzle on that animal from Memphis" (qtd. in Schechter 97). The white press, both South and North, routinely impugned Wells in attempts to neutralize her indictments of white racial supremacy during these British tours, calling her "the negro adventuress of decidedly shady character" ("Ida Wells Abroad") and "the mulatress missionary" (*New York Times* July 27, 1894, qtd. in Duster 218 n. 1).

Knowing well the power of coverage in the press and traveling to Britain, in part to secure the attention of the white press on both sides of the Atlantic, Wells referred to such "foul tirade[s]" as bringing "stronger supporters to the Anti-lynching cause than it perhaps would have had otherwise" and took them as opportunities to respond with "facts" of the "lynching record" ("Ida B. Wells . . . Reply"). Routinely put in the position of defending her reputation, it seems an understatement to say that Wells "was keenly aware of living within a web of social and political forces that affected her capacity to use words with the consequence she desired" (Royster, *Traces* 52). And certainly, as Linda McMurray notes in her biography of Wells, she "faced the dual suspicions of women speaking in public and of anyone speaking openly of rape" (170). That Wells's body, its acts and its very nature, was the focus of criticism and suspicion is significant, since her subject matter was the violent embodiment of African American men, women and children who, as victims of rape or the lynch mob, were made to serve as spectacular reminders of white control and black subservience.

If the dual and often conflicting imperatives of being both a "race woman" and an outspoken activist in the United States are registered in such responses to Wells at home, British press accounts also registered the risks of embodiment in her work abroad. In addition to calling her descriptions of the lynching of black men, women, and youth and the rape of black women "graphic," Scottish papers reported that "[n]othing more harrowing has been for years related from a Glasgow platform" (qtd. in Hopkins 280). English papers such as the *Liverpool Weekly Review* referred to the accounts Wells offered as "a lamentable, sickening list, at once a disgrace and degradation to nineteenth century sense and feeling" ("Ida B. Wells . . . Reply"), and to lynching as "fiendish saturnalia" ("Bitter Cry"). While McMurray speculates that the "details of . . . lynching titillated the Victorian public for whom frank discussions of violence and sex bordered on pornography," she raises this as a potentially "alienating" effect on Wells's audiences, rather than considering what effect such sensation may have had on Wells's work itself and upon her circulation on these tours (216). In her incisive study of nineteenth-century African American women rhetors, Shirley Logan highlights Wells's use of descriptive detail to invoke presence, an "especially important" rhetorical technique since "[w]ith subjects like lynching, . . that which is suppressed becomes very easy to ignore, dehumanize, and rationalize" (74). Logan also argues that Wells's descriptions would "persuade audiences geographically and emotionally removed" from American lynching (74) by "exhibit[ing] the actual scene" rather than simply narrating it (Logan 72). While McMurray's and Logan's points are important to consider, scholarship on Wells and early black feminism more largely also needs to ask what risks are involved in bridging or closing an emotional gap between audience and subject, and how black activists like Wells might have managed them. Moreover, given the bodied nature of Wells's lectures, however unimpassioned their delivery, we must also consider what it might mean to be a black woman on the platform rendering present or "exhibiting" the lynching of black men, women, and children.

Certainly, Wells's speeches in Scotland and England were bodied in subject; she unflinchingly focused her audiences on specific cases of lynching in the United States. "[O]ccupied . . . with the socially weak" or dispossessed, as was abolitionist discourse, I would argue that Wells's addresses also drew attention to their "plight [as] . . . inscribed upon the body, rendering [her lectures] highly bodied" in content (Peterson 126).[12] Accounts of her appearances suggest that her 1892 Lyric Hall address to African American women in New York and her subsequent pamphlet *Southern Horrors* formed the basis for her lectures on this first British tour.[13] As in her pamphlet, Wells presented lynching alongside the disenfranchisement and segregation of African Americans in the South, updating her lectures with accounts and statistics of new lynchings. In *Southern Horrors,* Wells cited twelve newspaper accounts of interracial relationships, proving "the assertion that there are white women in the South who love the Afro-American's company even as there are white men notorious for their preference for Afro-American women" (26). She went on to document the rape of five black women—describing four of these as young girls, little girls, or children—and the lynching of five black men, two black women, and one fifteen-year-old black girl. Finally, Wells closed with the lynching of thirteen-year-old Mildrey Brown of Columbia, South Carolina, accused of poisoning a white infant in her care (*Southern Horrors* 44–45). Wells would keep the assault, rape, and lynching of black women and girls in focus during her speeches, as reports of both her 1893 and 1894 tours noted.[14] During her 1894 tour, the lynching of a woman in San Antonio, Texas, "[w]ho was boxed up in a barrel into which nails had been driven and rolled down hill" (" Ida B. Wells . . . Lectures"), caught the attention of her audiences and was frequently repeated in coverage of her speeches, by Wells herself or by those introducing her addresses.[15]

Such accounts of the rape of, and mob assaults on, black women and girls refuted the notion that lynching "punishes" the black male rapist and, as Gunning notes, "argue[d] into public consciousness the black female body itself as a primary site of white aggression" (86). This strategy was evidently successful, for when Wells read the account of this lynching to a gathering of the Women's Liberal Association of Bristol, members said "in their speeches [that they] had imagined . . . lynchings . . . [answered] terrible crimes perpetrated by Negro men upon white women" ("Ida B. Wells . . . Lectures"). Part of arguing the black female body into public consciousness and making lynching and its victims present to British audiences is also to *be* a black woman on the platform and in the press. Wells's account of her own threatened lynching following her *Free Speech* editorial was also part of these addresses[16] and arguably facilitated her audiences' imagination and empathy thereby closing that emotional gap between "American Atrocities," as she titled some of her talks, and British sentiment.[17] Much like Ellen Craft, whose circulation as "the White Slave" deliberately capitalized upon her imagined enslavement, Wells presents herself as potential lynch victim alongside those she memorialized in her lectures.

However, neither the embodiment of a near-lynch victim in Wells's person nor that of actual victims in the accounts she read are unproblematic appeals. Simone Davis contends that lynching made its victims the embodiment of or "medium upon and through which 'the lyncher' transmits an economically motivated, political *message*" (83). Lynching's message extended beyond its ostensible warning to potential black rapists so that as public spectacle, the mutilated bodies of its victims threatened African Americans, both male and female, adults, youth and children, with violent consequences should they "step out of place." African Americans who might "aspire" to more than subservience to whites were "taught" by such spectacles that an equally violent fate awaited them. And as Robyn Wiegman has argued, detailed newspaper accounts of lynching conveyed and extended that message, so that spectacle simultaneously functioned "as a mode of surveillance by reiterating [lynching's] performative qualities" (91). Whether African Americans who feared the mob ever saw the violence it exacted was effectively rendered a moot point by the transmission of lynchings' details in the press and by word of mouth. Wiegman and Davis remind us what was at issue, beyond the physical safety of African Americans, during lynching's apex. The "constitution of the citizen as a disembodied entity, bound to . . . the larger body of national identity" (Wiegman 94), coded masculine and white, was at stake during "the nadir." Lynching, however, as "a forced invasion of the body . . . which seems to be coded female" in its affinity with rape, was part of a "continuum" of "violently imposed, bodily feminization" (Davis 92, 93). This violent, bodily feminization graphically underwrote the embodiment of African Americans within the national culture with consequences for their access to the public sphere and status as citizens. Since embodiment (coded feminine and racialized) is understood as antithetical to rational debate and discourse in the public sphere, an important concern for Wells would be preventing her own embodiment on the platform, and that of African American lynching and rape victims in the text of her speeches, from playing into just such a notion of "blackness." Rather, both need to remain part of an effective agitation for the end of such violence and the entry of African Americans into the national body politic.

Wells's use of quotation from white press accounts of lynchings, which critics frequently read as part of her objective style and the credible proof of what she argued,[18] should also be considered as just such a strategic counter to embodiment. However, this is not a strategy without risk. Like Remond often did before her, particularly in Britain, Wells likewise seemed to use the remove of a third-party account to render her addresses less "bodied" in form. The graphic details of press accounts that formed her highly bodied content come "out of their own mouths," as she would say, not her own (*Red*

Record 150). Wells, then, appeared to simply relate sensationalized white press descriptions of lynchings to her audiences, rather than to represent or evoke such violence herself. She could also be said to balance that sensation with the rational appeal of the "facts" offered by the statistics she quoted. Indeed, Wells stressed that she presented "facts" and "proof," that "statistics of lynchings prove" the claim that rape motivates lynching "is a falsehood" ("Ida B. Wells . . . Liverpool"). Like Craft, Remond, and other black abolitionists who appeared in Britain before her, Wells needed to avoid reducing the suffering and abuse of African Americans to sensation and spectacle, yet her audiences had to know of white supremacist violence in America if they were to be moved to voice their opposition. Wells knew very well that she spoke again and again to audiences who had never heard of such atrocities or, if they had, never conceived they could be true.[19] British press accounts of her lectures register her growing impact and a growing British understanding of lynching as an atrocity unlike others they had yet known of. Reports like *The Scottish Pulpit*'s of audiences "listen[ing] . . . with rapt attention to cruelties and outrages" without compare indicate Wells's success at insisting upon the uniqueness of violences her listeners could not condone (qtd. in Hopkins 280). However, given that the British press highlighted the "harrowing" details of her addresses, it is difficult to say that they were referenced in reports only as a way to register the growing impact and understanding of lynching among a British public and not offered by the papers as sensation.

Indeed, Wells addressed a public that from the mid-1880s had been scandalized by the moral panic of "white slavery." Stead's "Maiden Tribute," published in the *Pall Mall Gazette* over the course of a week in the summer of 1885, was, he claimed, the "first official report of a sexual traffic . . . in English girls" (Devereux 1). His exposé extended a rising concern with prostitution to include the duping and kidnapping of working-class girls who became trapped in London's sexual underworld. Rendering his accounts in melodramatic narratives and stressing the value of virgin girls to "procurers" in the "trade," Stead's account of white slavery presented victims a British public had yet to consider, conceiving as they did of a foreign trade in adult, not child, female prostitutes. "The Maiden Tribute" reached audiences well beyond the *Pall Mall Gazette*: the telegraph enabled its circulation on the Continent and in the United States, while "[u]nauthorized reprints were said to have surpassed the one and a half million mark" (Walkowitz 82). Stead's work roused a public demonstration numbering 250,000 in Hyde Park and "forced the passage of age-of-consent legislation," raising the age of consent for girls from thirteen to sixteen years, that had been "stalled in Parliament for years" (Walkowitz 82).[20]

Wells was undoubtedly familiar with "white slavery" and the rhetoric of agitators for its "abolition" by the time of her two British tours, given that "the United States produced what may be the biggest archive anywhere of white slave material . . . [in] newspaper reports, tracts, pamphlets, and books" beginning in 1885 (Devereux 2).[21] Gabrielle Foreman notes that "[c]ensus figures and surveys of the 1880s and 1890s charted the swelling concern and affirmed that prostitution was on the rise." By the 1880s "interest in and agitation for Black rights had dramatically declined" in the United States, while "progressive organizations and their constituencies rallied behind anti-white-slavery efforts . . . and 'former abolitionists . . . joined forces with "social purity" reformers to battle the new slavery.' . . . Increasingly, organizers distinguished white slavery as a subset of ex-Black slavery or positioned the two as equal evils" (Foreman 336).[22] Speaking in England Wells had to contend not only with preconceptions of "white slavery" as sexual danger to white girls and young women and social purity agitators as "new abolitionists,"[23] but also with an emerging socialist representation of the British working poor as the exploited white slaves of capitalism.[24] Attempts to draw attention to exploitation or victimization beyond this white lens would have to negotiate a public and reform focus on social purity and the "emancipation" of the British working poor.

Wells's turn to abolition in her American and British speeches is notable for its attention to the power of an existing discourse with both a history and new meanings that might be remotivated or revised for her purposes. While slavery and abolition had become metaphors in social purity campaigns and socialist literature, Wells sought to make abolition and anti-lynching agitation analogous thereby returning that rhetoric, as it were, to a renewed focus on the rights of African Americans. Wells may not have known much of Remond's specific appeals to her British audiences, or those of other black abolitionists offered several decades earlier, but she clearly knew that referring to abolition and its greats, like "Garrison, Douglass, Sumner, Wittier, and Philips" ("Lynch Law" 347) could have a rousing affect on white northern audiences and those across the Atlantic.[25] With Douglass as her supporter, Wells had access to former British abolitionists such as Eliza Wigham[26] and Ellen Richardson on both of her British tours, and she paid visits to Canon Wilberforce and the Clarks (Schechter 101). During her first British tour, she also spoke to the Edinburgh Ladies Emancipation Society (on April 28,

1893), which Remond had addressed in the late fall of 1860. Wells repeated this strategy during her second tour, writing an article for the *New York Independent* titled "Liverpool Slave Traditions and Present Practices" in which she made analogous her work and "Henry Ward Beecher's controversial antislavery lectures in Liverpool before the Civil War" (Schechter 101).[27]

Through her lectures in both the United States and Britain, Wells worked to foreground anti-lynching and antislavery as linked reforms, the one a fulfillment of the other. In "Lynch Law in All Its Phases," her February 1893 address to a predominately white audience at Boston's Tremont Temple a few months before she would begin her first British lecture tour, Wells quoted William Lloyd Garrison while likening those who "cannot conceive" of lynching to their "[a]ncestors . . . [who] refused to believe that slavery was the 'league with death and the covenant with hell.' . . . [T]he Nation was at last convinced that slavery was not only a monster but a tyrant." Wells continued: "That same tyrant is at work under a new name and guise. The lawlessness which has been here described is like unto that which prevailed under slavery. *The very same forces are at work now as then*" (344). As Patricia Schechter notes, "African American supporters [would later] pick up on" these analogies between slavery and lynching in their own anti-lynching work. Meanwhile, time and again during her first British tour and her second, Wells would insist that "the lot of the coloured people . . . is little better than when slavery was in full force" (*Peterhead Sentinel and Buchan Journal* 2 May 1893, qtd. in Duster 91). She would then liken the censure her British audiences might offer to "the criticism England levelled at America before the war for pretending to democracy while still holding to the old barbarism of slavery" ("Sentiment").

Wells more than simply reminded her audiences of their past reform impulses in order to link them to her current cause. She used two of abolition's strongest appeals, the sense of "moral right" and a concern for violated domestic space. Early in her first tour, Wells wrote the *Birmingham Daily Post* responding to a local councilor's letter to the editor that contended there was no "ground . . . for British people to dictate on questions of detail in the local police arrangements of certain towns in the United States" ("Wearied Councillor"). Wells was quick to point out that the conditions she outlined in her lectures were far more than local police arrangements. She then went on to say that since the American "pulpit and press . . . remains silent on these continued outrages . . . [i]t is to the religious and moral sentiment of Great Britain we now turn. . . . The moral agencies at work in Great Britain did much for the final overthrow of chattel slavery. They can, in like manner, pray and write and preach and talk and act against . . . the hanging, shooting, and burning alive of a powerless race" ("Lynch Law in the United States"). This stress on moral sentiment and moral agencies quite deliberately invokes that earlier abolitionist emphasis upon abolition as a "moral right."

Most often the outrages of slavery were conveyed in representations of imperiled domestic space or relations: families sold apart; children kidnapped into slavery under the 1850 Fugitive Slave Act; bondswomen denied the role of mother to their children. Such attention to the domestic linked these abolitionist appeals to existing discourses of sentiment and melodrama, particularly appealing for their opposition between good and evil. Significantly, these appeals also resonated with those offered by Stead's "Maiden Tribute" in its focus on young, unsuspecting girls lured away from family and home by procurers who made their living by satisfying the "immoral" desires of privileged men. As Judith Walkowitz notes, melodrama had been a popular form in radical politics since at least the 1830s, and "particularly appealed to female audiences . . . precisely because it foregrounded issues of gender and power and highlighted the role of the heroine, however passive and suffering she might be" (87). In choosing melodrama, Stead made a bid for popular appeal despite the fact that radicalism had, by the 1880s, turned from melodrama to scientific and realist discourses.[28]

However, we are reminded that this rhetoric positioned the suffering slave, whether the "white" slave of the new abolitionists or the black slave of the old, as virtuous, helpless, and in need of rescue. Such a representation of black Americans is hardly one Wells would advocate, having already encouraged African Americans to practice "self-help" by withholding their trade from white-owned businesses, refusing to use streetcars or the railway, withdrawing their labor, leaving southern states where the lynch mob prevailed, and giving "a Winchester rifle . . . a place of honor in every black home" (*Southern Horrors* 40–42). Yet by emphasizing the rape and lynching of black women and girls, and ending *Southern Horrors* and presumably many of her speeches with the lynching of thirteen-year-old Mildrey Brown, Wells "recontexutalize[d]" lynching as what Sandra Gunning has called "a state-sanctioned violation of domesticity and femininity" (87).

Moreover, her depictions of many African American rape victims as "girls" would appeal to audiences shocked by revelations of "white slavery" and its workings yet also would challenge them to see that sexual danger was not only threatening white girls in England but African American girls and women across the Atlantic. Strategically, Wells omitted the age of rape, assault, and lynching victims she referred to only as "girls," with the exception of "eight-year-old Maggie Reese" and "poor little thirteen year old Mildrey Brown" (*Southern Horrors* 27, 45). With Britons agitating to raise the age of consent from thirteen to sixteen years, and age of consent legislation across various states in America ranging from seven to thirteen years, Wells's black "girl" and "child" victims would surely shock her audiences as extreme cases that exceeded their knowledge and expectations. Indeed, a close look at the way Wells structures the accounts of white violence against black men and women in *Southern Horrors,* upon which her British lectures were based, reveals that she frames the lynching of men with the rape and lynching of women and girls. With this framing, Wells effectively sketches the black family—men, women, and children—as the targets of white violence, thereby using an appeal to the racialized violation of domestic space to forward her argument. In this kind of domestic appeal Wells both strongly echoed abolitionist rhetorical techniques, and worked to shift "new abolitionist" appeals from their exclusive white and working-class focus.

While critics often characterize Wells as working to "minimize [a] pathetic appeal" in favor of "an assertive and traditionally masculine persona" (Logan 86, 71),[29] her work with a combination of appeals, rather than any singular approach, is overlooked. That combination of appeals might at first seem contradictory. Well known is Wells's recollection of the tears she shed during her Lyric Hall address to African American women as an "exhibition of . . . woman's weakness" she sought to avoid (Duster 80). Yet in her *Inter-Ocean* column, she wrote of "the tears rolling down my cheeks," during an address in Manchester as she heard someone in the audience read a newspaper account of a woman lynched in San Antonio ("Ida B. Wells . . . Bishop"). Interestingly, in her column Wells highlights, rather than omits, this show of emotion. Moreover, her addresses, like *Southern Horrors,* represented the lynching and rape of black women and children through a domestic appeal that had a strong affect on her listeners' emotions. That use of affect was further strengthened by Wells's frequently restrained style. Described repeatedly by the press as speaking "with a singular refinement, dignity, and self-restraint," she was said to "by this marvellous self-restraint . . . move us all the more profoundly" (Armstrong). Wells's seemingly contradictory stand on revealing her emotions, and her efforts to elicit her audience's emotions while projecting an image of self-restraint, indicate that she needed to work carefully, as had Craft and Remond before her, to build and manage her audiences' empathy and identifications.

While affective appeals to violated domesticity and melodramatic accounts of female victimization were reassuringly familiar to her British audiences, indeed, a familiarity Wells actively worked to build upon in order to create a public for anti-lynching agitation abroad, these were also appeals that could result in a facile, empathic identification that supporters, such as Catherine Impey, had fallen into in the past and might so again. In 1883 Impey had written Frederick Douglass, saying that her trips to the United States had caused her "sympathies [to be] keenly alive" so that she could "really feel [herself] *more black than white*" (qtd. in McMurray 189). Wells shares with Craft and Remond before her the risk that empathy will become identification, that the differences she delineates between "white slavery" and the lynching and violent intimidation of African Americans will be ignored and these reforms simply be seen as analogous. A possible consequence of such empathic identification is that "American atrocities" will be compared to the conditions of working-class Britons as well as girls trapped in "the trade" in order to garner further attention for these reforms rather than understood in their own right. As a result Wells's efforts to induce British reformers and the wider public to exert pressure and influence on the United States could go unheeded as her audiences' emotions and resolve continued to be focused on the "white slavery" of Britain. This would be a particular risk, it would seem, with those female members of Wells's audiences interested in social purity and "white slavery" for the emancipationist opportunities it offered them. "Feminist supporters of Stead used the new 'license' to speak publicly on sexual matters to voice their own fears about sexual danger and to attack institutions of male power that encouraged violence against women," documents Walkowitz. "Exclusion from the social contract, liberal feminists insisted, made women vulnerable in public places. They identified the 'outlawed political condition of women' as the root cause of the crimes exposed in the 'Maiden Tribute'; legal indifference and female economic dependence, they charged, placed all women, regardless of class, at risk" (132).

Wells addressed audiences whose own investments, particularly those in (white) woman's rights, could make them more interested in analogies that would amplify their own platforms for agitation rather than join in Wells's efforts to outlaw lynching in the United States. This was a particular risk given the shift in strategy British feminists were undertaking at the time. With the attention to suffrage spectacle—"[p]ictorial leaflets, cartoons, posters and postcards, . . processions and banners"—or what was regarded as "agitation by symbol," suffragists pursued a mode of agitation or "object-lessons, by . . .

visible and audible displays," that they believed "could offer 'imaginative insight into the minds of others and the reconstruction of suffering which is not felt'" (Tickner 10). In other words, spectacle in public reform was becoming aligned with the attempt to facilitate an empathic identification that would enable those outside a cause to not only understand it, but to "feel" the suffering it championed. Whether Wells's audiences came to understand the sexual danger and violence she spoke of as analogous to "white slavery" or as distinctly "American atrocities," the risk remained that they would empathically "feel" themselves "into the minds" and suffering of others.

Astutely, Wells contains her audience's potential empathic identification through the very appeal that elicits it. Her representation of African Americans as suffering a violated domesticity turns on its head the familiar "justification" for lynching and narratives of the white slave's seduction and entrapment. In Wells's writing and speeches the violator of white domestic sanctity is white men or women who "love the Afro-American's company" (*Southern Horrors* 26), particularly white women, who as seductive "Delilahs" betrayed "Afro-American Sampsons" (*Southern Horrors* 19). According to Wells, the white race as family is betrayed repeatedly by the white woman it claims is in need of protection, an argument that significantly counters both white supremacist and "white slavery" rhetoric. In England, as Devereux argues, Stead's account of "white slavery" "met with an immediate and spectacular response . . . because [he] had struck a chord amongst Britons who were increasingly anxious about the ability of . . . the Anglo-Saxon 'race' to maintain its expanding empire . . . [through] what eugenicists by the mid-1880s were referring to as healthy racial stock" (14). The girl kidnapped into prostitution and the rape victim were the unwilling objects of desire for a nonreproductive or "diseased" sexuality. However, Wells was representing white American women as subjects, rather than the objects, of just such a "miscegenous" and so "unhealthy" desire. White women, conventionally seen as the victim of such desire, were themselves threatening the "purity" of the "white race."

Picking up on both white supremacist and eugenics rhetoric, Wells narrated accounts of white wives of prominent citizens, ministers, and physicians who imperiled the so-called sanctity and health of the white race through their willing relationships with black men.[30] She highlighted the wording of the white press accounts she offered which characterized such relationships as "fearful depravity," "rank outrage," and "loathsome disease" (*Southern Horrors* 23, 21). Depicting the white family as violated from within by its wives, mothers and daughters, Wells made it very difficult for her audiences to liken "white slavery's" narratives of privileged men threatening white domesticity to the dynamics of American lynching. She presented white womanhood as an active and privileged agent in the violation of black domesticity, rather than in peril and in need of protection from the black male rapist. Moreover, while the white woman violated the white "family" and race from within with her own desire, white Americans and the mob were external forces wrecking violence upon black domesticity from without. Wells stressed that in their murder of fathers, brothers, sons and raping of mothers, sisters and daughters, the white mob and America's most prominent white citizens violated the sanctity of the black family and outraged black womanhood. The domesticity threatened by sexual danger in Wells's accounts was a black domesticity and the villains of the piece were white men and women. Unique in her attention to the victimization of black women and to the sexual desire of white women, Wells gave voice to elisions and taboos that served the interests and power of white men within that larger network of violence and intimidation in which lynching was a primary tool.

Wells focused on women and children as victims of lynching and rape throughout her career. In "The Negro's Case in Equity" (1900), she defended African Americans as law-abiding citizens who witnessed white supremacist violence without resorting to mob-style vigilantism in response. Importantly, Wells presented "the negro" as witnessing "women and children stripped and strung up to trees or riddled with bullets for the gratification of spite, as in the case of Postmaster Baker's family two years ago, and in that in Alabama a few weeks ago, when an entire family was wiped out of existence" ("Equity" 1010). While African Americans are presented as law-abiding, though dispossessed, citizens of the nation, the nation itself is questioned in Wells's speech to the National Negro Conference on May 31, 1909, titled "Lynching, Our National Crime." Again, it is the African American family, particularly women and children, who, violated by the mob, indict the nation. "No other nation, civilized or savage, burns its criminals; only under the stars and stripes is the human holocaust possible," argued Wells. "Twenty-eight human beings burned at the stake, one of them a woman and two of them children, is . . . the gruesome tribute which the nation pays to the color line" ("Our National Crime" 262). Challenging all-too-familiar stereotypes of "depraved" African Americans threatening the white race, Wells rewrote familiar domestic appeals in ways that interrupted a facile identification with an attention to the difference a violently policed color line had made in America.

"A brown-faced little woman": Managing Sensation

Wells marshaled reports of interracial desire and sexual relations not only to recast familiar domestic appeals but also, it seems, to play on the sensation "miscegenation" caused among the British public at the time. The consequence would be the press coverage she sought but also an attention to her own "blackness." Wells's recollection of the second speech of her 1893 tour to the Aberdeen Men's Pleasant Saturday Evening meeting indicates the interest raised by her argument that "in spite of such laws to prevent the mixing of the races, the white race had so bleached the Afro-American that a race of mulattoes, quadroons, and octoroons had grown up within the race" (Duster 91). One of the other speakers of the evening was unable to be present and Wells was asked to extend her address by fifteen minutes. Wells's reference to miscegenation is preceded by points on "jim crow laws [and] ballot-box intimidation" and followed by the "cruel physical atrocities vented upon my race" (Duster 90–91). Isabelle Mayo, who with Impey was financing Wells's tour and arranging her speaking engagements, "was elated, said that it was the best I had done, and urged me to continue along those lines" (Duster 91). Since the only change Wells mentioned to what was a standard speech on this tour based on *Southern Horrors* was her attention to the white race "bleaching" the black, it seems that Mayo urged her to continue referencing miscegenation in America. During her second tour, *The Westminster Gazette* published an interview with Wells titled "The Bitter Cry of Black America. A New 'Uncle Tom's Cabin.'"[31] The article opened provocatively, quoting Wells as saying "'Taint, indeed! I tell you, if I have any taint to be ashamed of in myself, it is the taint of *white* blood!" The writer goes on to refer to Wells as a "brown-faced little woman . . . who bears strongly printed on her the partly Negro origin of which she speaks so spiritedly, though one would not guess that there is also a Red Indian strain in the odd racial composition of which she is the outcome." Finally, the interview comes to a close with the writer "admitt[ing] that, as a white, I was dead against" miscegenation. Wells reportedly retorted, "'Which race has sought it? Not ours. It is yours . . . and now, having created a mulatto population, you turn and curse it'" ("Bitter Cry").

Such interviews and speeches were controversial on these tours, since, as McMurray notes, "most Britons were repulsed by miscegenation" (220). Repulsed, perhaps, but certainly interested in ways that Wells could capitalize upon to gain further publicity for her work. Wells knew, from the clippings she kept, that British papers focused on her appearance, calling her "a young lady of little more than 20 years of age" (qtd. in Tucker 119) or "a good-looking mulatto, dressed with uncommonly good taste" ("Ida B. Wells's Crusade"). As she played to the fascination with her youthful appearance by "referr[ing] to 'my 28 years' in the South, which . . . shave[s] . . . four years from her actual age of 32" (McMurray 216), Wells's interview in *The Westminster Gazette* played to the sensation caused by her appearance and her references to "miscegenation."[32] Wells was repeatedly singled out in press reports as extraordinary, indeed, "uncommon," within a British racial imaginary. In fact, the *Chronicle* of London focused not only on Wells's "mixed blood" but also on her looks and youthfulness: "She is a very notable product of that mixing of the blood which is proceeding so rapidly in the Southern States of America. She claims relationship with the red Indian, the negro, and the Anglo-Saxon races. . . . She is under 30 years of age, very vivacious in manner, and decidedly good looking" (rpt. in "Ida B. Wells's Crusade"). As this article indicates, Wells herself drew attention to her so-called mixed blood and capitalized upon a continued fascination with blackness among the British public that we can trace back to the fad for fugitive slave lectures that black abolitionists used so effectively.

While Mrs. P. W. Clayden, wife of the editor of the *London Daily News,* "often remarked that she thought that my success would have been much greater if I had been a few shades blacker" (Duster 214), questions about "how black" Wells was fueled even greater interest. Wells noted this interest upon her return to New York from her first British tour, stressing, as did many traveling black abolitionists in that midcentury anglophilic style, that she encountered no "race prejudice anywhere in Great Britain": "[I]t was like being born again in a new condition. . . . In fact, my color gave me some agreeable prominence which I might not otherwise have had" ("Ida B. Wells's Crusade"). Speaking to an interviewer from the *New York Sun,* Wells shows her awareness that for many white Americans, even white northerners, the thought of receiving an African American woman on equal social footing, as Wells enjoyed in Britain, would be unusual if not shocking. For Wells, race prejudice as she knew it in America consisted of mob violence, Jim Crow, and social and political inequity. While she may have experienced heightened attention to her looks and color, positioning her as an oddity or as the embodiment of exceptional "black womanhood" as the "Negro lady lecturer," Wells was able to use that interest to her advantage. Taken to embody both "blackness" and its "mixing" as that "good-looking mulatto," Wells kept her work, not just her name and person, in the press, translating controversy into increased public interest in and coverage of her lectures.

Wells knew, then, how particular representations could affect an audience or readership and was insightful in her ability to capitalize upon the British press's attention, be it controversial, sensational, or otherwise. Adept at rechanneling the investments her listeners and readers had in particular discourses, she also worked to challenge their understanding of objectivity, facts, and an American press that claimed to promote both. As a journalist and editor herself, it is not surprising that Wells would use the press and her audiences' investments in it to her advantage. Exactly how she dealt with and exposed the white American press, however, is both intelligent and worthy of note.

As we have seen, Wells's lectures and her person, like her journalism, caused a degree of sensation, making her technique of quoting southern white press coverage of lynching significant in ways critics have yet to consider. Repeatedly in her speeches and pamphlets, it is the press itself, white editors and journalists, who are the purveyors of sensation, not Wells. As I have noted, critics have tended to see this as a strategy of "authentication" designed to convince her readership and audiences of her objectivity; however, contrary to such readings I would stress that Wells deliberately chose to quote press coverage that was anything but objective. Certainly Wells invites such readings when she refers to press coverage and statistics of lynching as "the facts." And she would appear to use these quotations in order to access a significant turn in the public perception of American journalism in the late nineteenth century. As David Mindich documents, "In the 1890s 'objectivity' became codified as the great law of journalism . . . [and] was a recognized ethic" in the profession (114). However, Wells took pains to point out that American papers, both North and South, suppressed reports of lynchings that were later determined to have been based on "falsehoods." Indeed, Wells revealed that the assistant editor of the *New York Tribune* "def[ied] the publication" of such cases in his paper (*Red Record* 200).

Wells's "facts" are slippery. The press both prints statistics enabling her to prove that less than one-quarter of lynchings "punish" rape, attempted rape, or alleged rape[33] and actively suppresses, distorts, or misrepresents cases of lynching in which the victim is innocent. Wells claims to take the opportunity to make herself "safe from the charge of exaggeration" (*Red Record* 150) by quoting the white press. Yet the effect of doing so is to gain the trust of her readers and listeners based on her ability to ferret out truth from the exaggeration not she but the white press has propagated. More often than not, Wells's corrections to lynching reports go unsubstantiated in her pamphlets and readers do not know exactly how she has garnered details that challenge them. However, I would argue it is the nature of the corrected coverage, rather than the verifiability of Wells's clarifications, that is compelling. "In a county in Mississippi during the month of July [1895] the Associated Press dispatches sent out a report that the sheriff's eight year old daughter had been assaulted by a big, black, burly brute who had been promptly lynched," writes Wells in *A Red Record*. "The facts which have since been investigated show that the girl was more than eighteen years old and that she was discovered by her father in this young man's room who was a servant on the place. But these facts the Associated Press has not given to the world" (*Red Record* 209).

Indeed, to argue that Wells's clarifications are somehow undercut by our inability to verify them is to accord those accounts we can document in newspapers of the day a status Wells repeatedly argues they do not deserve. More important, however, doing so would dismiss both the local knowledge Wells was able to gather and the resistance "from below" such knowledge represents (Kelley 9). In his caution to "question . . . common ideas about what are 'authentic' movements and strategies of resistance," Robin Kelley argues that we must cease "presum[ing] that the only struggles that count take place through institutions" (4). The details, when we are offered them, of Wells's work to discover the "truth" of particular lynchings reveal that African American resistance to lynching, when organized, was often not organized around what would ordinarily be seen as political institutions. Wells investigated reported lynchings like the 1909 torture and murder of "Frog" James in Cairo, Illinois, and gained access to information and viewpoints that the white press could not or cared not to report. Together, Wells and black residents of Cairo successfully agitated for the removal of Sheriff Frank Davis for failing to protect a prisoner in his custody. Wells, with the help of Dr. Will Taylor of Cairo, "spent the day talking with colored citizens and ended with a meeting that night. I was driven to the place where the body of the murdered girl had been found, where the Negro had been burned, and saw about twenty-five representative colored people of the town" (Duster 313). She gathered both information and support from African Americans who feared the mob's retaliation for their actions and presented the state's governor with the results of her investigation, a resolution supported by Baptist ministers, and petitions "circulated in three Negro barbershops" in Cairo and signed by "nearly five hundred Negro men" (Duster 316). Wells's marshaling of local knowledge and her mobilization of the local politics historically conducted in the black church and barbershop were instrumental in ousting Davis from his office and preventing his reinstatement.[34] Her "facts" and corrections to both the white press' record and that offered by Davis's attorney were duly considered by the governor, despite their undocumented nature. While those unaware of barbershops and churches as primary sites of black politics would not recognize the political organization involved in circulating petitions or resolutions there, Wells was able to access black resistance in Cairo through both these institutions and informal discussions with black residents.

Wells not only gained her readers' and listeners' trust by quoting and correcting the sensational and, at times, falsified reports of lynching printed in white American papers, hardly an authoritative third party to which she need appeal in order to fend off charges of exaggeration, but she also exposed the pedagogical qualities of the press. In her injunction to African American self-help, Wells stressed that "one of the most necessary things for the race to do is to get these facts before the public." For Wells, "there is no educator to compare with the press." While she urged black papers to "print the truth," saying that they were the "only ones" who would, she was also aware that the white press was an "educator" and that the white southern press employed a rather specific and disturbing pedagogy (*Southern Horrors* 42–43). Citing cases in which the crimes "motivating" lynchings were sensationally exaggerated in the white press, Wells established that such accounts both aim to justify the mob's actions and to further incite mob violence, representing it as warranted by the extremity of such crimes. In effect, these very graphic reports taught readers a technology of lynching, including the further outraging of the corpse in the gathering of souvenirs. As Wells's pamphlets and lectures detailed, the consistency of lynching's "ritualized violence" went well beyond the repeated hanging, burning alive, and castrating of its victims. Indeed, referring to such acts as ritualistic suggests that they are somehow beyond the acts of individuals; rather, her work demands that we revise our understanding of lynching so that responsibility for such acts is no longer deferred to the mob as unidentified, vigilante force outside the control of the law, social censure, or individual accountability.[35] In contrast, Wells worked to isolate lynching as a violent tool of control and intimidation wielded not only by some of the most prominent citizens of towns and cities in the South and North, but also by a press ostensibly governed by that "ethic" of objectivity on the rise just as lynchings reached their peak.

A Counter-pedagogy of the Press

From the beginning of her anti-lynching activism, and continuing into the early twentieth century, Wells foregrounded the press's active incitement of the mob in what I would call a counter-pedagogy to such schooling in white supremacist violence. *A Red Record* addresses the reader as the "student of American sociology [who] will find the year 1894" the culmination of "ten years" of lynching, an act that has become "so common that scenes of unusual brutality failed to have any visible effect upon the humane sentiments of the people of our land" (*Red Record* 140). Wells then offers her student a condensed history of African American dispossession and intimidation, "[b]eginning with the emancipation of the Negro" (*Red Record* 140–41). Presenting *A Red Record* as a pedagogical document offered to "students" of that new science, sociology, Wells positioned her readers as enhancing an already advanced education in American life and culture. As Fitzhugh Brundage documents, lynching's "increase in the late nineteenth and early twentieth centuries coincided with the maturation of American social sciences." Alluding to that institutional interest in lynching, seen by sociologists and psychologists as "a glaring example of social pathology that . . . [they] were committed to explaining" (Brundage, "Introduction" 6), Wells credits her readers with a similar knowledge or education and a commitment to understanding and ridding the nation of such violence. This framing is significant, for Wells will go on to quote reports in which the white press teaches its readers exactly how they might participate in a lynching and obtain a trophy as memorabilia of the event. The *New York Sun,* in its February 2, 1893, report of Henry Smith's lynching in Paris, Texas, effectively tells its readers that their participation in lynching can suit both their means and the variety of their interests: "Curious and sympathizing alike they came on train and wagons, on horse, and on foot to see if the frail mind of a man could think of a way to sufficiently punish the perpetrator of so terrible a crime" (*Red Record* 165). Even though the *Sun* protests that "[w]ords to describe the awful torture inflicted upon Smith cannot be found," the report goes on to graphically detail the violence to which he was subjected, pausing to mention that "curiosity seekers have carried away already all that was left of the memorable event, even to pieces of charcoal" (*Red Record* 167).

Wells closes her interrogation of the Smith lynching with a newspaper interview of Reverend King. This African American minister, who attempted to "interfere in the programme," speaks of children in attendance who "struggled forward to obtain places of advantage. 'It was terrible. One little tot scarcely older than [4] . . . clapped her baby hands as her father held her on his shoulders above the heads of the people. "For God's sake," I shouted, "send the children home." "No, no," shouted a hundred maddened voices; "let them learn a lesson"'" (*Red Record* 170). The pedagogy of lynching, this paper makes clear, extends to young children, who, accompanying their parents, can be lessoned in such violence and its ostensible justifications. *A Red Record* closes with "The Remedy," and heading the list of possible corrective action is the reader "help[ing to] disseminate the facts contained in this book by bringing them to the knowledge of every one with whom you come in contact" (248). The student in effect becomes the teacher, taking up and helping to extend Wells's counter-pedagogy in which "the facts speak for themselves," countering the press's sensationalized and incendiary coverage so that "public sentiment may be revolutionized" (*Red Record* 248).

The Paris, Texas, lynching of Henry Smith was an Ur-text of sorts for Wells, and a case she referred to frequently during her first British lecture tour. Attracting an unprecedented crowd of participants, gathered as the train carrying Henry Smith from Clow, Arkansas, where he had fled, traveled "through Texarkana where 5,000 people awaited the train" to Paris, where "the train was met by a surging mass of humanity 10,000 strong" (*Red Record* 166), this lynching became a community event. "Whisky shops were closed . . . [and] schools were dismissed by a proclamation from the mayor, and everything was done in a business-like manner," reported the *Sun* (*Red Record* 165). As Wells knew, lynchings on such a scale were possible only with the widespread transmission of details like the "crime" and the likely time and place of its "retribution," communication beyond the means of word of mouth. The ability of the press to incite mob violence would continue to be Wells's focus in later writings such as *Lynch Law in Georgia* (1899), a pamphlet published at Wells's expense and based on a detective's investigation of Samuel Hose's lynching in Palmetto, Georgia, on April 23, 1899.[36]

Taking the *Atlanta Constitution* as an example of press coverage of Hose's lynching, Wells quotes its repeated "predictions" that Hose will be lynched. "'When Hose is caught he will either be lynched and his body riddled with bullets or he will be burned at the stake'" read the *Constitution* on April 13 (qtd. in *Georgia* 7). By the fifteenth "burning and torture is confidently predicted [by the *Constitution*] in these words: 'Several modes of death have been suggested for him, but it seems to be the universal opinion that he will be burned at the stake and probably tortured before burned'" (*Georgia* 7). The *Constitution* did not limit itself to a daily encouragement to torture and burning but offered its readers the horrific details of Hose's death: "[T]he flames began to eat into his body. . . . his left ear was severed from his body. Then his right ear was cut away. . . . Other portions of his body were mutilated by the knives of those who gathered" (*Georgia* 9). The paper then proceeded to describe the gathering of souvenirs: "[T]hey almost fought over the ashes of the dead criminal. Large pieces of his flesh were carried away, and persons were seen walking through the streets carrying bones in their hands. . . . Not even the stake to which the Negro was tied when burned was left, but it was promptly chopped down and carried away as the largest souvenir of the burning" (*Georgia* 10). A group of two thousand people participated in Hose's lynching, a number Wells makes clear was possible only because of the *Constitution's* ten-day "coverage" of an event the paper incited with daily columns and a five-hundred-dollar reward for Hose's arrest.

Scholars such as Robyn Wiegman argue that lynching operates as both intimidation and surveillance, its performance a reminder of what may happen to other African Americans. Others like Jacqueline Goldsby rightly note that lynching's performative qualities extend to its representation: "[T]he representation of racial violence is part of the social experience of the event" (274). Yet a century ago, Wells went further in her analysis of lynching than scholarship ventures today. She interrogated newspaper coverage that preceded lynching as working in concert with reportage that represented its violence in order to educate "the mob," individual readers who might be incited to participate in these acts. She argued for an understanding of the active pedagogy of the press, so that her listeners and readers understood that lynching's power extended beyond the performative and "ritualized" qualities of the event itself, and even beyond the representation of particular lynchings in reports that followed them, to the repeated schooling the white press offered in exactly where and how one might take part in such atrocities. In her pamphlets and speeches both in the United States and Britain, Wells engaged in a counter-pedagogy through which she could educate her readers and listeners in not only what material violence African American men, women and children faced, but also what symbolic violence the press was exacting while ostensibly presenting objective coverage of the facts.

The effects of Wells's work are often difficult to gauge, largely because she was received as a controversial and somewhat threatening figure in African American politics, so much so that many of her supporters came to marginalize or exclude her as anti-lynching agitation continued through the early twentieth century.[37] Even though the risks and potential success of schooling British audiences in the lynching and rape of African Americans during her two lecture tours, audiences for whom such violence was, to a degree, spectacle and sensation, were many, Wells succeeded in effectively creating a public that donated funds and formed committees to advance the anti-lynching cause. Her 1893 tour resulted in the organization of the Anti-Lynching Committee of London; its membership included members of Parliament and the British elite, and it aimed to raise funds to investigate and expose lynching in the United States.[38] Following that first tour, she returned to America to much acclaim and launched a year long, cross-country lecture tour (McMurray 222, 223).

However, during Wells's second tour in 1894, despite gaining "the endorsements of . . . the Baptist and Congregational Unions, the British and Foreign Unitarian Association, the Aborigines Protection Society, The British Women's Temperance Association, and the 'women members of the Society of Friends,'" she found "Christian bodies [in Britain] less responsive by far than the Press" (qtd. in Schechter 99). In particular, Wells's indictment of American churches for refusing to condemn and for "actually abett[ing,] lynching" was controversial and drew sharp criticism from the National Conference of Unitarians in April 1894. Calling it a "terrible misrepresentation of" American Unitarians, their criticism questioned Wells's veracity and undermined her work (qtd. in Schechter 100). This second tour also saw Wells's public criticism of Frances Willard, American leader of the Women's Christian Temperance Union (WCTU), for her refusal to publicly condemn lynching while suggesting in speeches that southern whites were justified in "protecting" themselves against the black male rapist.[39] Wells's public exposure of Willard's position, carried in British papers and reprinted by the American press, angered Lady Henry Somerset, president of the British Women's Temperance Association, and may have cost her some support there. But ultimately, Wells was represented in the British press as the heroine of the battle, the "insignificant colored woman" who the powerful American and British temperance leaders were attempting to "crush" (qtd. in Schechter 102).

Again, Wells was able to generate publicity through controversy and managed it skillfully to advance her cause. Still, as Patricia Schechter notes, "strife in the British crusade never reached the bulk of Wells's readers in the United States" (103), so that Wells's ability to manage British press coverage was perhaps no more effective at home than the indictments in the white American press that sought to undermine her cause. The consequence was twofold and ambivalent: while African Americans, particularly club women, hailed her "as the 'modern Joan of the race,'" white audiences in the United States saw Wells as "just another 'negro,' a 'problem,' and, as a black woman, a favourite scapegoat" (Schechter 104). Nonetheless, the Memphis lynching of 1894, occurring shortly after Wells returned from England, resulted in "white business leaders" publicly condemning the violence and raising funds for "apprehending 'the criminals' and . . . for the benefit of the widows and orphans" of the six lynched men (Tucker 121).[40] Clearly Wells had brought the pressure of international scrutiny to bear on Memphis. David Tucker notes that "the Memphis press never again condoned lynch law and no lynching occurred until 1917, when Ell Person, an accused axe-murderer, was lynched just outside the Memphis city limits" (122 n. 42).

Overall, Wells's British lecture tours, including their impact in America, reveal how complex building a transatlantic anti-lynching network and taking black feminism international could be in the late nineteenth century. What is clear is how tenuous was the position an outspoken black female activist might occupy at the time. It is a credit to Wells that the risks she knew she faced never tempered the truths she told, as she brought her knowledge of and experience with the press, as well as her oratorical skills, to bear in her international campaign to outlaw white violence—both lynching and rape—as tools designed to intimidate and control black Americans. Even as support for Wells began to wane in 1895, just one year after her return from British platforms, African American club women remained her strongest supporters as she continued to produce pamphlets, conduct investigations of lynchings, and join in the anti-lynching efforts of the Afro-American Council and the NAACP.[41]

Wells's Complicated Legacy

The effects of Wells's anti-lynching pedagogy can also be seen in her work's influence on other African American women who would take up the anti-lynching cause, whether they condemned or supported and echoed Wells in public statements and their own efforts to end state-sanctioned violence against African Americans. Wells, while often seen as an isolated figure, worked with appeals activists such as Frances Harper made before her and pursued an analysis that came to be modeled by women such as Mary Church Terrell and the Anti-Lynching Crusaders in the early twentieth century.[42] Not always supported by black feminists who, like her, spoke publicly condemning lynching and rape, Wells made their work possible and created a revised understanding of lynching that enabled their appeals to be better understood.

Katherine Davis Tillman, along with Florida Ruffin Ridley, Josephine St. Pierre Ruffin's daughter and club leader, and Fannie Barrier Williams, lent Wells public support at a time when Wells would say she needed it. Yet she also alienated potential African American women supporters and activists to whom her work was indebted with her tendency to expose the equivocal positions on lynching taken by leaders of national organizations. Notably, Frances Harper's speech, "Duty to Dependent Races," delivered to the National Council of Women of the United States on 23 February 23, 1891, forged several arguments Wells would come to use only a year and a half later. Harper opened her speech by refusing to include "the negro" in the category of dependent races, arguing that African Americans be regarded as "member[s] of the body politic who ha[ve] a claim upon the nation for justice, simple justice, which is the right of every race, upon the government for protection, which is the rightful claim of every citizen, and upon our common Christianity for the best influences which can be exerted for peace on earth and good–will to man" ("Duty" 36). Wells, following Harper, would also refuse to characterize African Americans as "dependent" or second-class citizens, instead encouraging African Americans to practice "self-help" by recognizing the economic pressure they could exert.

But perhaps the strongest echo of Harper's speech in her anti-lynching work is Harper's stress on civilization: "Our first claim upon the nation and government is the claim for protection to human life. That claim should lie at the basis of our civilization, not simply in theory but in fact. Outside of America, I know of no other civilized country . . . where men are still lynched, murdered, and even burned for real or supposed crimes" ("Duty" 36).[43] Following Harper, Wells, too, would indict America for its hypocritical claim to be a civilized nation and appeal to Christianity in speeches like "Lynching, Our National Crime," delivered at the National Negro Conference in 1909: "No other nation, civilized or savage, burns its criminals; only under the stars and stripes is the human holocaust possible. Twenty-eight human beings burned at the stake, one of them a woman and two of them children, is the awful indictment against American civilization. . . . Why is mob murder permitted by a Christian nation?" (262). Yet despite Wells's obvious affinity with Harper's anti-lynching appeal in "Duty to Dependent Races," Harper would come to criticize Wells at a Purity Congress during the 1895 WCTU national convention in Baltimore. Harper was the only African American woman present at the Purity Congress sessions and was by this time a highly respected national figure in the WCTU. Her critique of Wells indirectly referenced Wells's charges against Frances Willard and took a more optimistic stand on race relations than lynching and racial violence would bear out at the time:

> "I do not approve of Miss Wells' vehemence in dealing with the subject," Mrs. Harper replied slowly and apparently measuring the effect of her words. ["]She is a little too sweeping in her charges . . . and her mind has

been set unduly against the whites. I look at the lynchings as the eruptions of a disease lingering in the body politic, caused by the war. The old-time prejudice still remains, but I believe that it is growing less and less day by day. I do not believe that lynchings of negroes who assault girls are brought about alone by the color of the criminals for I have noticed that some white men who, accused of similar offenses have had summary punishment meted out to them. No, I believe that the white man is coming to treat the opposite race more as brothers." ("About Southern Lynchings")

Whether criticized by those who enabled, in their earlier work, her lynching analysis or by those whose anti-lynching appeals were clearly indebted to her own, Wells occupied a rather fraught position in both African American politics and the anti-lynching movement.

At times Wells was both emulated and denied by those who knew her the longest. Mary Church Terrell echoed Wells in her 1904 article, "Lynching from a Negro's Point of View," published in the prestigious *North American Review,* but she acknowledged neither Wells's influence nor her accomplishments. Like Wells before her, Terrell debunked lynching mythology by citing statistics: "Since three-fourths of the negroes who have met a violent death at the hands of Southern mobs have not been accused of [rape] . . . it is evident that . . . rape is the most unusual of all the crimes for which negroes are shot, hanged, and burned" (855). Borrowing one of Wells's signature rhetorical techniques, Terrell also quoted newspaper coverage that offered horrifying details of mob behavior, including the gathering of souvenirs. And as Wells had in *Lynch Law in Georgia* (1899), Terrell pointed to the pedagogical powers of the press in the lynching of Sam Hose, citing the *Atlanta Constitution*'s five-hundred-dollar reward and its predictions that virtually guaranteed Hose's lynching and gathered thousands of people to participate (Terrell, "Lynching" 859–60). She also cited lynchings of women and children, and the rape and assault of black women and girls, as Wells had. Finally, Terrell linked lynching to slavery as its legacy, violence carried on by subsequent generations in "mobs . . . generally composed of the 'best citizens' of a place, who quietly disperse to their homes as soon as they are certain the negro is good and dead. . . . If the children of the poor whites are the chief aggressors in the lynching-bees . . . it is because their ancestors were brutalized by their slaveholding environment" (861).

If Terrell emulated many of Wells's techniques and repeated her arguments, her analysis was in many ways less sharp than her predecessor's. Offering a problematic argument designed to counter the belief that African American men raped white women because they desired social equality, Terrell's article took a class-based turn that Wells's anti-lynching work avoided. Terrell argued that "the best negroes" did not sympathize with rapists, be they black or white, and that African American rapists were not motivated by a desire for social equality because, as "near brute creation[s]," they had never "heard of social equality," or if they had, they "had no clearer conception of its meaning than [they] had heard of the binomial theorem" (855–56). While Wells would argue that mob violence did not respect class lines in either its victims or its participants, she avoided engaging with contentions that "low-class" African Americans were threatening white womanhood in the South. Nor did she draw a class line among African Americans and their censure of rape.

Terrell's analysis of the press and its pedagogical powers was also far less pointed than Wells's. Her arguments about the press read as equivocal, at once accusing the press of inciting lynching and mob violence and suggesting they simply erred on their "facts": "Instance after instance might be cited to prove that facts bearing upon lynching, as well as upon other phases of the race problem, are often garbled—*without intention, perhaps*—by the press" (860; emphasis added). Yet Terrell had not only published "Lynching from a Negro's Point of View" in a venue Wells's own writings had never appeared in,[44] but her article drew international attention and praise, interestingly enough, from W. T. Stead. While in London en route to address the 1904 International Congress of Women in Berlin, Terrell met Stead and wrote of his "encouragement" in her report for *Voice of the Negro.* "When I met him for the first time, he had already commented upon my articles [*sic*] on lynching, which appeared in the June number of the *North American Review,* in the kindest and most complimentary way," wrote Terrell. The appreciation seems to have been mutual, as Terrell continued: "The colored people of the United States have very few friends who champion their cause so loyally, so fearlessly and so eloquently as Mr. W. T. Stead" ("International" 456–57). Yet Stead, it seems, was slow to come to "the cause," having neither supported Wells nor her efforts nearly ten years earlier, nor recalling her lectures and presence in Britain. Such amnesia was definitive of the latter stages of Wells's anti-lynching career, as new voices and organizations took prominence in efforts to outlaw lynching and in the public imagination.

Anti-lynching efforts shifted in the early 1920s to reach more interracial audiences and promote efforts across the color line to end mob violence. While Wells continued to publish pamphlets at her own expense, and Terrell addressed a primarily white northern audience with "Lynching from a Negro's Point of View," women such as Charlotte Hawkins Brown spoke at inter-racial conferences and worked to enlist the efforts of white southern women in the anti-lynching cause. In an argument that, again, was clearly indebted to Wells's work, Brown referred to herself as a "radical" and accused white southern women of being unwilling to control their men, tempering that in-dictment with a stress on cooperation between women across the color line. "[W]e have become a little bit discouraged. We have begun to feel that you are not, after all, interested in us and I am going still further. The Negro women of the South lay everything that happens to the members of her race at the door of the Southern white woman. Just why I don't know, but we all feel that you can control your men," Brown said. "We feel . . . that, if the white woman would take hold of the situation that lynching would be stopped, mob violence stamped out and yet the guilty would have justice meted out by due course of law and would be punished accordingly" (C. Brown). She also spoke for an end to the insults and assaults upon black womanhood, urging white women to exert their influence with white men: "I want to say to you, when you read in the paper where a colored man has insulted a white woman, just multiply that by one thousand and you have some idea of the number of colored women insulted by white men. . . . I want to ask my friends that while you want to see the criminal who sets upon you punished, won't you help us, friends, to bring to justice the criminal in your race . . . when he tramps on the womanhood of my race. I want you to know, my friends, that we are anxious to work with you to bring about a better citizenship" (C. Brown). At once appealing to a shared sense of womanhood across the color line and stress-ing the differences in white and black women's experiences, Brown walked a fine line between accusation and the solicitation of "friendship" and will-ing cooperation in this speech. Jacquelyn Dowd Hall has called this confer-ence "historic," "the beginning of interracial women's activities" in the South ("Subversive" 363).

The following year, the Southeastern Federation of Colored Women's Clubs presented a position paper on interracial cooperation in anti-lynching and suffrage efforts titled "Southern Negro Women and Race Co-operation." Signed by club leaders such as Lucy Laney, Charlotte Hawkins Brown, Janie Porter Barrett, and Mary McLeod Bethune, the paper "appeal[ed] to white women to [r]aise their voices in immediate protest when lynchings or mob violence is threatened," to "[e]ncourage every effort to detect and punish the leaders and participants in mobs and riots," and to "[e]ncourage the white pulpit and press in . . . outspoken condemnation of these forms of lawlessness" ("Southern"). In a resolution indebted to Wells's analysis of the white press and its pedagogical powers, club women urged white women "to correct this evil" of the white southern press to "give undue prominence to crime and the criminal element among Negroes. . . . We feel that a large part of friction and misunderstanding between the races is due to unjust, inflammatory and misleading headlines and articles appearing in the daily papers" ("Southern"). The early 1920s, then, was a period of calls for interracial cooperation in the anti-lynching cause that ultimately lead to southern white women's organization for better race relations.

This period also saw the organization of the Anti-Lynching Crusaders, lead by Mary Talbert with "an executive committee of 15 supported by over 700 state workers," whose object was to "unite a million women to stop lynching . . . both white and black." *The Crisis* announced the formation of this organization whose first statement stressed the violences suffered by black women: "[T]hey put forward as the first fact in the lynching campaign the horrid truth that 83 American women have been lynched by mobs in the last 30 years in addition to 3,353 men" ("Anti-Lynching Crusaders" 8). Like Wells before them, the Anti-Lynching Crusaders quoted statistics, noting the alleged crimes for which men and women were lynched while asking, "*Is Rape the 'Cause' of Lynching?*" in their circular titled "The SHAME of AMERICA," which stressed the Dyer Anti-Lynching Bill "still before the United States Senate" as "THE REMEDY." "Run as a full-page ad in the *New York Times*," (Schechter 123), the circular directed contributors to send funds to Joel Spingarn, treasurer of the NAACP ("Shame" 167). The Anti-Lynching Crusaders were dubbed "The Ninth Crusade" by Du Bois's *Crisis*, which actively promoted their efforts from November 1922 through the spring of 1923. Intended as a "temporary campaign beginning October 1st [1922] and ending December 31st" of that year, these women were still receiving letters of support sent to *The Crisis* and the NAACP in the spring of 1923 ("Ninth Crusade" 213–14). In a statement seeking financial support mailed to individuals along with the Anti-Lynching Crusaders "Shame of America" circular, Mary Talbert wrote that the organization aimed "to raise at least one million of dollars . . . to help us put over the Dyer Anti Lynching Bill" ("Anti-Lynching Crusaders Statement"). By the spring of 1923, they had raised $10,803.38 ("Ninth Crusade" 214). Even though she fell short of her ambitious fund-raising goal, Talbert's organizing efforts were remarkable, as "within three months after its founding [in July 1922], the group's sixteen original members had expanded to nine hundred. Broader based than the NAACP, the Crusaders . . . had an unpaid staff and a leadership made up of veterans of settlement houses, state federations of Black women's clubs, the YWCA, the Woman's Committee on the Council of National Defense, and the NAACP" (J. Hall, "Anti-lynching Movement" 40).

Although, as Patricia Schechter observes, "almost no journalistic or academic treatments of lynching in this period credited her work in any way" and some "within the NAACP felt that her exposés in the 1890s had succeeded only in hardening southern defensiveness . . . making a new approach necessary" (122), those new approaches and their visibility were unmistakably indebted to Wells's earlier efforts and successes. African American women, whether writing articles, organizing committees, or addressing interracial conferences, worked, as Wells had before them, to keep the victimization of black women an issue of concern and necessary redress, to debunk the mythology of the black male rapist with lynching statistics, to indict the white press for deliberately misinforming and inciting their readers to mob violence, and to stress the responsibility of not just white men but also white women in the lynching and rape of black men, women, and children. Not the work of a solitary black woman alone in the anti-lynching cause, Ida B. Wells's pedagogy of American lynching made possible the analysis and appeals black women after her would pursue, thereby marking, even if leaving largely unacknowledged, her legacy. Yet scholarship on Wells's life and work continues to underscore her position as a lone figure, a controversial militant who became alienated from the very reform circles whose work she was instrumental in advancing. In order to unseat this narrative we must revisit her British tours and place them at the center of how we understand her as not only garnering international attention and press coverage for her work but as actively building a public for her anti-lynching politics by manipulating reform interests and rhetoric for that purpose.

While the marginalized militant is an image Wells herself cultivated, particularly in her autobiography *Crusade for Justice,* she was very much in the thick of British reform and a figure of note in British newspapers during these lecture tours, and it is on these tours that Wells developed and honed the strategies she would go on to use for the remainder of her career. Attending to Wells's work and the press coverage it received on these tours as elements of "making public" an anti-lynching politics shows us a rather different activist than the marginalized figure she would later become. Not simply an outspoken woman who alienated fellow reformers by insisting upon her independent initiatives for change, Wells was adept at appealing to and managing an existing public in order to gain a hearing, interest in her cause, and material support for her politics and she passed those skills to feminists who followed her. In this work, Wells renewed black feminism's visibility in an international reform arena, pulling the British and continental focus away from "white slavery" of trafficking in women to garner censure of "American atrocities." Like black feminists before her, Wells understood the condition of African American women as intimately linked to that of black men, the condition of southern African Americans as inseparable from that of African Americans in the North, and the violent intimidation of them all as a tool of political, social, and economic oppression.

Chapter 5

"We must be up and doing": Feminist Black Nationalism in the Press

"Even though we wish to shun them, and hold ourselves entirely aloof from them, we cannot escape the consequences of their acts. So, that, . . policy and self-preservation would demand that we do go among the lowly, the illiterate, and even the vicious to whom we are bound by the ties of race and sex, and put forth every possible effort to uplift and reclaim them," wrote Mary Church Terrell in the January 1900 issue of the *AME Church Review*. "The purification of the home must be our first consideration and care. It is in the home where woman is really queen, that she wields her influence with the most telling effect," she continued. "In the mind and heart of every good and conscientious woman, the first place is occupied by home" (Terrell, "Duty" 73, 76). Writing on behalf of the National Association of Colored Women (NACW) as its president, Terrell urged *AME Church Review* readers to practice domestic feminism even as she engaged in a view of working-class black women frequently indicted as elitist by contemporary scholars. Seen as the long-awaited moment of the African American woman's entry into public politics, the club movement at the turn into the twentieth century also has been regarded as the seedbed of a domestic black feminism that echoed notions of the republican motherhood by arguing the nation was the home[1] and, therefore, that woman, as caretaker of home and family, was ideally positioned to participate in national political concerns. Regarded as constructing a black middle-class or elite woman as its ideal, the club movement has been said to promote the middle-class woman's responsibility to "lift" the working-class woman "as she climbed," "correct[ing] many of the evils which militate so seriously against us" (Terrell, "Duty" 73).[2]

We would be mistaken, however, if we were to continue to hold the club movement as either the inaugural moment of black female "public" political agitation and organization or its primary form, and to regard domestic feminism as an elitist political discourse promoted exclusively by club women.

Mistaken, too, would be lauding African American women's participation in black nationalist politics as a "first" of the turn into the twentieth century (Romero 54–55).[3] Instead, a thriving feminist black nationalism developed in the journalism of black women as early as the 1830s, a feminist politics that advocated for the concerns of working-class women rather than positioned them as a "problem" that risked tainting "the race." This feminist black nationalism linked the migrant and working-class woman's economic self-sufficiency to the uplift of the race as a whole. Indeed, the writings of black feminist journalists reveal a very different picture of the working-class woman's position within a black nationalist and feminist politics, as they pursue a domestic feminism that does not depend upon her subjugation for its rhetorical force. Together they remind us how varied African American feminism was in the nineteenth century, underscoring the importance of Angela Davis's insistence that there are "multiple African American feminist traditions" (*Blues* xix).

While it is vital to recognize that those multiple traditions included black women promoting a nationalist and feminist politics with working-class women at its center, it is also significant that such a politics was pursued in the press. Here we see early black feminists actively creating a public for their politics in this media, in addition to their work accessing existing publics and reform networks to forward their goals. Indeed, black feminists who saw the press as an important political tool were arguably using its "reflexivity in the circulation of texts among strangers" to shape those readers into what Michael Warner calls "a social entity," a public (*Publics* 11–12), that comes to "exist *by virtue of being addressed*" (*Publics* 67). The "punctual rhythm of circulation" enabled by the press effectively produced "the sense that ongoing discussion [was] unfold[ing] in a sphere of activity" (Warner, *Publics* 96), that feminist black nationalism was a vital and developing politics addressing a like-minded public; and it is this sense of black feminism as building upon an established, while also forging a responsive and contemporary, feminist black nationalist politics that the press arguably made possible for those black feminists who used it.

African American women made significant use of the press from the 1830s onward as a venue for the development of black feminisms. Patrick Rael's argument about the importance of the black press to black politics in general also speaks to black feminism in particular: "Through public media like newspapers, African American elites gained access to the discourse of nation; by constructing those media themselves, they found the capacity to appropriate and reformulate ideas of nation in their own defense" (216). Yet studies of the nineteenth-century black press focus, overwhelmingly, on the male editors of papers and periodicals, giving little, if any, attention to the women who also contributed to them. While black feminist contributions to the American press, both white- and black-operated, were somewhat rare early in the century, by the 1880s and 1890s black women were journalists, edited women's departments, wrote regular columns and edited their own papers. The appearance of Josephine St. Pierre Ruffin's *Woman's Era* in 1894 is the oft-hailed crowning achievement of black women's independence in the periodical press. Focusing on the press as vital to a developing black feminism, this chapter traces the intervention of black feminists in the male-dominated discourse of black nationalism as they argued for improved material conditions for African Americans, drew attention to the particular concerns of black women in the South and North, and appropriated the black nationalist politics of respectability to reposition black women as the agents of a moral uplift that would foster community solidarity.

The black press rivaled only the church in its centrality to nineteenth-century African American political culture and to the black community in general. As Martin Dann observes, the black press was "one of the most potent arenas in which the battle for self-definition could be fought and won. . . . Indeed, black papers were usually the only source of information about the repression of the black community" (13). Early black papers were fostered by the black convention movement, those eleven national conventions held in the Northeast between 1830 and 1861 frequently led by editors of the emergent black press at which "an organized political response to American racism" was formulated. These papers printed convention resolutions, pursued the political agenda set there, and worked to unite free northern blacks (Dann 17). As Frankie Hutton points out, the early black press was a middle-class institution that saw its readership as the free black population of the North even as it sought white readers both for its financial survival and to achieve its goal of shaping white Americans' view of African Americans (39). Hutton estimates that the circulation of most black newspapers from 1827 to 1860 ranged from 1,500 to 3,000, but the actual readership of such papers was "considerably wider" due to the prevalent practice of sharing newspapers within a community.[4] Frederick Detweiler notes this practice was particularly common in the South, where later in the century black papers were routinely read aloud to people gathered in public places like barbershops, a long-established informal site of black political debate (7). This effective lending library of black papers led some editors to estimate that for every "100 copies of the paper" an average of "1,000 readers" existed (qtd. in Detweiler 6).

How many of these readers were African American women is as difficult to determine as is the actual total readership of such papers. However, given that black papers developed "women's departments" and hired African American women to write them, as well as published their letters to the editor, essays, and articles, it is clear that editors saw women as a significant portion of their readership. Indeed, the explosion of the American "mainstream" press at midcentury was the consequence of rising literacy rates; advances in the printing press and resultant mass-production of daily, evening, and penny papers; lowered postal rates; and the rise of American women as a new readership of the newspaper and periodical (Mott 303–4).[5] These factors were also at play in the later growth of the African American press in the 1880s and 1890s. African American literacy was growing at spectacular rates by the late nineteenth century. While 30 percent of the black population was considered literate by 1880, that figure rose to 42.9 percent in 1890 and to 55.5 percent by 1900 (Detweiler 61). Roland Wolseley documents the rate at which black newspapers were established after the Civil War, with 12 founded between the spring of 1865 and January 1866, 68 founded in 1887, and a total of 575 established by 1890 (38).[6]

"By the last decade of the [nineteenth] century, the secular African American press rivaled the pulpit" (Potter 7) in political power and influence, but throughout the nineteenth century, as John Ernest has argued, it was the twinned forces of print culture and oratory that "constituted" and "maint[ained] . . . that imagined nation" that fueled black nationalism (*Liberation* 238). African American women capitalized on the combined rhetorical force of press, platform, and pulpit. However, the power and influence of the press cannot be taken straightforwardly as of and for "the" African American community, North and South. The positioning and address of African American papers was complicated by the fact that, even late in the century, white Americans were the main patrons of black American papers and periodicals while "two-thirds of literate African Americans support[ed] white dailies and weeklies even though they cost more" than black-owned papers (Penn 493). One notable result of this pattern of subscription was the black press's consistent focus on African American women in a politics of racial respectability. Black women were represented as both potential problems in, and the solution to improving white American attitudes toward African Americans. The black press throughout the nineteenth century promoted rather conservative images of women, frequently stressing their place in the home as agents of morality and respectability among the race,[7] rather than presenting African American women as potential or actual participants in public politics. Indeed, Patrick Rael has called respectability "a master value . . . [that] occupied a central place in antebellum black nationalism" (291). We should not underestimate the effect of such representations on both the women and men who read these papers, but neither should we take such images as evidence that African American women acquiesced to such pedagogy in their proper place rather than refashioning it for their own political purposes.

A Feminist Nationalism: Maria Stewart in *The Liberator*

If the African American women contributing to William Lloyd Garrison's "Ladies Department" of *The Liberator* is any indication of how they saw such pronouncements on their role, black women ignored the injunction to keep quiet and to the home.[8] Instead, they ventured into the public space of a white-owned and -operated abolitionist paper and reached their own community as well as white Americans. One such woman, renowned as the earliest American woman, black or white, to take the public platform, was Maria W. Stewart. Born free in 1803 in Hartford, Connecticut, Stewart was orphaned at the age of five and bound out to a clergyman's family until she was fifteen years old. She afterward worked as a domestic servant and at the age of twenty-three married James W. Stewart in Boston, a marriage that would last little more than three years, ending with her husband's death in December 1829. A year later Stewart would suffer the loss of her friend and political mentor, David Walker, whose *Appeal to the Coloured Citizens of the World* (1829) sought to incite African Americans to an armed revolt against the slave system and quite likely resulted in his mysterious death. Stewart was a spiritual woman, whose essays and speeches might well be termed sermons on the condition of African Americans and their role in bettering it. She was affiliated with the Methodist, Baptist, and Episcopal churches and was clearly intimately familiar with the Bible, Watt's hymns, and the political culture that surrounded her in 1830s Boston.

Often hailed as a lone figure effectively run out of Boston just two years after she began speaking in public, Maria Stewart is known primarily as an orator and for her abolitionist arguments, her indictments of the free black population including its male leadership, and her calls to improve black women's material condition and position within the black community. However,

Stewart was also using the press to forward a black feminist politics in the early 1830s, and she was not the only African American woman to do so, nor would she be the only black feminist who would adopt a traditionally male form of invective—the black jeremiad—for her public addresses and writings on black women's rights and black civil rights.[9] We must take care to consider Stewart within the larger context of early black feminism, which includes those preaching women discussed in chapter 1, Sojourner Truth's use of the black jeremiad considered in chapter 3,[10] and early black feminists like Sarah Mapps Douglass and Mary Ann Shadd Cary, who used the press in the 1830s and 1850s to enter the male-dominated discourse of black nationalism and further develop a black feminist voice in the public politics of their day. In his study of antebellum black political culture in the North, Patrick Rael defines black nationalism as comprised of "three general elements": "group conscious-ness built on racial identity and pride," "a desire to develop social and politi-cal institutions autonomous from those of whites," and a "valoriz[ation of] a distinct black cultural heritage" (210). Though black nationalism "often envi-sions the eventual formation of a black state," this is not always an element of this politic.

Stewart's addresses and tracts opened with what are often taken to be disclaimers regarding her intent to enter into political debate. She stressed that while she hoped to "arouse" her readership and audiences "to exertion" (*Religion* 28), she was doing so by divine instruction. "Methinks I heard a spiritual interrogation—'Who shall go forward, and take off the reproach that is cast upon the people of color? Shall it be a woman?' And my heart made this reply," said Stewart to her audience at Franklin Hall on September 21, 1832. "'If this is thy will, be it even so, Lord Jesus!'" ("LECTURE"). Like those preaching women who gained hearings and spiritual strength from the Holi-ness revival and the Second Great Awakening, Stewart's initial communica-tion with the free blacks and whites of Boston emphasizes her conversion and its direct link to her politics. In fact, Stewart published *Religion and the Pure Principles of Morality* in the same year she was converted: "[I]n 1831 [I] made a public profession of my faith in Christ. From the moment I experienced the change, I felt a strong desire, with the help and assistance of God, to devote the remainder of my days to piety and virtue, and now possess that spirit of independence that, were I called upon, I would willing sacrifice my life for the cause of God and my brethren" (*Religion* 29). Stewart suggests that she was not only converted but also, perhaps, sanctified in the phrase "[I] now possess that spirit of independence." She was arguably a product of the same wave of religious enthusiasm that swept the Northeast, bringing women like Rebecca Cox Jackson, Jarena Lee, Zilpha Elaw, Julia Foote, and others before a public to whom they preached conversion, sanctification, black civil rights, and the right of women to preach as we saw in chapter 1.[11]

Taken in such company, we must consider that Stewart was not simply claiming an authority to speak and write as one given her by God, but that her spirituality demanded she labor to ameliorate the condition of her fellow African Americans in a social gospel, placing her firmly within the black nationalist politics of her day. Eddie Glaude notes that the centrality of religion to black politics and black nationalism was marked in the early nineteenth century: "What sets it apart from the ideas of nation that have come to dominate black political debate is its moral component; that is, the nation is imagined not alongside religion but precisely *through* the precepts of black Christianity. . . . [O]ut of black religious life emerged a conception of black national identity" (6; emphasis added). For antebellum northern blacks, political discourse and "political languages were tied to a black Christian imagination" (Glaude 111). Given that black political debate was male dominated at the time, it is hardly surprising that Stewart's gospel was, at times, militant in ways that were conventionally masculine. She dared not only to take to the platform and to the press, but, in doing so, dared also to appropriate to her own purposes the existing political rhetoric and discourse of contemporary black male leaders.

Marilyn Richardson, whose archival work brought the writings and addresses of Maria Stewart to light, has argued that "it is not possible, nor would it be appropriate, to separate [Stewart's] secular documents from the pervasive religious consciousness which informs her analyses. Stewart's intense piety shaped her decidedly evangelical style" ("Preface" xvii). Richardson goes on to contend that Stewart defended herself against the criticism she knew she would receive as a woman speaking in public by "defining herself as a passive instrument in God's hands" ("Introduction" 19). Yet I would argue Stewart's spirituality and evangelism was more than a matter of style or self-defense; rather, it must be regarded as part of that larger black nationalist political discourse that saw black national identity emerge from black Christianity. Stewart sought to "convert" her listeners and readers to the necessity of black Americans to unite, better their condition, resist the colonization movement, and regard the black woman as integral to racial uplift. What Joycelyn Moody refers to as Stewart's "theology of survival" (*Sentimental* 26), we would do well to recognize as a theology of black nationalist solidarity. She repeatedly argued, using the black jeremiad as form, that black self-determination was possible only with a renewed belief and faith in God, a God who would visit retribution upon those who impeded the progress of African Americans.

Rael has traced religious language in black nationalism in the antebellum North, noting that "theodicy and jeremiads" were "meld[ed] . . . with important principles of nationalism" in the rhetoric of black leaders that "told African American northerners they were part of a special community with a divine mission" (266–67). Stewart's jeremiads are black nationalist in Rael's sense, yet they also threatened white Americans who held African Americans in bondage or failed to challenge the slave system with such retribution as well as members of free black communities in the Northeast. And while she knew that men like David Walker, who used the black jeremiad, might pay for such risks with their lives, Stewart was not daunted. She not only risked the anger of slaveholding and proslavery whites but also risked alienating her African American listeners and readers by using a black-male form of politicized critique to call the African American community, particularly its male leadership, to action.

As I noted in chapter 3, the black jeremiad was a "mainly pre–Civil War phenomenon . . . often directed at a white audience. . . . Sometimes its warnings were militant and direct. . . . At other times . . . the tone was that of a friendly warning, couched in the rhetoric of Christian conciliation" (Moses 31, 37). Stewart's warnings were far from "friendly," and as Carla Peterson has pointed out, her "texts constitute invectives directed *primarily* against her own people" (66). In sharp contrast, white Americans were more often the targets of the black jeremiad as men wielded it. Yet even as she gave the black jeremiad this intraracial focus, Stewart pursued the more militant style of the genre favored by male leaders like David Walker, thereby paving the way for its use by black feminists who followed her like Sojourner Truth. Ebony Utley has argued that "Stewart's contribution to black feminist discourse extends . . . [to] her expansion of the jeremiad to include races as well as genders," thereby modeling "the inclusivity and coalition building" foundational to black feminisms (69). Yet that politics appeared particularly challenging at the time and in the form Stewart used.

Stewart's great challenge to free African Americans was to see their own role in their "degraded" material condition rather than continue to blame white Americans for it. In this sense, Stewart was a proponent of religious black nationalism, which "told its adherents . . . [that] maintaining unity required the subordination of individual wills to the greater project of group elevation" (Rael 277). Stewart was both firmly in step with and ahead of her time, undertaking her public career in militant evangelical speaking and writing just two months after Nat Turner's religiously inspired rebellion and two years after Walker published his *Appeal,* yet turning her critique upon her own community while those black male leaders around her were indicting white Americans for the slave system and the colonization scheme that sought to remove African Americans from the United States. Far from a "style" that appealed to divine authority as a sanction for her entrance into public politics, Stewart's social gospel refused to adhere to gender proscriptions of woman's place or established conventions regarding the use of black political rhetoric like the black jeremiad. Stewart's faith was more than self-defense or a "feminine rhetoric of inadequacy" that she used selectively (Peterson 67), but was a politicized belief that she must risk the censure and alienation of her community to bring them her divinely inspired message of racial uplift. Even though Stewart's politics eventually saw her ostracized from Boston's free black community, they nonetheless show us her efforts to enter into the black political debates of her day that fused Christianity with an emerging black nationalism. Stewart referred to her faith as "worth dying for" (*Religion* 33) and repeatedly invoked her martyrdom as inevitable: "I have enlisted in the holy warfare, and Jesus is my captain; and the Lord's battle I mean to fight, until my voice expire in death. I expect to be hated of all men, and persecuted even unto death, for righteousness and the truth's sake" ("Afric-American Female Intelligence Society"). As Marilyn Richardson has observed, "[R]eligious and social justice are so closely allied in her analysis that to her mind, one could not be properly served without a clear commitment to the other" ("Maria" 18).

Stewart used the press astutely to forward that social gospel. Shortly after William Lloyd Garrison opened *The Liberator* offices in Boston, and after she quite likely read of his interest in woman's influence in abolition,[12] Stewart approached Garrison and Isaac Knapp in October 1831 with a completed manuscript. Garrison "struck off in tract form" Stewart's *Religion and The Pure Principles of Morality, The Sure Foundation On Which We Must Build* that year (Garrison qtd. in Richardson, "Introduction" 11). Stewart approached a white abolitionist paper undoubtedly because there was only one African American paper operative at the time, the *African Sentinel and Journal of Liberty* (1831–32), and it was published in Albany, New York (Pride and Wilson 28 n.16).[13] But since 80 percent of *The Liberator*'s initial 450 subscribers were free African Americans, with black "organizations, churches, societies, and prosperous Negro businessmen either donat[ing] funds or [buying] blocks of subscriptions" to *The Liberator* (Pride and Wilson 26), Stewart clearly sought to reach a predominantly African American audience with her publications there.[14]

While Stewart's oratorical critiques of the free black community of the Northeast are celebrated in scholarship on her life and work, she was a "published writer before she was a public speaker" (Richardson, "Introduction" 26). We should not underestimate her decision to use the press to forward her aims. Stewart was familiar with *Freedom's Journal,* the first paper owned, operated, and edited by African Americans and in print from March 16, 1827, to March 28, 1829. In what may have been her first foray into the pages of a newspaper, Stewart wrote the paper's editors to caution against the exclusion of black women in a politics of racial uplift (Moody, *Sentimental* 26). *Freedom's Journal* would hardly have encouraged its female readers to take to public politics, however, given its tendency to publish pieces chastising women who did not hold their tongues: "A babbling tongue is the 'object of my implacable disgust'" ("Observer No. V").[15] Yet it did publish the proceedings of female benevolent society meetings, an early form of black women's political culture and often the training ground for black women who would enter public politics through reform. Such societies enjoyed community approval and support from the late 1820s into the 1840s.[16]

As James and Lois Horton document, "[B]lack women not only contributed to the welfare of their community" but also "participated in the political discourse of the day" through benevolent societies and associations, "a role unfamiliar to most American women of the time" (128). In this way, Stewart would have been aware of the tendency of African American male leaders and the black press to permit women public roles that appeared to leave the status quo and its male-dominated nationalist politics unchallenged, even as those roles enabled African American women to participate in central political debates via benevolent and mutual-aid societies. She identified *The Liberator* early in its publication as sympathetic to women, even though it, too, permitted women a voice in its pages in socially sanctioned ways through its Ladies' Department. In other words, even as Garrison and Knapp would prove supportive of Maria Stewart's work and goals, she knew that publishing in the press far from guaranteed an African American woman the liberty of expressing her political views or of having them favorably received. Still, Stewart ventured well beyond the sanctioned space of the benevolent society to speak to her community and to white Bostonians not only in person from the platform but also in print, thereby reaching more people than could, or were inclined to, attend her addresses.[17]

The Liberator was a powerfully militant antislavery weekly that promoted immediate emancipation for a remarkable thirty-five-year run. Subscriptions were two dollars per year for a "lively mixture of excerpts from the religious and temperance press, factual material on slavery, reports of meetings held to protest the slave trade or register opposition to colonization schemes, inspiring verses from Cowper and Byron and the black literary societies, and provocative letters from readers and the editorial fraternity" (Mayer 114). *The Liberator* expanded by its second volume, enabling Garrison to give "increasing prominence to women's voices, both black and white," and to devote some of that additional space to "a weekly column of news about female antislavery societies" (Mayer 133). African American female abolitionists published under pseudonyms in Garrison's paper: Sarah Mapps Douglass as Zillah and Sophanisba and Sarah Forten as Ada and Magawisca. Garrison envisioned *The Liberator* as a forum for black activists and an interracial political coalition and represented the free northern African American community as politically active and organized by reporting on their meetings denouncing colonization. Such representations of abolition politics, black, white, and interracial, reached not only *The Liberator's* readers in Boston and the Northeast but also southerners who had come to see the paper as threatening the stability of the slaveholding system.[18] As Henry Mayer documents, "Southern editors not only saw the paper but reprinted material from it—accompanied by bitter condemnation—which was then picked up by other papers and eventually worked over again by Garrison in a lively cycle that . . . enabled *The Liberator* to make a noise out of proportion to its size or subscription base" (117). It is important to remember, then, that Stewart's addresses, excerpt and essay had the potential to reach readers not only in Boston and New England, but also across the Mason and Dixon line.

The way in which Garrison presented Stewart's addresses to *The Liberator's* readership suggests that their reprinting was a deliberate part of her politics, much like her first approach to him. In the October 9, 1831, issue of *The Liberator,* Garrison advertised "a tract addressed to the people of color, by Mrs Maria W. Steward [*sic*], a respectable colored lady of this city." Stewart's tract, *Religion and the Pure Principles of Morality,* sold for six cents, and Garrison promised "extracts in the paper hereafter" ("For sale"). He published the first, and what appears to be the only, extract in the Ladies' Department of the January 7, 1832, edition. Whether Garrison chose it or Stewart did is something we cannot know, yet the extract's focus on African American women suggests it may well have been Stewart who selected it.

This extract opens and closes with Stewart's call to the free black community to "unite, heart and soul, and . . . let us promote and respect ourselves," a classic black nationalist tenet of self-sufficiency ("Essays"). The black community of Boston had entered a period of political dissension come the late 1820s and early 1830s, of which Walker's *Appeal* "was the most public manifestation . . . [as it rent] black organizing activity" (Reed 68). Yet Stewart had feminist goals in mind as she called for community solidarity at what James and Lois Horton call a "watershed" moment for "black identity" (191),[19] when a rising generation of political activists saw Africa as "heritage" and their "home" as the United States. Reed argues that this generational shift was also marked by a shift from interracial cooperation to a more radical politics (69). In *Religion,* Stewart argued that the liberation of African Americans from slavery was possible only with the unification of the black community (30) but particularly focused on the liberation of African American women from domestic service to whites: "How long shall the fair daughters of Africa be compelled to bury their minds and talents beneath a load of iron pots and kettles?" ("Essays"). Stewart foregrounded the effective segregation of black women in northern labor markets, limited mainly to domestic service that working white women shunned, and the competition they also faced as an influx of German and Irish immigrants brought African Americans into more serious competition with whites for employment after 1820 (Horton and Horton 165).[20] The liberation Stewart spoke of was possible, for her, only with the unification of the free black community, whose members would "promote and patronize each other."

But for Stewart the black woman was the object of neither a male-led racial uplift nor white philanthropy. Rather, she saw African American women contributing a part of their earnings for a school that would educate them: "Shall it any longer be said of the daughters of Africa, they have no ambition, they have no force? By no means. Let every female heart become united, and let us raise a fund ourselves . . . that the higher branches of knowledge might be enjoyed by us" ("Essays"). Stewart advocated what Gayle Tate has identified as a link between black women's labor and activism in the antebellum North: "Black women were laborers and activists in all phases of the community's development and utilized economic and political participation as a springboard to their political and social agenda" (67). Stewart had been a domestic laborer and knew, firsthand, free black women's material conditions even as she envisioned their political potential. While the black national convention movement and the black press was targeting African American women as the objects of moral concern, responsible for either the improved reputation of "the race" or its moral downfall depending upon whether black women heeded black men's call for moral improvement, Maria Stewart was focused on their mental and material elevation through their own economic solidarity.

Marilyn Richardson has argued that Stewart drew significant attention to, and critiqued, the "domestic double standard" to which black women were subjected by Boston's labor market and a gendered politics of respectability that saw "the home their proper sphere" even as it was their necessary workplace, given their wages were crucial to "keep[ing] their households afloat" ("Maria" 29). Yet with her call for women's education Stewart explicitly challenged both that gender politics of racial respectability and the black convention movement's exclusive focus on the education of African American men, a focus that would develop into the 1833 proposal of a "mechanical arts" high school and a college in New Haven, Connecticut. Stewart's call for the higher education of African American women also emerged in the context of Prudence Crandall's academy for black women, founded in 1833 in Canterbury, Connecticut, when her school for girls, first established in 1831, drew censure because she had admitted an African American pupil. For Stewart, any program to educate African Americans must include women and should not be limited strictly to a program of manual arts; rather, the black woman must be elevated beyond such labor by her own efforts and through her pursuit of "higher branches of knowledge." Effectively, Stewart's call both supported Crandall's academy but also marked the necessity for more such opportunities for African American women.

Stewart's argument for black female self-help, self-sufficiency, and access to higher education also had a particular resonance by appearing in *The Liberator*'s Ladies' Department headed, as it was, with the "Am I not a Woman and a Sister?" emblem. The emblem—depicting a kneeling, chained female slave, arms clasped in a pleading gesture—was designed to convey the need for the black female slave's liberation by sympathetic white women, thereby recruiting white women to abolition. While Stewart might present the "good [white] women of Wethersfield, Connecticut," who cultivated and sold enough onion seed to build a church, as an example "worthy of imitation," it was the black woman who would free herself from "iron pots and kettles," not the white woman who would break her chains ("Essays"). Often contrary

to the politics *The Liberator* and Garrison espoused, Stewart pursued her own
political messages. Refusing to position the African American as passive victim and object of white philanthropy, Stewart called upon black women to
raise themselves through diligence and economy.

Publishing her addresses after their delivery seems also to have been
Stewart's idea, as the disclaimer Garrison published in the April 28, 1832,
edition indicates: "It is proper to state that the Address of Mrs. Stewart, in our
Ladies' Department to-day, is published at her own request, and not by desire
of the Society before whom it was delivered" ("It is . . ."). Evidently Garrison
found it necessary to include this disclaimer to reinforce the heading "For the
Liberator" that preceded the text of Stewart's address to the Afric-American
Female Intelligence Society of Boston. In addition, Stewart's lecture at Franklin Hall appeared in the November 17, 1832, edition of *The Liberator* "BY
REQUEST," as the parenthetical heading ran for this speech delivered on September 21. Clearly, Stewart was deliberately seeking out the press as a venue
for her politics, thereby reinforcing her platform appearances and giving her
political program additional force.[21]

Though a significant part of Stewart's political message, her black nationalism has been largely ignored by a body of scholarship that attends, instead,
to her abolitionism and her texts as spiritual narratives.[22] I would argue, however, that key to understanding Stewart's work and importance is an attention
to her decision to publish her addresses and excerpt from *Religion,* with their
black nationalist messages, in a newspaper given the work of this genre in the
formation of what Benedict Anderson has called the "imagined community"
of the nation. Particularly, the act of reading the paper, or what Anderson
calls an "extraordinary mass ceremony [of] . . . simultaneous consumption,"
unites readers unknown to each other and separated by space and situation.
"It is performed in silent privacy. . . . Yet each communicant is well aware that
the ceremony he performs is being replicated simultaneously by thousands (or
millions) of others of whose existence he is confident, yet of whose identity he
has not the slightest notion. . . . What more vivid figure for the . . . imagined
community [of the nation] can be envisioned?" asks Anderson. "At the same
time, the newspaper reader, observing exact replicas of his own paper being
consumed by his . . . neighbours, is continually reassured that the imagined
world is visibly rooted in everyday life . . . creating that remarkable confidence of community in anonymity which is the hallmark of modern nations"
(35–36). The convention movement and the early black press it conceived
and supported were the twinned forums for early-nineteenth-century black

nationalist politics, such that the link Anderson writes of between nationalism and the newspaper was one actively forged by black male political leaders from the 1830s through to the Civil War. Indeed, as John Ernest has documented, by the late 1830s papers like the *Colored American* in articles titled "Elevation of Our People" stressed the importance "for African Americans to 'cultivate a reading disposition' as the foundational step toward a long process of elevation and communal self-determination" (*Liberation* 295).

It is striking that the agenda for the first national black convention in Philadelphia held September 20, 1830, is also Stewart's political agenda as forwarded in her speeches and publications in *The Liberator:* "emigration, opposition to the American Colonization Society, and issues of education and self-help" (Glaude 113). Clearly, Stewart aimed to take a central position in the black political debates of her day. Established to build black solidarity and community in the face of white mob violence in the late 1820s,[23] the national black convention movement's largest delegations were from New York and Pennsylvania, but the movement was not exclusively a northern one; rather, delegates also participated from Virginia, Maryland, and the District of Columbia (Horton and Horton 208). The conventions began debating the advantages of African American emigration to Canada as a response to such violence. Northern free African Americans had opposed the African Colonization Society (ACS) almost at its inception in late December 1816, believing that the ACS, with its slaveholder membership, aimed to "remove free blacks, the strongest voices against slavery in the nation" (Horton and Horton 188).[24] Indeed, as Patrick Rael documents, the ACS understood free African Americans as "especially dangerous" and characterized them "as . . . more vicious and degraded than any other which our population embraces . . . a ragged set, . . . notoriously ignorant, degraded and miserable, [and] mentally diseased" (qtd. in Rael 160). By the 1830s the ACS had become quite powerful, and African American leaders campaigned to diminish its influence, while free African Americans called local meetings to protest African colonization and support Canadian emigration in its stead. Those debates were also pursued at the national black conventions. However, by 1832 the focus of convention meetings would shift to promote a politics of respectability. The convention movement came to reject emigration to Canada, focusing instead on the formation of temperance societies and the establishment of a high school and "mechanical arts" college for men.

From 1835 to 1842, the convention movement was known as the American Moral Reform Society, a "controversial transmutation" which took "education, temperance, and economic self-sufficiency as its rallying points" (Glaude 127). While the society took up "the full sweep of Garrisonian multi-reformism," it was seen as having abandoned the black nationalism of the convention movement (Ernest, *Liberation* 251). However much African American women may have been seen as the objects of a politics of racial respectability, as reflected in their representation in early black newspapers, they were not permitted to participate in the convention movement itself until 1840. For Stewart to pursue a similar political agenda in the early 1830s and insist that it include African American women, on both the platform and in the press, is nothing short of extraordinary. That she was not the only African American woman to do so at the time, but was joined by Sarah Mapps Douglass, as we shall see, is remarkable. Yet histories of black feminism have made little if anything of this fact.[25] Indeed, scholars continue to place the emergence of "female uplift ideology" at the turn into the twentieth century, or "woman's era," as Frances Harper dubbed it: "At the turn of the century, African American periodicals contained numerous articles linking the needs and aspirations of black women to the advancement of the race. As a result, womanhood and domesticity became powerful tropes in the language of racial uplift during the Progressive period" (Wolcott 14). Yet at least sixty years earlier, Maria Stewart was contending that women, working women in particular, were central to the achievement and success of community self-sufficiency and racial advancement.

In the excerpt of *Religion* published in *The Liberator,* Stewart urged the free black community to pursue a program of economic self-help in the form of a store selling "dry goods and . . . groceries"[26] and a program of political self-interest: "Sue for your rights and privileges. Know the reason that you cannot attain them. Weary them with your importunities. You can but die, if you make the attempt; and we shall certainly die if you do not" ("Essays"). Stewart's vision of an economically self-sufficient black community challenged that promoted by the black convention movement in one significant regard: she argued for that self-sufficiency in the urban centers where African Americans already worked and lived, while convention delegates like Austin Steward and Bishop Richard Allen "urged blacks to leave the city and acquire farms," believing that the effects of racial prejudice in the North were "less potent in the country" than in the city and that through farming African Americans could "act with a degree of independence" (qtd. in Horton and Horton 209).

The reality of urban African American women's labor opportunities and resulting skills made farming an unrealistic form of self-support, since they were primarily limited to the wage labor of domestic service, as Stewart well knew. The convention movement's promotion of farming as a "solution" to the northern urban racism and violence affecting free African Americans was strongly gendered, a viable option for black men, perhaps, but less so for black women. For Stewart, the black woman was central to a politics of self-sufficiency that included urban businesses operated and supported by blacks and an educated community of both men and women as key forms of African American self-improvement. Given that education was a long-held value that African Americans linked to freedom, Stewart effectively made the African American woman key to the liberation of "the race" from both slavery in the South and menial labor in the North. Far from the object of concern for the race's respectability, the black woman was cast as an active player—wage earner and student—in Stewart's model of racial uplift and as political activist by Stewart's example. Both models of black womanhood directly challenged the supportive and secondary roles women were expected to play in black politics. Implicitly casting African Americans as an independent "nation" by referring repeatedly to whites as "the Americans," Stewart outlined her program for black liberation and put educated and self-sufficient black women at its center: "Possess the spirit of independence. The Americans do, and why should not you?" ("Essays").

In her first Boston address at the invitation of the Afric-American Female Intelligence Society, reprinted in the April 28, 1832, edition of *The Liberator,* Stewart indicted African American clergy for advocating what she saw as inaction when "there was no peace," cited historical examples of nationalist movements including the French and Haitian revolutions as she urged blacks to unite, and contended that even though African Americans were "despised above all the nations upon the earth," they were a nation nonetheless.[27] In her second Boston address at Franklin Hall on September 21, 1832, the site of regular monthly meetings of the New England Anti-Slavery Society, Stewart pursued a black nationalist politics on several fronts, opening with her opposition to colonization and her call for African American solidarity and self-help: "Why sit we here and die? If we say we will go to a foreign land, the famine and the pestilence are there, and there we shall die" ("LECTURE"). Indicting the inaction she saw around her, Stewart called on her community to improve their condition, one she saw as "little better" than "southern slavery," for "there are no chains so galling as the chains of ignorance" that bind African Americans to "lives of continual drudgery and toil" ("LECTURE").[28] While the black male leaders of the convention movement promoted a politics of respectability that emphasized black manhood as "self-assertive and independent, capable of leading and protecting their families and . . . the nation" and "disciplined the activities of black women with such notions as 'protection' and 'true womanhood'" (Glaude 121), Stewart charged both black men and women with improving the race's image in the eyes of whites. She left the black nation, "the American free people of color," unmarked by gender, insisting implicitly that it include not only black men but black women as active agents: "[W]ere the American free people of color to turn their attention more assiduously to moral worth and intellectual improvement, this would be the result:—prejudice would gradually diminish, and the whites would be compelled to say,—Unloose those fetters!" ("LECTURE").

Finally, Stewart closed her address with a direct invocation of black nationalism as forged in opposition to oppression by likening the political effort she called for to the founding of the United States itself. "Did the pilgrims, when they first landed on these shores, quietly compose themselves, and say, 'The Britons have all the money and all the power, and we must continue their servants forever'? . . . No—they first made powerful efforts to raise themselves, and then God raised up those illustrious patriots, Washington and Lafayette, to assist and defend them. And, my brethren, have you made a powerful effort?" asked Stewart. "Have you prayed the legislature for mercy's sake to grant you all the rights and privileges of free citizens, that your daughters may rise to that degree of respectability which true merit deserves, and your sons above the servile situations which most of them fill?" ("LECTURE").

The "nation" that Stewart "re-presented" to *The Liberator*'s African American readership injected a black feminist voice into black nationalist political debates, repeatedly recasting black women as full participants in the pursuit of an economically self-determined, educated, and politicized black nation within the United States. Stewart's calls to "unite" were also issued within the pages of a newspaper read weekly, so that her readership could "perform" a shared imagining of a liberated black community and a solidarity with others engaged in similar activities and sharing similar political views. In fact, Stewart directly invited the audience, and subsequently her readership, of her Franklin Hall address to partake of just such imagining by invoking her own participation in a shared community as a newspaper reader. Immediately following a powerful assertion of her place in both the larger nation and the black community she was calling to unite, Stewart took on colonizationist notions of black inferiority. "I can but die for expressing my sentiments: and I am as willing to die by the sword as the pestilence; for I am a true born American; your blood flows in my veins, and your spirit fires my breast," insisted Stewart.

"I observed a piece in the Liberator a few months since, stating that the colonizationists had published a work respecting us, asserting that we were lazy and idle. I confute them on that point. Take us generally as a people, we are neither lazy nor idle," she continued, "and considering how little we have to excite or stimulate us, I am almost astonished that there are so many industrious and ambitious ones to be found" ("LECTURE"). Stewart presented herself, exemplary of black women in general, as abreast of and fully engaged with the most significant political situations facing free black Americans at the time. She invited her listeners and readers to educate themselves, as she did, by reading the newspaper and contributions like hers and through that act to become part of a community she and other black nationalists were urging to fight for their rights as "true born" Americans.

Clearly, Maria Stewart went too far, as evidenced by the rejection she suffered by Boston's free black community. Like central black feminist figures who were her contemporaries and those who would follow, Stewart was rejected by her fellow African Americans.[29] Even before she daringly indicted black male leaders in her Masonic Hall lecture, reprinted in two *Liberator* installments in late April and early May, Stewart was registering the effects of entering male-dominated debates in the early 1830s, telling her audience at the Afric-American Female Society lecture that "my soul has been so discouraged within me, that I have almost been induced to exclaim, 'Would to God that my tongue hereafter might cleave to the roof of my mouth and become silent forever!'" ("For the Liberator"). Demanding that her audience not "applaud the dandy that talks largely on politics, without striving to assist his fellow in the revolution" in her Masonic Hall speech when secret societies, like the Masons, were favored by African American men and central to black male political culture, Stewart imperiled her position in Boston even further ("An Address . . . Concluded").

While I would argue that Stewart's rather scathing critique of male leadership in such a "distinctively male space" was daring, to say the least, and not "a fatal rhetorical miscalculation" (Peterson 68), it does seem to have effectively ended her political career in Boston. She gave her farewell address seven months later. Advertised in *The Liberator* as focused "on her own christian experience, and the all important subject of religion," Stewart's farewell address was her final opportunity to espouse her feminist black nationalism in "the African school room" of the African Meeting House on the evening of September 18, 1833 ("Notice"). Marilyn Richardson notes the importance of this venue as the "center of community activity and protest in antebellum black Boston" ("What If?" 202). Even as she took her leave from Boston and the most public moments of her political career, Stewart took her feminist arguments to the black community's political center: "[B]e no longer astonished then, my brethren and friends, that God at this eventful period should raise up your own females to strive by their example both in public and private, to assist those who are endeavoring to stop the strong current of prejudice that flows so profusely against us at present. No longer ridicule their efforts, it will be counted for sin" ("Farewell Address" 69).

Maria Stewart left Boston in 1833 for New York City, where she joined a Female Literary Society, attended the 1837 Woman's Anti-Slavery Convention (Richardson, "Introduction" 27), went to school for seven years (Hatton 93), and taught in Manhattan and Brooklyn. Her departure from Boston was not the end of her public recognition as a black woman of note, nor was it the end of her political career. Stewart continued to be visible in the press and to lecture after she left Boston, becoming a "regular contributor" to the AME Church's *Repository of Religion and Literature, and of Science and Art* in the late 1850s to mid-1860s (Richardson, "What If" 205 n. 1).[30] Abolitionist William C. Nell wrote *The Liberator* on March 5, 1852, to recall that in the early 1830s, "Mrs. Maria W. Stewart—fired with a holy zeal [—delivered] . . . public lectures [that] awakened an interest acknowledged and felt to this day" (Richardson, *Maria W. Stewart* 90). Stewart had this letter reprinted in the 1879 edition of her collected works, *Meditations from the Pen of Mrs. Maria W. Stewart,* which she financed with her hard-won widow's pension and sold for thirty-five cents a copy.[31] The effect was to suggest that she had never left the minds of abolitionists during the forty-odd years since her controversial Boston lectures.

Sarah Mapps Douglass, Mary Ann Shadd Cary, and Jennie Carter

Just three weeks before Stewart's Afric-American Female Intelligence Society lecture appeared in *The Liberator* (April 28, 1832), with its focus on African American women's roles in black nationalist efforts, Sarah Mapps Douglass published "Moonlight" in the Ladies' Department. Born free in Philadelphia on September 9, 1806, Sarah Douglass was a member of the interracial Philadelphia Female Anti-Slavery Society, which her mother, Grace Bustill Douglass, had helped found in 1833. Douglass was a teacher and in the 1820s had opened a school for African American children in Philadelphia (Lerner,

Notable 1: 511). She not only dared to be active in abolition at a time when attending abolition meetings was "a life-threatening activity" (Yee 21), but, like Maria Stewart, also entered the male-dominated debates over emigration and colonization. Like Stewart, Douglass would today be regarded by some scholars of black nationalism as an integrationist or "weak" nationalist, one who "believ[ed] that blacks had to become fully integrated" in American society (Conaway 227).

Such scholarship tends to oppose integrationist or assimilationist nationalism to separatist nationalism, an opposition that Patrick Rael argues is a misleading, retrospective reading of black nationalism in the nineteenth century through a twentieth-century political lens.[32] "Calls for separate black institutions are often taken as evidence that black leaders pursued a strategy of cultural separation. In noting that their calls for separate institutions were qualified by their universalism, it would be easy to suggest the opposite—that spokespersons ultimately pursued a strategy of integration and cultural assimilation, even if they used separation as an intermediate stop-gap," writes Rael. "Yet neither claim will suffice. To argue that black leaders sought separation only as a temporary and pragmatic response to oppression is not to argue that black thought was ultimately integrationist or assimilationist, for to do so would be to remain bound by modern-day terms of debate, which fail to appreciate the mental world of the antebellum North. Black leaders viewed their efforts, and hence constructed their identity as a race, as the public struggle for their political liberty and rights in a republic" (52). Indeed, in the feminist black nationalism this chapter explores, varied positions on emigration and integration are taken yet all are recognizably black nationalist in their politics. "Moonlight," Douglass's first foray into black nationalist politics in *The Liberator*'s pages, was rather subtle. Ostensibly contemplating the death of friends, Douglass recalled her "happy schooldays,—my school companions. . . . O, my heart! where are they now? Two or three have left their native city for a foreign land; others have passed away" ("Moonlight"). Likening emigration to death, Douglass closed with her understated "hope" that African Americans would yet become citizens of the nation, rather than be forced to establish colonies in "foreign" lands: "Hope whispers,—'The time is not far distant, when the wronged and enslaved children of America shall cease to be a "by-word and a reproach" among their brethren'" ("Moonlight").

Signing her *Liberator* contributions "Zillah" and "Sophanisba," Douglass contributed regularly to the Ladies' Department throughout 1832 and contributed as Zillah to *The Emancipator* in 1833.[33] Come late July 1832,

Douglass would debate emigration with *The Liberator*'s readers. "You do not agree with me in regard to emigration. Would that I had eloquence enough to convince you that I am right!" she wrote. "If we should bend our steps to Hayti, there is no security for life and property. . . . If we go to Mexico, it is the same there. Why throw ourselves upon the protection of Great Britain, when thousands of her own children are starving? Do you suppose she can feel more love for us than she does for her own?" ("Extract"). As James and Lois Horton document, Haiti had actively sought to attract African American immigration since 1804. By 1818, the Haitian government was offering African Americans land and their passage paid, and in the 1820s Jonathan Granville, a charismatic Haitian military officer, traveled through the American Northeast and the upper South lecturing on the advantages of Haitian emigration to "large and enthusiastic" African American audiences (Horton and Horton 193). The Haitian Emigration Society was formed in Philadelphia in 1824, and by the 1830s some eight thousand to thirteen thousand African Americans had emigrated to Haiti, only to experience sickness and hardship. In order to keep African American immigrants in the rural areas they were expected to settle, the Haitian government instituted the Rural Code of 1826, which African Americans experienced as enforcing "slave-like plantation labor" (Horton and Horton 196).

By the early 1830s, when Sarah Douglass was writing on emigration for *The Liberator,* the disappointments of Haitian emigration and opposition to the ACS had rendered debates over emigration and colonization highly charged. Some African Americans were participating in Liberian colonization, yet reports raised fears of their endangered health. Canada emerged as a viable alternative, said to have a healthier climate (Horton and Horton 197–99). At the national black conventions Canadian emigration was seriously discussed as a route to African American independence in the early to mid-1830s. However, black leaders were also ambivalent about Canada as a site for black settlements, fearing it would create the perception that African Americans had relinquished their fight for rights in the United States. From the 1830s through the 1860s, forty thousand African Americans emigrated to Canada, more than emigrated to either Haiti or Africa, while the vast majority of African Americans remained in the United States (Horton and Horton 211).

Finding Haiti and Canada wanting as suitable colonies for African Americans, Sarah Douglass rejected emigration altogether in her *Liberator* writings, and stood firm when a reader, "Woodby," wrote to challenge her.

Just as Stewart fused her social gospel with her black nationalist arguments, Douglass invoked God as ordaining that African Americans remain in their "own, native land": "I firmly believe it is his will that we remain. I would not give up this belief for a thousand worlds. . . . Cease, then, to think of any other city of refuge. Listen to the voice of our dear Redeemer! . . . 'Fear not, little flock; it is your Father's good pleasure to give you the kingdom'" ("Reply to Woodby"). With Douglass's debate with "Woodby," *The Liberator*'s readers saw enacted that "imagined" community actively engaged in black nationalist political debates as they were being infused with women's voices and a black feminist politics, a community with which they were being invited to identify by contributions like Douglass's and Stewart's.

Perhaps inspired by Stewart's *Religion* excerpt and her essay "Cause for Encouragement," Douglass also argued for the importance of religion as a unifying force for social change in "Family Worship," published in the September 8, 1832, edition of *The Liberator*. Inviting her readers to watch the Lindsey family through their "open window," Douglass depicted the Lindseys reading the Bible and praying together as her ideal of "christian religion productive of . . . good." The race, like a family, if engaged in such prayer and worship would "disperse the mists of prejudice which surround us! Yes, religion and education would raise us to an equality with the fairest in our land" ("Family"). Fusing both a black nationalist politics of respectability and an emphasis upon education as liberating and equalizing with a social gospel that advocated religion's role in social amelioration, Douglass joined Stewart in the Ladies' Department, amplifying the messages of Stewart's January, April, and July publications.[34] Yet Douglass also offered a difference. While Stewart repeatedly called for African Americans to unite in self-sufficient community, Douglass called for a future of interracial cooperation in the June 30, 1832, edition. For Douglass, the races must come to interact socially rather than allow the racist "persecution" that African Americans "have suffered" to continue. "I see black and white mingle together in social intercourse, without a shadow of disgust appearing on the countenance of either," wrote Douglass. "And what has wrought this mighty change? Religion, my sister; the religion of the meek and lowly Jesus" ("Extract").

Douglass and other black feminists of the 1830s and 1840s seemed to have well understood the power and importance of the press as a venue for black feminism. While Douglass would advocate religion as instrumental in the interracial cooperation she promoted in the summer of 1832, she also clearly valued black feminist community and its continued participation in, and transformation of, a black nationalist politics. As we learned in chapter 2, Sarah Mapps Douglass helped found the all-black Women's Association of Philadelphia in 1848 to support "Frederick Douglass's call for black nationalism" (Dunbar 95). Its constitution's preamble, written by black nationalist Martin Delany, stressed "self-elevation" and "self-exertion" and a program of fund raising through fairs and bazaars that would "support . . . the Press and Public Lecturers devoted to the Elevation of the Colored People" (qtd. in M. Jones 83). The association clearly articulated its intention to participate in black nationalist efforts and its sense that the press was central to such a politics: "Whereas, believing Self-Elevation to be the only true issue upon which to base our efforts as an oppressed portion of the American people; and believing . . . that the Press and Public Lecturer are the most powerful means by which an end so desirable can be attained" (qtd. in Sterling 117).[35]

Come the 1850s, African American women would not only recognize the importance of contributing to the press in order to advance their feminist politics, but one would venture to edit and publish her own newspaper. Mary Ann Shadd Cary, best known as the first African American woman to establish her own paper, *The Provincial Freeman,* was free born in Wilmington, Delaware, on October 9, 1823.[36] Her father, Abraham Shadd, was an abolitionist, active in both the black national convention movement and debates regarding black emigration to Canada. The Shadd family's move north to West Chester, Pennsylvania, in 1833 was likely precipitated by "the increasing severity of Delaware's black codes" (Rhodes 13); once there, they became active in the Underground Railroad and Mary Ann was educated. She taught school in the 1840s and early 1850s as she became active in abolition. In September 1851, Shadd Cary attended the Great North American Anti-Slavery Convention in Toronto, and "within a few days" of its end she had decided to leave the United States for Canada West to "join the emigration movement in body as well as spirit" (Rhodes 34).

Before she left the United States, Shadd Cary became visible in the black press with her March 24, 1849, letter to Frederick Douglass's *North Star* on improving the condition of free blacks in the North. Like Maria Stewart nearly two decades earlier, Shadd Cary would indict the black community's central political institution, the black church, charging that its clergy was "corrupt . . . sapping our every means, and . . . inculcating ignorance as a duty. . . . [I]t does really seem to me that our distinctive churches and the frightfully wretched instruction of our ministers . . . is attributable more of the downright degradation of the free colored people of the North, than from the effect of public opinion" ("Power"). And like Stewart, Shadd Cary also published a pamphlet, *Hints to the Colored People of the North*—on the self-determination of free northern African Americans—that was excerpted in Douglass's *North Star* in the early summer of 1849.[37] Jane Rhodes summarizes Shadd Cary's notion of racial uplift: "Education, moral refinement, and economic self-sufficiency were, in her view, inextricably connected to the fight against slavery and racism" (22). Undoubtedly these ideas were influenced by the black national convention movement in which her father participated, given the way they echo the black nationalist politics developed there. I want to underscore, however, that Shadd Cary's racial uplift also echoed Maria Stewart's even as her entrance into public politics via the press mirrored Stewart's earlier political program in Boston. Shadd Cary may have "inherited" a black nationalist political stance, but it was one inflected with a feminist politics and was arguably indebted to the work of Maria Stewart decades earlier.

The *Provincial Freeman* was initially published listing abolitionist Samuel Ringgold Ward as its editor on March 24, 1853. Subscriptions for the weekly four-page broadsheet of seven columns per page were $1.50 per year (Rhodes 74). Shadd Cary would not identify herself as the *Provincial Freeman*'s editor in its pages until August 26, 1854, when in response to a letter to the editor addressing her, as such letters always did, as Mr. M. A. Shadd, Shadd Cary corrected this "misapprehension . . . occasioned, no doubt, by the habit we have of using initials, we would simply correct, for the future, our error, by giving here, the name in full, (Mary A. Shadd) as we do not like the Mr. and Esq., by which we are so often addressed" ("Remarks"). The *Freeman*'s inaugural issue identified its concerns as "the elevation of the Colored People; . . . TEMPERANCE . . . ANTI-SLAVERY" and the emigration of both free blacks and "refugees from the southern plantations" ("Introductory"). Shadd Cary would go beyond that mandate, however, and focus attention on woman's rights through published letters to the editor, articles, and reprints. She sought to establish a subscription list of three thousand readers and secured traveling agents to do so. Rhodes notes that the paper reached readers, via these agents, in "Detroit, Philadelphia, Pittsburgh, Cincinnati, and other American cities" (88).

Though it was moved from Windsor, to Toronto, to Chatham and weathered an interrupted publication history, the *Provincial Freeman* was one of the longest running antebellum black newspapers (Rhodes xii), in print from March 24, 1853, until the summer of 1860. As William Still would note in a letter published in the March 24, 1855, issue of the *Freeman,* sustaining a black newspaper for this long was exceptional, but that a woman edited such a successful paper was truly remarkable. "How you have thus long and well succeeded, to me is a matter of wonder. As I glance over the wrecks which have marked the career of not a few of the 'sterner sex' . . . in almost every instance those enterprises have hopelessly failed ere they had existed twelve months—indeed most of them before six months," wrote Still. The hard fact, he concluded, was that "the masses of our people are quite indifferent as to whether their Presses are supported or not" ("Miss M. A. Shadd"). Indeed, as Rhodes documents, the "only black newspapers that survived this period in the United States were those with strong support from white abolitionists and philanthropists, like *Frederick Douglass's Paper,* or from established institutions, like the A.M.E. Church, which published the *Christian Recorder*" (100). Shadd Cary succeeded with neither form of support, and sustained the *Provincial Freeman* for an astounding seven years. Along the way, she not only contended with the difficulties facing all black antebellum papers—securing subscriptions and their payment as well as undertaking fund-raising tours to remain in operation—but also faced resistance and, at times, vocal opposition to her visibility as editor and activist. According to Rhodes, Shadd Cary saw her gender as her "greatest obstacle" and came to be convinced "that her role as editor was threatening the newspaper's very existence" (98).

Two and a half months after publishing Still's letter with its pointed attention to gender, she announced she would no longer be editor of the paper and turned that office over to William P. Newman in order to begin a fundraising tour to ensure its continued publication. Taking her readers' leave in the June 30, 1855, issue, she encouraged other black women to enter journalism: "To colored women, we have a word—we have 'broken the Editorial ice,' whether willingly or not, for your class in America; so go to Editing, as many of you as are willing, and able, and as soon as you may if you think you are ready" (qtd. in Rhodes 99).[38] By May 1856 she would again be listed on the *Freeman's* masthead as coeditor, along with her brother Isaac Shadd and H. Ford Douglass (Rhodes 116). Shadd Cary's complicated history as editor, both "silent" and public, of the *Provincial Freeman* marks the difficulty African American women continued to have as public activists within black politics and the black press some twenty years after Maria Stewart felt forced to leave Boston and the pages of *The Liberator.* Yet her determination, like Stewart's, was a defining precedent in the development of African American feminism in the press.

Even before she began work on the *Provincial Freeman,* Shadd Cary, like Stewart before her, was well aware of the newspaper press's importance to African American politics. In a lecture in Windsor in the fall of 1851, "Miss Shad [*sic*] . . . alluded to the various instrumentalities which should be used as means of elevation, among which was the Press," citing the *Voice of the Fugitive* and the AME *Christian Herald* as exemplary papers ("Donation Party"). Shadd Cary consistently used the power of the press to advocate a politics of black self-determination, including black female self-determination, as had Maria Stewart before her.

Pursuing that black nationalist politics in the pages of the *Provincial Freeman,* Mary Ann Shadd Cary challenged the dominant abolitionist image of the enslaved African American as passive victim awaiting emancipation at the hands of her white sympathizers, instead characterizing fugitive slaves who had escaped to Canada as self-sufficient. Shadd Cary's refusal to simply reinscribe existing images of the enslaved and to argue for the refugee black American as self-determined importantly parallels the work Sarah Parker Remond was doing on British podiums around the same time. While Remond used Margaret Garner's particular case to render the fugitive slave far from passive, Shadd Cary offered her firsthand knowledge of those refugees who arrived at Canada West. Importantly, for her to reconfigure that stock image of the fugitive also meant that she was challenging the position of African American activists in Canada West like Henry Bibb of the Refugee Home Society.[39] Shadd Cary saw the society as a "begging system" that represented and treated fugitive slaves as helpless, dependant upon white philanthropy, and she accused Henry Bibb of dishonesty and corruption (Rhodes 66).[40] In "Fugitive Slaves in Canada," in the March 25, 1854, issue of the *Freeman,* Shadd Cary undertook, first, to educate her readers on the numbers of enslaved African Americans traveling north to Canada, "from thirty . . . to thirty-five thousand, of whom from three to five thousand have annually escaped since the passing of the Fugitive Slave Law" in 1850. While fugitives arrived in Canada "destitute," having "undergo[ne] numerous privations on their painful and wearisome journey," they were quickly provided "food, clothing, tools" by the "Anti-Slavery Society of Canada and a Ladies' Society at Toronto." Shadd Cary stressed that such assistance was "only temporary. . . . Labour of every kind is in great demand, and . . . they seldom fail to procure employment on advantageous terms. In no instance within the last year and a half has the Society been called upon to extend relief for more than six days" ("Fugitive Slaves").

Shadd Cary's article not only reconfigured the fugitive slave as self-sufficient individual rather than passive victim but also recast fugitives as refugee settlers who proved by example "the equal capacity of the negro for self-advancement . . . [and] the unreasonableness of the prejudice against him. Lastly, his social elevation, by his own industry and enterprise, is even now triumphantly proving the fitness of the slaves for freedom, the righteousness and the practicability of immediate emancipation . . . and the perfect capability of the negro to live and to advance under the same government, and upon terms of political and social equality with the Anglo-Saxon race" ("Fugitive Slaves"). Shadd Cary insisted upon referring to escaped slaves not as fugitives but as refugees. While a fugitive "flees" or runs away, particularly from duty or a master, a refugee, instead, seeks refuge from political troubles in another country.[41] Essentially, Mary Ann Shadd Cary used her newspaper to reconfigure the escaped slave as a political agent rather than a violator of "duty," a criminal, or a vagrant. Such a distinction, emphasized within an antebellum newspaper, is significant given that "the prevalence of runaway slave advertisements," with their "trade cuts of slaves[,] . . . became a standard element of print culture" in the antebellum United States (Wood 89). Those advertisements and wood cuts announced "within the terms of an established legal code . . . an act of theft, albeit self-theft" (Wood 79). For Shadd Cary, however, the refugee African American not only undertook *the* most radical abolitionist act in escaping enslavement but also came to epitomize the goal of black nationalist politics—a self-sufficient and self-determined African American and a legitimate settler of Canada West. Effectively, both the refugee's escape and his or her successful settlement at Canada West were rendered highly political acts in Shadd Cary's paper at a time when the enslaved and the fugitive circulated as passive and negative figures, respectively, in both abolitionist and proslavery discourses as well the popular imaginary.

While Shadd Cary stressed that the refugee slave's escape struck a political blow against the slave system, she indicted white Americans with self-interest in their antislavery agitation and support for colonization in the May 27, 1854, issue of the *Freeman*. Taking aim at the hypocrisy of emancipating the enslaved only to deem them, as the ACS effectively did, "'an undesirable part of the *free* population,'" and to declare "the land of his forefathers . . . the best country for him, could it only be 'fixed up a bit,'" Shadd Cary forcefully opposed African colonization: "[W]e want that the colored man should live in America—should 'plant his tree' deep in the soil, and whether he turns white, or his neighbors turn black by reason of the residence, is of no moment." Ultimately, African Americans must be free to exercise choice, she argued, "not be driven to Africa, nor obliged to stay in the States if he desires to go elsewhere" ("Humbug"). Shadd Cary was particularly concerned for the welfare of African American women in the colonization scheme, who, she underscored, were not being consulted when it came to such "solutions." "What will you do, or what will your women say, for they must go along, when surrounded by . . . all manner of creeping and biting things?" she asked in the April 15, 1854, edition of the *Freeman* (qtd. in Rhodes 87).

As Carla Peterson points out, the emigration debates of the 1850s "replayed in similar terms" those of the 1830s (111) and reconsidered the viability of African colonization and Haitian and Canadian emigration in the face of legal developments like the 1850 Fugitive Slave Law, the Kansas-Nebraska Act (1854), and the Supreme Court's *Dred Scott* decision (1857). These debates were more complicated than those of the 1830s, as Peterson notes, with several possible destinations available for consideration, all of which were ideologically inflected: "emigration to a white country, Canada, to which Shadd Cary added her voice, or to a land where blacks already constituted a majority of the population [the British West Indies, Haiti]; western emigration, where the transplanted population would remain close to slaves in the South; or eastern emigration back to Africa." Some scholars have argued that in the 1850s black emigration was still a male-dominated political debate, while "black women refused by and large to endorse emigration" (Peterson 112). Yet Martha Jones has recently documented women's participation at emigration conventions in the 1850s, contending that "women figured prominently" and at some conventions, such as the 1854 National Emigration Convention of Colored People convened by Martin Delany in Cleveland,[42] "nearly one-quarter (39 of 171) of the 'executive delegates' were women; Canadian activist Mary Bibb was elected vice president, and four additional women served as members of the finance committee" (105). Though "most female delegates were in the company of male relatives, most often husbands," marking the way in which a politics of respectability shaped women's access to the emigration movement, they were present and taking an active role in this debate (M. Jones 105). Opposed to colonization, Shadd Cary represented it to her readers as a dangerous undertaking, like Maria Stewart and Sarah Mapps Douglass before her, and one that risked abdicating the fight for black civil rights in the United States while ignoring the rights and interests of African American women altogether.[43] However, she proved the exception to what Carla Peterson tells us was the general rule of black women's opposition to emigration (112) by actively promoting Canadian settlements to free and refugee African Americans alike.

Shadd Cary's *Provincial Freeman* writings, then, mark her complicated position as a black woman and political activist. Registering her affinity with her black female abolitionist contemporaries, like Remond, and with her feminist black nationalist predecessors, like Stewart and Mapps Douglass, Shadd Cary was unlike the majority of black women in her day who opposed emigration. That political position did not mean she was at odds with a black feminist politics, however. Shadd Cary also worked to establish the black press as a viable venue for woman's rights agitation. In this sense, she is a key transitional figure who helps us trace a line from the feminist black nationalism of a Maria Stewart in the 1830s to that of established African American female journalists in the 1880s and 1890s. With the letters to the editor she chose to publish and the articles she reprinted, as well as by her own example and pointed comments, Shadd Cary used the *Provincial Freeman* from the mid- to late 1850s to advocate for woman's rights and to encourage African American women to participate in public politics. Indeed, Martha Jones argues that Shadd Cary be credited with "extending the woman question debate into the realm of publishing while also creating a forum in which women's voices were being heard with unprecedented clarity" (88). I would stress, however, that Shadd Cary be understood within a black feminist tradition that begins earlier than her work in the 1850s. Rather than marking her work as unprecedented, it is best understood as part of an established and ever-growing black feminism.

In the late spring and early summer of 1854, Mary Ann Shadd Cary not only drew her readers' attention to "woman's rights" but also purposefully linked agitation for married women's property reform in the United States, Great Britain, and Canada with the articles she wrote and chose to reprint. Woman's rights was thus represented in the *Freeman* as having achieved a kind of critical mass and international scope that could not be ignored. In the May 6, 1854, issue, "Woman's Rights" appeared on the front page, detailing the New York Assembly's consideration of a bill ensuring "any married woman, whose husband, either from drunkenness, profligacy, or any other cause, shall neglect, or refuse to provide for her support and education, or for the support and education of her children, and any married woman who may be deserted by her husband, shall have the right, by her own name, to receive and collect her own earnings, and apply the same for her own support, and the support of her children, free from the control and interference of her husband" ("Woman's Rights"). This bill also sought to ensure that children could not be indentured or apprenticed without the written consent of their mothers.[44] One month later, Shadd Cary reprinted Caroline Norton's "One of Our Legal Fictions" in the June 10, 1854, edition of the *Freeman*. Her timing of this reprint is significant, given that Lord Cranworth's Matrimonial Causes bill was introduced and tabled in the same month in the British House of Lords. Norton's autobiographical essay narrativized the loss of her three children and her inheritance to her abusive estranged husband under British common law. Hers was a vivid and scandalous example of what could happen to married women who, under "the idea of an English marriage," entered into a "strict union of interests" that meant "the absorption of the woman's whole life in that of the man's . . . the entire annihilation of all her rights, individuality, legal existence, and his sole recognition by the law" (Norton, "Fictions").[45]

Married women's property rights were a focus of woman's rights agitation not only in Great Britain and the United States at midcentury[46] but also in Canada. As Constance Backhouse points out, even though scholarship assumes "that the organized women's movement did not appear in Canada until 1876[,] . . a series of petitions [was] presented by Elizabeth Dunlop and other women to the Legislative Assembly between 1852 and 1857" (223). Mary Ann Shadd Cary was, then, effectively using her paper to participate in organized feminist agitation in what is now Ontario on women's property rights during the mid- to late 1850s and to extend its concerns to a wider public. Using the New York Assembly and Caroline Norton's individual case[47] together to build for her readers an understanding of the importance of such rights for women, Shadd Cary emphasized that such reforms were neither local nor limited to individual cases of distress that could be explained away and treated as exceptional. Instead, "they assert that the education and elevation of women are not the offspring of legislation, but of civilization," she argued ("Woman's Rights"). The *Freeman's* wider public, Shadd Cary insisted, surely shared in "civilization" as a value. And by addressing her readers as though they shared this common value that, by extension, would ensure woman's rights, Shadd Cary was effectively creating a public for such a politics. As Michael Warner argues, a public's "reality lies in just this reflexivity by which an addressable object is conjured into being in order to enable the very discourse that gives it existence" (*Publics* 67). Shadd Cary was able to convey woman's rights as having achieved a critical mass through the reflexivity of the forms she chose to use—the Norton reprint and the citation of proposed reforms to New York state law. For Warner, newspapers as a structured form "developed reflexivity about their circulation through reviews, reprintings, citations, controversies.

These forms single out circulation both through their sense of temporality and through the way they allow discourse to move in different directions. I don't just speak to you; I speak to the public in a way that enters a cross-citational field of many other people speaking to the public" (*Publics* 95).

In those late spring and early summer months of 1854, when *Freeman* readers were being encouraged to consider married women's property rights, Mary Ann Shadd Cary chose to print two letters to the editor on woman's "sphere" and her "elevation" she very likely wrote herself, one from a Henrietta A. W––S in the April 22, 1854, issue and the other in response from a Dolly Bangs in the April 28, 1854, issue. Henrietta styled herself as having "taken up my pen with a trembling hand and a fearful heart," this being her "first communication for the press." She protested that she was not "seeking to make innovations upon the long and time honored customs of society" but was "content to operate in the sphere to which my humble circumstances have assigned me." Finally, she dared to criticize the "stern opposition from almost every quarter" to woman's education, arguing that "as a class, we make no unreasonable demands of those who style themselves our superiors; all we ask is to receive that encouragement to which our merit entitles us." Having thus screwed up her courage to offer this very brief criticism, Henrietta then abruptly closed her letter ("MR. EDITOR"). In the next issue, Dolly Bangs replied to Henrietta, clearly impatient with "her extreme modesty, which . . . led her . . . to beg as a favor that which is hers by right." Dolly was particularly perturbed by Henrietta's query as to whether the *Freeman* received correspondence from its female readers, a question she found "ridiculous," given that "woman [should be] taught that her mental faculties are God-given, and are therefore to be used." She, consequently, worried that "there may be a vast amount of latent talent which might be used with advantage" going to waste and argued that it is woman's "right, nay, her duty, to press boldly forward to her appointed task, otherwise she is guilty of burying her talent." For Dolly, this included writing for the press, both professionally and as an interested reader, and she closed with her hope that the *Freeman* would "continue to be . . . a medium through which the rights of all may be discussed" ("MR. FREEMAN").

These letters to the editor are important in several ways. They show us that despite Jane Rhodes's assertion that Shadd Cary was "especially cautious about taking a public stance in favor of women's rights" (91–92), she, in fact, deliberately created a space in which women readers were represented as feeling able to voice their position on this issue.[48] Henrietta's and Dolly's letters also mark the range of possible *Freeman* readers, from those "modestly" interested in the "encouragement" of woman by her "superiors," though certainly not in "innovations" upon social custom, to those readers who would advocate for woman's education and the free exercise of her faculties, despite what social custom might endorse or prohibit. Shadd Cary's paper deliberately appealed, then, to readers aware of available rhetorical positions on woman's rights, from the "reasonable" appeal that will leave woman's sphere and masculine superiority unchallenged to the divinely sanctioned exercise of woman's faculties as only appropriate "in the afternoon of the nineteenth century" ("MR. FREEMAN"). Such letters conveniently enabled the *Freeman* to represent "its own circulation . . . to characterize [its] own space of consumption" (Warner, *Publics* 100), conveying the distinct sense to its readers that woman's rights was a vital, contemporary, circulating public discourse. Since Shadd Cary is acknowledged as often having written such letters to the editor herself, the political work they enabled was more than happenstance.

Finally, the letter to the editor as form is important to attend to when considering the significance of Shadd Cary's work. While Benedict Anderson argues more generally for the newspaper as facilitating a "mass ceremony" of "imagined community" (35), he does not consider the significance of certain forms within the newspaper itself. Pressing on his contention that the ritual of reading the newspaper enables readers to imagine themselves as part of a larger community partaking of the same solitary activity, I would argue that letters to the editor are evidence of that very community writ large. Such letters make visible and tangible what Anderson argues readers can only imagine, a community of which one is a part. Henrietta's and Dolly's letters in the *Freeman* offer Shadd Cary's readers "real women" with whom they might share interests, opinions, a certain politics, or a debate. Michael Warner's notion of public discourse in general also applies to the particular form of the letter to the editor, which "gives a general social relevance to private thought and life. Our subjectivity is understood as having resonance with others, and immediately so" (*Publics* 77). Rather than ducking a public avocation of woman's rights in the *Freeman*, Shadd Cary was actively building a public interested in this issue by not only writing and reprinting articles on woman's rights, but also rendering visible and embodied—in letters to the editor—that community that Anderson argues is only "imagined" in the act of reading the newspaper.

At the same time that Shadd Cary was publishing and writing letters to the editor and articles on woman's rights, she was using her paper to encourage

African American women to participate in public politics. In the late summer and early fall of 1854, the *Freeman* both reported on Shadd Cary's own political activities and printed a spirited letter from her criticizing what she called black female "apathy." It covered the organization of the Provincial Union in the August 19, 1854, edition, highlighting Shadd Cary's own role in it, unsurprising given that it was "concocted" by her (Rhodes 94). The union pledged its members would "encourage and support a Press . . . *in Canada* . . . do all in our power to remove the stain of Slavery from the face of the earth . . . encourage the rising generation in literary, scientific, and mechanical efforts . . . [and] support the '*Provincial Freeman*' as our organ" (Shadd Cary, "Meeting"). Shadd Cary was the only woman of the seventeen listed who took up a role outside the union's Ladies' Committee, as "Special Agent to organize Auxiliaries" and its treasurer. She was also the only woman to participate in the program, reading "the Constitution, Pledge, &C, which, after a harmonious discussion, were unanimously adopted," documents she had drafted (Shadd Cary, "Meeting").

The Provincial Union espoused black nationalist principles of self-help, racial uplift, and abolition, and evidenced Shadd Cary's interest in playing an instrumental role in the development of black politics in Canada. That desire made her impatient with other black women who did not share her aspirations for a developing black feminist activism. In late October 1854, Shadd Cary harshly criticized black women for failing to think for themselves, to educate themselves on current political issues by reading the newspaper, or to question their prescribed roles. "If there is any one thing that tends to intensify one's contempt for the *muslin multitude,* it is the nothingness the delicate creature displays when invited to aid in a work for the general good," she railed. "You would be surprised at the pains they take to impress you with their 'feebleness.' . . . Must not think of helping without getting Mr.——'s consent. . . . Young ladies who have no Mr.——s to think for them, really do not know,—they never read the newspapers. . . . What a set!" ("Dear 'C'").

If, as Michael Warner argues, publics "exist by virtue of their address" (*Publics* 67), what public was Mary Ann Shadd Cary striving to create with this report on the Provincial Union and her letter on female apathy? Clearly, Shadd Cary was working to create a public who saw women as active participants in black politics, who would find it not only acceptable but also expected that women would take up both leadership roles, as she did, and those more socially sanctioned positions for women in auxiliaries like the Ladies' Committee. Moreover, by couching her criticism of her black female peers in a letter to the editor, rather than in an editorial or article, Shadd Cary could promote her belief that women should become educated and politicized as a shared view held by *Freeman* readers. Shadd Cary was strategically present-ing her ideal of black women as potential activists as though it came from that "imagined" community of newspaper readers not from an idiosyncratic individual. As Henrietta's and Dolly's letters to the editor functioned, Shadd Cary's paper made tangible a public who shared a sense of woman's political responsibility and thereby created "a general social relevance" for her own views. What is more, by publishing the Provincial Union report and this let-ter to the editor in the *Freeman* separated only by a few months, Shadd Cary was also creating a sense that woman's political role was a timely and vital topic, for as Warner argues, "the punctual rhythm of circulation is crucial to the sense that ongoing discussion unfolds in a sphere of activity" (68). For Warner, the circulation of public address "allows participants in its discourse to understand themselves as directly and actively belonging to a social entity that . . . has consciousness of itself" (75). *Freeman* readers would see the is-sue of women in public politics as not only a significant and contemporary issue but also one directly relevant to them in their own active participation in abolition, woman's rights, black nationalism, and other political concerns promoted by the paper. In these ways, Shadd Cary astutely used her news-paper to promote a black feminist politics that circulated as a shared concern central to black politics at midcentury.

What is distinctive about Shadd Cary's contribution, and what links her to black feminist activists such as Ellen Craft, Sarah Parker Remond, and Ida B. Wells, is her work to take black feminism public beyond a national arena. Shadd Cary's readership was transnational, largely comprised of read-ers in Canada West and the United States, but since Canada West was at the time a British colony, Shadd Cary's work also had a potential transat-lantic and international reach. The *Freeman*'s nominal editor after Shadd Cary removed her name from its masthead, Samuel Ringgold Ward, was touring Great Britain in 1853 when she relocated its offices from Windsor to Toronto.[49] As Rhodes documents, Shadd Cary "kept the myth of Ward's editorship alive as his reputation was the main selling device for the fledgling newspaper" (83). But Shadd Cary further sought to amplify an international reach for her feminist black nationalist politics by urging black Americans to "consider the opportunity to be '*part* of the Colored British nation'" (qtd. in Rhodes 87), aligning Canada West with Great Britain rather than North America in her feminist-emigrationist stance.

Shadd Cary remained active in black nationalist politics, even as she re-signed as editor of the *Freeman*. She became the first woman elected a mem-ber of the National Convention of Colored Men at the organization's meeting in Philadelphia, October 16–18, 1855. This organization sought to promote black nationalist principles of autonomy and solidarity. During the mid to late 1850s she continued to lecture on abolition and emigration, but with limited success. The emigration movement marginalized her, but undaunted, she continued to participate in black politics and to advocate women's inter-ests in fields like the black labor movement during the late 1860s and early 1870s. Shadd Cary also continued to use the press to call for black women's participation in the advancement of black political concerns. She published "Trade for Our Boys" in the March 21, 1872, issue of *New National Era*. In it, Shadd Cary bemoaned "the death-like silence of colored women," who could be instrumental in raising public interest in securing trades for young Afri-can American men. But Shadd Cary went further, urging African American women "to let the nation know how they stand. White women are getting to be a power in the land, and colored women cannot any longer afford to be neutrals" ("Trade"). As late as the 1880s, Shadd Cary continued to insist upon feminism's place in the black nationalism that first motivated her to enter black public politics. In 1880 she formed the Colored Women's Pro-gressive Franchise Association, whose promotion of "women's political and economic rights" alongside a nationalist focus on "religious and moral values" (Rhodes 199) stressed woman's centrality to black public politics.

Shadd Cary's work in the press as an advocate for emigration and her feminist black nationalist politics that stressed community solidarity and up-lift were part of a wider tradition than is often recognized in scholarship that understandably celebrates her individual achievements with *The Provincial Freeman*. In addition to placing her in a tradition of feminist black national-ism in the press that reaches back to Stewart and Douglass, she is part of a black feminist journalism that also extended to the West and which is only now beginning to be recovered. Eric Gardner has recently documented that black newspapers in the West, such as San Francisco's *Mirror of the Times,* were also "direct outgrowth[s] of the convention movement" (xiii). Gardner's research has brought to light the work of Jennie Carter, who through the late 1860s and early 1870s wrote under the pen names Mrs. Ann J. Trask and Semper Fidelis for San Francisco's black weekly, *The Elevator* (founded in 1865), and for the Philadelphia-based AME *Christian Recorder* on "California and national politics, race and racism woman's rights and suffrage, temper-ance, morality, education, and a host of other issues" (vii).

Attuned to the expediency politics of the white woman suffrage movement, Carter supported black male suffrage but not woman suffrage (Gardner 76–77), even though she argued forcefully for women's economic rights: "The wife has the right to the husband's money, to use judiciously. . . . All women should know their husband's pecuniary affairs" ("Letter from Nevada County," *Elevator* 5 June 1868, in Gardner 35). And she could be understood within a black feminist politics that advocated migration for improved opportunities because, like emigrationists such as Shadd Cary, she offered her readers views of a life possible in black communities outside the Northeast. Carter often contributed pieces to *The Elevator* depicting the life of African Americans in towns in the West, such as Oroville, California. "Mr. Editor," wrote Carter, "California as a part of Uncle Sam's domains is truly an important part, and . . . she will furnish homes for thousands of Europe's poor, Asia's industrious, and Africa's once despised" (*Elevator* 25 June 1869, in Gardner 73).

Finally, Carter also promoted black nationalist tenets in her journalism. Seeing the Fifteenth Amendment as an opportunity upon which African Americans must capitalize, Carter criticized the San Francisco black community for its "indifference on the subject of education" and for a larger regression since the 1850s in which she saw "no desire for knowledge, a hatred towards those who try to make themselves useful, [and] a spirit of envy towards those who succeed in life." Carter's call to "Organize! Organize!! Present a united front to the enemy. Let all mankind know we are in earnest and are not to[o] lazy to progress" was a strong one. Yet she tempered it with a domestic feminism that stressed the importance of hearth and home in that larger political progress for which she called: "We want out altars and hearths to remain a sacred legacy to our children. We want all our rights, education, civil and religious. We want them to-day, and we want to transmit them unsullied to our children's children forever" (*Elevator* 7 May 1869, in Gardner 69–70).

Carter's critiques of her community place her in the company of Maria Stewart and Mary Ann Shadd Cary. Her consideration of viable alternatives for African American community share affinities with the writings of Stewart, Douglass and Shadd Cary. And her attention to black civil rights and suspicion of the white woman's rights and suffrage movement keep company with the likes of Sojourner Truth and Frances Harper. As a black woman entering the press it is also significant that Carter chose the form of letters to the editor for her journalism, actively creating, as did Shadd Cary in the 1850s, the sense that her views were part of a tangible, unified, and visible black community that was linked nationally through the black press. "Black newspapers," Patrick Rael has argued, "thus served as the great mechanism for constructing a unified, even pan-African black identity, one that could protest the interests of the free and slave, African and African American" (216). What women like Shadd Cary and Carter show us is the reach of this unified communal identity beyond Rael's antebellum North and into Canada and the postbellum U.S. West. Carter's activity in the late 1860s and early 1870s positions her at the cusp of what would be an explosion in the growth of the black press in general and the growth of black feminist journalism in particular.

Racial Respectability: Migrancy and Black Women's Labor

As Hazel Dicken-Garcia documents, the black press grew at an astonishing rate following the Civil War. While a dozen new publications were established in the nine months following the War's end, from the late 1880s through the early 1890s, the black press experienced unprecedented and astonishing growth.[50] This explosion facilitated the work of black women in journalism, both North and South. In fact, southern African American women were a distinct phenomenon in late-nineteenth-century black journalism, as Gloria Wade-Gayles has noted. "Of twenty-three black women in the nation who had achieved status as journalists by 1891, *sixteen were native Southerners,*" emphasizes Wade-Gayles. "[F]rom 1883 to 1905, of forty-six black women journalists in the United States, *thirty . . . were Southerners* by birth and up-bringing" (139). Black women journalists from the mid-1880s through the early twentieth century pursued a feminist nationalism and a politics of re-spectability, as had their predecessors earlier in the nineteenth century, but the predominance of southern women writing for black publications produced a particular focus within that politics—the migrant, working-class black woman who traveled north to urban centers, such as New York and Chicago, for improved employment opportunities.[51]

All of the writings on black migrant women upon which this chapter focuses were published on the cusp of and during the early years of what is known as the Great Migration.[52] The Great Migration, which many scholars argue spanned 1910 to 1970, saw "over 2.5 million southern-born blacks living outside of the region by 1950" and culminated in "over 4 million by 1980" (Tolnay 210). During the first wave of the Great Migration, between 450,000 and 500,000 southern African Americans relocated to northern urban centers between 1915 and 1918, with another 700,000 migrating north during the 1920s (Arnesen 1). Published between 1885 and 1914, black women's journalism that addresses this first wave of migration clearly marks a growing concern for the material conditions and employment opportunities of black women in northern cities as implicated in the promotion of a feminist-nationalist politics that emphasized both a domestic feminism and a politics of racial respectability. While those documenting the Great Migration contend that northern urban life was "unappealing for African Americans in the pre–World War II decades" (Arnesen 6), African American women journalists reveal a far different situation in which black women were not only migrating north but doing so in sufficient numbers to constitute a "concern." The tendency of much of this journalism to advocate for the migrant woman rather than pathologize her in a bid for black middle-class respectability in the eyes of white Americans is importantly distinctive.

This is not to say that no black female journalist from this period raised the specter of the migrant woman as "contagion." However, by and large black women journalists brought to light black migrant and working-class women's living and working conditions to advocate for their improvement and to educate young southern women about the pitfalls that awaited them in the North. Black women's journalism on migrancy circulating on the cusp, and during the early years, of the Great Migration significantly challenges the established critical reading of the black female migrant as central figure in a moral urban panic that arose in response to the "general crises of social displacement and dislocation that were caused by migration" (Carby, "Policing" 118).[53] While that moral panic is said to have situated the migrant woman as threat, be it to racial progress, black middle-class respectability, interracial relations, or black masculinity (Carby, "Policing" 118), black women's journalism on the migrant woman often represented her as a figure of potential. Moreover, while many "female uplift ideologues . . . attempted to police" migrants and their behaviors, "which they believed would undermine the effort to uplift the race" (Wolcott), this black feminist journalism marks racial uplift and racial respectability as hardly the sole purview of the middle class. Instead, working-class and migrant black women were represented as having already accomplished uplift in the South and, so, uniquely able to continue that work in northern cities upon their arrival. In this way, the domestic feminism of this journalism sharply counters such scholarly narratives of migrancy and significantly countered the predominant wielders of domestic feminism in its day, the club movement, which, as Mary Church Terrell's remarks opening this chapter indicate, repeatedly positioned working-class black women as "the lowly . . . the vicious" whose influence upon public perceptions of "the race" must be countered.

Scholars have begun to revisit longstanding conceptions of the Great Migration, given the recent accessibility of census data from 1850 to 2004 through the Integrated Public Use Microdata series project. The release of 1920 census information has been particularly transformative, since the 1920 census was the first to ask respondents to indicate their residence five years prior, in addition to their birthplace and current residence, thereby enabling researchers to identify recent first-wave migrants to the North and trace where they came from, in addition to knowing their occupation, education, and marital status. This work has begun to alter received knowledge and understanding of African American migrants' realities.

The prevailing image of black migrants from the South, which emerged primarily from social scientists writing about the first wave of the Great Migration as it was unfolding, has tended to dominate scholarship that followed,[54] an image of the "typical" migrant as an "illiterate sharecropper, displaced from the rural South because of agricultural distress or reorganization" (Tolnay 211). Migrants as a whole have been characterized as "a relatively uneducated and morally slack population riddled with unstable families that created many problems for northern cities and their inhabitants" (Curtis White 416). Whether these images speak to migrants' realities, to prevailing social sentiment regarding migration at the time among both whites and blacks, or to the predispositions of these social scientists themselves and those they influenced is important to consider, though such questions have not received much attention in scholarship until recently. Scholars of the Great Migration cite what they refer to as "push and pull" factors that caused this monumental shift. Northern labor markets opened new opportunities for African Americans, particularly in manufacturing, and northern labor agents became active in the South, even offering to finance the move north from migrants' future wages; newspapers spread word about work, housing, and life in northern cities, with Chicago's *Defender* using editorials and stories as well as organizing what it called the "Great Northern Drive" of 1917. While these factors "pulled" migrants to the North, others, such as deteriorating economic and political conditions marked by boll weevil infestation of cotton crops, floods, racial violence, Jim Crow, and political disenfranchisement, "pushed" migrants out of the South.[55] The dominant motivation amid these interacting influences has been said to be economic.

Recent research on southern migrants has begun to challenge these longstanding characterizations of the Great Migration, especially its first wave. As Thomas Maloney has recently noted, migration virtually tripled between

1910 and 1920, when seventy per one thousand African Americans migrated north in contrast to twenty-five per one thousand between 1900 and 1910 (2). While the majority of those migrating were between twenty and forty-four years old, migration was most attractive to those between the ages of twenty-five and twenty-nine during the first wave; and while migrants were leaving all regions of the South, the increase in out-migration was particularly marked for the east south-central states (Alabama, Kentucky, Mississippi, and Tennessee) (Maloney 2). Even though this data may appear to confirm that prevailing image of the young, usually single, southern male sharecropper pushed out of the rural South, Maloney's work also documents that, contrary to that image, migration rates rose at least as much among the literate as among the illiterate (and perhaps more), and migration increased more for married African Americans than for the unmarried (11). In other words, migrants of the first wave were far more likely to be literate and married, challenging that image of migrants as illiterate and unable or unwilling to maintain "stable" family structures.

For African American women, Maloney found that "increased probability of Northern residence was concentrated among literate women as well as married women" (5), which directly contradicts that image of the migrant black woman as "pathology" or "contagion," dangerous because she migrated on her own and because her lack of education, both moral and formal, threatened to degrade those urban African American communities she joined. As Victoria Wolcott notes, we know little of migrating African American women beyond caricatures because "most historians have largely left women out of their narratives" or position them, at best, as secondary figures—the "supportive wives and mothers or family members left behind" (50)—and as secondary or supplemental wage earners.   However, Katherine Curtis White's recent work comparing African American and white female migrants offers a corrective to such prevailing understandings. Contrary to that popular image of the female migrant as exclusively an African American woman, she reveals that white women migrated at rates double that of black women in 1920, near the end of the Great Migration's first wave. As we might expect, her work documents limited employment opportunities for black female migrants who were segregated primarily in domestic service work and undesirable factory labor in "the hog head, bone, and hair departments of packing houses" (418). Yet black women were more likely to work than their white counterparts. Perhaps most telling is Curtis White's finding that for African American women, children rarely "negatively impact[ed] a woman's occupational status" (439), by which she means African American women neither reduced their work hours nor left employment around the birth and raising of their children. Clearly, African American working-class women could not afford to do so, but their higher paid white migrant "sisters" could and did, suggesting that it may have been white female migrants whose wages were secondary or supplemental to their families' incomes while those of black female migrants were crucial to family survival. Curtis White's research also complicates that rather straight-forward assumption that southerners migrated north for better economic opportunities, since African American women left predominantly domestic service employment in the South only to be limited to such employment in the North. And while she notes that "between 25 and 50 percent of the female southern-born migrant population did not have a spouse present" (445), we must remember that white women migrants doubled the number of black women migrants in the north. Even though she does not note how many of that 25–50 percent of unmarried female migrants were African American, to imagine that the unmarried migrant is always an African American woman would be a misperception.

Yet it is the black female migrant who scholars maintain was perceived as the greatest social threat. Was this, in fact, as widely held a perception as scholarship has suggested? Was the black woman migrant indeed vilified by the black middle class and black feminists, policed and feared by African Americans and whites alike? Or have we taken the writing of particular individuals, and that disseminated in certain venues, as definitive when African American urban communities in the North and black feminists themselves held a more complicated and diverse social view of black women migrants? Turning to the journalism of African American women in both specialized periodicals and some of the most successful black newspapers of the day, we see a very different picture that, again, shows us our critical lenses can risk producing limited understandings of black feminist politics and strategy.

In the mid-1880s, Gertrude Mossell used her regular column, "Our Women's Department," in the *New York Freeman* to draw attention to black women's working and living conditions in the urban North and the elision of such conditions in a black nationalist politics of racial respectability. Indeed, that politics had a deep reach, extending back to the debates over preaching women and reforms in the AME Church examined in chapter 1 and into re-form circles, as work such as Xiomara Santamarina's has argued. Santamarina has importantly called for an examination of "the cultural role of labor in discursive constructions of black femininity," with particular attention to "labor's conflicted representational status during a period of profound social, economic, and cultural transformations" (24). While her focus has been on black women's autobiographies at midcentury, the migrations of African Americans north at the turn into the twentieth century is another moment of such "profound transformation" when we again encounter a "cultural conundrum—in which emancipatory rhetorics reproduced a different form of subjugation" (Santamarina 18) for black women.

I would argue that black feminist journalists who challenged representations of working black women in a discourse of racial respectability understood that respectability and the values that were its markers colluded with "an expanding market economy" that stressed individual ability to achieve "material and moral success" and left "little room for analyzing anonymous and impersonal structures of domination" (Rael 131). Unlike Rael, I do not see such analyses as emerging from "a handful of radicals and working-class labor theorists (many of them European)" (131); rather, critiques of market capitalism and its effects upon working black women are a hallmark of the black feminist journalism of Mossell and her contemporaries. We must recall that the politics of respectability that Mossell challenged was dominant in both the black press and black nationalist politics early in the century, and that work such as hers is indebted and connected to that of Maria Stewart some fifty years earlier. A member of Philadelphia's black elite, Mossell had been writing for black publications since she was sixteen years old and was woman's editor of the *Freeman* from 1885 until 1889, when she left to take up the same post at the *Indianapolis World* until 1892. Mossell's was the first woman's column in the black press (Streitmatter, *Raising* 40), one she declared would "aim to promote true womanhood . . . of the African race" ("Woman Suffrage"). Despite the seemingly conservative aims of her *New York Freeman* column, Mossell used it as a forum for promoting woman suffrage, encouraging women into business and journalism, and covering the controversial ordination of women in the AME Church.

Mossell's column "Woman Suffrage" in the December 26, 1885, edition of the *Freeman* is significant for its attention to the elision of black working-class women's concerns in a middle-class discourse of racial respectability. The column opened with a celebration of Senator Blair's woman suffrage motion before Congress and then moved to "Care of Children." Ostensibly offering child care advice to parents, Mossell related two cases in which working black women "dosed" their children so that the children could be left at home while they went to work. One woman who "gave her three children

doses of laudanum and then went to washing . . . was spoken of in the community 'as such a hard working, industrious woman.' . . . In another case
a little one was given a dose of Mrs. Winslow's Soothing Syrup and passed
away into its eternal sleep" ("Woman Suffrage"). While Mossell offers these
stories with little comment other than to caution against "dosing," several
issues emerge clearly from her strategic decision to offer them in this particular column. Mossell unmistakably, though indirectly, indicts an employment
market that not only gives the black woman little choice save menial labor
but also ignores her domestic situation in order that she may be relied upon to
improve her employer's by doing the week's washing. Clearly, these women's
wages do not enable them to both support their families and secure care for
their children, leaving them little choice but to sacrifice the latter in order to
eke out a subsistence wage. In fact, in mentioning the mother who gives her
children laudanum in order to go to work washing, Mossell may also subtly
be invoking the desperation of fugitive slave mothers who would dose their
children with laudanum in order that they all might more readily escape.

A reader noticing this echo may ask, how different are the "opportunities"
of northern labor markets from slavery? Yet such working women are lauded as
admirable, for they present the image of "hard working, industrious" African
Americans to society at large, an image of racial respectability that effectively
disciplines such women to accept the very material conditions such an image
elides. Marking her awareness that reformers sought to "redefine domestic labor as a noble pursuit that was essential to racial uplift," a pursuit that would
elevate not only the race, "but also the women who performed it . . . in standing" (Wolcott 19), Mossell foregrounds the dependence of a politics of racial
respectability on the labor of working-class black women and the enforced neglect of their children. Exposing the catch-22 in which the working-class black
woman is caught, Mossell tempers the celebration of Blair's woman suffrage
motion with which her column opened, and underscores the importance of
using whatever political rights woman might secure to address the particular
concerns of the working-class black woman and her children. Presenting these
issues in a regular column, Mossell effectively insists that woman suffrage and
the material conditions it might be exercised to ameliorate are central to the
day-to-day concerns of African Americans rather than exceptional. The result
is to create a certain expectation that working-class women will become part
of a politics that thus far has tended to ignore or vilify them.

Mossell's "Woman Suffrage" column was also, effectively, a caution to
her readers on the perils of a working-class, urban life for black women, one

that many southern girls were choosing as they migrated north to cities such as New York.[56] Her contemporary, Victoria Earle Matthews, would be much more explicit in her caution to migrating women some thirteen years later. Matthews was born a slave in Georgia, the daughter of her mother's master and reared as white in his house. Her mother fled slavery, but returned to regain custody of four of her nine children. Victoria was later educated in New York, where she was forced to take on domestic work to help support her mother and siblings. Remarkably, Matthews found time to write and began publishing in the early 1890s. Known more as a club woman and social worker in scholarship documenting her life and work, Matthews was also one of the most esteemed African American female journalists of her day, writing for dailies such as the *New York Times* and Boston's *Advocate* before working for T. Thomas Fortune's *New York Age*.[57] Matthews was particularly concerned for the welfare of female migrants and their children, establishing the White Rose Mission in New York City in 1897. The mission was operated as a settlement house, offering "mother's meetings, . . . vocational courses in cooking, sewing, dressmaking, woodcarving, cobbling, chair caning, basketry, and clay modeling" (Cash, "White Rose" 1258–59). Matthews also formed the first travelers' aid service in 1905, "a chain of service centers from Virginia to New York, designed to support and protect young women" migrating from the South (Fuchs para. 7).

In July 1898 Matthews published "Some Dangers Confronting Southern Girls in the North" in the southern black periodical *Hampton Negro Conference,* the published proceedings of the annual Hampton conferences begun in 1897.[58] Painting the plight awaiting migrant African American women as "heart broken, disgraced . . . sin-stained years of city life," Matthews exposed the "hordes of unscrupulous" individuals who prey upon black working-class "needs and limitations" in the South, luring men and women north and particularly targeting "young innocent girls from the South for immoral purposes" (63). Indeed, Matthews likens this exploitation of working-class southern African Americans to a form of neoslavery in which they are regarded "as 'crops.' A 'crop' will ordinarily last about five years. There are always new recruits and the work of death and destruction goes on without let or hindrance" (964). Migrant women are frequently employed through a "Society" that collects their wages against the "debt" of their board and lodging, Matthews informs her readers, keeping them bound to such a scheme and often coercing them into "camps," groups of female migrants who are used in "petty gambling schemes," employment scams, and, if fair skinned, as "diversions" in prostitution rings (66–67). Matthews insists that escape from such a life is nearly impossible, as northern "ladies refuse to employ colored help" because they assume all come from such a life in the "tenderloins." Migrating women seeking such employment find doors shut and inevitably, she warns, fall into this life whether directly recruited to it by "traveling agents" in the South or not. No northern urban center is free of such pitfalls for migrating black women, as Matthews indicts "New York, Boston, San Francisco, Chicago, and other cities of lesser note" as well as an "employment system" that developed first in Virginia and spread throughout the South (68–69). Such exploitation is so entrenched, and the employment system network so complex, that Matthews calls naïve the hope of "bringing the guilty ones to justice" (68).

Matthews's article is significant for the ways in which it differs from those characterizing female migrancy as social pathology and contagion. First, she recognizes the need of young African American women to find employment, often outside the rural South of their birth and upbringing. Second, Matthews maintains that such women are neither naturally "depraved" nor immoral, contrary to popular opinion, and need only frank and honest accounts of life and work in northern urban centers in order to steer their way clear of "traveling agents" and their traps. By the early twentieth century, female migrants would become pathologized by social workers like Frances Kellor, general director of New York City's Inter-Municipal Committee on Household Research, as the targets of specific reforms that discounted and, indeed, sought to manage, the migrant woman's agency.[59] In "Southern Girls in the North: The Problem of Their Protection," Kellor proposed the use of "practical and sympathetic women" who would direct migrants upon their arrival to a "controlled system of lodging houses" that would then monitor and curtail their movement, particularly at night. These matrons would also enroll migrant women in "training schools to make" them "more efficient" (585). In Kellor's view, migrant black women "desire to avoid hard work," a trait which leads them to "rely upon odd jobs and employment in the questionable house" and into the hands of employment agencies that encourage "immoral habits, vice and laziness" (584, 585).

In sharp contrast to this discourse of moral panic wielded by Kellor and others, a discourse that would become more entrenched by the teens and twenties, Matthews locates the "problem" of migrancy in a corrupt employment market, not in the female migrant's supposed "desire to avoid hard work." She insists that migrant women can protect themselves and their interests if they are sufficiently informed of the pitfalls they may encounter in the North and stresses the importance of enlightening "women and girls" on the dangers of migrancy so that they may "begin to think, and stop placing themselves voluntarily in the power of strangers" (69). For her, unlike Kellor, migrant women are not a problem to manage but a fully thinking and responsible group of women who have the potential to "purify" the tenderloins and "elevate" the "common standard of life" by arriving in the North aware and trained for labor there, or apprised of where to attain such training, like at Matthews's own White Rose Mission (68).

If we do not attend to where articles on black migration appear as shaping the positions their writers take and the characterizations they offer of migrant women, we can mistake what are politicized positions for a general public response. Matthews's article was published in a southern periodical, a transcript of her address to a southern school offering industrial education to young black men and women. This venue underscores her interest in reaching female migrants and empowering them with full information on working-class living and employment conditions in the urban North. In contrast, Kellor's article addressed its concern for "inefficient" migrant women to northern urban audiences of interested philanthropists through the ten-cent weekly *Charities,* published by the New York Charity Organization Society, presenting migrants as a "concern" to be dealt with by others and thereby contributing to the ostensible "moral panic" that surrounded discussions of black migrancy. Kellor's career, by the time her article appeared in *Charities,* had focused on the investigation of employment agencies and their exploitation of African American women, and on "household research" in New York and Philadelphia.[60] She addressed, in other words, individuals and groups predisposed to see African American migrants, and black female migrants in particular, as a social problem to be solved. Her audience was not black female migrants themselves or, in the main, African American communities North or South, but rather philanthropic whites, fellow sociologists, and interested government officials through whom Kellor worked to effect what she saw as necessary national reforms. Given her audience, her training, and the research that had established her career and reputation, it is unsurprising that Kellor presented black female migrants as she did. Unlike Kellor, Matthews sought to reach migrant black women themselves before they left the South when they were still able to avoid the difficulties they would undoubtedly encounter in the urban North. She addressed them as potential agents in securing decent employment and living conditions rather than as the objects of a controlling social philanthropy that clearly perceived them as pathological and a contagion to be guarded against.

Journalists such as Mossell and Matthews, then, offered their readers a different view of black women migrants, stressing that they made "active choice[s] for economic betterment" rather than depicting them as "vulnerable and naïve" and, so, in need of rescue and reform as Victoria Wolcott has argued the "general discourse about female migration" tended to do (100). Was there such a monolithic discourse on black female migration and its "threat" to racial respectability? Or have we mistaken writings from particular locations as indicative of a more uniform response to migration than may have actually existed at the time? Wolcott herself raises such a question when she notes that "respectability encompassed a set of ideas and normative values that had tremendous power among African Americans and was particularly open to competing definitions, inflections, and meanings. Individual black women understood respectability in very different ways depending on their social, political, and cultural contexts" (4). And scholars before her, such as Sharon Harley, have stressed the standards of respectability and the domestic ideology of "even . . . the poorest blacks . . . [were] not always diametrically opposed to middle-class norms of behavior" (46). In fact, working-class African Americans understood that discourses of racial respectability were tools to social mobility, as Stephanie Shaw has argued (*Ought* 15), and used these "class-coded" discourses "for their own ends" even as they saw the potential for "the new reform organizations" designed to police their behaviors as routes to "white-collar and industrial employment" that would enable them to "leave domestic service behind" (Wolcott 15).

Yet if we look primarily to the writings of a figure such as Frances Kellor, to the writings of club women such as Mary Church Terrell or, as we shall soon see, those of Fannie Barrier Williams, or to specialized periodicals such as *Charities* as representative responses of northern middle-class African Americans and of northern whites to black female migrants, we shall reduce the actual complexity and range of responses to black working women migrating north. Instead, we will have mistaken a particular politics, and at that a rather limited view of that politics, for a larger social view. In other words, a continued focus on the club movement and the writings and speeches of its "greats," as well as a scholarly predisposition to generalize the "moral panic" that social scientists and club women wielded for political purposes, will necessarily miss the rich body of black feminist writing on migracy for the periodical press and tell a partial and skewed story of responses to African American women during the first wave of the Great Migration.

In contrast to the scholarly narrative of anxious responses to and views of black migrancy, at the root of black feminist journalism like Gertrude Mossell's and Victoria Earle Matthews's was both a concern for working black women and an insistence that even though particular material and labor conditions limited their choices with often devastating results, these women were nonetheless subjects with the potential to better not only their own conditions but those of their communities. In this way, their work echoes that of their predecessors like Maria Stewart, who argued that working black women were key to a nascent black nationalist movement. The importance of such writings must not be understated, for they circulated at a time when African American working women in northern cities were publicly blamed, by both "concerned" blacks and whites, for the circumstances in which they and their children lived.

Indeed, black working-class women became the objects of social concern not only for white philanthropists and social workers, such as Frances Kellor, but also for some black club women. Women such as Fannie Barrier Williams, a member of Chicago's black elite who helped found both the National League of Colored Women in 1893 and the National Association of Colored Women in 1896, wrote of migrancy as doomed to failure and of urban segregated housing as corrupting the "decent element of the colored people" who are forced to live among the so-called vice-ridden working classes ("Social Bonds" 40). A journalist and sociologist influenced by the Chicago School, Williams "became a leading intellectual black voice through her writings in newspapers" such as the *New York Age* and the *Defender* and periodicals like *Woman's Era, Voice of the Negro,* and the *Colored American Magazine* (Deegan xxxiii).

Williams published "Social Bonds in the 'Black Belt' of Chicago" in the October 7, 1905, special issue of *Charities* devoted to black migration, just seven months after Kellor's article pathologizing female migrants appeared in that same journal. *Charities'* special number titled "The Negro in the Cities of the North" positioned black working-class men and women who had migrated to the North as a social problem for interested parties to correct through articles titled "Some Causes of Criminality Among Colored People" and "Negro Dependence in Baltimore." In "Social Bonds," Williams ambivalently praised migrants arriving in Chicago for "their efforts for self-help and self-advancement" yet deplored the fact that the "decent element" of Chicago's black community was forced to live in the "Black Belt" along with working-class migrants, where they "witness[ed] the brazen display of vice of all kinds" (40). A strong proponent of and active within the social settlement movement, Williams had already written in the September 1904 issue of *Southern Workman* that the "large proportion of the people who flock to our large cities are utterly incapable of adapting themselves to the complex conditions of city life" ("Social Settlement" 502). Thus representing migrants themselves as inevitable "failures," Williams called for "directing agencies to save and protect" the "poor colored people who come to these cities of the North," and underscored the need of a "settlement institution located right in the midst of the blackest of the black belts of our city's population" ("Social Settlement" 504). In these articles Williams lauded the respectability of that "decent" class of African Americans by indicting the vice-ridden migrants and working classes as a "problem" in dire need of management.

The *Southern Workman* (1872–1939) was a monthly periodical published by the Hampton Institute and was clearly addressed to readers who saw African Americans as potential "problems." Its editorial committee chaired by Hampton Institute's three successive white principals, the *Southern Workman*'s masthead noted it was "a magazine devoted to the interests of undeveloped races" that "provides an open forum for the discussion of ethnological, sociological, and educational problems" of African and Native Americans. The monthly claimed to have "an important influence both North and South on questions concerning the Negro and Indian races," and quoted the *New York Times* as praising its "description and discussion of their nature, their work, their needs, their life" ("*Southern Workman*" 466). Though Hampton Institute's goal was to teach African Americans "how to educate their own race . . . and to equip them with agricultural and mechanical skills by which they could support themselves" (Engs 243), it was supported by northern white philanthropy and government funding, making neither the *Hampton Negro Conference,* where Matthews published her warnings to migrants in 1898, nor the *Southern Workman,* where Williams's work was published in 1904, unproblematic venues for addressing the conditions of migrating African Americans. Clearly, Hampton Institute effectively marked black migrancy as a "social problem" within a larger and ongoing discussion of the "nature" of the "undeveloped" black race. And even though, by this time, the *Southern Workman* had begun to publish articles by black leaders like Lucy Laney, Booker T. Washington, and Robert R. Moton, its focus remained "convinc[ing] white philanthropists that Hampton's endowment drive was a worthy cause" (Daniel 357). Consequently, the *Workman* and the Hampton Institute itself did little to challenge their view that "the Negro" was a "problem" to be solved, and it was the individual interventions of essays like

Matthews's that contested the Institute's overriding tendency to represent migrancy and migrants themselves as social ills.

Williams's position was not simply a product of the time in which her articles on migrancy appeared, for nearly ten years earlier she had characterized working-class black women as "the unfortunate women of the slums" and middle-class club women as "noble women" whose efforts mark the beginning of "lift[ing] women out of a state of social dependency into the larger world of social independence, duties, and responsibilities . . . of civilization" (393, 396). In this article, "The Awakening of Women," published in the *AME Church Review* in 1897, Williams represented working-class black women as the objects of a philanthropy that had as its goal not the ostensible bettering of "slum" life but the political emancipation of the black middle-class woman through a domestic feminism that would challenge racial prejudice. Williams's rhetoric was part of a larger trend in which arguments for the recognition of black middle-class respectability turned on a demarcation of differences in morality, self-sufficiency, and diligence along class lines. Both Williams's early writings, such as "The Awakening of Women," and her later publications, such as "Social Bonds in the 'Black Belt' of Chicago," mark this tendency to ground a politics of middle-class racial respectability in an indictment of the black working classes and, in particular, migrants.

Even though club women and influential journalists such as Fannie Barrier Williams used the "moral panic" of migrancy to argue for the respectability of the black middle class, whose club women could "purify" the black community of this supposed contagion, a feminist black nationalism indebted to women such as Maria Stewart, linking black female working women to a solidarity and self-sufficiency that would better "the race," persisted in the feminist journalism of several other African American women writing at this time. Indeed, the migrant and working-class black woman as agential subject and figure of potential continued to be a strong theme in the early twentieth-century journalism of African American women.

Addie Hunton, who wrote for preeminent black periodicals such as *The Colored American Magazine, The Voice of the Negro,* and *The Crisis,* pursued a line of argument that echoed Victoria Earle Matthews's earlier advocacy for migrant black women in *Hampton Negro Conference.* Hunton, educated in Boston, became a teacher in Alabama and then moved to Atlanta in 1899 with her husband, where she became active in the YWCA.[61] Hunton was an activist on several fronts, as a member of the NAACP, a pan-Africanist, and a supporter of woman suffrage. Her regular column, "Women's Clubs," in *The*

Crisis marks her importance as a club woman, a member of the NACW, and a recognized writer on issues facing African American women in the early twentieth century. *The Crisis* "embraced . . . a militantly integrationist vision," and was the official organ of the NAACP edited by the eminent black leader, W. E. B. Du Bois. It "promoted pan-Africanism, the liberation of Africa, and the solidarity of 'the darker races' against worldwide white domination" (Hutchinson 145).

In January 1911, Hunton used her *Crisis* column to draw attention to the employment opportunities of black working women in Chicago. She stressed that African American women, whether educated or not, had "no choice but housework," for which they were frequently paid lower wages than those earned by "white maids" when they could find employment. African American domestic workers were paid "$3–4.50 per week" while white women earned six dollars per week ("Employment" 24, 25). "In many cases, especially when the women were living alone," wrote Hunton, "the earnings, plus the income from the lodgers [they would take in], barely covered the rent" (25). While Hunton identified the racism that limited black working-class women's employment opportunities in Chicago, she, like Matthews before her, refused to represent black women as less than active agents with the potential to better their condition. Like Matthews, Hunton stressed the importance of "industrial training" as a route to improved employment opportunities and self-sufficiency (25). And like Matthews, Hunton was not ignorant of the challenges migrating women faced as they worked to establish themselves in the North. She drew her readers' attention to the Traveler's Aid and Protective Association in her July 1911 column. In Norfolk, Virginia, alone, Traveler's Aid met "702 steamers and trains" and assisted "479 girls . . . in various ways" during one year, reported Hunton, primarily focusing on "giving its large number of migratory young women respectable and comfortable rooms" ("Women's Clubs" 122).

Indeed, Hunton worked, as had Matthews before her, to educate her readers on the working conditions of black women migrating to the North, taking care to insist upon the southern black woman's "high virtue" and refuting those who presumed the independent migrant woman was inherently immoral. In an article titled "Negro Womanhood Defended," published in the hallmark "Our Woman's Number" of *Voice of the Negro*,[62] Hunton characterized the southern working woman as having "early realized that the moral and conservative qualities of a race reside in its womanhood, and with this realization came a longing and a reaching after a virtuous home-life; hence, we have thousands of homes dotting this Southland, some mere cottages . . .

all are citadels of purity and virtue" (282). She then linked the black working woman's labor and "thrift" to the education and elevation of "the race," as had Maria Stewart some seventy years earlier: "By her thrift she has helped to . . . raise nearly $14,000,000 for the education of her children. She has educated more than 25,000 teachers of her own race, and all of this, in her hampered condition, in less than a half century. With her deeper interest in her people, her larger knowledge of their needs . . . she is constantly at work for the uplift of her race" (282). Under Hunton's able pen, the uplift of the race, intellectually, morally, and socially, became the responsibility not of middle-class club women but of working women of the South, who were more than up to the task. Working-class and migrant women need not be saved from themselves by interested club women and philanthropists but were already busy at work educating their communities in the South and making the best of stifling labor markets in the urban North. For Hunton, as for Mossell and Matthews before her, migrant women did not need "protective" monitoring but access to industrial training and stopovers in the rooming houses of traveler's aid associations as they continued to pursue their self-determined goals.

Addie Hunton also linked the accumulation of property by working women in the South to racial uplift, an argument Josephine Silone-Yates would make just three years later in the *Colored American Magazine*. Together, Hunton and Silone-Yates were writing on working-class women's political potential for the two African American periodicals with the widest circulation in the early twentieth century, *Voice of the Negro* and the *Colored American Magazine*. In 1904, Hunton credited Southern women with a "thrift [that] has helped to accumulate property, real and personal, to the value of more than $700,000,000" ("Negro Womanhood" 282), and in 1907 Silone-Yates put that thrift into historical context while she also underscored the black working-class woman's contributions to the future of "the race." "This [accumulation of millions of dollars in property] means much more than presents itself on the surface, when we reflect that one of the greatest curses of slavery to the slave was, that by denying him even the God-given right to own himself, the acquisitive faculty largely was destroyed," wrote Silone-Yates. "[A]nd no one . . . will question whether . . . the colored woman has done her part. . . . Our wage-earning women . . . are doing their part towards putting the race on a firm financial basis" (133). Born on Long Island, New York, in 1852, Josephine Silone-Yates was educated at the Institute for Colored Youth in Philadelphia while living with her uncle and his family. She then completed high school in Newport, Rhode Island, and attended the state Normal School at Providence. From 1880 to 1889, she was chemistry professor and head of the department of science at Lincoln Institute in Jefferson, Missouri, some seventeen years before Anna Julia Cooper would chair the modern languages department there. As Hallie Quinn Brown wrote in *Homespun Heroines,* Silone-Yates "had been writing for the press" for "the greater part of her life," and was also "a zealous club worker" and the second president of the NACW (179).

In this article for the monthly *Colored American Magazine* (1900–1909), Silone-Yates adeptly brought together an attention to working-class women as central to racial uplift with the domestic feminism promoted by African American club women. The result was a powerful argument for a feminist black nationalism in which the nation becomes the "home" where woman wields the greatest influence and power. Silone-Yates first establishes woman's "moral, intellectual and industrial emancipation," which has resulted in "a great multiplication of her legal rights and industrial privileges" (132). After making her case for "honor[ing] and prais[ing] the Afro-American mother" (133), she moves to bring these important figures of the working woman and the mother together in her model of the African American family and home as a "profit sharing" enterprise. "Profit sharing between the employer and the employed in a firm or company is one of the most recent methods of securing an equitable distribution of wealth, and the home in many respects should be looked upon as a firm, or cooperative union," she writes, "in which, on some substantial and equitable basis, husband, wife, and children are to share in the accruing profits. . . . In the professions, in the industries, in commercial pursuits . . . woman is proving herself a factor to be reckoned with; but in the midst of all this, let us not forget that there is still a crying need for homes . . . where intelligence and morality rule . . . [and] peace presides" (134). Directly linking the working-class black woman to the domestic feminism that has often been regarded as an exclusively middle-class discourse, Silone-Yates brought together two of the most prevalent concerns of black feminist journalism at the turn into the twentieth century. While women such as Gertrude Mossell and Addie Hunton would write of domestic feminism and working-class and migrant women in separate articles, Silone-Yates's journalism is significant for linking these elements in a feminist black nationalism for *Colored American Magazine*'s nearly eighteen thousand subscribers.

Taken together, the black feminist journalism examined in this chapter offers several important challenges to received understandings of domestic feminism, a politics of racial respectability, and the continuing development of a feminist black nationalism. Focusing on journalism rather than solely on the club movement as the location of a turn-of-the-century black feminist politics, we see that the club movement was not the site of an African American feminist *emergence* into public politics, nor did it represent a consensus of voice for African American feminists. Club women variously advocated for the migrant and working-class woman as agent in racial uplift and the development of the African American "home" and nation *and* vilified her in an attempt to argue for a middle-class respectability she was seen to threaten. Moreover, the domestic feminism the club movement seems to have exclusively championed through a "discourse on raising the standards of home, family life, and motherhood . . . that insist[ed] that the future of the race was moored to African American mothers' moral guardianship" (Knupfer 12) had been in circulation for some sixty years by the time it was promoted by clubs and club women. We see it in the controversial journalism and public lectures of Maria Stewart in the 1830s, and it had its roots in the republican motherhood well before that.

Significantly, Stewart saw domestic feminism as not simply a route into black nationalist discourse (Romero 63), which was espousing a gendered discourse of racial respectability, but as the foundation of the feminist black nationalism she would espouse and pass on to those feminists who followed her. For Stewart, improving the material and working conditions of black women, and encouraging them to devote some of their earnings to their own education and to "strive to excel in good housewifery, knowing that prudence and economy are the road to wealth" ("Essays"), were the central tenets to racial uplift. The working African American woman was not the object of "concern" or a "problem" in Stewart's mind but was the figure whose economic self-sufficiency and care for home and family would ensure the viability of the African American nation. Thus it was crucial that she be intellectually and economically liberated, not "compelled to bury [her] mind and talents beneath a load of iron pots and kettles" ("Essays"). Stewart did not envision the working-class black woman as a rhetorical stepping stone to the increased political participation of the middle-class black woman. Even though "nineteenth-century black women featured discursively almost entirely in relation to the work or 'labor' of racial reform," as Santamarina has argued, a significant body of black feminism did value women "as self-supporting or independent" and endeavored to counter those discourses of racial respectability that tended to marginalize "black women *workers*" (Santamarina 20).

If we trace a line of descent from the journalism of Maria Stewart, through that of Mary Ann Shadd Cary focused on the welfare of refugee African Americans and the participation of black women in public politics, to the black feminist journalism of the late nineteenth and early twentieth centuries, the centrality of free labor and the working woman to a feminist black nationalist politics becomes clear. That link between black women's economic self-sufficiency and black feminism takes several forms, as we have seen, but it persists with such strength in the late nineteenth century that we can no longer maintain that the working black woman circulated primarily as a figure to be managed and contained in the arguments of middle-class black club women who contended for their own right to political participation through her vilification. It has, perhaps, been too tempting to mistake the sheer volume of calls to domestic feminism and the presumed class of the woman such a discourse invokes as the *first* articulation of a public black feminism at the turn into the twentieth century.

Certainly domestic feminism was advocated in the journalism of all the women discussed here and many others,[63] but it was hardly a feminist discourse that emerged only late in the nineteenth century with the national club movement, nor one that was believed to apply only to women of the middle and elite classes. Instead, domestic feminism was central to feminist black nationalism very early in the century and continued to be so as that feminism developed both in the press and in the club movement. As Stephanie Shaw has noted, the Colored Women's League (1892) "was a coalition of 113 organizations" and the National Federation of African-American Women (1895) "of 85 organizations." "When these two federations combined in 1896 to form the NACW, the inclination and impetus for black women to form a collective was more than a few years old" (Shaw, "Black Club Women" 433–44), and predated by generations what Elsa Barkley Brown has argued is often mistakenly hailed as this "inaugural moment or even height of black women's participation in politics" (137). Indeed, we must look to the benevolent societies of the early nineteenth century and to the feminist black nationalism espoused in the press alongside their development as forms, and not the only forms as I have argued, of a black feminism that would continue to be viable and to develop as the century progressed.

An examination of black feminist journalism shows us that African American women were, indeed, not only participating in black public politics well before the turn into the twentieth century but also creating publics through the "reflexive circularity" of the newspaper and periodical. Black feminists were using the press to insist that a domestic feminism and an attention to working black women as potential "mothers" of the nation were central to black nationalist goals of racial uplift and self-sufficiency. In an important sense, the potentiality of both black working-class women and a feminist black nationalism were realized in the pages of the press and through publics these articles not only addressed but created. For, as Michael Warner argues, "the achievement of this cultural form," the press, "is to allow participants in its discourse to understand themselves as *directly and actively* belonging to a social entity *that exists historically in secular time and has consciousness of itself*" (*Publics* 105; emphasis added). African American women journalists made the material conditions of working-class black women central to nationalist politics in a concrete, rather than abstract or symbolic, way; offered their readers the sense that they, too, were participating in a vital debate about black women's political potential; and drew readers—strangers separated by space and circumstance—together on that common ground.[64] In doing so, these black feminists exercised a "new, creative, and distinctly modern mode of power," the "projection of a public" for whom women were necessary political agents (Warner, *Publics* 108). For African American feminist journalists, black women were far from asking to enter into such a politics; rather, they had already proven their ability to realize its goals.

Conclusion

Feminist Affiliations in a Divisive Climate: Anna Julia Cooper's "Woman versus the Indian"

"It is not the intelligent woman vs. the ignorant woman; nor the white woman vs. the black, the brown, and the red,—it is not even the cause of woman vs. man. Nay, 'tis woman's strongest vindication for speaking that *the world needs to hear her voice.* . . . Hers is every interest that has lacked an interpreter and a defender. Her cause is linked with that of every agony that has been dumb—every wrong that needs a voice," wrote Anna Julia Cooper in late 1891 in her essay "Woman versus the Indian" (Cooper, "Woman" 107). An educator, activist for the poor, leader in the social settlement movement and the black women's club movement, and a journalist, Cooper had taken up what she believed to be a low point in the fight for woman suffrage that saw the rights of "woman" pitted against those of "the Negro" and "the Indian" at the National Council of Women's first triennial meeting in Washington, D.C., held February 22–25, 1891.

Women attending the council's meeting heard addresses ranging from the control and care of "Vicious and Dependent Classes" to charities, social purity, "dependent races," women in the church and missionary work, temperance, women's education and employment, suffrage, and women's clubs and associations. While the meeting's agenda lists a range of causes and locations for women's political participation that, it is important to note, also informed the political complexity of black feminisms, the National Council of Women was dominated by white women whose racism had or would soon be called into question by black feminists such as Sojourner Truth, Frances Harper, Ida B. Wells, and Josephine St. Pierre Ruffin. The 1891 meeting was the site of just such conflicts and the venue, effectively, for legitimating expediency arguments and conservative, exclusionary strategies that would be employed by the newly reunited (white) woman suffrage movement in its efforts to win over women from the South to the movement. Anna Howard Shaw, the "queen" of the suffrage platform and later president of the National

American Woman Suffrage Association (NAWSA), gave an address titled "Women vs Indians" in which she denounced the recent enfranchisement of Native Americans in South Dakota at the ostensible expense of "eminent [white] women," such as NAWSA's own Susan B. Anthony (*HWS* 4: 182).

At this same gathering, Frances Ellen Watkins Harper, one of the greats of black feminism and apparently the only black woman to take the platform, also spoke as part of a panel asked to address woman's "Duty to Dependent Races." In this speech, given at a time when lynching was at an all-time high, Harper asserted the claim of "the negro" upon the nation, contending that African Americans were no "dependant race" but worthy citizens deserving of justice and protection from the violent tyranny of the lynch mob. By implication, Harper's silence on "the Indian" seemingly positioned Native Americans as, indeed, one of the "dependent races" of her panel's title with a lesser claim on the franchise and its promised protections than "the negro" could assert. Focusing on that panel, "Duty to Dependent Races," Shaw's speech, and Cooper's essay, this conclusion draws out several important threads in this study of early black feminism and its publics in order to remind us of those central considerations we have seen black feminists working with throughout the century even as we turn our attention to a crucial moment in the overlapping and competing of feminist publics. The expediency arguments of the (white) woman suffrage movement in the early 1890s made rather specific demands of black feminists, even as they created what some would see as opportunities for forging new publics and coalitions. The positions two very different figures like Frances Harper and Anna Julia Cooper took are instructive not only for the picture of black feminism at the century's close they offer us but also for our understanding of what challenges certain politics and appeals continue to present to the histories of early black feminism we create.

A complex picture of black feminism near the close of the nineteenth century emerges from Anna Julia Cooper's response to Shaw's and Harper's National Council of Women addresses in her essay "Woman versus the Indian." Likely in attendance at the council meetings, Cooper saw these addresses as marking a pivotal moment for American feminisms. When expediency arguments had come to define the newly reunited white suffrage movement and the lynching of African Americans was at a frightening peak, Cooper insisted that her readers consider the costs of prioritizing rights—be it the white woman's over all others or "the negro's" over those of other "dependent races." Cooper's essay also drew attention to the unevenness of black feminism, and of American feminisms in general, in the century's last decade as the suffrage movement made its bid for southern support by adopting extreme expediency arguments that prioritized the political enfranchisement of "native-born" white women over women of color, immigrant women, and women of the working classes. Together, Cooper's essay and Harper's speech remind us of the central issues facing black feminists throughout the century: To understand black feminism in its complexity as it reaches and actively creates publics necessitates that we consider the work of appeal, both to gain a hearing at all and to register one's political position and argument; what it is possible and strategic to say in what locations and to what audiences; and the complex position of African American feminists within reform movements, such as abolition, woman's rights, and the suffrage movement. What Cooper's essay uniquely underscores, however, are the possibilities for coalitions amongst feminists in a political climate that thwarted even as it made such affiliations all the more crucial. Cooper's "Woman versus the Indian" enables us to draw together and reconsider the concerns of taking black feminism public as we turn to consider its further grounds and possibilities near the close of the nineteenth century.

A Turning Point for Suffrage at the Nation's Capital

The National Council of Women of the United States was founded along with the International Council of Women (ICW) in 1888 at the second international conference of the National Woman Suffrage Association (NWSA), called by Susan B. Anthony, May Wright Sewall, and other prominent white suffragists. The aim of this conference was to form a National Council of Women in each self-governing country of the world to further the goal of woman's rights.[1] With Frances Willard as president and Susan B. Anthony as vice-president, the National Council of Women of the United States held its first meeting in late February 1891, explicitly addressed to a public interested in "the advancement of women's work in education, philanthropy, reform, and social culture" (Avery 10). The council's meeting immediately preceded the twenty-third annual suffrage convention, both of which were held in Albaugh's Opera House in Washington, D.C., and, consequently, a predominantly suffragist audience was in attendance. Indeed, as the *History of Woman Suffrage* put it, the audience for the National Council of Women meeting "kept on coming, scarcely knowing the difference" between it and the suffrage convention that followed, hardly surprising given the suffrage focus of many council addresses (4: 175).

Eighteen ninety one, the year the council first convened, was a key year for woman suffrage in several important ways. The previous year had seen Wyoming become the first state to grant women the vote; the American Woman Suffrage Association (AWSA) had also merged with its rival the National Woman Suffrage Association (NWSA) to become the National American Woman Suffrage Association (NAWSA) in 1890; and at the National Council of Women meeting NAWSA resolved to focus on bringing women from the southern states into the movement during the coming year (*HWS* 4: 184). The woman suffrage movement had healed its split, dating back to 1869, over the Fifteenth Amendment enfranchising African American men but not women. However, that unification was reached with compromise, one significant compromise being the strategy to bring southern white women on side at the expense of African American women's priorities. Conservative strategies also included expediency arguments premised on racism and nativism, such as the active recruitment of "native born," middle-class American women to the movement at the exclusion of African American women, foreign-born women, and working-class women (Terborg-Penn 56). Woman suffrage in the United States was celebrating its first victory and setting its sights on a renewed and problematically "unified" fight for the vote.

The early 1890s were also significant for black suffragists and their strategies. As Rosalyn Terborg-Penn documents, some African American women continued to attend NAWSA meetings despite the rise in conservatism,[2] while others concentrated on their own agendas including "more radical ideas that connected suffrage and the economy with the status of Black women" (56). The Colored Women's League (1892), which Anna Julia Cooper had helped organize, and the National Federation of African American Women (1895) united in 1896 as the National Association of Colored Women's Clubs, as black women's clubs became prime mobilization sites for suffrage.[3] And in this decade black feminism would see the emergence of what Terborg-Penn calls a third generation of black suffragists, a diverse group of women who were, in the main, middle-class women connected in "nationalist ways" (57) to the reform tradition out of which suffrage grew. These women, "many of whom had been born in the South" (Terborg-Penn 79), would fight for women's rights as they were connected to black nationalist goals of "racial uplift" and community self-sufficiency, pursuing those arguments increasingly through the press.[4] In other words, their work was clearly indebted to the efforts of so many of the women in this study, particularly those of chapter 5, given their use of the press. As has been the case throughout the century from the work of preaching women to that of black feminists involved in abolition, woman's rights, anti-lynching, and a feminist black nationalist politics, in the 1890s we see black feminists taking their politics public through existing and emerging networks, the social bonds facilitated by the press, and the active building of black feminist publics and reform affiliations in varied ways.

Yet the National Council of Women meeting is important to an understanding of black feminism at the close of the nineteenth century not only because it marks a turning point for the woman suffrage movement and for black suffragists but also because it was held in Washington, D.C. As Terborg-Penn has emphasized, "[M]ore than any other southern city of the times, Washington was home to a significant number of African American women suffragists, who networked in various ways" (65).[5] This combination of location—the nation's capital—and critical mass has meant that our understandings of third generation black suffragist strategies and politics are in many ways defined by what was said at meetings in Washington, D.C., for, as Terborg-Penn notes, these women gained hearings in both white and black public spheres and their work was recorded and preserved (65). Given the potential homogenization of black feminism that can result from such a phenomenon, it becomes all the more important to understand that black feminism's strategic affiliations and politics continue to be diverse at the close of the century, rather than coalescing in primary investments in suffrage and the black women's club movement as its mobilizer. Though Cooper is part, then, of that Washington network of black feminists most of whom had southern roots, her "Woman versus the Indian" makes clear that a complex and hardly monolithic black feminism continues to thrive in this divisive climate, debating questions of political affiliation, political goals, and rhetorical strategy.

In several important ways Frances Harper and Anna Julia Cooper represent just that diversity. Coming from very different backgrounds, Harper and Cooper achieved rather different public reputations, in part creating the unique rhetorical situations in which they addressed woman suffrage and black civil rights in 1891. What a figure like Frances Harper, well established and nationally recognized as a prominent abolitionist, advocate of the rights of freedmen and women of the South, and temperance leader, chose as the focus of her remarks at the National Council of Women, and what Anna Julia Cooper, then only emerging as a leading member of Washington's black intelligentsia, could take up in an essay she would later publish as the centerpiece of her collection *A Voice from the South,* are importantly distinctive. That Cooper called for a red-black feminist coalition while Harper believed she must, yet again, demand her nation and white feminists recognize and work to end the violence and intimidation under which African Americans lived, draws attention to the range of political positions black feminists adopted, what they chose to say, and, indeed, what was possible and most strategic for them to say at particular moments and in particular venues. Though white women reformers ostensibly "championed" the rights of "the negro" and "the Indian," black feminists were not necessarily predisposed to link their political interests with those of Native American women. To explore a highly visible moment in which Anna Julia Cooper called for a red-black feminist coalition demands that one not only understand the possible limitations on such affiliations in the political climate of the early 1890s, but also that one examine the diversity and complexity of black feminisms. What Cooper is able to step back and say in the context of an essay for imagined readers, and what Harper chooses as the focus for her remarks at a meeting in which she is, in several ways, a lone voice with perhaps few sympathizers, matter not simply for their content but for what they tell us is possible to say in certain locations and from the position gained from activist work of a particular nature.

Feminist Affiliations and Exclusions at the Dawn of Woman's Era

Anna Julia Cooper was born a slave on August 10, 1858, in Raleigh, North Carolina, only to become regarded by some scholars as one of the most radical African American feminists of her day. After having completed a bachelor's degree in 1884 and a master's degree in mathematics in 1887 at Oberlin College, Cooper moved to Washington, D.C., to teach at the M Street High School. Upon her arrival, Cooper lived for a year in the home of Alexander Crummel,[6] and her social circle included the Grimké family: Angelina Grimké was her close friend and Charlotte Forten Grimké her mentor. From 1901 to 1906 she would be M Street School's principal until a curriculum controversy saw her dismissed. She would not return to Washington and the school until 1910, where she would remain until her retirement in 1930.[7] Cooper began building a reputation as a popular public speaker during those early years in Washington, and many of her most well known and highly regarded lectures were given from the mid-1880s through the 1890s at venues such as the American Negro Academy, of which she was the only elected female member, the Conference of Educators of Colored Youth (1890), the World's Congress of Representative Women (1893), and the First National

Conference of Colored Women (1895).[8] In 1900 Cooper would represent African American men and women at the Pan African Conference in London.

Yet contemporary scholars position Cooper as "more a scholar than a public figure," whose work "for racial uplift [focused on] . . . lecturing and writing provocative essays" (Logan, "What" 150). They speculate that "Cooper's activism was never as widely recognized as Mary Church Terrell's or Ida B. Wells-Barnett's," nor her writings "as numerous or as well known as [W. E. B.] Du Bois's" because her social activism was largely "local" and because her insights were unique.[9] Indeed, scholars have called her political positions "isolating" because they "anticipated by nearly a century today's debates" regarding the intersections of race, gender and class (Lemert, "Colored" 7, 14–15). Yet Cooper was clearly highly regarded by her activist and intellectual contemporaries, as indicated by her invitations to speak at such important events as the World's Congress of Representative Women alongside preeminent feminists and reformers such as Frances Harper and Fannie Barrier Williams, her membership in the American Negro Academy with the likes of Alexander Crummel and W. E. B. Du Bois, and her organizational role in the Colored Women's League of Washington, whose members included Mary Church Terrell and Coralie Franklin Cook.

Even though Cooper also has been hailed by scholars as "the" prototypical black feminist for her sustained considerations of race, class, and gender's interimplications in *A Voice from the South,* she has occupied a vexed position in scholarship on black feminism. Cooper tends to be alternately read as elitist for what appear to be her wholesale endorsements of the standards and values of bourgeois or "true" womanhood, and as an astute critic of imperialism who, "unlike Frances Harper, . . identified the intimate link between internal and external colonization, between domestic racial oppression and imperialism" (Carby, *Reconstructing* 101).[10] Rather than considering that Cooper's range of arguments reflect the diversity of black feminism at the close of the nineteenth century, particularly given the rise of the black woman's club movement, which has itself been criticized for elitism, scholars have labeled these positions "contradictions" in Cooper's work. Consequently, Cooper has been somewhat underexamined in studies of black feminist thought and activism.[11]

These opposed readings of Cooper are also made possible, in part, by her subtlety as she preferred to catch her readers and audiences off guard with what some have called "rhetorical traps" (Lemert, "Colored" 28). In an essay like "Woman versus the Indian," that subtlety can mean that readers are left perplexed by Cooper's choice to bookend an essay apparently bemoaning the racist treatment of African American women on the railway with indictments of white suffrage leaders for their racism and a call for an antiracist feminism that understands "woman's cause" as "the cause of every man or woman who has writhed silently under a mighty wrong" ("Woman" 108). Cooper may appear to be arguing that the black woman's experiences on the railway—confined to smoking cars, ejected from trains, and left "wondering under which head" she comes when faced with washrooms marked "'FOR LADIES' . . . and 'FOR COLORED PEOPLE'"—are examples of the racism the woman's movement should aim to eradicate, a racism that notably affects privileged black women through the style and comfort in which they may travel ("Woman" 95). Indeed, Mary Helen Washington has indicted Cooper for betraying "her sympathies . . . with the poor and uneducated" with "images in *A Voice* . . . of privileged women" excluded from railway cars and "culture clubs" (xlix). Or Cooper is taken to move from indictments of suffragists like Anna Howard Shaw to "other subjects—principally to a complicated theory of race and sex caste in American society" (Lemert, "Colored" 31). How the essay's opening and closing come together with what still other scholars have called Cooper's critique of imperialism in "Woman versus the Indian" is left largely unexplored.

Yet in what seems like an essay wholly occupied with the indignities elite African American women suffer in the late nineteenth century, particularly in the American South, Cooper's "Woman versus the Indian," in fact, takes up a central issue for American feminism in the early 1890s. Cooper obviously saw herself as participating in the central feminist debates of her day, given that she claimed to speak for and as "the black woman of the South" in *Voice* at precisely the moment when the suffrage movement had declared itself to be wooing southern white women. That *Voice* appeared in 1892, the very year NAWSA promised it would bring southern states into the movement, is hardly accidental despite its being rarely, if ever, remarked upon in scholarship on Cooper's work. Given this context, it is all the more significant that in this essay Cooper argues for the importance of a red-black feminist coalition—another possible public for black feminism at the dawn of woman's era—a coalition forged not only in opposition to the racism within the woman suffrage movement but also one in and for itself. Indeed, Cooper's essay enacts a coalitional feminism, urging its readers to recognize the linked oppressions of Native Americans and African Americans in a contemplation of the railway, American manners, and competition for the suffrage and citizenship so central to the woman suffrage movement at the close of the nineteenth century.

Despite its importance and its frequent citation as the essay Cooper desired to be the centerpiece of *A Voice from the South,* "Woman versus the Indian" has been contextualized in ways that limit critical understanding of the work she may have been pursuing through it. Cooper opens the essay with an indirect indictment of Anna Howard Shaw, Susan B. Anthony, and the woman suffrage movement as racist. Cooper notes the inconsistencies between Shaw's address, "Women vs Indians," to the National Council of Women in 1891 calling for the primacy of the white woman's vote in baldly racist terms and her earlier repudiation of an African American woman's exclusion from Wimodaughsis, a woman's club of which Shaw had been president. Although Shaw's speech prioritizes the (white) woman's vote over the suffrage for "Indians" and, in fact, all people of color, the working classes, and immigrants, she also once threatened to resign as national president of Wimodaughsis because the Kentucky branch of the club refused to admit an African American applicant. [12] As Cooper writes with biting sarcasm, "the Kentucky secretary" of Wimodaughsis failed to "calculate that there were any wives, mothers, daughters, and sisters, except white ones," and upon seeing a "solitary cream-colored applicant" before her, refused her membership (Cooper, "Woman" 88).

This critical accusation in Cooper's essay has been poorly contextualized. Charles Lemert, editor with Esme Bahn of the only collection of Cooper's essays, papers, and letters, including *Voice* (1998), speculates that Wimodaughsis was Cooper's creation and, by extension, that the African American woman rejected by the club was simply an archetype for the racism black women experienced in the feminist movement more largely at the time (Lemert, "Colored" 28–29). Lemert footnotes Cooper's reference to Wimodaughsis by noting that "it is hard to imagine that Cooper is not joking here, either by making up the ridiculous acronym or, if it was indeed the name of a club, by using it without comment" (Lemert, "Colored" 28 n. 50). In fact, Wimodaughsis was a very well known club needing little comment for Cooper's readers at the time. A suffrage-oriented national woman's club, Wimodaughsis was founded in 1890 by Emma Gillett and headquartered in Washington, D.C. Branches of Wimodaughsis continue to be active today.[13] Its name is an amalgam of wife, mother, daughter, and sister, and the club purported to disregard members' race, religion, or class. Incorporated as an educational society to help working women further their education, the D.C. headquarters of Wimodaughsis provided courses for women in areas such as

French and Journalism. Stockholding members contributed their five dollars per share to the building of the Washington, D.C., clubhouse, and its members included Elizabeth Cady Stanton and Susan B. Anthony.

Cooper goes on to note that while "Susan B. Anthony and Anna Shaw are evidently too noble to be held in thrall by the provincialisms of women who seem never to have breathed the atmosphere beyond the confines of their grandfathers' plantations" in the Wimodaughsis affair, they nonetheless have stooped "from the broad plateau of light and love" to become "as fearful of losing caste as a Brahmin in India" (Cooper, "Woman" 89, 91). For Cooper, Shaw's speech, "Women vs Indians" amounts to nothing "less than a blunder," for in delivering it Shaw has failed her responsibility as a feminist and leader of the suffrage movement: "Miss Shaw is one of the most powerful of our leaders, and we feel her voice should give no uncertain note. Woman should not, even by inference, or for the sake of argument, seem to disparage what is weak" (Cooper, "Woman" 105). By implication, Susan B. Anthony has similarly failed by pursuing expediency arguments that contend the suffrage for (white) women take precedence over the suffrage for all other groups, including "the Indians" of Shaw's speech. Yet Cooper's editors also question whether Shaw's speech was, in fact, given at the first meeting of the National Council of Women of the United States in 1891: "It is possible that Cooper's reference to the 'National Woman's Council' could have been a mistaken allusion to the NWSA before which Shaw was a prominent lecturer in 1891" (Lemert, "Colored" 28 n. 50). The implication is that Shaw's speech, like Wimodaughsis, may have been Cooper's creation, in this case an amalgam of Shaw's speeches while national lecturer for NWSA, which had, Lemert fails to note, become NAWSA by 1891. Although Shaw's speech is not included in the National Council of Women's transactions for this meeting, it can be found in the *History of Woman Suffrage*'s account of the gathering. Far from a convenient straw man for Cooper's purposes, Shaw's speech is part of the established, mainstream account of the American suffrage movement compiled by its leaders.

Shaw, however, circulates phantom-like in the editorial apparatus of Cooper's collected work, leaving the reader to wonder what Shaw did say and to what audience, and in turn raising the possibility that Cooper's critique of white feminists and the racism within the suffrage movement—both the pro-suffrage Wimodaughsis and the National Council of Women of the United States—may be a convenient creation for her purposes. Yet the importance of documenting the context to which Cooper speaks extends from Shaw's particular address to the larger discourse on Native American rights circulating in the early 1890s. We cannot understand Cooper's essay as moving beyond an indictment of white women reformers to a performance of a coalitional feminism if we do not know how her extended treatment of discrimination against African American women on the railway connects both to discourses of Native American "civility" and to the effects of the transcontinental railway upon Native Americans.

Suffrage, Citizenship, and "Dependent Races"

Touted as the most renowned American woman speaker of all time and "queen" of the suffrage platform, Anna Shaw was one of the strongest reform and suffrage voices the American public heard at the close of the nineteenth century. Like many of her contemporaries, Shaw's reform roots were in abolition. Her parents were abolitionists who had assisted fugitive slaves, and the family had also established a colony in northern Michigan in 1858, "half a dozen miles from any neighbor, save Indians, wolves and wildcats" (Linkugel and Solomon 4). Shaw became a licensed Methodist preacher in the early 1870s and attended Boston University Theological School. By the 1880s she was an established temperance lecturer, and in 1885 she became a full-time lecturer for suffrage, temperance, and social purity. In 1890, Shaw was appointed national lecturer by NAWSA and in 1892 became the organization's vice president. During Shaw's tenure as president of NAWSA from 1904 to 1915, the number of states with full suffrage nearly tripled and the organization's membership rose from 17,000 to 183,000 (Linkugel and Solomon 76).

On February 23, 1891, Shaw addressed suffragists in Washington, D.C., on "Women vs Indians." Focusing on the enfranchisement of "the Indians" in South Dakota in 1890, Shaw noted that "45 per cent. of the votes cast the preceding year were for male Indian suffrage and only 37 per cent. for woman suffrage." Going on to complain that "Indians in blankets and moccasins were received in the State convention with the greatest courtesy" while "Susan B. Anthony and other eminent women were barely tolerated," Shaw depicted Native Americans in South Dakota as undeserving of the ballot. "[W]hile these Indians were engaged in their ghost dances, the white women were going up and down in the State pleading for the rights of citizens," she argued (A. Shaw 182). Then, willfully ignoring that in South Dakota, at least, "the Indian" was now the political better of the white woman, she declared that "the solution of the Indian Question" be left "to a commission of women with Indian reformer and suffragist Alice Fletcher at its head," whose aim would be to "mete out to the Indian, to the negro, to the foreigner . . . the justice which we demand for ourselves" (A. Shaw 182–83). Shaw's denigration of Native Americans themselves, and of their spiritual and cultural practices, is a bald and obvious attempt to position (white) woman as not only more deserving of the ballot but, indeed, already engaging in her civic responsibilities. That image of the white woman as more responsible than "the Indian" continues in Shaw's deliberate selection of Alice Fletcher as the head of her proposed commission to solve "the Indian Question." Fletcher, a respected anthropologist, had some ten years earlier drafted what became the blueprint for a national severalty program that would bargain away Native American lands for Native American citizenship. Through plans like Fletcher's, "the Indian" could only "prove" his fitness for citizenship by being a responsible, individual landowner; "the Indian" could not achieve this status without the guidance of the more "civilized," in this case the white woman and the nation state upon whose behalf and in whose interests she acted.

Commissions formed in the interests of Indian reform were, as Shaw well knew, already in place and "met[ing] out to the Indian" a rather different "justice" than that Shaw demanded for (white) women. One such commission was the Woman's National Indian Association (WNIA), founded in 1879 by interested white women to ostensibly protest the encroachment of railroads and settlers into Indian Territory in violation of federal treaties.[14] By 1883, The WNIA had called for recognition of Native American rights under the law, the universal education of Native American children, the dismantling of the reservation system, and the reallotment of tribal lands to individual Native Americans. Under the Dawes Severalty Act of 1887, in exchange for renouncing their tribal holdings, Native Americans would receive individual land grants of 160 acres to family heads, 80 acres to single men, and 40 acres to dependent children. After twenty-five years, individual landholders would be given title to the land and become citizens.[15] When all allocations had been made, the extensive lands remaining were declared surplus and opened for sale to non–Native Americans. By 1934, allotment had left 100,000 Native Americans without land and had exacted from Native American tribes and nations over 90 million acres of former reservation lands (Hirschfelder and Kreipe de Montano 22). And while the WNIA also advocated for the legal protection of "suffering, undefended, ever-endangered Indian women and children" in the early 1880s, that "protection" became the WNIA's domestic missionary work encroaching on Native American homes and tribal communities with a "christianization" ostensibly designed to "hasten" Native American "civilization . . . and enfranchisement" (qtd. in Mathes 5).

The question of citizenship and enfranchisement for Native Americans at the time Shaw gave her speech was fraught, linked as it was to forced assimilation and the promotion of citizenship as individualism at the expense of Native American sovereignty and lands. Fraught, too, was the framing of arguments for "woman's" citizenship and enfranchisement in the 1890s. Shaw's "Women vs Indians" is not simply an example of the white suffrage movement's expediency arguments arising with its reunification, which contended that a scarcity of resources in the struggle for political rights made it expedient to enfranchise (white) women before "dependent races." Rather, Shaw's speech, given her status and reputation, functions as NAWSA's justification for the ever more racist and nativist politics it was only just beginning to embark upon as it made its move to draw white southerners into the movement, thereby expanding and securing its base and support for the struggle ahead. Shaw's speech also reveals the willful ignorance upon which that anxiety over resources rested to which expediency arguments were then appealing. Shaw and NAWSA had little to fear from Indian reform and its yoking of potential citizenship to land reallotment. Yet the National Council of Women's meeting in 1891 reveals how successful that anxious-making appeal to competing rights among the "oppressed classes" could be.

Opening the panel on "Dependent Races," Alice Fletcher—Shaw's proposed head of the commission to solve "the Indian Question"—delivered her speech "Our Duty to Dependent Races." Fletcher's remarks focused on "the Red Man" and his ability to "bre[e]d evil among" whites "by turning loose the lightly-leased savage elements of our nature" as evidenced by "the conduct of white men . . . in the West among the Indians" (Fletcher 83–84). Fletcher, an anthropologist and Indian reformer, was active in implementing land allotment among the Omaha and Nez Percé. She had drafted the Omaha Severalty Act of 1882, regarded as the precursor to the national allotment program initiated by the Dawes Act. Fletcher had also proposed that when Native Americans returned from boarding schools they be lent funds to "build white-style houses" in order to exemplify "civilized living" in their communities and stressed the role of Native American women in assimilating "the Indian" (Landsman 270). At the Hampton Institute of Virginia, dedicated to the vocational education of Native and African Americans, Fletcher and the WNIA had raised money to "build model cottages so that young, married Indian couples could be trained in the art of Victorian domesticity." However, "over half of the adults from the model family program died within a few years of their return home" due to the impoverishment and resulting poor health conditions consequent to allotment (Olund 163, 164). Still, Fletcher praised the Dawes Act and the WNIA for their shared efforts to usher "the Indian" into civilization and "the rights of citizenship" (Fletcher 84).

Immediately following Fletcher's speech urging white women to fulfill their duty to the Indian, Frances Harper reminded them of theirs to "the negro," then being lynched in the name of a feared "negro supremacy." By 1891, Frances Harper was sixty-six years old and had been politically active in reform since the mid-1850s, when her outrage over the Fugitive Slave Act drew her into abolition and antislavery lecturing.[16] Harper was also, by the 1890s, a highly respected national figure known for her activism as well as for her poetry, novels, and short fiction.[17] Like Sojourner Truth, Harper had sold her books at her antislavery lectures (Peterson 122), and because she earned her livelihood by her writing, her economic independence and survival was very much a consequence of her public reputation. Harper was also well regarded outside of reform circles, with her "work regularly appear[ing] in—and her activities . . . respectfully reported by—the white press in the United States and in England" (Foster, "Gender" 48). Although Harper had been a vocal critic of racism within the woman's rights movement and was active in the black women's club movement, becoming vice-president of the National Association of Colored Women in 1897, scholars also mark her awareness that "in order to transform the social and political condition of black women alliances with white women were important, if not crucial" (Carby 118). As Frances Smith Foster documents, Harper "was one of the very few African-American women able to gain some measure of acceptance in the American Women's Suffrage Association, the National Council of Women, and the Women's Christian Temperance Union." In fact, Harper was an internationally recognized temperance leader; serving as the superintendent of the "Philadelphia and the Pennsylvania 'colored' chapters" from 1883 to 1890, she remained active within the WCTU until at least 1893 (F. Foster, "Introduction," *Brighter* 21).

Harper opened her speech by refusing to include "the negro" in the category of dependent races, arguing that African Americans be regarded as "member[s] of the body politic who ha[ve] a claim upon the nation for justice, simple justice, which is the right of every race, upon the government for protection, which is the rightful claim of every citizen, and upon our common Christianity for the best influences which can be exerted for peace on earth and good-will to man" (Harper, "Duty" 86). Not once does Harper mention "the Indian" and, instead, argues that the greatest claim on the white woman and the nation is "the negro." Harper's attention to lynching in 1891 presses the demand to end the butchering and burning alive of hundreds of black men, women, and children.[18] Indeed, Harper's stress in this speech is on the nation's claim to civilization, an ironic and perhaps deliberate choice given Fletcher's sketch of the "Red Man's" savagery as contagion spreading among whites in the West. "Our first claim upon the nation and government is the claim for protection to human life," urged Harper. "That claim should lie at the basis of our civilization, not simply in theory but in fact. Outside of America, I know of no other civilized country . . . where men are still lynched, murdered, and even burned for real or supposed crimes" (Harper, "Duty" 86–87). It is hardly surprising that Harper should focus on lynching in this speech, given its use as a tool of political intimidation and one soon to draw international censure through the anti-lynching efforts of Ida B. Wells as we have seen.

Yet I would argue it remains significant that Harper contends for the greater claim of "the negro" at the expense of an opportunity to align African American claims on the nation's "civility" with those of Native Americans. Here it is important to understand that Harper was not alone as a black feminist to urge "the negro's" greater claim to rights, for Mary Ann Shadd Cary had also done so in the *Provincial Freeman* in 1854 as she promoted emigration to Canada.[19] Yet neither was Harper ignorant of nor unsympathetic to the oppression of Native Americans. In fact, Harper had written about the "wrongs of the Indian" in 1862, at a time when we might have expected her to have focused primarily upon the condition of African Americans given this was the midst of the Civil War. Yet she did not—aware, perhaps, of the further devastating effects the Homestead Act of 1862 would undoubtedly have upon Native Americans who had already been driven from their lands under the Indian removals decades earlier[20]—and instead linked those "wrongs of the Indian" to the "outrages of the negro" in a jeremidical warning to the nation. In this 1862 letter to the *Christian Recorder,* the longest running black newspaper in the United States and then an eight-page weekly, Harper warned of the consequences of the nation's lacking "contrition for the wrongs of the Indian or the outrages of the negro." For Harper these were lessons that America "should have learned amid the wrecks of ancient empires, buried beneath the weight of their crimes" (qtd. in Peterson 134). She warned that America awaited a fate similar to Egypt and Babylon for its crimes against "the Indian" and "the negro." Nor was Harper averse to taking controversial positions in lectures before woman's rightists.

In her May 1866 speech, "We Are All Bound Up Together," given at the Eleventh National Woman's Rights Convention in New York, Harper linked her critique of white women within the movement to an avocation of rights for all, regardless of race or position, much as Cooper would nearly thirty years later. "This grand and glorious revolution which has commenced, will fail to reach its climax of success, until . . . the nation shall be so color-blind, as to know no man by the color of his skin or the curl of his hair. It will then have no privileged class, trampling upon and outraging the unprivileged classes, but will be then one great privileged nation," contended Harper. She immediately followed with her position on suffrage: "I do not believe that giving the woman the ballot is immediately going to cure all the ills of life. I do not believe that white women are dewdrops just exhaled from the skies. I think that like men they may be divided into three classes, the good, the bad, and the indifferent" (Harper, "All Bound Up" 218). Yet in this speech Harper closed with a focus on black civil rights and, interestingly, her experience on the southern railway and Philadelphia's streetcars. "You white women speak here of rights. I speak of wrongs. I, as a colored woman, have had in this country an education which has made me feel as if I were in the situation of Ishmael, my hand against every man, every man's hand against me," said Harper. "Let me go tomorrow morning and take my seat in one of your street cars—I do not know that they will do it in New York, but they will in Philadelphia—and the conductor will put up his hand and stop the car rather than let me ride. . . . Going from Washington to Baltimore this spring, they put me in the smoking car. Aye, in the capital of the nation . . . they put me in the smoking car!" (Harper, "All Bound Up" 218).

Why, then, does Harper link the "outrages of the Negro" to "the wrongs of the Indian" in her 1862 letter but appear to equivocate on that position four years later by moving from championing the rights of all "unprivileged classes" to the seemingly greater "wrongs" she "as a colored woman" has experienced in this country at the national woman's rights convention of 1866? Harper, like the other black feminists upon whom this study has focused, was carefully attuned to both audience and venue as key considerations for the appeal she would present in any given speech or writing. While the politics appear to shift, it is important to notice that the venue for Harper's statements shifts as well, from a black newspaper and the black public sphere to a white-dominated woman's rights convention and the overlapping and competing publics of white and black feminisms. And Harper seems to have known and judged well her audience, for it was her closing remarks on her ejection from Philadelphia streetcars and her confinement to the smoking car in the nation's capital that drew a response from those woman's rightists gathered in New York. Indeed, one woman interjected, "[T]hey will not do that here," while the crowd cried loudly, and repeatedly, "Shame" as Harper related her experiences ("All Bound Up" 218). Those women were better able to sympathize with a woman suffering such indignities than they were able to imagine themselves as part of the racial climate that made them possible in the first place, remaining silent as Harper suggested that not each and every one of them were "dewdrops exhaled from the skies." Yet Harper refused to allow them such selective outrage by saying of segregated public transportation, "Have women nothing to do with this?" ("All Bound Up" 218).

Still, in 1866 Harper stopped short of using the railway to explicitly connect, in her listeners' minds, those "wrongs of the Indian" and "outrages of the Negro" as Cooper would do in 1891, even though the Railroad Enabling Act of 1866 and its appropriation of Native American lands for the use of railway corporations is clearly part of those linked wrongs as Cooper points out. In other words, while the railway circulated with some of the same cultural meanings in 1866 as it would when Cooper indicted America's national symbol of progress in 1891, Harper did not confront her audience with the same imperialist consequences the railway marked as Cooper later would. And by 1891, Harper herself would not take the opportunity to mention the "wrongs of the Indian" together with the "outrages of the Negro," instead refusing "the negro" be classed as a "dependent race" yet saying nothing of whether "the Indian" were or not. What white suffragists would hear, what they could sympathize with and so see as an affiliate cause, in part determined what Harper would argue in 1891 as it apparently had in 1866. Certainly, by then Harper had decades of experience working within predominantly white reform networks and was well aware of the need to shape carefully her political appeals to overlapping and competing publics.

American Manners and the Railway

Given Frances Harper's focus on the greater claim of "the negro" at the National Council of Women in 1891, then, it is all the more significant that Anna Julia Cooper's essay published a year later would not only indict the racist treatment of African American feminists within the woman's rights movement but also critique the battle over rights in an ostensible climate of scarcity pitting white suffragists against "dependent races" and black against red.[21] Cooper's essay marks her astute reading of not only Shaw's speech but also Fletcher's and Harper's speeches as well as white women's reform of "the Indian" more largely. Appearing to focus on the indignities African American women suffer on the American South's railway system, Cooper's essay plays on that mode of transport as an historical source of oppression for Native Americans and African Americans and as a symbol of "national progress." Cooper clearly recognized that the development of the railway in the United States came at a severe cost to Native Americans well beyond the Railroad Enabling Act of 1866 that appropriated Native American lands for such corporate use. It is then quite to the point that Cooper casually observes that "there can be no true test of national courtesy without travel" and seemingly by the way suggests that while white Americans see "our well-nigh perfect railroad systems" as the epitome of "the comfort and safety of American travel, even for the weak and unprotected," she has "some material [she] could furnish" on the railway's realities, "though possibly it might not be just on the side" the American public may "wish to have illuminated" (Cooper, "Woman" 94, 92). Cooper goes on to elaborate upon the discrimination she has endured while riding the railway of a Jim Crow South, thus subtly presenting her readers with this mode of comfortable and safe American travel as, in fact, a tool of oppression. The "weak and unprotected" of Cooper's essay, who at first glance appear to be (white) women reassured they can travel safely on the railway, are in fact those "dependent races" with which white female reformers like those attending the National Council of Women meeting are so concerned. Far from comfortable and safe as a result of the railway's expansion across the nation, "the Indian" and "the negro" are the more firmly kept in dispossessed place by it.

Cooper argues that the national genocide, exploitation, and dispossession of African Americans and Native Americans is a responsibility for white American women to shoulder. If the railway is a true test of national courtesy, and if, as Cooper argues following the rhetoric of domestic feminism at the time, the "American woman . . . is responsible for American manners" (Cooper 90), then the oppression of Native Americans and African Americans can no longer be viewed as competing with the white woman's in a hierarchy of victimization fueling expediency arguments in the suffrage movement. Rather, the oppression of the so-called dependent races is the direct result of the "American woman's" now-questionable civilizing effects upon the nation: "[L]ike mistress, like nation," as Cooper says ("Woman" 92). The white woman is responsible for the way in which America treats her "weak and unprotected," not simply one of her nation's victimized number. Consequently, argues Cooper, the white woman's civilizing impulse should be turned not to the uncivilized and unchristianized "Indian" but rather to her own back yard.

With an attention to tracing the effects of a white American incivility, Cooper refers to the conductor who would eject her from the ladies' car as "an American citizen who has been badly trained . . . sadly lacking in both 'sweetness' and 'light'" and then turns her gaze out the car window to a chain-gang of African American youths "working on private estates . . . not in 1850, but in 1890, '91 and '92." Cooper makes a mental memo that "the women in this section should organize a Society for the Prevention of Cruelty to Human Beings, and disseminate civilizing tracts, and send throughout the region apostles of anti-barbarism," exclaiming under her breath, "What a field for the missionary woman" (Cooper, "Woman" 95). Indeed, a richer field for those missionary women of the WNIA would be the nation itself, the "least courteous . . . on the globe" according to Cooper and one in need of a "national . . . department for . . . GOOD MANNERS" (96). Under Cooper's witty and able pen, then, that bugbear of disqualification for citizenship and fair treatment, incivility and "barbarism," is the state of white Americans, not Native or African Americans, and it is best witnessed on that symbol of national and imperialist progress that has dispossessed and daily oppresses America's "dependent races," the railway.

Anna Shaw's "Women vs Indians" is all the more dangerous in Cooper's view given that it manipulates its audience into seeing the white woman as potential victim of the newly enfranchised "Indian." Instead, Cooper contends that "woman's cause" is to see the struggle for rights as an affiliated rather than competing one: "[W]hen the weak shall have received their due consideration, then woman will have her 'rights,' and the Indian will have his rights, and the Negro will have his rights, and all the strong will have learned at last . . . the secret of universal courtesy which is after all nothing but . . . regarding one's neighbor as one's self" (Cooper, "Woman" 105). Moreover, the effect of a scarcity of rights or expediency argument upon African American feminists themselves is also Cooper's target in this essay. She contends repeatedly that "the cause of freedom is not the cause of a race or a sect, a party or a class," that "it is not the intelligent woman vs. the ignorant woman; nor the white woman vs. the black, the brown, and the red," but rather "the cause of human kind" (Cooper, "Woman" 106, 107). In what is surely a caution against positions like that taken by Frances Harper in arguing the greater claim of "the negro" on the nation or Mary Ann Shadd Cary's view of "the negro" as more "progressive [in] character" than "the red man" (qtd. in Conaway 239), Cooper calls instead for connections between races and classes. Refusing the opposition between white women and "the black, the brown, the red," Cooper also implicitly calls for affiliations between those women of "dependent races," whom white suffragists like Anna Shaw seek to pit not only against the white woman but against each other. Just as "woman" cannot "rest her plea . . . on Indian inferiority, nor on Negro depravity," so too must African American feminists not effectively seek to capitalize upon the suffrage movement's racism by turning their backs on other women of color in favor of appealing to white women on behalf of "the negro's" greater claim.

In a larger sense, that refusal of competing claims is also a refusal of individualism itself. Cooper's stance—using a discourse of universalism even as she repudiates the abstract individualism to which it appeals—is no small gesture for a feminist at the close of the nineteenth century since, as Joan Scott has noted, "the revolutionary promise to realize the individual human rights of liberty, equality, and political participation has been the basis for woman's claim for citizenship in Western democracies since the eighteenth century. . . . [F]eminism, even as we know it today, would not exist without abstract individualism" ("Universalism" 1). Indeed, as we have seen it is virtually a hallmark of early black feminism to present a double-voiced appeal in order to be heard by, yet also critique, the politics of those existing reform networks that were, in part, black feminism's publics. Yet Cooper refuses individualism with an awareness of what it exacts in the claim for and realization of citizenship. Effectively, the condition of Native American citizenship under the Dawes Act and "Indian reform," such as that promoted by the Indian Rights Association and the WNIA, becomes individualism through land severalty, a promised inclusion of individual Native American land owners in the US nation only at the expense of Native American sovereignty, culture, and tribal community. The Dawes Act was the first of a series of acts and declarations that rescripted Native American citizenship as potential, a potential realized only through what it called the adoption of "the habits of civilized life," which would ensure "the absorption of the Indians into our national life, not as Indians, but as American citizens" (qtd. in Benn Michaels 31).[22] Citizenship for Native Americans, then, rested on "one's own actions," as Walter Benn Michaels puts it, on the individual's potential and choice to *become* "civilized" and thereby become a citizen (32).

Were Cooper's focus on the railway and the experiences of African American women under its Jim Crow policies to advance an argument for a citizen's rights of access in "Woman vs the Indian," she too would be pursuing a politics of individual rights and one that must necessarily ignore that such access—to the railway, which is both tool and realization of genocidal expansionism—is always both the promised result and constitutive of an imperialist exploitation. Cooper quite rightly recognizes that any black feminist activism seeking rights of access as a marker of citizenship risks colluding with a white imperialist project, so that recognizing the black woman as individual citizen due "comfort and safety" comes at the continued exploitation and dispossession of Native Americans. This may be why Cooper subtly, though with devastating acuity, rewords Shaw's speech title, changing it from its original "Women vs Indians" to "Woman versus the Indian." Doing so not only signals the individualism driving an expediency of rights argument in the white suffrage movement but also warns against a similar individualist ethic in a black feminist politics that would argue "the negro's" greater claim at the expense of the rights of other "oppressed classes." Cooper ends her essay by reminding her readers that such "wrongs" as those she has contemplated will always be "indissolubly linked with *all* undefended woe" ("Woman" 108; emphasis added). The "civility" of the nation is a direct consequence of its barbarity to "the Indian" and "the negro" and in greater need of the white woman's missionary work than she supposes the reservation or the un-Reconstructed South to be. The positions of African Americans and Native Americans within the nation are linked historically as well as by present circumstances, making the need for coalition rather than competition between black and red all the more urgent at the dawn of "woman's era."[23]

Why was this an argument Cooper could forward in 1891 while Harper clearly believed the more pressing work for her to undertake was reminding "the nation" that "our ['the negro's'] first claim upon the nation and government is the claim for protection to human life" ("Duty" 87)? Near the end of her highly respected career as a reformer, at the age of sixty-six, Frances Harper knew the risks of taking a position that could alienate those she addressed.[24] Part of an earlier generation of black women reformers who had worked both within black politics and alongside white women in abolition, temperance, and woman's rights, Harper knew only too well the need for and limits of "sisterly sympathy" across the color line. That she raised the specter of lynching before a predominantly white and female audience a full year before Ida B. Wells's infamous article in the *Free Speech* and two years before Wells would begin a national and, eventually, international anti-lynching campaign that would dispute the myth of the black male rapist was certainly risk enough. Harper's audience was hardly what we might today call diverse; while there were undoubtedly some of those Washingtonian black feminists, indeed, likely Cooper herself, in attendance at the National Council of Women meeting, they would have been a distinct minority. Moreover, Harper must have been aware that she had secured and needed to maintain the acceptance of black women—even if only of herself—within national feminist organizations like the National Council of Women. Harper could take her audience only so far, and it is a testament to her experience, her incisive understanding of the complexities of audience, venue, and self-positioning, and her oratorical skill that she was able to argue her case without being dismissed by her listeners. This is not to say that Harper was one to pull her punches but that she had for years worked with multiple and, at times, competing publics and such work makes particular demands with which Harper was intimately familiar.

In contrast, Anna Julia Cooper's public career was in its early stages in 1891 as Harper's was nearing its close. Living until 1964, Cooper's productivity as a writer and speaker continued until 1930 and is regarded as having begun in 1886 with "Womanhood: A Vital Element in the Regeneration and Progress of a Race," a speech delivered to a convention of African American clergymen in Washington, D.C. Harper was a first-generation black suffragist, and Cooper was part of that third generation of whom Terborg-Penn writes and has been described as "the most widely recognizable symbols of the new black woman" (Lemert, "Colored" 4). And while Harper's livelihood depended upon her public reputation, since she made her living by her writing and speaking, Cooper's career was in education. Even though Cooper fell victim to political controversy at the M Street School, she was able to secure another teaching post, chairing the Modern Languages Department at Lincoln Institute, and eventually returned to be principal of M Street. She was able to pursue graduate work and attain her doctorate. In other words, the risks Cooper managed were distinctly different than those Harper had to consider. Cooper, it is important to remember, made her arguments in an essay, not a speech, to an imagined audience rather than, as did Harper, to women seated before her with whom she had worked or who had come to know and respect her through a lengthy and established career in reform. Who Cooper may have imagined her audience to be for "Woman versus the Indian," and for *A Voice from the South* in general, would have undoubtedly included her fellow black feminists and her fellow black intellectuals both male and female, since *Voice* was published by Aldine Publishing House,[25] as well as white women reformers and suffragists.

In many senses, then, Frances Harper and Anna Julia Cooper can be seen to represent the complexity and diversity of black feminism at the century's close—with its different goals and strategies—even as they also represent the longstanding concerns black feminists managed throughout the century as they addressed publics and worked to maintain a voice in the varied politics of their day. And even as we consider their differences as, in part, generational or as differences of position, there are consequences to the very different places Harper and Cooper have come to occupy in an historical memory of early black feminism. In a very real sense, their differences in strategy and address have been taken for differences in politics itself, even as we can find them pursuing remarkably similar agendas albeit in work reaching publics at times several decades removed from each other. While Frances Harper has been lauded as one of black feminism's "greats" and frequently praised for her commitment to working among "the people," as she did during her antislavery lecture tours and with her temperance work, Anna Julia Cooper's position within that history remains vexed and contested, her politics often dismissed as elitist. Yet if we allow that there is no universal blueprint for nineteenth-century black feminisms, neither a singular politics pursued nor homogeneous public addressed, we must not only reconsider the places we have accorded certain figures like Harper and Cooper but also ask why we have made such choices and with what results. Have we risked limiting our understanding of black feminists and their work, foreclosed our knowledge of their publics and strategies of address?

One consequence of according Anna Julia Cooper a lesser position within this history is to risk occluding the possibility of coalitions between feminists of color, such as those for which she called. References to "the Indian" in the work of nineteenth-century black feminists are rare. Were such coalitions limited because expediency arguments resting on, indeed creating, anxieties over competing rights in a climate of scarcity were difficult to overcome? Did red-black feminist coalitions or publics develop? Or are understandings of rights and their stakes and achievement for black and red feminisms so different that they have difficulty coming together in the nineteenth century or at its close? Perhaps the more challenging question is not how to find evidence of such publics or coalitions—though that is, of course, very important work—but how to grapple with what may have hindered their formation. If, as Cooper makes clear in this essay, an unrestricted access to the protections and privileges of citizenship can become black feminism's goal, including unhampered access to the railway, does a black feminist agenda also risk capitalizing upon imperialist expansion and genocide? Cooper indirectly suggests that an unexamined black feminist politics will not only risk succumbing to a competition over rights but also risk colluding with that larger imperialist project and its production of "American citizenship." This is the challenge Cooper's "Woman versus the Indian" ultimately offers its readers—not only the challenge to the white woman to eradicate racism from the woman's rights movement, though surely that is an end Cooper would have desired, but also the challenge to black feminists to seek affiliation between black and red as well as between black and white.

Yet our ability to imagine that an African American feminist like Cooper not only critiqued the white feminist movement but also did so with a view to marking important links between African American and Native American women has been affected by the narratives of American feminism's "first wave" we have inherited. When we do hear those voices of dissension within the first wave, we more often hear of black feminist critiques of white racism without attention to whether those critiques are an end in themselves or calls for affiliations outside extant white feminist networks and their power dynamics. What feminist publics we can conceive of, and can then work to document, have largely been determined by the critical lenses employed in their study. An essay like Cooper's "Woman versus the Indian" raises the stakes for contemporary studies of black feminism and the narratives they will tell. Cooper's essay, and Shaw's and Harper's speeches, tell us much about the ongoing challenges of coalitions between women, even as they address us from a past shaped carefully to support particular narratives of African American and American feminisms. This is a history we must first examine more fully by considering that black feminism's publics were not limited to networks with predominantly white reform movements or to a more "local" black nationalist politics serving the interests of African American communities, nor were black feminism's publics and politics uniform. Rather, as Anna Julia Cooper's work suggests, black feminism's publics may also have included affiliations that saw black feminism going public beyond a white-black color line. By reconsidering her work, as well as that of her foremothers and contemporaries, both within networks and independently, we stand to gain a much richer understanding of black feminism's development and achievements in the nineteenth century.

Notes

Introduction

1. That Truth includes accounts of both speeches in her 1878 *Narrative* is telling in this regard. Clearly Truth knew both incidents were familiar to her readers and had become important elements of her national reputation.

2. Further accounts of her speeches indicate that her self-presentation as a slave type may have included exaggerating her enslavement as forty rather than thirty years.

3. Elsa Barkley Brown makes an argument similar to Sandra Gunning's (*Race* 78) in her study of African American women in Richmond, Virginia, during the 1880s in "Negotiating and Transforming the Public Sphere." For her, Richmond women had long occupied important positions in black public politics, but "the nadir" posed particular challenges to them.

4. This emphasis upon the late nineteenth century as black feminism's moment of emerging into visibility is still active in recent work such as Martha Jones's important new study of the "woman question" in black political culture, *All Bound Up Together* (M. Jones 2, 9). And in incisive recent collections on nineteenth-century black feminist thought, such as Waters and Conway, some pieces follow that well-established historiography by arguing, for example, that "the earliest and most visible manifestations of black feminist consciousness appeared in the written scholarship of Anna Julia Cooper," who was active at the turn into the twentieth century (Simien 421). This position is also part of an established way of reading Cooper's significance as the "prototypical" black feminist.

5. See, for example, Carby, *Reconstructing*; Ann D. Gordon with Bettye Collier-Thomas, John H. Bracey, Arlene Voski Avakian, and Joyce Avrech Berkman, eds., *African American Women and the Vote: 1837–1965* (U of Massachusetts P, 1997); Higginbotham, *Righteous Discontent*; M. Jones; Knupfer; Salem; Terborg-Penn, *African American Women*; Yee; Jean Fagin Yellin and John Van Horne, *The Abolitionist Sisterhood: Antislavery and Women's Political Culture* (Ithaca: Cornell UP, 1994); and Yellin.

6. See Neverdon-Morton; Higginbotham, *Righteous Discontent*; Peterson; and Knupfer.

7. See, for example, Painter, *Sojourner;* Mabee; Boyd; and Frances Ellen Foster, ed., *Brighter;* McMurray; Schechter; Thompson; B. Jones; Richardson, *Maria;* Beardin and Butler; and Rhodes.

8. Extant scholarship that attends to lesser-known black feminists includes Terborg-Penn's essential study of black women suffragists, *African American Women in the Struggle for the Vote;* Martha Jones's more recent *All Bound Up Together;* and historical scholarship focused on particular cities, such as Dunbar's *Fragile Freedom,* which is focused on antebellum Philadelphia.

9. New scholarship that focuses on the nineteenth century in black feminist tradition is deeply indebted, as is mine, to the groundbreaking work of Carla Peterson's *"Doers of the Word,"* which examined black women's oratory and writing in the Northeast from 1830 to 1880, and Shirley Wilson Logan's *"We Are Coming,"* which focused on central black women orators in "the last two decades of the [nineteenth] century" (xiv). That new work on black feminism in varied spaces throughout the century includes Martha Jones's *All Bound Up Together* and Waters and Conaway's *Black Women's Intellectual Traditions.* These books are joined by scholarship that takes a specific focus, such as McHenry's *Forgotten Readers,* on the significance of nineteenth-century literary societies to black political culture; Moody's and Bassard's work on black women's spiritual narratives; and Santamarina's work on class and labor in black women's autobiographies at midcentury.

10. This notion of early black feminist oratory and writing as "double-voiced" derives from Henry Louis Gates Jr.'s *Signifying Monkey,* in which he argues that African American texts necessarily derive from and address two very different readerships and textual traditions: one Anglo-American and the other African American. The result of such a positioning is the predominance of a double-voiced strategy of address within the black American rhetorical tradition. Gates, xxv–xxviii, 110–13. See also Peterson.

11. An important exception is the work of Shirley Wilson Logan and Jacqueline Jones Royster.

12. Jürgen Habermas's notion of the bourgeois public sphere elaborated in his *Structural Transformation of the Public Sphere* has come under criticism, particularly by feminists, who have argued that his democratic "ideal" is constituted through exclusions and inequities that not only fail to account for the political participation and styles of women, the working classes, and racial and ethnic minorities but also willfully ignore multiple publics. On the constitutive exclusions of the Habermasian public sphere, see, for example, Joan Landes, *Women and the Public Sphere in the Age of the French Revolution* (Ithaca: Cornell UP, 1988); Ryan, "Gender," and Geoff Eley, "Nations, Publics, and Political Cultures: Placing Habermas in the Nineteenth Century," both in *Habermas and*

the *Public Sphere,* ed. Craig Calhoun (Cambridge: MIT, 1992); and Michael E. Gardiner, "Wild Publics and Grotesque Symposiums: Habermas and Bakhtin on Dialogue, Everyday Life and the Public Sphere," *After Habermas: New Perspectives on the Public Sphere,* ed. Nick Crossley and John Michael Roberts (Oxford: Blackwell, 2004) 28–48. Habermas has also responded to his critics, but without forfeiting "the" public sphere, as Mike Hill and Warren Montag point out: "Habermas has come to recognize that if there is indeed a plurality of spheres there is also a sphere of all spheres. The public sphere thus conceived is the totality formed by the communicative interaction of all groups, even nominally dominant and subaltern" ("Introduction" 3). See Jürgen Habermas, "Concluding Remarks," *Habermas and the Public Sphere,* ed. Craig Calhoun (Cambridge: MIT, 1992) 466. For work that attends to the political styles and interventions of women, the working class, and racial and ethnic minorities, see, for example, Nancy Fraser, "Rethinking the Public Sphere: A Contribution to the Critique of Actually Existing Democracy," *Social Text* 25–26 (1990): 56–80; Nancy Fraser, *Unruly Practices: Power, Discourse, and Gender in Contemporary Social Theory* (Minneapolis: U of Minnesota P, 1989); Higginbotham, *Righteous Discontent;* Ryan, "Gender" 259–89; Ryan, *Women;* Young, *Justice;* and Young, "Impartiality" 57–76. For critiques of feminist scholarship on the public sphere, see Park and Wald 226–50. For considerations of the viability of public sphere theory for African American studies, see Holt's and Dawson's essays in *The Black Public Sphere;* and Squires.

13. On the public sphere as a contested site, see also M. R. Somers, "Citizenship and the Place of the Public Sphere: Law, Community, and Political Culture in the Transition to Democracy," *American Sociological Review* 58 (Oct. 1993): 587–620. For further work on counterpublics, see, for example, Robert Asen, "Seeking the 'Counter' in Counterpublics," *Communication Theory* 10.4 (Nov. 2000): 424–46; and Asen and Brouwer. In her work on nineteenth-century American culture, Mary Ryan, like Fraser, affirms there was never an "ideal bourgeois public sphere but this variegated, decentered and democratic array of public spaces" ("Gender" 264). Bruce Robbins has also been a central advocate for taking up the notion of a "multiplicity of distinct and overlapping public discourses [and] public spheres" (Robbins xii). Attention to multiple publics has produced studies of the "proletarian" public sphere, "subaltern counterpublics," the black public sphere, "tiny publics," "wild publics," "intimate publics," and, more recently, the reading of Bakhtin together with Habermas to press on not only a critique of *the* public but also of "rational discussion" within the public sphere. On proletarian publics, see, for example, Oskar Negt and Alexander Kluge, *Public Sphere and Experience: Toward an Analysis of the Bourgeois and Proletarian Public Sphere* (Minneapolis, U of Minnesota P, 1993); and Mike Hill and Warren Montag, eds., *Masses, Classes and the Public Sphere*

(London: Verso, 2000). "Subaltern counterpublics" is Nancy Fraser's term in "Rethinking the Public Sphere," and "wild publics" is Iris Marion Young's in "Impartiality and the Civic Public," 57–76. On "tiny publics," see Fine and Harrington 343–56. On "intimate publics," see Berlant, *Female*. On the black public sphere, see Marie "Keta" Miranda, *Homegirls in the Public Sphere* (U of Texas P, 2003); Gwendolyn Pough, *Check It While I Wreck It: Black Womanhood, Hip-Hop Culture, and the Public Sphere* (Boston: Northeastern UP, 2004); and Black Public Sphere Collective, ed., *The Black Public Sphere* (Chicago: U of Chicago P, 1995).

14. Young also ascribes this style of speech culture to women and "non-Western" people in general.

15. Asen ("Seeking") also cautions against identity as a marker for counterpublic membership. Squires, in working to examine the black public sphere as heterogeneous focuses on enclaves—communications that use spaces and discourses hidden from the dominant public, counterpublics—which "project the hidden transcripts, previously spoken only in enclaves, to dominant publics" (460), and satellite publics, which "aim to maintain a solid group identity and build independent institutions" (463). While this appears to be a progressivist narrative of black public sphere development, early black feminism shows us the simultaneity and contiguity of these publics.

16. See, for example, Miranda, *Homegirls;* and Pough, *Check It.*

17. In "The Black Press and the State," Catherine Squires makes a related claim that "a national Black pubic did not arise immediately after slavery" but that "the black public still acted more like an enclaved public for the remainder of the nineteenth century, expressing its oppositional consciousness mainly in safe spaces and rarely supporting open confrontations with the white public . . . until the Great Black Migration . . . and Ida B. Wells's anti-lynching crusade" (113). Squires's emphasis upon the late nineteenth century as the moment when a "national" black public emerges seems to ignore the national black convention movement at the century's opening but it also interestingly echoes the emphasis on the turn into the twentieth century as black feminism's public emergence into visibility that is stressed in narratives of black feminism. In contrast, Craig Wilder has positioned secret societies, like Prince Hall Freemasonry, as precursors to the black church as political center for a black public sphere that emerges in the late eighteenth and early nineteenth centuries. Of course we should note that while Wilder enlarges our historical scope, he continues to gender the black public sphere by marking its origins in the male-only secret societies. See Craig Steven Wilder, *In the Company of Black Men: The African Influence on African American Culture in New York City* (New York: New York UP, 2001).

18. For detailed work on women's access to the black convention movement, see Martha Jones. Jones notes that as early as 1836 women were "seated as delegates and signing petitions" (45). For women's role in the American Moral Reform Society, founded in 1835 at the fourteenth black convention, see M. Jones 47–60.

19. See, for example, A. Davis, *Women;* Jacquelyn Dowd Hall, "'The Mind that Burns in Each Body': Women, Rape, and Racial Violence," *Powers of Desire: The Politics of Sexuality,* ed. Ann Snitow et al. (New York: Monthly Review, 1983) 328–49; duCille; Giddings; Guy-Sheftall; Evelyn Brooks Higginbotham, "African-American Women's History and the Metalanguage of Race," *Signs: Journal of Women in Culture and Society* 17.2 (1992): 251–74; Karla F. C. Holloway, *Codes of Conduct: Race, Ethics and the Color of Our Character* (New Brunswick: Rutgers UP, 1995); Holloway, "Body Politic" 482–95; bell hooks, *Ain't I a Woman: Black Women and Feminism* (Boston: South End, 1981); Omolade; Spillers, "Interstices" 73–100; and Spillers, "Mama's Baby" 65–81. Of course "the great divide," as Mary Ryan coins it, has also been considered critically in women's history circles, most recently in a special issue of *Journal of Women's History* 15.2 (2003).

20. As Martha Jones documents, both the black church and the black convention movement were developing national networks by the 1830s, and black women participated in and challenged the politics of both (15–16).

21. Even though Peterson identifies "the 'brave' who form the subject of this book [as women who] worked and wrote from positions of marginality, from social, psychological and geographic sites that were peripheral to the dominant culture and, very often, to their own" (6–7), her work makes further critical attention to the places and publics of early black feminism possible by problematizing notions of the margin and challenging hierarchies mobilized by center versus margin binaries.

22. This is also true of some work on the black public sphere. See, for example, Dawson for his assertion that the club movement provided the "crucial link between the women's suffrage and Black rights movement" (205). Of course black feminists were actively forging such links between feminist abolitionism, woman's rights, temperance, and black civil rights much earlier.

23. Chapter 1 of this study focuses on this question of the politics of preaching and spiritual writings, and that critical trend is examined there. Claudia Tate's *Domestic Allegories of Political Desire: The Black Heroin's Text at the Turn of the Century* (New York: Oxford UP, 1992) challenges the tendency to dismiss black domestic fiction for its questionable politics or lack of a politics.

24. See Salem; and Giddings.

25. See Sanchez-Eppler.

Chapter 1

1. As examples of this scholarship Grammer cites Catherine Brekus, *Strangers and Pilgrims: Female Preaching in America, 1740–1845* (Chapel Hill: U of North Carolina P, 1998); Nancy Cott, *The Bonds of Womanhood* (New Haven: Yale UP, 1977); Nancy Cott, "Young Women in the Second Great Awakening in New England," *Feminist Studies* 3 (1975): 16–22; Nancy A. Hardesty, *Women Called to Witness: Evangelical Feminism in the Nineteenth Century* (Knoxville: U of Tennessee P, 1999); Nancy A. Hardesty, *Your Daughters Shall Prophesy: Revivalism and Feminism in the Age of Finney* (Brooklyn: Carlson, 1991); Janet James, ed., *Women in American Religion* (Philadelphia: U of Pennsylvania P, 1980); Dana Robert, *American Women in Mission: A Social History of Their Thought and Practice* (Macon: Mercer UP, 1997); Rosemary Ruether and Rosemary Keller, eds., *Women and Religion in America,* vol. 1 (New York: Harper, 1981); Rosemary Ruether and Eleanor McLaughlin, eds., *Women of Spirit* (New York: Simon, 1979); Mary Ryan, "A Women's Awakening: Evangelical Religion and the Families of Utica, New York, 1800–1840," James, *Women in American Religion;* Carroll Smith-Rosenberg, *Religion and the Rise of the City* (Ithaca: Cornell UP, 1971); Carroll Smith-Rosenberg, "Women and Religious Revivals: Anti-ritualism, Liminality, and the Emergence of the American Bourgeoisie," *The Evangelical Tradition in America,* ed. Leonard I. Sweet (Macon: Mercer UP, 1984.); and Deborah Valenze, *Prophetic Sons and Daughters: Female Preaching and Popular Religion in Industrial England* (Princeton: Princeton UP, 1985).

2. See also Bassard, "Gender"; Joanne M. Braxton, *Black Women Writing Autobiography: A Tradition within a Tradition* (Philadelphia: Temple UP, 1989); F. Foster, *Written;* Jean McMahon Humez, "'My Spirit Eye': Some Functions of Spiritual and Visionary Experience in the Lives of Five Black Women Preachers, 1810–1880," *Women and the Structure of Society,* ed. Barbara J. Harris and JoAnn K. McNamara (Durham: Duke UP, 1984) 129–43; Hunter; McKay; Joycelyn K. Moody, "Twice Other, Once Shy: Nineteenth-Century Black Women Autobiographers and the American Literary Tradition of Self-Effacement," *A/b: Auto/Biography Studies* 7.1 (1992): 46–61; Moody, "On the Road"; and Peterson.

3. Many of the African American preaching women we know of began to preach in their thirties and forties, often after their husbands died or their marriages ended, thereby freeing them from domestic duties and a significant source of opposition. Many also, however, continued to care and provide for their children, securing homes and care givers for daughters and sons when they undertook itinerancies.

4. Although I refer to Elizabeth's narrative as a spiritual autobiography, it is important to note that it was written by an amanuensis who declares, in a single-

sentence preface to the text, that it "was taken mainly from her [Elizabeth's] own lips in her 97th year" (Elizabeth 3).

5. More recent work with women's spiritual autobiographies, such as that of Elizabeth Grammer, reaffirms and builds on Foster's insights.

6. See Frances Smith Foster's discussion of Jarena Lee's spiritual autobiography in *Written by Herself.* Here Foster notes that in an African American spiritual auto-biography tradition, race became central in various ways to narratives of spiritual quest. It is clear from the women's spiritual autobiographies I examine in this chapter that concerns of gender also were made significant in what we might recognize as a distinct tradition of African American spiritual autobiography.

7. William Andrews defines the position of exhorter as follows: "Exhorters occupied the lowest position in the church's preaching hierarchy and had to have permission before addressing individual congregations. They could lead Sunday school classes and prayer meetings, but in formal church services they usually spoke at the sufferance of the presiding minister and only in response to the biblical text that he had selected" ("Introduction" 14). An exhorter is also defined as "a person who encourages through personal testimony . . . [and] is examined and licensed by the Quarterly Conference" of the AME ("Ministry of the A.M.E.").

8. Albert Raboteau underscores the richness of the enslaved's religious experience: "The religion of the slaves was both institutional and noninstitutional, visible and invisible, formally organized and spontaneously adapted. . . . Preachers licensed by the church and hired by the master were supplemented by slave preachers licensed only by the spirit" (212).

9. Like Lee, Elaw cited preaching women from scripture, including Phoebe, Paul's helpmeets "in the Gospel," Tryphena, Hereus and her sisters, the hand-maids mentioned by Joel, and Priscilla (Elaw 124).

10. The exception is, of course, biographical work like that of Painter, Mabee, Stetson and David, and Fitch and Mandziuk.

11. Truth, like other African Americans, was likely drawn to millennialism because "the starkness of racial injustice made the need for God's judgment all the more imperative," speculates Nell Irvin Painter (*Sojourner* 81). However, she found the Millerites' ecstatic worship excessive during an 1843 camp meeting which became known for an outbreak of fanaticism and she dis-identified with them (Painter, *Sojourner* 84). This was the second instance in which Truth sought community with a more radical religious group, the first being her affiliation with the Kingdom of Matthias. See Painter and Vale.

12. According to Carleton Mabee, we have little record of what Truth preached during this itinerancy and her recollection of preaching abolition at this time has not been substantiated (47).

13. The Burned-over District was that region of New York west of the Catskills and Adirondacks, but it has also come to be seen by scholars as including Pennsylvania and Ohio's Western Reserve. Reform as well as religion thrived there among people "open to unusual religious beliefs, enthusiastic worship practices and crusades aimed at the perfection of mankind" (M. Jones 78).

14. The woman with whom Foote was staying had a daughter who had run away from her master, occasioning his forceful entry of the house and Foote's bedroom at midnight one evening.

15. It is important to note that the club movement was facilitated by black churches. The National Association of Colored Women's 1896 convention was held at the Nineteenth Street Baptist Church of Washington, D.C., and eight of fifteen national meetings from 1901 to 1930 were held in churches (Townes 162).

16. The obvious exception here would be Sojourner Truth, who integrated her preaching with her public speaking engagements on abolition, women's rights and black civil rights.

17. See, for example, Andrews, *Sisters;* Braxton, *Black Women.*

18. See the citations in note 1 for examples of such arguments.

19. Like Chanta Haywood, I have in mind the work of Frances Smith Foster, Hazel Carby, Patricia Hill Collins, Carla Peterson, Deborah McDowell, and Paula Giddings as "rightfully recogniz[ing] this period as a critical moment in the development of black feminist thought" (91). But giving this moment its due should not come at the expense of acknowledging the political import of African American preaching women's work. For an examination of the way in which scholars focused on black preaching women have also "downplayed their roles as social activists," see Haywood 93–95.

20. On Hughes and Wilson, see Angell.

21. On the formation of the AME Church, see, for example, Doris Andrew, "The African Methodists of Philadelphia, 1794–1902," and Will B. Gravely, "African Methodisms and the Rise of Black Denominationalism," both in *Perspectives on African Methodism,* ed. Russell E. Richey, Kenneth E. Rowe, and Jean Miller Schmidt (Nashville: Kingswood-Abingdon, 1993). Richard R. Wright Jr.'s *Centennial Encyclopedia* notes that "during the first fifty years [1816–66], the church was confined almost entirely to the Northern States, as it was not allowed to operate among the slaves in the South, though in Charleston, New Orleans, and one or two other places, there were small organizations among free Negroes" (5). During this period the church grew from 7 churches and 400 members to 286 churches with 73,000 members. By 1916 AME churches would number 7,300, claiming 650,000 members with 6,650 ministers and 6,400 local preachers (Wright 5).

22. In the late fall of 1787, trustees of the church pulled Allen and Absalom Jones from their knees in prayer at a service, demanding they return to their gallery seats where blacks had been relegated to worship. Allen and Jones left the service. They formed Bethel AME and St. Thomas African Protestant Episcopal Church, respectively. Significantly, the AME's first home, before its official formation, was the house of "Sarah Dougherty . . . from May of 1788 through December" (Dodson, "Power" 38–39). Gravely also points out that although Methodist bishop Francis Asbury ordained "at least eight . . . black local preachers" as deacons, "the Methodist Episcopal general conference never . . . accepted the deacons into annual conferences . . . and never advanced the black deacons to eldership or full priesthood" ("African Methodisms" 137). This inequity also contributed to the formation of the AME Church.

23. A deacon is licensed by the AME Church and serves two years on a trial basis. If after this period the candidate "achiev[es] the level of education as dictated" by the church and has "passed those duties brought before them by the Ministerial Institute, the candidate is reviewed and if approved ordained a Deacon. As Deacon, the ministerial candidate can do everything but consecrate the elements of Communion. They can marry, bury, and serve communion . . . and if needed, Pastor a church" ("Ministry of the A.M.E."). The position of elder is the highest level of ordination within the AME. One can be ordained an elder after "achieving the ordination of Deacon and . . . serv[ing] an additional two years on trial." Again, an elder must fulfill educational requirements ("Ministry of the A.M.E.").

24. In the meantime, resolutions proposed, like Rev. Henry Davis's in 1864, which sought to temper the licensing of women to preach by creating monitoring safeguards controlled by male church leaders, including "recommendations from male class leaders, an examination, a 'majority of votes' obtained at 'a special meeting,' and 'final examination' by the quarterly conference's presiding elders" (M. Jones 148–49), all to obtain a license subject to yearly renewal, were defeated.

25. The *AME Church Magazine* (begun June 1844) and the *AME Church Review* (founded in 1881) register the decades-long opposition to preaching women. In its second issue the *AME Church Magazine* endorsed woman's role as one of influence and example in the home ("Power of Woman"). At least twice, in the mid-1880s and early 1890s, Rev. James H. A. Johnson wrote articles for the *AME Church Review* arguing against women preaching, citing danger to the church in women entering the pulpit: "[T]he bolstering up of female preachers can but enervate the ministry and damage the church" ("Female Preachers" 105). Yet even here, in its official organ, bishops favoring woman's licensing were heard, like the Rev. John M. Brown of Washington, D.C., who in 1886

marshaled both scriptural and historical evidence of women taking leadership roles in the church ("Two questions" 356–61).

26. Through the recuperative work of Jualynne Dodson we know of Mary Palmer, Melinda Cotton, Emma Johnson, and Mary Harris preaching in the North and Charlotte Riley and Lillian Thurman ministering in the South ("Nineteenth-Century AME" 287–88), and of Sophie Murray, Elizabeth Cole, Harriet Felson Taylor ("African Methodist Episcopal" 12), and Emily Calkins Stevens ("Introduction" xxxiii). Rev. Revels Adams notes that Rachael Moman of Mississippi was "Class Leader, Stewardess, Missionary President, President of the W.C.T.U. and Deaconess" in the nineteenth century (139–400), and Bishop John Mifflin Brown mentions Millie Wolfe, "Rev. Mrs. J. Lee[,] . . . Mrs Martha Low . . . [and] Mrs Emily Rodney Williams" as preachers (355). In *Scraps of African Methodist Episcopal History,* Rev. James A. Handy notes Annie Dickerson and Miss Mary Ann Prout were exhorters at Bethel AME, while Doritha Hill exhorted and held band meetings in Baltimore (344). Handy also praises Rachel Evans as "a preacher of no ordinary ability. . . . There were but few of the preachers of that day who were her equal" (345), and Alexander Wayman's *Cyclopedia of African Methodism* attests that "she could rouse a congregation at any time" (57). Daniel Culp includes an entry for Lena Doolin Mason in his *Twentieth-Century Negro Literature,* noting that Mason began preaching in 1887 at the age of twenty-three, and has since "preached in nearly every state in the Union. . . . [T]he preachers are few who can excel her. . . . She has . . . been instrumental in the conversion of 1,617 souls" (444). Priscilla Baltimore was known as "mother Baltimore in many parts of Illinois and Missouri" for having opened her home to the first organized AME church in Illinois (Wayman 18). Sarah Early credits her for having founded "the first church in Missouri, the 'Oldest AME Church west of the Mississippi River,'" in her home in May 1841 (4).

27. Smith's work was endorsed by several AME bishops, and in 1889 Baker was appointed "to take charge of St. Paul's church" in Lebanon, Pennsylvania (Acornley 46).

28. As Elizabeth Grammer notes, "[M]ore and more women found themselves baptized by the Spirit" during the Second Great Awakening. "Joining local churches, organizing praying bands and missionary societies, women were also awakened in greater numbers to the possibility of preaching the gospel" (8). The result was that "'probably hundreds of women' preached, if only in a local church or revival, 'grassroots practice' differing sharply from . . . prescriptions against women's preaching" (Billington qtd. in Grammer 8).

29. See those texts listed in note 1 above.

30. Diane Sasson has pointed out that Jackson's "use of biblical imagery[,] . . the folk preacher's rhetorical devices [and] its exceptional poetic qualities suggest that Jackson may have delivered versions of her conversion as testimonies and sermons during the 1830s and 1840s" (165–66).

31. Jackson notes the meeting was held on a Tuesday, but it was likely not a holiness "Tuesday Meeting" since she notes these revival meetings had been going on for several days (76).

32. In her writings Jackson refers to her return from a preaching tour to New York and Providence: "And when I came home, it seemed as though my very life was at stake. . . . [F]rom that time, Samuel sought my life day and night. And if I had not had the gift of foresight . . . I must have fell in death by his hands" (145).

33. As Diane Sasson documents, Shaker theology "maintained that perfection did not come suddenly and completely but was attained slowly through discipline and self-denial," a tenet conflicting with Jackson's experience of sanctification (166 n. 11).

34. Jarena Lee opposed Jackson's labors, and likely on the grounds of her controversial avocation of celibacy and her belief that the church, in its worldliness, was failing believers. Jackson writes of a meeting between the two in early 1857 during which she recalls Lee "was one of my most bitter persecutors" (262).

35. Here we must remember that African American preaching women repeatedly tell of beginning to preach once their husbands were dead, or of their marriages ending because of that decision, and of having children to support. Their livelihoods were dependant upon the contributions of others to their ministry, with no domestic support, and frequently those contributions paid for their itinerant travel and base subsistence while on the road. If preaching women could access education as women, they certainly could not afford to pay for it. Consequently, we read of these women having had only a few months schooling as children, or of their self-taught attainment of functional literacy (see, for example, the narratives of Jarena Lee, Elizabeth, and Amanda Berry Smith).

36. Habermas acknowledged and responded to these challenges in his *Structural Transformation of the Public Sphere.*

37. *The AMEC Book of Worship* defines love feasts as "devotional services, not sacraments such as Holy Communion or Baptism, that are customarily observed to spiritually prepare the church for Holy Communion. Love Feasts may be conducted by the Pastor, a class leader, or the Pastor's appointee" (40). "In the early church," love feast was "a meal eaten together as a sign of Christian affection and cordiality, also called AGAPE. Water and bread are used" (235).

Chapter 2

1. I draw this phrase from the title of chapter 6 of Shirley Yee's seminal study, *Black Women Abolitionists*. I would argue that the recent trend in trans-Atlantic studies has been to position black women like Craft and Remond as oddities within a negrophilic United Kingdom cultural imaginary that was more entertained by their appearances than reached by their politics.

2. Sarah Mapps Douglass, Harriet Purvis, and sisters Sarah and Margaretta Forten signed its charter.

3. Susan Paul, Louisa Nell, and Nancy Prince, among other lesser-known African American women, were members of the Boston Female Anti-Slavery Society. Shirley Yee documents the following black female societies in the Northeast, active between 1833 and 1860: the Female Colored Union Society of Nantucket, the Union Anti-Slavery Society of Rochester, and the Female Wesleyan Anti-Slavery Society of the Methodist Episcopal Church in New York City (88).

4. Dunbar documents that "between 1836 and 1840, 86 new members joined the PFASS, only one of whom was African American." 1842 was the last year an African American woman joined the association (93–94).

5. For example, Sarah Mapps Douglass and Hetty Burr maintained membership in both the racially mixed Philadelphia Female Anti-Slavery Society and in the Women's Association of Philadelphia, an all-black association founded in 1848 (Yee 111).

6. By the mid-1840s the sister slave image had become so popular that the Boston Type Foundry included it among other cuts "for sale in its *Specimen Book*. . . . [T]he female slave entered commercial discourse and became both figuratively and literally a stereotype" (Yellin 23). Yellin details the ways in which American antislavery women used the emblem of the female supplicant slave ambivalently to both address and avoid "issues of race, sexual conformity, and patriarchal definitions of true womanhood." These strategies coalesced around two distinct appeals that positioned white female abolitionists as "chain-breaking liberators and as enchained slaves pleading for their own liberty, then asserting it and freeing themselves" (25).

7. See Gerda Lerner, *The Grimké Sisters from South Carolina: Rebels against Authority* (U of North Carolina P, 1967).

8. For work focused on the tragic mulatta within feminist abolitionist rhetoric and Victorian culture more widely, see Sanchez-Eppler; Brody; and Zackodnik.

9. For example, Anne Knight of Chelmsford corresponded with Angelina and Sarah Grimké, as well as Maria Weston Chapman, and she admired black abolitionist Margaretta Forten of the Philadelphia Female Anti-Slavery Society for

her bravery. Chartist sympathizer Elizabeth Pease also corresponded with the Grimké sisters (Midgley, *Women* 157).

10. As Kathryn Kish Sklar documents, the 1840 World Anti-Slavery Convention was called by the BFASS: "[F]ounded in 1839 to celebrate the emancipation of slaves in British colonies six years earlier and the abolition of an 'apprentice' system of semislavery that year, the BFASS now turned attention of local English anti-slavery organizations to 'universal abolition,' with particular attention to slavery in the United States" (461).

11. This very question had fractured the movement in the United States a year earlier.

12. For example, Anne Knight, Elizabeth Pease, Elizabeth Reid, Mary Howitt, Matilda Ashurst Biggs, Elizabeth A. Ashurst, and Marion Reid.

13. See Midgley, *Women;* and Sklar, "Women Who Speak" 453–99.

14. Prior to the Fifteenth Amendment in 1870, universal male suffrage proceeded state by state as property qualifications were rescinded. Vermont had practiced universal male suffrage since its entry into the Union in 1791, while Tennessee (established in 1796) permitted suffrage for the vast majority of its taxpayers. New Jersey, Maryland, and South Carolina all abolished property and taxpaying requirements between 1807 and 1810. States entering the Union after 1815 either had universal white male suffrage or a low taxpaying requirement. From 1815 to 1821, Connecticut, Massachusetts, and New York abolished all property requirements.

15. William Wells Brown's daughters, Clarissa and Josephine, of whom he had legal custody following the dissolution of his marriage, joined him in the UK in 1851 and again from 1852 to 1855 following their schooling in the north of France; Harriet Jacobs briefly visited England in 1858 in an attempt to secure a publisher for her *Narrative;* a former slave listed only as Josephine was in the UK in 1856; Caroline Putnam, lifelong companion of white abolitionist lecturer Sallie Holley, once an agent for the American Anti-Slavery society and an activist for the freedmen in the 1860s, was in the UK from 1859 to 1860; Frances Russell, a former slave, visited in 1854, while Mary E. Webb accompanied her abolitionist husband Frank J. Webb to the UK and toured as an elocutionist publicly reading, among other things, selections from Harriet Beecher Stowe's *Uncle Tom's Cabin* from 1856 until her health necessitated she travel to the south of France in 1858.

16. Martha S. Jones documents that women in general, not only black women, had come by the mid-1840s to be a draw on antislavery lecture circuits. AME Church minister Jeremiah Sanderson wrote Amy Post after the 1845 meeting of the AASS: "What a change has come over the face of the Society's character; a few years ago men . . . hissed at the mere idea of woman's speaking in

public, . . now men come to anti-slavery convention[s] attracted by the announcements that women are to take part . . . and they are often more desirous of hearing women than men" (qtd. in M. Jones 69).

17. For assessments of Ellen Craft and Sarah Parker Remond as exploited by British negrophilia and the management of their public appearances, see, for example, Fisch, *American* and McCaskill, "'Yours Very Truly.'"

18. Willi Coleman documents that Remond herself had this perception of the British Isles before she crossed the Atlantic to take up her work there: "By the end of 1858 . . . Remond admitted to 'an intense desire to visit England, that I might for a time enjoy freedom'" (qtd. in Coleman 177).

19. William Wells Brown was born a slave in Lexington, Kentucky, and escaped to the North on New Year's Day in 1834. He became a successful and well-known abolitionist lecturer, novelist, and playwright.

20. When Ellen's appearances became silent ones is difficult to determine.

21. As I have argued elsewhere, this resonated with American women through a feminist-abolitionist register in which Ellen embodied the fears of her white female audience members who lacked a legal right to bodily integrity and would not yet risk a public debate about such rights. If slavery would sink so low as to enslave a "white" woman such as Ellen Craft, white women were, indeed, enslaved. If Ellen Craft bore in her features the evidence of a male desire that took all precedence over a woman's bodily integrity, then sexual "slavery" was real. See Zackodnik chap. 2.

22. See Saidiya Hartman's work on melodrama, violated family bonds, sympathy, and empathy in abolitionist discourse in *Scenes of Subjection,* particularly chapter 1.

23. Ellen Samuels notes there is "no critical consensus on the authorship of the Crafts' narrative," citing some seven central scholars of *Running,* herself included, who believe the narrative was a collaborative effort (42 n. 1).

24. The Virginia Act of 1662 repealed the longstanding English law of descent which held that a child inherits the father's status: "'Whereas some doubts have arisen whether a child got by an Englishman upon a negro should be free or slave, be it therefore enacted by this present grand assembly, that all children born in the country shall be bound or free according to the condition of the mother'" (qtd. in Johnston 167).

25. See, for example, McCaskill.

26. Indeed, in 1853 Ellen met Stowe at a party held at "Mrs. Reid's in London" for the purpose of introducing the author to the likes of "Lady Byron, Mrs Jameson, Mrs Bayne, Dr. King, Dr. Estlin and twenty or thirty others" ("Our Boston Correspondence"). Elizabeth Jesser Reid, reformer, abolitionist, and

founder of Bedford College; Anne Isabella Noel Byron, wife of the poet George Byron and abolitionist; Anna Jameson, woman's rights activist and author of *Sisters of Charity;* Dr. John Estlin, anti-BFASS radical and founder of the *Anti-Slavery Reporter's* rival publication the *Anti-Slavery Advocate.*

27. Farmer describes McDonnell as "a most influential member of the executive Committee of the National Reform Association" ("Fugitive Slaves").

28. As we shall examine in chapter 4, by the 1890s the English remained highly anxious about miscegenation, and the fascination with the mulatta that Jennifer Brody's work details indicates this anxiety was operative throughout the century.

29. See Toole for a very useful summary of the positions taken by labor historians on the link between antislavery and labor reform.

30. While the Cotton Famine is frequently understood as resulting from the Civil War, given its effects on supply, others argue it began earlier, in 1857, when the Indian Mutiny first curtailed exports to India and then significantly increased them, causing an explosion of capital and labor in Lancashire coinciding with the largest cotton yields in the United States from 1857 to 1859 (Toole 166).

31. Unemployment in the weaving districts was extremely in the midst of the American Civil War. Alan Rice documents that "in Burnley during the summer of 1862, 10,000 out of 13,000 operatives were out of work" (Rice n.p.). And Rosalind Hall, noting the Lancashire cotton district's dependence upon American cotton (80 percent of Lancashire mills' cotton came from the United States in 1860, fully 71 percent of the American crop that year), underscores that with "2,300 mills and 450,000 operatives concentrated in Lancashire . . . [i]n December 1862 one-fifth of the population . . . was receiving parochial relief. . . . In the long term there were about 330 permanent mill closures" due to the war (227–28).

32. Remond's lecture tour from 1859 to 1861 included the following, though this list is not comprehensive: Liverpool, Warrington, Dublin, Waterford, Clonmel, Cork, London, Southwark, Bristol, Manchester, York, Edinburgh, Bolton, Bedford, Leeds, Glasgow, Hawick, Dumfries, Carlisle, and Ulverstone.

33. Clark documents that "in 1858, able-bodied men were only 6% of South Dublin workhouse inmates, but children were 34%. . . . The Famine broke up families and left orphans to be raised in the workhouse" ("Wild" 390).

34. Even in the post-Famine years, industrialization based on linen mills took hold primarily in the North (Belfast and eastern Ulster) with the exception of the "Malcolmson cotton empire at Portlaw, County Waterford." Otherwise, manufacturing tended to go into decline from as early as 1820, amounting to what R. F. Foster calls a "process of actual deindustrialization" (342).

35. This prioritizing of Repeal caused Wendell Phillips to call him the "Great Beggarman" and James Haughton to plead that he end "such an unholy contamination" (qtd. in Nelson 69).

36. Irish American Repeal associations disbanded under this pressure in states such as South Carolina, Mississippi, and Louisiana. Those associations that didn't disband repudiated O'Connell and his views (Murphy 13). The nativist threat was quite real and far from limited to the slaveholding South, with rioting in Philadelphia led by nativists in 1844 and articles detailing the nativist threat dominating Irish American papers such as the *Boston Pilot* and the *New York Freeman's Journal* (Murphy 11).

37. Its members included cultural nationalists Thomas Davis, John Blake Dillon, and Charles Gavan Duffy (together cofounders of the *Nation*).

38. Mitchel settled in America in 1853 and founded the *Citizen,* a radical Irish nationalist newspaper in New York. It was seen as controversial in its defense of slavery; Mitchel's rhetorical technique was to stress the hypocrisy of abolitionists. However, Mitchel also believed that African American slaves, even in the South, were better cared for and fed than Irish cottiers or industrial workers in English cities such as Manchester.

39. Scholars such as R. J. M. Blackett have noted that the BFASS had "lost much of its vibrancy, many of its regional affiliates going to seed in the 1850s" ("African Americans" 55). Indeed, the BFASS never announced the arrival of Brown and the Crafts in the *Anti-Slavery Reporter,* as this piece in London's *Morning Advertiser* reprinted in September 26, 1851, edition of *The Liberator* bemoaned: "Affecting as their [the Crafts'] whole history has been, and especially desirable as it was that the friends of the slave in this country should clearly understand the working of the Fugitive Slave Law in their case . . . the *Anti-Slavery Reporter,* the organ of the British and Foreign Anti-Slavery Society, has never yet alluded to the arrival of the Crafts in England, so that whatever knowledge of these individuals such portion of the public as did not attend their meetings may possess, has been derived from appears unconnected but by sympathy with the antislavery cause. The British and Foreign Anti-Slavery Society have thus again left other parties to perform their duties, and have shown an especial favor to slaveholders, who are not at all pleased to have it known that any attention is shown to their *property* by Englishmen" ("William and Ellen Craft").

40. The exception would be her first lecture in Dublin sponsored by the Dublin Ladies' Anti-Slavery Society. In that city philanthropic causes, such as antislavery, mounted public lectures and distributed tickets for them on a donation basis as a fund-raising endeavor (this was particularly common in the funding of fever hospitals and orphanages). This practice created an audience of the "better classes" who could afford such donations and would, in Dublin, have

made for a mixed Protestant and Catholic audience. Dublin, unlike other parts of the country, claimed a population of wealthy Irish Catholics. I thank Robert Brazeau for these insights on Irish Catholics in Dublin and the shift from Remond's first free lecture under the auspices of the Dublin Ladies' Anti-Slavery Society to the meetings held at the Mechanics Institute in Dublin, where admission was charged.

41. Margaret Garner attempted to kill her children following her family's failed escape from slavery. The house at which they took refuge in Cincinnati, Ohio, was under siege by her master, two of his friends, three deputies, and several other men comprising a posse of eleven; and as gunfire was being exchanged, Garner slit the throat of her two-year-old daughter, Mary, and attempted to kill her two sons, Tom and Sam (ages six and four), and her nine-month-old daughter Cilla. Garner became an abolitionist cause célèbre, as her case focused attention on the "horrors" of slavery and the Fugitive Slave Law of 1850. Even though her lawyer attempted to have her tried for murder, a capital crime that would override her master's attempt to have her remanded to slavery as a fugitive, he was unsuccessful. For information regarding the popularity of the Garner case among American abolitionists, see Steven Weisenburger, *Modern Medea : A Family Story of Slavery and Child-Murder from the Old South* (Toronto: Douglas & McIntyre, 1998).

42. For an analysis of Remond's appeals to white women's concerns and white feminist political interests, see Zackodnik chap. 2; Bacon 190–96; Fisch 84–88; and Peterson 140.

43. This is a rhetorical technique Remond would have brought with her from her experience in the United States as an antislavery lecturer and from her involvement with woman's rights. We need only return to Karen Sanchez-Eppler's work to document the ways in which feminist abolitionists negotiated their own embodiment by putting the body of the enslaved to specific rhetorical use in order to recognize how Remond is very aware of a nascent white feminist ambivalence when it comes to sexual desire and anxiety: "[F]eminist abolitionists emphasise the similarities in the condition of women and slaves; nevertheless, their treatment of the figure of the sexually exploited female slave betrays an opposing desire to deny any share in this vulnerability. . . . Thus in the writings of antislavery women the frequent emphasis on the specifically feminine trial of sexual abuse serves to project the white woman's sexual anxieties onto the sexualised body of the female slave" (33).

44. Founded in 1763 by Dr. Charles Lucas and Henry Brooke, *The Freeman* was known as Ireland's "patriotic paper" for many years (R. Foster 183). Lucas, a native of County Clare, attacked constitutional dependence on England and was declared a public enemy and forced into exile by 1749, just eight years

after being elected to the Common Council of the City of Dublin (R. Foster 238–39).

45. Dred Scott, a slave, unsuccessfully sued for his freedom, a case that went to the Supreme Court. His case raised the issue of a slave's free status while in a free state; Congress had not asserted whether a slave was free once setting foot on northern soil. The Supreme Court decision ruled that people of African descent, whether bound or free, could never be American citizens and that Congress had no authority to prohibit slavery in federal territories. The decision further polarized the North and South division over slavery and arguably violated the Missouri Compromise, as it suggested that a southern slave owner could purchase slaves in a slave state then transport them to a free state without losing his ownership rights. Remond evokes the *Dred Scott* case through her paraphrase of Chief Justice Taney's delivery of the Supreme Court's decision, often quoted, that the Constitution had viewed African Americans as "beings of an inferior order, and altogether unfit to associate with the white race, either in social or political relations, and so far inferior that they had no rights which the white man was bound to respect" (*Dred Scott v. Sandford*).

46. In 1859, Remond would have traveled by Bianconi coach. Charles Bianconi revolutionized public transport in Ireland with the use of horses and carriages on a network of routes, which eventually covered most of the country from Belfast to Cork.

47. This is unmistakable for Remond, given that she met with the Neapolitan exiles (Blackett, *Building* 199) who were covered heavily in Irish newspapers while she was on tour there. Often her appearances and discussion of their exile were covered in the same papers.

Chapter 3

1. Studies that focus in whole or in part on nineteenth-century black feminism and black women's political culture include the following (though this list is not comprehensive and does not include studies focused on single figures): Giddings; Gordon et al., *African American Women;* Higginbotham, *Righteous Discontent;* Darlene Clark Hine, Barkley Brown, and Rosalyn Terborg-Penn, eds., *Black Women in America: An Historical Encyclopedia,* 16 vols. (Bloomington: Indiana UP, 1994); Darlene Clark Hine, Wilma King, and Linda Reed, eds., *"We Specialize in the Wholly Impossible": A Reader in Black Women's History* (New York: Carlson, 1995); Knupfer; Lerner, *Black Women;* Logan; Lowenberg and Bogin; Neverdon-Morton; Peterson; Salem; Sterling; Terborg-Penn, *African American Women;* Yee. Truth's predecessors and contemporaries include Maria Stewart, Frances Ellen Watkins Harper, Sarah Parker Remond, Mary Ann Shadd Cary, Harriet Forten Purvis, Margaretta Forten, Charlotte

Forten, and itinerant preachers such as Old Elizabeth, Jarena Lee, Amanda Berry Smith, and Zilpha Elaw.

2. For example, in her new forward to the 1999 revised edition of her *Ar'n't I a Woman? Female Slaves in the Plantation South* (New York: W.W. Norton & Co., 1999), Deborah Gray White calls Truth's Akron speech "discredited," taking Mabee's and Painter's biographies as having "demonstrated that twelve years after the 1851 Akron, Ohio, Women's Rights meeting, Frances Dana Gage, not Sojourner Truth, wrote the famous 'A'n't I a Woman?' speech" (5, 11). In contrast, Erlene Stetson and Linda David caution against dismissing Gage's account and taking the *Anti-Slavery Bugle* version as the more reliable, for this account had its "own agenda . . . to elevate the anti-slavery cause" and, consequently, "suppressed the radical intent of [Truth's] challenge to the white patriarchy" (112–13). Stetson and David nevertheless register their own preference for Gage's account through a focus on Truth's idiom. While they acknowledge that Gage's plantation dialect did not accurately transcribe "Truth's speech patterns," they claim, without explanation or elaboration, that "a few fragments" in this version "seem somehow uncannily authentic" (112).

3. This is true also of Truth's *Narrative*. Recent scholarship on this work, such as that of Naomi Greyser and John Ernest, argues that however much the *Narrative* is a complex representation of Truth by her amanuenses, and however much it may read as a fragmented text, it nonetheless offers us Truth's self-representation in important, but far from straightforward, ways. Xiomara Santamarina has persuasively argued not only that this text has been overlooked as part of the larger archive of Truth's work, including speeches and reform activities, as does Ernest, but also that this critical omission repeats a kind of silencing Truth met in reform and activist circles in her day that were challenged by the way she "countered representations of uneducated black workers' inferiority by emphasizing the legitimating properties of what was disparaged as manual and menial labor" (38). Santamarina's argument is very much to the point, and while I do not consider Truth's *Narrative*, I do find that representations of Truth's body and her own arguments about authority and rights based in her self-identification as a worker are central to her black feminist politics, as I argue both in the introduction and in this chapter.

4. For example, see Donna Haraway, "Ecce Homo, Ain't (Ar'n't) I a Woman, and Inappropriate/d Others: The Human in a Post-Humanist Landscape," *Feminists Theorize the Political,* ed. Judith Butler and Joan W. Scott (New York: Routledge, 1992) 86–100; Constance Penley, *The Future of an Illusion: Film, Feminism, and Psychoanalysis* (Minneapolis: U of Minnesota P, 1989); and Denise Riley, *"Am I That Name?" Feminism and the Category of "Women" in History* (Minneapolis: U of Minnesota P, 1988).

5. Far from a "popular" understanding of Truth, even scholars pursuing studies of her as an orator situated within nineteenth-century public politics persist in crediting her greatest achievement as embodying, in an uncomplicated way, what she argued for. Drema Lipscomb, in "Sojourner Truth: A Practical Public Discourse," argues that Truth's oratory "illustrates the power of *enactment. . . .* [S]he was *herself an immediate and dramatic proof* of the ills resulting from woman's position . . . particularly [for] poor slave women" (238; my emphasis). Stetson and David call Truth's Akron speech "a historic joining of abolitionism and feminism *bodied forth in her own person*" (112; my emphasis). And Shirley Logan introduces her study of nineteenth-century black women's persuasive rhetoric by focusing on embodiment as distinguishing Truth from other early black women reformers: "To a greater extent than any of the other black women activists discussed here, Truth, female and formerly enslaved, embodied the arguments she made in support of abolition and women" (11). See also Painter, *Sojourner* 4; White, *Ar'n't I a Woman?* 161–62; Patricia Hill Collins, *Fighting Words: Black Women and the Search for Justice* (Minneapolis: Minnesota UP, 1998) 239; and Nick McCarthy, "Authority, Orality, and Specificity: Resisting Inscription in Sojourner Truth's 'Ar'n't I a Woman?'" *Sage* 9.2 (1995): 34.

6. I am referring to "intelligible subjectivity" as materialized through an "exclusionary matrix" as Judith Butler develops the concept in *Bodies that Matter:* "[T]he exclusionary matrix by which subjects are formed thus requires the simultaneous production of a domain of abject beings, those who are not yet 'subjects,' but who form the constitutive outside to the domain of the subject. The abject designates here precisely those 'unliveable' and 'uninhabitable' zones of social life which are nevertheless densely populated by those who do not enjoy the status of the subject, but whose living under the sign of the 'unliveable' . . . will constitute the defining limit of the subject's domain; it will constitute that site of dreaded identification against which—and by virtue of which—the domain of the subject will circumscribe its own claim to autonomy and to life" (3).

7. This was often the opening focus of press accounts of Remond's British lectures.

8. There were four accounts of this address reported by papers at the time. See the *New York Daily Tribune* 6 June 1851; *The Liberator* 13 June 1851; *Saturday Visiter* [sic] 14 June 1851; and *Anti-Slavery Bugle* 21 June 1851.

9. Gage's account was later published in the *National Anti-Slavery Standard;* the text of the speech is the same, though the dialect differs somewhat. See "Woman's Rights Convention," *National Anti-Slavery Standard* 2 May 1863: 4, rpt. in Fitch and Mandziuk 103–4. Painter points out that the *Independent* was the "nation's foremost religious newspaper" at this time (*Sojourner* 175). Gage's

piece not only drew further attention to Truth and her activities but also forwarded Gage's own literary career as a writer. She had been publishing short pieces in *Saturday Visiter* [*sic*] since 1849 and wrote under the pseudonym "Aunt Fanny" for both feminist and agricultural papers during the 1850s and 1860s (Painter, *Sojourner* 121 and 175). Gage's "Reminiscences" initially participated in a moment of heightened national attention to African Americans during the Civil War and, in effect, capitalized upon the focus on Sojourner Truth created by Stowe's very popular article. Rather quickly, Truth became a recognizable figure, not only as a result of Stowe's article but also due to the popularity of William Wetmore Story's statue, *Libyan Sibyl* (1860–61). Story's statue, inspired by Stowe's recollection of first meeting Truth, was exhibited to large audiences at London's Great Exhibition of 1862, where it marked his first major recognition as a sculptor. By 1863, the statue was being hailed by American periodicals such as *Harper's* as America's national symbol (Mabee 114). Through the mid- and late 1860s, newspapers and reformers alike called Truth the Libyan, Sable, African, and American Sibyl (Painter, *Sojourner* 162).

10. Naomi Greyser argues that in placing Gage's account at the front of the "Book of Life" section of Truth's 1875 *Narrative* rather than chronologically according to its publication, Frances Titus made it definitive of Truth's reform activities recorded through press clippings that Truth kept and reproduced in that second section of the *Narrative* along with correspondence and "Autographs of Distinguished Persons" (281).

11. As Karen Sanchez-Eppler notes, "[I]ntersections between antebellum feminism and abolition are legion: the Grimké sisters [were] antislavery lecturers. . . . In the 1830s and 1840s, Susan B. Anthony and Lucy Stone worked as paid agents of the American Anti-Slavery Society. . . . Elizabeth Cady Stanton and Lucretia Mott first met at the World's Anti-Slavery Convention of 1840, at which the female delegates were refused seats; legend has it that the idea of a woman's rights convention . . . was first discussed in the London hotel rooms of these excluded women" (51–52 n. 4).

12. In contrast, Marius Robinson, secretary of the Convention, specifically noted that "the business of the Convention was principally conducted by the women" and quoted attendants as praising the convention's "female 'army of talent'" (qtd. in Painter, *Sojourner* 125). Moreover, *The Liberator* characterized the convention as "crowded . . . with an audience of the most intelligent and earnest men and women, all faces beaming with joyous gladness," and pronounced it a meeting that "has never been surpassed or equalled in point of talent and importance. . . . [N]o person could have attended this Convention, and then said that woman was unqualified to sustain an equal position with man" ("Woman's Convention"). *The Liberator* also notes the addresses of nine women over

the course of the two-day convention, including Gage, Sarah Coates, Jane Swisshelm, Truth, Emma Coe, and Hanah Tracy Cutter.

13. See Mabee 76–78. Here Mabee examines Gage's speeches and writings in order to argue that her style, not Truth's, was marked by the "rhythmic repetitions" we see in her account of this speech.

14. I differ from Naomi Greyser in reading Gage's account as rendering the "A'n't I a Woman?" question as a request for recognition, given it is cast as delivered by a "voice like rolling thunder." Greyser, in her examination of the "ethical bind of sentimentalism" and Truth's *Narrative,* argues Gage renders this a "sentimental plea" to "'include *me,*'" which then enables "the white woman," and by extension "the woman's rights movement," to be positioned as the "heroine" who is "abl[e] to sentimentally embrace and understand her" (282).

15. Swisshelm had declared that "in a Woman's Rights Convention, the question of color has no right to a hearing" (qtd. in M. Jones 92).

16. Writing to *The Lily* (June 1852), Gage opens her rebuttal of Mrs. M.A. Bronson's assertion in the *Saturday Visiter* that women could not lecture without being mobbed by marking her position in the home: "I drop my broom and duster, now right in the midst of house cleaning time, to tell you what a spirited temperance meeting we have had in our little village." Only after this careful nod to her place does Gage go on to note that "I am known here as an earnest advocate of 'Woman's Rights,' yet I was called out, sustained and listened to by all classes, without a word or sign, so far as I know of disapprobation" ("Letter from Mrs Gage").

17. Neither this passage nor the representations of conventional bourgeois womanhood represented in it appear in any of the other reports of Truth's speech. See Mabee 75.

18. Truth's speech has been the subject of debate and various representations. While Gage represents it as plantation-style dialect, Robinson rendered it in standard English for the *Anti-Slavery Bugle.* Painter argues that Truth's speech would have been inflected with elements of Dutch, her first language (*Sojourner* 7).

19. Truth frequently cited her slave past as the grounds of the citizenship and authority to speak she claimed, as we see in the opening of her address to the Mob Convention: "I was born in this State. I've been a slave in this State, and now I'm a good citizen of this State" ("Women's Rights Convention"). Truth also began her address to an African American audience in New York City on November 7, 1853, by "detail[ing] much of her practical experience as a slave" ("Lecture").

20. In her *Mules and Men,* Zora Neale Hurston records "The Hawk and the Buzzard" folktale in which the hawk, who "takes" his living, looks down upon the

buzzard who "waits on de salvation of de Lawd." The buzzard maintains he'll "live to pick yo' bones, Brer Hawk," and does just that after the hawk impales himself on the dead limb of a tree while hunting a sparrow (116–17). Here the hawk preys on smaller, weaker birds only to meet an end from which the buzzard will benefit. Peterson has based her interpretation on a very similar tale ascribed to the Gullahs and quoted in Levine (92).

21. See, for example, Karlyn Kohrs Campbell, "Style and Content in the Rhetoric of Early Afro-American Feminists," *Quarterly Journal of Speech* 72.4 (1986): 435; A. Davis, *Women;* Eleanor Flexner and Ellen Fitzpatrick, *Century of Struggle: The Woman's Rights Movement in the United States* (Cambridge: Belknap, 1996) 85; Giddings 54; hooks, *Ain't I a Woman;* Lipscomb 237–39; Painter, *Sojourner* 171; Peterson 52; Stetson and David 114; White, *Ar'n't I a Woman?* 14; Yellin 80.

22. Hartman quite convincingly documents the ways in which empathy often gave way to sensation and made the slave's suffering an object of peculiar "enjoyment" in this dynamic of "kindred possession or occupation of the captive body. . . . Thus the desire to don, occupy, or possess blackness or the black body as a sentimental resource and/or locus of excess enjoyment is both founded upon and enabled by the material relations of chattel slavery" (21). For Hartman, empathic identification might, far from working towards freeing the enslaved, simply repossess him or her as the means of a fantasized brush with violence, pain, and suffering.

23. My phrasing of this focus on racial difference as both partial and additive, as though "gender" remains both racially uninflected and as such the primary concern of what McDowell refers to as "academic feminism" (97), is deliberate.

24. Space does not permit me to sketch, however briefly, the examples these black feminist critics cite as indicative of the larger problematic trends they are addressing.

25. Scarry's concept of analogical substantiation informs work on abolition and abolitionist feminist discourses. See, for example, Karen Sanchez-Eppler, *Touching Liberty: Abolition, Feminism, and the Politics of the Body* (Berkeley: U of California P, 1993); Lindon Barret, "African-American Slave Narratives: Literacy, the Body, Authority," *American Literary History* 7.3 (1995): 415–42; and Hartman.

26. The *History of Woman Suffrage* styles the "mobbish" opposition to this convention as indicative of the slavery of sex: "This Convention, interrupted throughout by the mob, has an unique and historic value of its own. It was the first overt exhibition of that public sentiment woman was then combating. The mob represented more than itself; it evidenced that general masculine opinion of woman, which condensed into law, forges the chains which enslave her" (*HWS*

1:547). It would seem the *History*'s writers want it both ways—Akron in 1851 was so threatened only an Amazonian Truth could save it, yet the Mob Convention in 1853 is the signal "first" of open hostility toward woman's rights.

27. Esther becomes King Ahasuerus's queen but is charged by her father Mordecai not to "shew her people nor her kindred" in the royal court (Esther 2:20). Mordecai has also saved the king's life by exposing a plot against him, for which Haman gets the credit and a promotion of sorts. Mordecai refuses to "reverence" Haman, and Haman, incensed at this lack of respect and knowing that Mordecai is Jewish, enlists the king's armies to "destroy" the Jews "scattered abroad and dispersed among the people . . . of thy kingdom" (Esther 3:8). Mordecai appeals to Esther to speak to the king, and she, knowing that to petition the king without having been called into his presence is to risk execution, agrees. In the meantime Haman, unsatisfied with the slaughter of the Jews in Ahasuerus's kingdom, has a gallows "fifty cubits high" built from which to hang an insubordinate Mordecai (Esther 5:14). Esther invites Haman to a banquet with the king at which she reveals she is a Jew and exposes Haman: "For we are sold, I and my people, to be destroyed, to be slain, and to perish. . . . The adversary and enemy is this wicked Haman" (Esther 7:4–6). King Ahasuerus then commands that Haman be hanged from the gallows built for Mordecai and gives Esther Haman's "house" to which she appoints Mordecai, who then decrees that the genocide end and the Jews begin "to avenge themselves on their enemies" (Esther 8:13).

28. See also "American Equal Rights Association," *New York Evening Post* 9 May 1867, which differs very little from the *History of Woman Suffrage* account. Painter has speculated that Truth may have said she had been enslaved for forty years in order to echo "the biblical experience of the children of Israel in their forty years of bondage" (*Sojourner* 141).

29. See also "Woman Suffrage."

30. Painter explains that New York state began the process of gradual emancipation in 1799: "Slavery would end on the Fourth of July 1827. For those born before 1799, emancipation would be unconditional; but those born after 1799 might have to serve a further period of indentured servitude: until they were twenty-eight, if male, or twenty-five, if female. This legislation would have kept Isabella [Sojourner Truth] and [her husband] Thomas slaves until 1827. Their children owed indentured servitude for much longer: Diana until about 1840, Peter until about 1849, Elizabeth until about 1850, and Sophia until about 1851. . . . When Sojourner Truth became an abolitionist, some of her children were still not free" (*Sojourner* 23).

31. The *New York Times* notes that the conference was "well attended, the audience for the most part being composed of ladies" ("Anniversaries").

32. In addition to calling for slavery's destruction "root and branch" in her May 9 speech, in her evening speech of May 10 Truth went on to invoke the war as a bloody battle to end slavery, saying, "We are now trying for liberty that requires no blood—that woman shall have their rights" (*HWS* 2: 225; "Woman Suffrage").

33. See Giddings 65–66; Darlene Clark Hine and Kathleen Thompson, *A Shining Thread of Hope* (New York: Random, 1999) 157–58 (this 1867 AERA speech is mistakenly noted as a speech Truth delivered at the 1870 AERA meeting, at which Truth was not present according to the *History of Woman Suffrage*); Bettye Collier-Thomas, "Frances Ellen Watkins Harper Abolitionist and Feminist Reformer 1826–1911," Gordon et al., *African American Women* 50. For interrogations of the way the *History of Woman Suffrage* has represented Truth's position on the proposed Fifteenth Amendment, see Terborg-Penn, *African American Women* 30–35; and Painter, *Sojourner* 225–30.

34. This line of argument is consistent across several accounts of this speech. See also "American Equal Rights Association," *New York Evening Post* 9 May 1867; "American Equal Rights Association" ("AERA"), 10 May 1867; and *HWS* 2: 193–94.

35. In the summer of 1864, Truth left Michigan for Washington, where she visited Lincoln at the White House, worked with the freedmen, and spoke in government camps where freed slaves were living.

36. The *History of Woman Suffrage* account of this speech also has Truth opening with these words. See *HWS* 2: 224–25.

37. This letter is reprinted as part of an appendix in *The History of Woman Suffrage* titled "National Conventions, 1866–1867" (*HWS* 2: 926–28).

38. See Peterson 47–52; McCarthy, "Authority" 30–35; and Painter, *Sojourner* 128–29.

39. The American Woman Suffrage Association supported the "'Negro suffrage' cause" and argued universal suffrage should be the goal, while the National Woman Suffrage Association cofounded by Anthony and Cady Stanton "divorced itself entirely from the 'Negro suffrage' question, concentrating on woman suffrage" (Terborg-Penn, *African American Women* 34).

40. Terborg-Penn "speculate[s] that free Black women who lived in the upstate New York area—perhaps in cities like Rochester—attended the [Seneca Falls] meeting along with the male abolitionists of color, but the chroniclers of the movement made no mention of them. However, there is evidence that, throughout the 1850s, a growing number of Black female abolitionists joined the small circle of suffragists" (14). She goes on to note that while Harriet Forten Purvis and her sister Margaretta Forten were key organizers of the Fifth National

Women's Rights Convention in Philadelphia, the "Pennsylvania state suffrage records . . . did not indicate that they were Black." In addition to the Forten sisters, Nancy Prince, Sarah Parker Remond, and Mary Ann Shadd Cary joined the woman's rights movement, yet like Harper, their participation receives scant attention in *The History of Woman Suffrage* in comparison to the attention paid Truth (Terborg-Penn, *African American Women* 14–21).

Chapter 4

1. Though Wells married in 1895, changing her name to Wells-Barnett, I will use Wells throughout for consistency as I consider her lectures and writings both before and following her marriage.

2. In her speeches and pamphlets, Wells would quote statistics published by the *Chicago Tribune* that documented lynchings according to state, victim, and "offence." For example, in a *Red Record,* Wells notes that in 1892 and 1893 "not one third of the victims lynched were charged with rape, and further that the charges made embraced a range of offenses from murders to misdemeanors" (156). That range included "attempted robbery . . . arson . . . incendiarism . . . alleged stock poisoning . . . poisoning wells . . . burglary . . . self-defense . . . insulting whites . . . malpractice . . . alleged barn burning . . . unknown offense . . . no offense" (*Red Record* 156).

3. See McMurray 177, 195–96, 214–5, 219; and Schechter 104–5.

4. See McMurray 213–14; and Schechter 105. In particular, the *New York Times* was quite critical of Wells.

5. See McMurray 115–16, 152–53, 156, 206–7, 217–18, 232–33; Schechter 95, 97, 106–9; and Streitmatter 53.

6. Wells addressed audiences in Boston; Wilmington, Delaware; Chester, Pennsylvania; New Bedford, Massachusetts; Providence and Newport; New York; and Washington, D.C.

7. There is some disagreement about when Wells had *Southern Horrors* reprinted in London as *United States Atrocities: Lynch Law* by Lux Publishing. McMurray notes the reprint appeared in 1892, importantly before her first tour (187), while Schechter notes it appeared in 1894, during Wells's second tour, and was sold at her lectures (99). Vron Ware offers the most information on this publication, documenting that Celestine Edwards—a black British temperance advocate, popular speaker and editor of *Lux,* a "'weekly Christian Evidence Newspaper' that . . . expressed anti-imperialist views"—wrote the introduction for *United States Atrocities* "published in Britain during her second trip" (193, 197).

8. An English Quaker, Impey knew Frederick Douglass and had come to know Wells's work during a visit to the United States. In September 1892, Impey

heard Wells speak at the National Press Association conference in Philadelphia and met her at William Still's home in Philadelphia two months later. Impey published a journal, *Anti-Caste,* "devoted to the interests of coloured races" (qtd. in Schechter 91–92). See also McMurray chap. 9. *Anti-Caste,* and particularly Impey's reports on American lynching, caught Mayo's attention. She contacted Impey suggesting they "arous[e] public sentiment" on the issue. Impey favored bringing Wells to Scotland and England as a speaker, and Mayo agreed to finance her tour (Schechter 92).

9. It is important to note that by the late 1890s and early 1900s, British suffragists had begun a campaign of public demonstration, rather than continuing to agitate through petitions. As Lisa Tickner documents in *The Spectacle of Women,* suffragists had come to understand the importance of "embodying their political commitment" through demonstrations that were "founded on a politics of 'seeing as believing which, if carefully attuned to the sensibilities of the watching crowds, could be a powerful instrument in winning their sympathy to the cause" (55). Consequently, the risks Remond and Craft faced taking to the platform before a public who saw such an act as "unwomanly" or "unsexing" the speaker were no longer this straightforward. Even though by the early twentieth century "the association between women and the streets in the public mind was an almost entirely degrading one," this changed "in a very short space of time" as suffrage spectacles became a "credible" and effective means of gaining public attention and sympathy for woman suffrage (Tickner 58).

10. The same can be said of women's access to public politics in the United States. Gabrielle Foreman documents American female reform societies, like "the New England Female Moral Reform Society [with] its bimonthly journal *Friend of Virtue* (1836–91)," that mark the organizing of nineteenth-century white women around social purity issues like "white slavery" (338).

11. See, for example, "Fortune and His Echo," *Indianapolis Freeman* 19 Apr. 1890, rpt. in Schechter 63. In this cartoon Wells is depicted as both a dog and as dressed in a suit saying, "I would I were a man." Notably, *The Freeman* was an African American paper.

12. Peterson is quoting Philip Fisher on sentimentality; however, this definition of a "bodied form" seems applicable to Wells's work on lynching and rape, even though Wells rarely delivered what we could call a sentimental appeal apart from her focus on the domestic, to which I will later return. See Philip Fisher, *Hard Facts: Setting and Form in the American Novel* (New York: Oxford UP, 1985).

13. In her autobiography, Wells wrote that her first address in Isabelle Mayo's parlor "told the same heart-stirring episodes which first gained me the sympathy and good will of my New York friends" (Duster 90).

14. See the *Birmingham Daily Post* 18 May 1893; *Westminster Gazette* 10 May 1894; and Wells's own "Ida B. Wells Abroad" column in *Inter-Ocean* [Chicago] 28 Apr. and 19 May 1894.

15. See *Westminster Gazette* 10 May 1894; and *Inter-Ocean* [Chicago] 19 May and 28 Apr. 1894.

16. See "Bitter Cry."

17. Wells also titled her talks during this first tour "Lynch Law in the United States." See "Miss Ida B. Wells, a negro lady."

18. See, for example, Braxton, *Black Women* 125; Carby, *Reconstructing* 111; Davis 79; Thomas C. Holt, "'The Lonely Warrior': Ida B. Wells-Barnett and the Struggle for Black Leadership," *Black Leaders of the Twentieth Century*, ed. John Hope Franklin and August Meier (Urbana: U of Illinois P, 1982) 47; Logan 76; Royster, "To Call" 180; and Streitmatter 54.

19. One of Wells's most outspoken British supporters during her second tour was the Reverend C. F. Aked, pastor of Pembroke Chapel, Liverpool. Aked introduced Wells's first address on this tour to his congregants, saying that "when [Wells] was in Liverpool last year friends of his who had heard me speak in London . . . wished him to invite me to speak in his church. He refused because he didn't . . . believe what I said was true. Since that tie he had been to America and was in Chicago to see the World's Fair. . . . He there read confirmation of all I had said in the reports of the Miller lynching in Birdwel, Ky., July 7. . . . I knew that what Miss Wells said was true" ("Ida B. Wells . . . Nemesis").

20. In most of the United States at this time, the age of consent was lower than it was in Britain: "In most of the States . . . the 'age of consent,' in cases of assault, is ten years, in a few twelve, in Iowa and Massachusetts it was by their last legislatures raised to thirteen, and in Washington Territory (where women are voters) to sixteen. In the District of Columbia, the national capital, . . it is ten years. In one State, Delaware, it is at the shockingly low period of SEVEN years!" ("Protection of Girlhood" 2).

21. Gabrielle Foreman notes, "Census figures and surveys of the 1880s and 1890s charted the swelling concern and affirmed that prostitution was on the rise" (336).

22. Just such a slippage occurred in Britain as well between working-class conditions and enslavement as evident in the *Oxford English Dictionary*'s definition of the term "slave" based upon its use in socialist discourse condemning the "white slavery" of English factory work, such as G. B. Shaw's *Fabian Essays on Socialism*: "3. One whose condition in respect of toil is comparable to that of a slave. . . . 1889 G. B. SHAW in *Fabian Ess.* 192 The white slaves of the sweater" (*OED* 15: 666).

23. In 1876, Josephine Butler, whose work Stead was indebted to for his accounts of white slavery in "The Maiden Tribute," published accounts of the Paris brothels and their horrors under the title *The New Abolitionists*. Stead, writing to Butler that year, contended that prostitution "wanted its *Uncle Tom's Cabin*," further underscoring the link between an earlier discourse on slavery, particularly American slavery, and the white slavery of British and European prostitution(qtd. in Walkowitz 96).

24. See Devereux 6.

25. Wells delivered a speech much like her Lyric Hall address to a predominantly white audience in the prestigious Boston Monday Lectureship series at Tremont Temple in Boston on February 13, 1893. In May it was published as "Lynch Law in All its Phases" in *Our Day: A Record and Review of Current Reform,* a monthly periodical whose editors included Frances E. Willard, president of the Women's Christian Temperance Union. The periodical's stated mission was "to provide a record that would 'form a comprehensive register of Criticism, Progress, and Reform, secular and religious, national and international.'" It also published the Boston Monday lectures delivered annually in March and February, lectures "which for several seasons have had a circulation of a million copies at home and abroad, [and] will discuss, as they have done for the last twelve years, whatever is at once new, true, and strategic in the relations of Religion to Science, Philosophy, and Current Reform." (qtd. in Royster, "To Call" 177–78). The first account of Wells's anti-lynching crusade to appear in a white northern newspaper ran in the *Boston Transcript and Advertiser* after this speech.

26. In praising Wells's anti-lynching work in her *Work of the Afro-American Woman* (1894), Gertrude Mossell noted that during her first tour Wells was "entertained" by "Miss Eliza Wigham, Secretary of the Anti-Slavery society" (7).

27. During this second tour, Wells again visited Ellen Richardson and wrote in detail of the meeting in her *Inter-Ocean* column. See "Newcastle Notes," *Inter-Ocean* [Chicago] 28 May 1894, rpt. in Duster 161–69.

28. See Walkowitz 94.

29. See also, for example, Campbell, *Critical Study* 147.

30. In her *Southern Horrors,* Wells cites the cases of "Mrs J. S. Underwood, the wife of a minister of Elyria, Ohio" (20), "the wife of a practicing physician in Memphis, in good social standing " (21), "A farmer's wife in Alabama" (23), and a Mrs. Marshall described as "one of the creme de la creme of" Natchez, Mississippi (25).

31. The article's title is evidence of the way in which the British press was accommodating Wells's anti-lynching appeals to the "new abolitionist" work on behalf of the working poor. *The Bitter Cry of Outcast London: An Inquiry into the*

Conditions of the Abject Poor, a pamphlet written by Congregationalist minister Andrew Mearns, appeared in 1883 and exposed the crime, prostitution, and disease of slum life in London. The pamphlet caused a public outcry and is regarded as having fueled the 1884 Royal Commission on the Housing of the Working Classes. See *Housing the London Poor,* a web site that includes primary documents, such as Mearns's pamphlet, Forest Crozier's *Methodism and "The Bitter Cry of Outcast London"* (London: T. Woolmer, 1885), and "'Outcast London.'—Where to Begin," *Pall Mall Gazette* 23 Oct. 1883, <http://www.people.virginia.edu/~djs2q/slums.html>.

32. During her first tour, an article in the *Ladies' Pictorial* also quotes Wells as saying, "Some of the 'coloured' people are not distinguishable from the whites, so far as their negro blood been diluted, but they are all 'African Americans'—that is Americans of African descent" ("Miss Ida B. Wells").

33. In her pamphlets, Wells would cite these statistics originally published in the Chicago *Tribune.*

34. When we learn of Wells's activities in Cairo we see how to the point Martha Jones's observation about the importance of the black church for black men during the Nadir is: "Men . . . turned their sights on the church as a critical site of African American resistance to the degradations of Jim Crow" (193).

35. As Larry Griffin, Paula Clark, and Joanne Sandberg point out, the sociological study of lynching in particular, with its emphasis on aggregate rates and statistics, has tended to "strip lynchings of their historical specificity, and relegate context and narrative to the void of 'background' . . . and 'illustration,' [so that] we seldom see what actually happened as lynchings unfolded. . . . We perceive the powerful and anonymous . . . forces at work behind the backs of southerners but not enough of their own moral and causative agency and thus too little of what racial violence reveals about the makeup and subtle operation of white supremacy" (24). Ironically, then, one of Wells's strongest tools—statistics that "proved" allegations of rape motivated far fewer lynchings than other alleged acts—became a research design that has tended to empty white mob violence of attention to the accountability of individuals.

36. "Black Chicagoans, led by Wells-Barnett and Reverdy Ransom, hired a detective to establish the facts surrounding the Hose lynching, which Wells-Barnett complied and published as a pamphlet" (Schechter 116).

37. For a thorough documentation of Wells's political marginalization in the black women's club movement and the NAACP, see Patricia Schechter's critical biography and Holt, "Lonely Warrior" 39–62.

38. The committee raised a "treasury of five thousand pounds" (Tucker 121) and sent a delegation to the United States in August 1895 to investigate mob violence and interview state governors about lynching. The black press "credited

Wells for the Briton's action," while the *New York World* polled state governors of whom only three welcomed the committee—two southern governors, "who felt their states would be vindicated," and the governor of Illinois, who took the opportunity to criticize Britain's record in Ireland (McMurray 227).

39. See Hazel Carby's summary of Willard's remarks at the 1894 WCTU conference in Cleveland. Carby, *Reconstructing* 114.

40. Thirteen men were indicted by grand jury for the lynchings, though they were never convicted.

41. Wells's position in the black women's club movement was, eventually, fraught, as Patricia Schechter details. While Wells published *A Red Record* (1895), *Lynch Law in Georgia* (1899), *Mob Rule in New Orleans* (1900), *The East St. Louis Massacre* (1917), and *The Arkansas Race Riot* (1920), many of these publications were self-financed. She was elected head of the Afro-American Council's Anti-Lynching Bureau in 1899 but left in 1903 (Schechter 116, 123). Wells's participation in the NAACP was hindered by that organization's marginalization of her. See Schechter 135–37, 141–45.

42. Wells also had an affect upon other African American newspaper editors, given how closely Alexander Manly's 1898 editorial in a Wilmington, North Carolina, paper echoes her rhetoric: "If the alleged crimes of rape . . . were so frequent as is oftentimes reported, her plea would be worthy of consideration." But, argued Manly, the fact that African American men were "sufficiently attractive for white girls of culture and refinement to fall in love with them . . . is well known to all" (qtd. in B. Jones, 189).

43. For an analysis of Wells's stress on civilization, see Gail Bederman, "'Civilization,' the Decline of Middle-Class Manliness, and Ida B. Wells's Antilynching Campaign (1892–94)," *Radical History Review* 52 (1992): 5–30.

44. In July 1892, Frederick Douglass had published "Lynch Law in the South" in the *North American Review,* yet despite Wells's often acknowledged position as his successor in anti-lynching agitation, her writings did not appear in this prestigious publication.

Chapter 5

1. For an examination of how the republican motherhood informed the domestic feminism of the black women's club movement in particular, see Knupfer.

2. The club movement, for both black and white women, had its roots in what were commonly known as self-improvement clubs, which filled the need for continued learning for women denied a college education. Club women developed study plans that emphasized literature, history, or the arts. During the Progressive Era, black women's clubs, like the benevolent and mutual-aid societies that preceded them, focused on the betterment of their communities,

advocating safe workplaces, particularly for women, establishing kindergartens, youth clubs, and homes for the elderly and engaging in fund-raising activities to benefit working-class and poor African Americans. The black women's club movement also pursued anti-lynching activism and has been regarded as the prime mobilizer for suffrage politics among African American women at the turn into the twentieth century. Black club women were predominantly middle-class and elite women in their communities, though they came from a variety of class and regional backgrounds. There is a rich body of scholarship on the black women's club movement, including Lynda F. Dickson, "Toward a Broader Angle of Vision in Uncovering Women's History: Black Women's Clubs Revisited," *Black Women in United States History: From Colonial Times through the Nineteenth Century,* ed. Darlene Clark Hine, Elsa Barkley Brown, Tiffany R. L. Patterson, and Lillian S. Williams, vol. 9 (New York: Carlson, 1990) 103–19; Kevin K. Gaines, *Uplifting the Race: Black Leadership, Politics, and Culture in the Twentieth Century* (Chapel Hill: U of North Carolina P, 1996); Willard B. Gatewood, *Aristocrats of Color: The Black Elite, 1880–1920* (Bloomington: Indiana UP, 1990); Giddings; Ruby M. Kendrick, "'They Also Serve': The National Association of Colored Women, Inc., 1895–1954," *Black Women in United States History: From Colonial Times through the Nineteenth Century,* ed. Darlene Clark Hine, Elsa Barkley Brown, Tiffany R. L. Patterson, and Lillian S. Williams, vol. 3 (New York: Carlson, 1990) 817–25; Knupfer; Gerda Lerner, "Early Community Work of Black Club Women," *Journal of Negro History* 59 (Apr. 1974): 158–67; Salem; Charles Harris Wesley, *History of the National Association of Colored Women's Clubs: A Legacy of Service* (Washington, D.C.: NACW, 1985); Deborah Gray White, "The Cost of Club Work, the Price of Feminism," *Visible Women: New Essays on American Activism,* ed. Nancy A. Hewitt and Suzanne Lebsock (Urbana: U of Illinois P, 1993) 247–69; and Jeremiah Moses Wilson, "Domestic Feminism, Conservatism, Sex Roles, and Black Women's Clubs, 1893–1896," *Journal of Social and Behavioral Science* 24 (1987): 166–77.

3. For such arguments regarding women in black nationalist politics, see Eric Sundquist, *To Wake the Nations: Race in the Making of American Literature* (Cambridge: Harvard UP, 1993); and Wilson Moses, *The Golden Age of Black Nationalism, 1850–1925* (New York: Oxford UP, 1978).

4. Within the larger context of American journalism, black press circulation figures approach those of the average weeklies and dailies. Between the 1830s and 1860s, "the great mass of weeklies had only a few hundred circulation each, and most of the dailies only a few thousand" (Mott 303).

5. Between the mid-1830s and 1860, American newspapers tripled in number. By 1860, the *New York Herald,* with a circulation of 77,000, was the largest daily in the world (Mott 303).

6. Mott also marks 1870–90 as a period of spectacular growth for the "mainstream" American press. The circulation of American dailies grew by 222 percent, while the nation's population increased by only 63 percent. "Illiteracy declined in these years from 20 to 13.3 percent" (507).

7. See, for example, James Horton, "Freedom's Yoke: Gender Conventions Among Antebellum Free Backs," *Black Women in United States History: From Colonial Times through the Nineteenth Century,* ed. Darlene Clark Hine, Elsa Barkley Brown, Tiffany R. L. Patterson, and Lillian S. Williams, vol. 2 (New York: Carlson, 1990) 667–92; Santamarina, "Introduction"; and M. Jones chap. 1.

8. Garrison published black women's contributions in *The Liberator's* Ladies' Department and actively sought them with this report of Philadelphia's Female Literary Association in the June 30, 1832, edition of the paper: "Nearly all of [the members of this 'society of colored ladies'] write . . . original pieces, which are put anonymously into a box, and afterwards criticized by a committee. Having been permitted to bring with him several of these pieces, he ventures to commence their publication, not only for their merit, but in order to induce the colored ladies of other places to go and do likewise" (qtd. in Richardson, *Maria* 126–27 n. 68). Stewart joined a similar literary society in New York city after leaving Boston in 1833.

9. For a close examination of Stewart's use of the black jeremiad, see Utley.

10. Lena Ampadu also sees Stewart as a rather unmistakable precursor to Truth in their shared use of a "similar provocative sermonic style" (41).

11. Gayle Tate also suggests that Stewart be considered as emerging in a context of black female evangelical activism (177). I would caution, however, against reading her, as many scholars have, only through the lens of evangelism and the study of spiritual narratives. Instead, Stewart might more productively be read as a transitional or bridging figure who makes clear the development of an early black feminism from preaching and evangelism to black civil rights and antislavery agitation.

12. Garrison opened the Ladies' Department with an assertion of woman's "influence" as an important factor in the abolition of slavery. See, for example, "The fact . . ." *The Liberator* 2.1 (7 Jan. 1832); and "Female Influence," *The Liberator* 2.1 (17 Mar. 1832).

13. In scholarship on Stewart, this paper is overlooked and, instead, the folding of *Freedom's Journal* and *Rights of All* by March and October 1829, respectively, are cited as evidence that no black newspaper existed to which Stewart could submit her writings. *Freedom's Journal* was the first black-owned and -operated newspaper in the United States. Edited by Samuel E. Cornish and John B. Russwurm in New York City, *Freedom's Journal* was a weekly that sold subscriptions for three dollars per year. Initially opposed to colonization, the

paper began to promote the movement in the fall of 1827 when Russwurm took over as sole editor. The paper could not sustain its readership with this shift in politics and it folded in the spring of 1829. Cornish returned to revive the paper as *The Rights of All* in May 1829, but it folded after less than a year's publication. Armistead Pride and Clint Wilson note that "following the demise of *Rights of All,* the next Black newspaper of any consequence did not appear until the arrival of the *Colored American* in 1837" (25). They do mention the *African Sentinel and Journal of Liberty* (1831–32) and the *Struggler* (1835–36) of New York city (Pride and Wilson 28 n. 16).

14. Benjamin Quarles notes that by the spring of 1843, African Americans formed three-quarters of *The Liberator*'s 2,300 subscribers (20). Joycelyn Moody contends that the readers of Stewart's tract would have been "generally New England whites' (34).

15. See also "A Sketch of Comfort," *Freedom's Journal* 22 June 1827.

16. See "Notice. . . . The African Dorcas Association," *Freedom's Journal* 1 Feb. 1828.

17. In addition to giving lectures to which whites were expressly invited, like the Franklin Hall lecture, Stewart's pamphlets undoubtedly reached a white readership. See Moody 34 and *The Liberator* 15 Sep. 1832.

18. Georgetown (a district in D.C.) passed a law in October 1831 prohibiting free African Americans from picking up copies of *The Liberator* at the post office and imposing a twenty-five-dollar fine and thirty days' imprisonment for those who did so. If found in violation of the law and unable to pay the stipulated fine, free African Americans in Georgetown would be "sold into slavery for four months" (Mayer 122). Other southern cities offered rewards for whites found circulating the paper, rewards for Garrison's arrest, and raised calls for Boston's mayor to suppress the paper. The Washington, D.C., *National Intelligencer* called for the paper's suppression; a Raleigh, North Carolina, jury indicted Garrison and Knapp for distribution of incendiary material; a vigilance association in Columbia, South Carolina, posted a $1,500 reward for whites found circulating the paper; and the Georgia legislature offered a $5,000 reward for Garrison's arrest. Garrison received death threats from both the South and within New England (Mayer 121–23).

19. Reed notes that the post–Revolutionary War generation of African American leadership in the Northeast was growing too old to be effective by the late 1820s, causing a shift in leadership with a move away from a politics of interracial cooperation toward a more radical politics, epitomized by the emergence of the Massachusetts General Colored Association founded in 1826 (69). Political consensus became much harder to achieve in this period, and "after 1829 [it] consisted of coalitions of individuals and organizations around

specific issues" (70). Horton and Horton cite this same generational shift as commensurate not only with a shift in black politics but also with a shift in black identification, as the new generation was largely American-born and saw Africa as "more their heritage than their home." As a result, opposition to the American Colonization Society and its aim to foster a mass black migration to Africa grew alongside interest in Caribbean or Canadian emigration (191).

20. See also M. Jones 96 for documentation of such labor competition in Boston in the 1840s and 1850s, and Santamarina 173 n. 19 for statistics on this competition in the Boston domestic labor market by 1860.

21. Marilyn Richardson notes that advertising the lectures of a black woman and printing them along with her essays gave Garrison not only "news in and of themselves" but also "strong statements in support of his publication's stands" (Richardson, "What If" 193). Yet Stewart as frequently contradicted Garrison's politics as she supported them, calling for militancy and invoking the jeremiad to imply a violent end for white America's oppression of blacks. Stewart may have also planned to publish the occasional essay for *The Liberator*. In the July 14, 1832, edition, Garrison published Stewart's essay, "Cause for Encouragement," which she noted was inspired by reading his account of the second national black convention in Philadelphia June 4–15, 1832 (Richardson, *Maria W. Stewart* 126 n. 68). By March 1832 Garrison was advertising Stewart's *Meditations: From the Pen of Mrs. Maria W. Stewart* and calling her a "highly intelligent colored lady." He "commend[ed] her 'Meditations,' which partake largely of a devotional spirit to the patronage of the people of color, and of all those among the whites who are disposed to encourage genius and piety in a person of her complexion." Stewart's *Meditations* sold for ten cents a copy ("Just published").

22. The scholars who focus on black nationalism in Stewart's addresses are few and include Lora Romero, Gayle Tate, Lena Ampadu, and Ebony Utley, though Carla Peterson does refer to it obliquely as "community building" (72).

23. Glaude cites the "Bucktown" riot in Cincinnati and others in places like Philadelphia in the fall of 1829 (113), as the violence against African Americans that motivated the organization of the first convention.

24. The ACS, however, enjoyed the support and interest of African Americans in the upper South, where "opportunities for free blacks were extremely limited" and where they were regarded as a threat to slaveholders (Horton and Horton 189).

25. Gayle Tate's work is a notable exception.

26. Interestingly, the *Colored American* reported on a co-operative grocery store established by black women in New York City, as Gayle Tate documents (*Unknown* 123–24). The one-hundred-member Female Trading Association sold "Dry *Groceries* of every description. . . . cheap for cash" (qtd. in Sterling 218).

27. Marilyn Richardson documents the founding of the Afric-American Female Intelligence Society of Boston in September 1831. The preamble to their constitution, published in *The Liberator*'s January 7, 1832, edition, noted their collective commitment to "the diffusion of knowledge, the suppression of vice and immorality, and . . . [the] cherishing of such virtues as will render us happy and useful to society" (*Maria* 127–128 n. 73). Harry Reed notes that the society "rented halls and sponsored lectures by William Lloyd Garrison" and others (78), promoted "abolitionist debates, dramatic readings, fundraising" and the establishment of "reading rooms, and other community welfare projects" (77), but "did not itself participate in public debates or lectures" (78). Shirley Yee documents that Boston black women were also active abolitionists, helping to organize the interracial Boston Female Anti-Slavery Society in 1833: "At least eleven black women participated in the Boston Female Anti-Slavery Society, including Susan Paul, Louisa Nell, and Nancy Prince" (90).

28. As Gayle Tate notes, labor conditions were much worse for free blacks in the North, even though they migrated there for better economic opportunities: "Leonard P. Curry's perusal of city directories between 1800 and 1850 led him to conclude that 'employment opportunities for blacks were clearly superior in the Lower South cities, worst in those of New England, and better in the urban centers of the Upper South than in New York and the Lower South'" (*Unknown* 101).

29. Like Elaw, who found white congregations more receptive to her preaching than black, and like Sojourner Truth, who was ignored by African Americans in New York City and preached, instead, at revivalist camp meetings and eventually as an itinerant, Maria Stewart was not welcomed as an activist by the free black community in Boston.

30. The *Repository* was published monthly from 1858 to 1864 and sold for one dollar per yearly subscription and twenty-five cents per copy.

31. Stewart successfully claimed eligibility for a pension as "widow of a veteran of the War of 1812" in 1878 (Richardson, *Maria* 79). Her pension was eight dollars per month.

32. The way in which the terminology applied to various black nationalist positions carries with it a none-too-implicit valorizing of separatist politics should give us pause, since they also tend to position feminist black nationalism as "weak" nationalisms against the "strong" or "radical" black nationalism of male leaders. I have in mind, for example, the work of Tommie Shelby in *We Who Are Dark: The Philosophical Foundations of Black Solidarity* (Cambridge: Belknap P of Harvard UP, 2005). For Shelby, strong black nationalism is separatist, whereas weak black nationalism is not concerned with the establishment of a distinct, self-governing black state and is regarded, as a result, as integrationist.

33. In 1849 and 1850 Douglass reported on the activities of the Women's Association of Philadelphia, as its corresponding secretary, to Frederick Douglass's paper *The North Star,* and in the spring of 1859 she wrote under her own signature for the new monthly *Anglo-African Magazine. The Emancipator,* edited by Joshua Leavitt in New York City, was a weekly publication of the American Anti-Slavery Association. Frederick Douglass's *North Star* was published in Rochester, New York, from 1847 to 1851. The *Anglo-African Magazine,* edited by Thomas Hamilton in New York City, was established in January 1859 and "appeared only sporadically for the next six years. Thomas Hamilton died in 1861, but his brother, Robert, saw the publication through the Civil War and into the first stages of freedom for the slaves" (Pride and Wilson 46).

34. Douglass can be understood as participating in a black nationalist discourse that stressed "concern for the soul" and individual virtue as an important component of the respectability and self-elevation it sought to cultivate among African Americans (Rael 132).

35. Shirley Yee notes the association's inaugural meeting was held in Rachel Lloyd's home and that Sarah Douglass and Hetty Burr "held leadership positions" in it. Delany addressed its members at this meeting (Yee 108).

36. Mary Ann Shadd married Thomas Cary on January 3, 1856. Even though I partly focus on her work before her marriage, for consistency I will refer to her as Mary Ann Shadd Cary.

37. There is no extant copy of this pamphlet. See Rhodes 22–23.

38. Shadd Cary's call to women to enter journalism was not a lone one. In 1892, for example, writing for the Kansas *Atchison Blade* edited by her father, Charles Langston, Carrie Langston wrote that "the time is not far distant when the intellect of woman shall cope with that of man's, and woman shall wield her scepter over man, as a philosopher, scientist and journalist. As woman sways her pen in writing, men see words fall from that delicate touch that conveys [*sic*] meanings that he is powerless to express, and when the earnest heart of true womanhood is beating with ambition to do something good or be something great . . . she decides that she can accomplish more good and win laurels and conquest by her work in journalism" (qtd. in McMurray 88).

39. The Refugee Home Society (RHS) was formed in 1852 in order to facilitate blacks settling in Canada West. It purchased farm land near Windsor and sold it to fugitives. The RHS "was controlled by whites in Michigan and administered locally by the Bibbs and David Hotchkiss . . . in Amherstburg." It was a controversial organization seen, by some black intellectuals, as promoting separatism (Rhodes 41–42).

40. On the complex relationship between Shadd Cary and Henry and Mary Bibb, see Rhodes.

41. See the *Oxford English Dictionary's* definition of "fugitive" and "refugee," both of which circulated with the connotations I note at the time Shadd Cary used them.

42. Martha Jones notes that in 1848 Cleveland hosted the National Colored Convention which heard Delany's call for women to participate equally in the meeting. This stance is also reflected in the 1854 convention, again hosted by that city, in which five of the nine member Cleveland delegation were women (105).

43. Like Stewart before her, Shadd Cary also used the black jeremiad to forward her anti-colonization arguments in speeches she delivered in her former home town of West Chester Pennsylvania during the summer of 1853 (Rhodes 79–80). She appears not to have used this rhetorical device in her newspaper writings, however.

44. The first Married Women's Property Acts were passed in the United States during the 1830s and 1840s. Feminists such as Elizabeth Cady Stanton and Susan B. Anthony were active in improving the 1848 and 1849 Married Women's Property Acts in New York State during the 1850s, agitation for change which this article reprinted by Shadd Cary undoubtedly reflects. As Carole Shammas documents, "Between the 1840s and 1880s, most states passed a series of acts that went beyond debt protection and recognized the right of married women to manage, enjoy the profits, sell, and will personal and real property that they had owned prior to marriage or had been given or inherited from a third party during marriage. Later versions often added earnings from wage work or businesses to what could be considered women's' separate property. Some states also included in the legislation safeguards against husbands unilaterally preventing their wives from being guardians of their children" (11). In New York state, the 1848 act was limited to women married after 1848 or to property of married women acquired after 1848; the Earnings Act of 1860 stipulated that the earnings must be paid by a third party and unconnected to household activities, thereby, for example, excluding earnings by boarding and the sale of staples like eggs and butter (Shammas 15). Peggy Rabkin argues that the 1848–62 married women property acts in New York were motivated by fathers seeking to protect their property from the claims of sons-in-law. On married women and property rights in the United States, see Joan Hoff, *Law, Gender, and Injustice: A Legal History of U.S. Women* (New York: New York UP, 1991); and Peggy A. Rabkin, *Fathers to Daughters: The Legal Foundation of Female Emancipation* (Westport: Greenwood, 1980).

45. As Mary Poovey notes, Norton's pamphlet, *Letter to the Queen on Lord Chancellor Cranworth's Marriage and Divorce Bill* (1855), "helped Barbara Bodichon convince the Law Amendment Society to take up the issue of married women's property." A year after the publication of *Letter to the Queen,* "more than seventy petitions" were presented to the Commons "about women and property;

one of these was signed by three thousand women. . . . another was signed by twenty-six thousand men and women" (70). On British married women's property law, see Lee Holcombe, *Wives and Property: Reform of the Married Women's Property Law in Nineteenth-Century England* (Toronto: U of Toronto P, 1983); and Mary Lyndon Shanley, *Feminism, Marriage, and the Law in Victorian England, 1850–1895* (London: I. B. Tauris, 1989).

46. An Act to Secure to Married Women Real and Personal Property Held in Their Own Right was enacted in 1851 in New Brunswick and ensured that "a married woman who was deserted or abandoned could sue for debts or damages in her own name" and "was authorized to retain any property she accumulated as a result of her own labor, safe from the control of her husband or his creditors" (Backhouse 218). Constance Backhouse details the provincial statutes and rulings that gradually gave married women "significant control over their real and personal property, wages, and business profits by 1900" (241).

47. It is worth noting that Caroline Norton becomes a symbol, for Shadd Cary, of married women's precarious legal position in what is an interesting reversal of the tendency amongst white British women to use the woman of color as symbol of white women's dispossessed position in society.

48. Even though Rhodes notes these letters to the editor and Shadd Cary's articles on women's rights, she nonetheless argues that Shadd Cary's tendency to mask her gender "by using her initials" and her rare direct address of gender in her editorials marks this cautiousness to weigh in publicly on woman's rights (91).

49. Ringgold Ward was "born a slave in Maryland in 1817, but his parents escaped to freedom when he was three years old, and he was educated by Quakers in New York. . . . his reputation came from his success as an antislavery lecturer and organizer. . . . Ward's lecture tours . . . earned him the reputation as an outstanding thinker and orator, second only to Frederick Douglass in stature among black public figures" (Rhodes 59–60).

50. As I have already noted, Roland Wolseley documents 68 newspapers founded in 1887 alone, and a total of 575 established by 1890 (38).

51. It must be noted that black women wrote on various topics for the black press, including lynching, woman suffrage, the convict-lease system, interracial cooperation, racial uplift, the club movement, women's education and employment opportunities, civil rights, and social settlement. Women like Fanny Alexander, of *Alexander's Magazine* (1906–8), also wrote regular women's columns offering housekeeping advice and grooming tips.

52. Some scholars refer to the Great Migration as extending from 1910 to 1970; others differentiate between the First Great Migration (1910–30) and the Second Great Migration (1930–70).

53. Even more recent scholarship, such as Victoria Wolcott's *Remaking Respectability,* that challenges prevalent images of African American migrants as well as the tendency to leave women out of histories of migration altogether tends to flatten what it characterizes as "reformers'" and "club women's" responses to migrants in northern cities. While it is true that this population was "managed" in various ways, this management and concern was far from a uniform response to migrants in existing, urban African American communities.

54. See, for example, *The Negro in Chicago: A Study of Race Relations and a Race Riot in 1919* (Chicago: Chicago Committee on Race Relations, 1922); A. Epstein, *The Negro Migrant in Pittsburgh* (New York: Arno, 1918); E. Franklin Frazier, *The Negro Family in Chicago* (Chicago: U of Chicago P, 1932); E. Franklin Frazier, *The Negro in the United States* (Chicago: U of Chicago P, 1939); and T. J. Woofer, *Negro Migration: Changes in Rural Organization and Population of the Cotton Belt* (New York: Negro UP, 1920).

55. See Maloney for a useful summary of this "push and pull" explanation of the Great Migration.

56. See also Mossell's column, "A Word of Counsel," *New York Freeman* 13 Feb. 1886 for an explicit warning to young migrating African American women.

57. For information on the *Age,* see chapter 4.

58. The first Hampton Negro Conference was held in 1897 at the Hampton Institute, founded near Hampton, Virginia, by the American Missionary Society in 1868 and directed by General Samuel Armstrong. It offered freedmen moral training and an industrial education that focused on domestic and agricultural practices. One of its most famous graduates was Booker T. Washington, who headed Tuskegee Institute, which shared Hampton's focus on training black men and women to become teachers or self-sufficient craftspeople and industrial workers. Hampton was a boarding school that also offered instruction to Native American students, who first attended in 1878. By the turn of the century nearly a thousand students were attending Hampton, of whom 135 were Native American ("Hampton Institute"). Hampton was also committed to women's education and admitted "large numbers of women" to its programs, endorsing the position that "women's influence was a key factor in the progress of Afro-Americans" (Neverdon-Morton 23).

59. From 1902 to 1904, Kellor studied employment agencies in New York City, Chicago, Philadelphia, and Boston and exposed the exploitation of black migrant women in her book *Out of Work* (1904). In the spring of 1905, the Inter-Municipal Committee on Household Research started to organize associations to protect black women in New York City and Philadelphia, with Kellor acting first as secretary and later as chair of the committee. The Associations for the Protection of Negro Women consisted of "travelers' aid, lodging houses, edu-

cation [and] employment agencies" for African American women migrating North. In 1906 the separate associations united as the National League for the Protection of Colored Women, for which Kellor acted as secretary (Cash, "Associations" 52).

60. It must be noted that Kellor played an instrumental role in the establishment of the National Urban League in 1911, formed as it was from the uniting of the National League for the Protection of Colored Women (founded in 1905), with the Committee on Urban Conditions Among Negroes (founded in 1910), and the Committee for the Improvement of Industrial Conditions Among Negroes in New York (founded in 1906), all originally founded by philanthropists in New York City.

61. On the YWCA and black women's activism, see Giddings 155–58.

62. This special issue also included articles on black women and morality by Josephine Bruce, Mary Church Terrell, and Sylvanie Williams.

63. See also, for example, the journalism of Anna Julia Cooper, Cornelia Bowen, Josephine Bruce, Ione Gibbs, Anna H. Jones, Josephine St. Pierre Ruffin, Mary Church Terrell, and Margaret Murray Washington. Space does not permit me to pursue a full discussion of domestic feminism in the black feminist journalism of the late nineteenth and early twentieth century, though it is ubiquitous at this time.

64. Warner identifies as "important needs of Publics" the "concretiz[ing of] the world in which discourse circulates, . . offer[ing] members direct and active membership, . . [and] plac[ing] strangers on a shared footing" (*Publics* 108).

Conclusion

1. By 1893, Canada had formed a National Council of Women. In Great Britain the National Union of Women Workers federated with the National Council of Women in 1898; it later changed its name to the International Council of Women (ICW). By 1938 the number of councils affiliated with the ICW had risen to thirty-six. The ICW's aims were the unification of women's organizations to promote human rights, sexual equality, peace, and women's involvement in the international sphere. Regarded by other women's groups as conservative, primarily for its early refusal to take a stance on suffrage, it continues today to organize women around the world with a focus on education and health. See Amy Hague, "International Council of Women Records, 1888–1959 Finding Aid," Sophia Smith Collection, <http://asteria.fivecolleges.edu/findaids/sophiasmith/mnsss96.html>. Even though the ICW was regarded as politically conservative in its early years, the National Council of Women of the United States was known as a prosuffrage organization and, consequently, regarded as radical.

2. For example, as Terborg-Penn documents. Adella Hunt Logan is listed in the *History of Woman Suffrage* as "the only life member of the NAWSA from Alabama" (60). Mary Church Terrell and Coralie Franklin Cook were also active in the NAWSA (Terborg-Penn 63).

3. See Terborg-Penn chap. 5.

4. That third generation of black suffragists identified by Terborg-Penn includes Gertrude Mossell, Mary McCurdy, Carrie Langston, Ida B. Wells, Adella Hunt Logan, Margaret Murray Washington, Lottie Rollin, Georgia Stewart, Angelina Weld Grimké, Anna Julia Cooper, Mary Church Terrell, Coralie Franklin Cook, Nannie Burroughs, Mary P. Burrill, Maria Baldwin, Mary E. Jackson, Lucy Diggs Slowe, Jeanette Carter, S. Willie Layton, Eugenia Burns Hope, Charlotte Hawkins Brown, Marion B. Wilkinson, Lucy Laney, Mary J. McCrarey, Janie Porter Barret, Mrs. Robert B. Moton, Minnie Lou Crosthwaite, Mary McLeod Bethune, Rosalie Jonas, and Pauline Hopkins.

5. Terborg-Penn includes Mary Church Terrell, Coralie Franklin Cook, Angelina Grimké, Nannie Helen Burroughs, and Anna Julia Cooper as part of this third generation based in Washington, some of whom were mentored by women such as Charlotte Forten Grimké. These women all migrated to Washington from elsewhere in the South, with Angelina Weld Grimké being the exception; she moved from Boston in 1905 with her father.

6. The first African American to be ordained an Episcopalian priest, Crummel was a leading black intellectual, writer, educator, and missionary who founded the American Negro Academy in Washington, D.C., in 1897. Regarded as one of the foremost black intellectuals of the nineteenth century, Crummel believed the academy would become an intellectual center for African Americans providing political direction. Its constitution described the American Negro Academy as an organization of black male intellectuals for the promotion of science, literature, and art. Its leading male members included W. E. B. Du Bois, Booker T. Washington, Paul Laurence Dunbar, James Weldon Johnson, Carter G. Woodson, Alain Locke, Arthur Schomburg, and Archibald H. Grimké. Cooper was its only female member.

7. Cooper also pursued a doctorate in modern languages and literature, with a specialization in French literature. She began studying in the summers at the Guilde Internationale in Paris from 1911 to 1913; she then undertook doctoral work at Columbia In 1914. However, Cooper was, by 1915, caring for five young children—great nieces and nephews—and could not complete the one-year residency requirement. She did not resume her studies until 1924, when she left for Paris and completed her degree at the University of Paris in a year. Cooper was by then sixty-six years old and was the fourth African American woman to earn a doctorate degree.

8. The first Conference of Educators of Colored Youth met in Washington, D.C., March 25–27. Instructors gathered, chiefly those from the southern states, to review the educational progress of African Americans since Emancipation and plan for the future. The conference stressed the need for permanent educational institutions for African American youth in the South, since existing institutions had been, for the past twenty-five years, operating with uncertain financial support. The 1893 World's Congress of Representative Women was held in Chicago in conjunction with the World's Columbian Exposition, at which African American leaders protested the exclusion of black Americans. Ida B. Wells and Frederick Douglass circulated their hallmark pamphlet *The Reason Why the Colored American Is Not in the World's Columbian Exposition* there, and Frances Harper delivered "Woman's Political Future," a speech in which she addressed lynching. Fannie Barrier Williams, Sarah J. Early, Fanny Jackson Coppin, Anna Julia Cooper, and Hallie Quinn Brown all gave addresses on "The Intellectual Progress of The Colored Women of the United States." The First National Conference of Colored Women was held in Boston on July 29, 1895, and led by Josephine St. Pierre Ruffin, editor of *Woman's Era*. A year later its membership, along with that of the National League of Colored Women, the National Federation of Afro-American Women, and over one hundred local clubs, would form the National Association of Colored Women.

9. In crediting Cooper with a "local" politics, scholars have in mind her advocacy of the rights and needs of poor black Washingtonians and her work with the settlement movement there.

10. Carby (*Reconstructing*) notes that Cooper's critique extended to condemning the United States' "imperialist expansion to Asia and the Pacific with its . . . appeal to a manifest destiny to civilize the uncivilized" (101). For arguments that Cooper was elitist, see, for example, Washington xlix.

11. As Charles Lemert notes, even though Paula Giddings takes Cooper's words for the title of her foundational history of black feminism, *Where and When I Enter,* and Hazel Carby has credited Cooper for her insights into the multiple oppressions of women of color, there are "few studies devoted exclusively" to her feminism and "the most serious scholarly works on the emergence of black feminist thought and fiction at the turn of the century tend to leave readers somewhat in the dark with respect to Cooper's specific contributions to black feminist theory" (17). As examples, Lemert cites bell hooks's *Ain't I a Woman,* Patricia Hill Collins's *Black Feminist Though,* Ann duCille's *Coupling Convention,* and Claudia Tate's *Domestic Allegories of Political Desire.* A recent exception is the section devoted to Cooper in Waters and Conaway's collection, *Black Women's Intellectual Traditions,* which reprints earlier scholarship on Cooper and adds one new essay by Janice Fernheimer.

12. Shaw's position was sustained by the club's board of managers, and it was "the Kentucky secretary," not Shaw, who resigned over the controversy.

13. In 1881, Gillet became the first female notary public in the United States and in 1890 the seventh female member of the Supreme Court. She was active in drafting married women's property legislation enacted in 1896, and cofounded the Women's Law Class at the Washington College of Law in 1896 with Ellen Spencer Mussey.

14. Mary Lucinda Bonney founded the WNIA at a meeting of the Woman's Home Mission Circle of Philadelphia's First Baptists Church. Her friend Amelia Stone Quinton joined Bonney in her organization's efforts, bringing her experience as a state organizer for the Women's Christian Temperance Union in the mid-1870s to the developing WNIA. Bonney funded the WNIA's efforts and Quinton undertook the research that fueled their petitions to Congress. The WNIA's first petition in February 1880 had been signed by thirteen thousand citizens in fifteen states. See Mathes 1–2.

15. Allotment, like "Indian reform" in general, was highly gendered. Three-quarters of adult men on a reservation were needed to agree to allotment before it was enacted. See Bonita Lawrence, "Gender, Race, and the Regulation of Native Identity in Canada and the United States: An Overview," *Hypatia* 18.2 (2003): 17. Title to allotted land was held in the name of the male head of the family, forcing a patriarchal relation and a nuclear family model upon those Native Americans who "elected" allotment. See Olund 154. As Angie Debo documents, however, Native Americans opposed the patriarchal underpinnings of allotment policy, arguing that "in their society married women and children had property rights" and "in 1891 the act was amended to provide equal shares to all—80 acres of agricultural, 160 acres of grazing land" (300).

16. Harper's first lecture was given in 1854 in New Bedford, Massachusetts, and in the early 1850s, Harper had already published an essay, "Woman's Rights," in the *Christian Recorder* (Peterson 120).

17. Publishing ten collections of poetry between 1846 and 1891, "the first short story by a black woman in 1851, three serialized novels in 1859, 1877, and 1887–88," and *Iola Leroy* in 1892, "probably the best-selling novel by an Afro-American written prior to the twentieth century," Harper earned her living by writing and by lecturing throughout the North and South to white and African American audiences. (Boyd 12; Foster, "Introduction" xxvii). Harper also was included in Phebe Hanaford's *Daughters of America* in 1883, in which Hanaford lists her as "one of the most eloquent women lecturers in the country" and "one of the colored women of whom white women may be proud" (326).

18. The Tuskegee Institute's records indicate that in 1891, 113 African Americans were lynched. Lynching was at its highest in the 1890s, with numbers ranging from 85 to 134 African Americans lynched per year. See http://www.law.umkc. edu/faculty/projects/ftrials/shipp/lynchingyear.html. In the 1890s, black feminist and anti-lynching activist Ida B. Wells would bring international attention to lynching as political intimidation in the United States and to its victims, who were not only black men but also black women and children.

19. Carol B. Conaway quotes Shadd Cary's 1854 editorial, "Our Free Colored Emigrants," in her contribution to *Black Women's Intellectual Traditions.* Shadd Cary characterized African American men as having a "progressive character, and in glaring contrast with the red man, they go onward, planning, improving, accumulating and enlarging" (qtd. in Conaway 239). For Conaway, this is Shadd Cary's view of Native Americans, in choosing not to leave the United States, as failing to "make any progress in fighting white racism and exploitation" (239). As my argument regarding Cooper's work will bear out, Shadd Cary's valorizing of accumulation and enlargement as twinned ideals of progress is quite problematic. Patrick Rael notes that antebellum black newspapers in the North "regularly reprinted tales of exotic Asian foreigners and seemed more than willing to cite white authorities who supported the potential of black intellect at the expense of that of Native Americans" (284), yet that propensity in antebellum newspapers should be weighed carefully against what we might think possible in black feminist thought later in the century, particularly when it would be difficult to ignore that such views had served white feminism's expediency arguments since the Fifteenth Amendment was debated and had riven the movement.

20. Between 1814 and 1837 some forty-six thousand Native Americans were removed from their lands.

21. While my focus is on this particular moment in woman suffrage, it should be noted that Cooper worked elsewhere to enter into that larger late-nineteenth-century debate in the United States over "the race problem." In "Has America a Race Problem? If So, How Can It Be Solved," the first chapter in part 2 of *A Voice,* Cooper argues, "Progressive peace in a nation is the result of conflict . . . produced through the co-existence of radically opposing or racially different elements" (Cooper, "Has America" 122). For her, *"equilibrium, not repression among conflicting forces is the condition of natural harmony, of permanent progress, and of universal freedom"* (Cooper, "Has America" 126). In this essay, Cooper argued for "universal freedom" in the United States by challenging existing discourses such as nativism, social Darwinism, and determinism as Fernheimer has observed (288). And again Cooper raised the question not only of African American claims on the nation but also those of Native Americans:

> *"Who are Americans?"* comes rolling back from ten million throats.
> . . . Who are the homefolks and who are the strangers? Who are
> the absolute and original tenants in fee-simple?
>
> The red men used to be owners of the soil,—but they are
> about to be pushed over into the Pacific Ocean. They, perhaps,
> have the best right to call themselves "Americans" by law of pri-
> mogeniture. They are at least the oldest inhabitants of whom we
> can at present identify any traces. If early settlers from abroad
> merely are meant and it is only a question of squatters' rights—
> why, the Mayflower, a pretty venerable institution, landed in the
> year of Grace 1620, and the first delegation from Africa just one
> year ahead of that,—in 1619. The first settlers seem to have been
> almost as much mixed as we are on this point; and it does not
> seem at all easy to decide just what individuals we mean when
> we yell "America for the Americans." (Cooper, "Has America"
> 127–28)

22. Boarding schools at this time also echoed the Dawes Act on civilization and
    assimilation, as General Richard Henry Pratt did in his educational philoso-
    phy for Carlisle, founded in 1879: "I suppose the end to be gained, however
    far away it may be, is the complete civilization of the Indian and his absorp-
    tion into our national life, with all the rights and privileges guaranteed to
    every other individual, the Indian to lose his identity as such, to give up his
    tribal relations and to be made to feel that he is an American citizen" (qtd. in
    Batker 17).

23. For example, slave owners perceived the proximity of Native American tribal
    communities and nations as dangerous potential refuges for escaped slaves,
    which they frequently were, and they feared armed revolt could result from
    sympathies and affiliations between Native and African Americans. William
    Katz documents the 1729 support of the Chickasaw Nation for black insur-
    rectionists in Louisiana. See William Loren Katz, *Black Indians: A Hidden
    Heritage* (New York: Atheneum, 1986).

24. Harper died in 1911, and Frances Smith Foster notes that "the public record of
    Harper's activities after 1901 is virtually empty" (*Brighter* 22).

25. Aldine was located in Xenia, Ohio, home of Wilberforce University. The press
    would publish such leading black intellectuals and feminists as Hallie Quinn
    Brown. See H. Brown.

Works Cited

"A Bitter Cry of Black America. A New 'Uncle-Tom's Cabin.'" *Westminster Gazette* 10 May 1894.

"About Southern Lynchings." *Baltimore Herald* 20 Oct. 1895. *Women and Social Movements in the United States, 1600-2000.* Alexandria: Alexander Street Press, 1997–2009. Document 38.

Acornley, John H. *The Colored Lady Evangelist, Being the Life, Labors and Experiences, of Mrs Harriet A. Baker.* 1892. New York: Garland, 1987.

Adams, Rev. Revels A. *Cyclopedia of African Methodism in Mississippi.* Natchez, Miss., 1902.

"Address by a Slave Mother. First Congregational Church, New York City. September 6, 1853." *New York Tribune* 7 Sep. 1853. Rpt. in Fitch and Mandziuk, *Sojourner Truth as Orator.* 145–47.

"A Distinguished Woman Honored." *American Citizen* 21 Oct. 1892.

A Lady of Boston. *Memoir of Mrs Chloe Spear, A Native of African Who Was Enslaved in Childhood, and Died in Boston, January 3, 1815 . . . Aged 65 Years.* Boston: James Loring, 1832.

The AMEC Book of Worship. Nashville: AMEC Sunday School Union, 1984.

"American Equal Rights Association." *The History of Woman Suffrage.* Ed. Elizabeth Cady Stanton, Susan B. Anthony, and Matilda Joslyn Gage. 1882. 10 vols. New York: Arno P, 1969. 2:182–228.

"American Equal Rights Association" ("AERA"). *New York Daily Tribune* 10 May 1867.

"American Fugitive Slave Bill." *Glasgow Herald* 10 Jan. 1851.

"American Slavery." a. *Clonmel Chronicle* 13 Apr. 1859.

"American Slavery." b. Rpt. in *The Liberator* 25 July 1851.

"American Slavery in the World's Fair in London." Rpt. in *The Liberator* 28 Feb. 1851.

Ampadu, Lena. "Maria W. Stewart and the Rhetoric of Black Preaching." *Black Women's Intellectual Traditions: Speaking Their Minds.* Ed. Kristin Waters and Carol B. Conaway. Burlington: U of Vermont P, 2007. 38–54.

"Anchor Brewery." *Thrale.com.* 25 Nov. 2007. <http://www.thrale.com>. 14 Aug. 2008.

Anderson, Benedict. *Imagined Communities.* London: Verso, 1983.

Andrews, William L. "Introduction." Andrews, *Sisters of the Spirit* 1–22.

———, ed. *Sisters of the Spirit: Three Black Women's Autobiographies of the Nineteenth Century.* Bloomington: Indiana UP, 1986.

Angell, Stephen Ward. "The Controversy Over Women's Ministry in the African Methodist Episcopal Church During the 1880s: The Case of Sarah Ann Hughes." *This Far by Faith: Readings in African-American Women's Religious Biography.* Ed. Judith Weisenfeld and Richard Newman. New York: Routledge, 1996. 94–109.

"Anniversaries. The Equal Rights Convention." *New York Times* 10 May 1867.

"Anti-Lynching Crusaders." *The Crisis* 25.1 (Nov. 1922): 8.

"Anti-Lynching Crusaders Statement." <http://womhist.alexanderstreet.com/lynch/doc7.htm> November 16, 2010.

"Anti-Slavery Meeting." *Cork Herald* 20 Apr. 1859: 2.

Armstrong, Rev. Letter to the *Christian Register* 21 Mar. 1894.

Arnesen, Eric. "Introduction: The Great American Protest." *Black Protest and the Great Migration.* Ed. Eric Arnesen. Boston: Bedford/St. Martin's, 2003.

Asante, Molefi Kete. *The Afrocentric Idea.* Philadelphia: Temple UP, 1987.

Asen, Robert, and Daniel C. Brouwer, eds. *Counterpublics and the State.* New York: SUNY P, 2001.

"Aunt Dinah." *Anti-Slavery Advocate* 45 (2 June 1856): 370.

Avery, Rachel Foster, ed. *Transactions of the National Council of Women of the United States, Assembled in Washington, D.C. February 22 to 25, 1891.* Philadelphia: Lippincott, 1891.

"A Wearied Councillor's Protest." *Birmingham Daily Post* 12 May 1894. Box 8, Folder 10. Ida B. Wells Papers. Special Collections, University of Chicago.

Backhouse, Constance B. "Married Women's Property Law in Nineteenth-Century Canada." *Law and History Review* 6.2 (Fall 1988): 211–57.

Bacon, Jacqueline. *The Humblest May Stand Forth: Rhetoric, Empowerment, and Abolition.* Columbia: U of South Carolina P, 2002.

Baker, Houston A., Jr. "Critical Memory and the Black Public Sphere." *The Black Public Sphere.* Ed. Black Public Sphere Collective. Chicago: U of Chicago P, 1995. 5–38.

Barkley Brown, Elsa. "Negotiating and Transforming the Public Sphere: African American Political Life in the Transition from Slavery to Freedom." *The Black*

Public Sphere. Ed. Black Public Sphere Collective. Chicago: U of Chicago P, 1995. 111–150.

Bassard, Katherine Clay. "Gender and Genre: Black Women's Autobiography and the Ideology of Literacy." *African American Review* 26.1 (1992): 119–29.

———. *Spiritual Interrogations: Culture, Gender, and Community in Early African American Women's Writing.* Princeton: Princeton UP, 1999.

Batker, Carol. *Reforming Fictions: Native, African, and Jewish American Women's Literature and Journalism in the Progressive Era.* New York: Columbia UP, 2000.

Beardin, Jim, and Linda Jean Butler. *The Life and Times of Mary Shadd Cary.* Toronto: NC, 1977.

Benhabib, Seyla. "Models of Public Space: Hannah Arendt, the Liberal Tradition, and Jürgen Habermas." *Habermas and the Public Sphere.* Ed. Craig Calhoun. Cambridge: MIT, 1992. 73–98.

Benn Michaels, Walter. *Our America: Nativism, Modernism, and Pluralism.* Durham: Duke UP, 1995.

Berlant, Lauren. *The Female Complaint: The Unfinished Business of Sentimentality in American Culture.* Durham: Duke UP, 2008.

———. *The Queen of America Goes to Washington City: Essays on Sex and Citizenship.* Durham: Duke UP, 1997.

Blackett, R. J. M. "African Americans, the British Working Class and the American Civil War." *Slavery and Abolition* 17.2 (1996): 51–67.

———. *Beating Against the Barriers: Biographical Essays in Nineteenth-Century Afro-American History.* Baton Rouge: Louisiana State UP, 1986.

———. *Building an Antislavery Wall: Black Americans in the Atlantic Abolitionist Movement, 1830–1860.* Baton Rouge: Louisiana State UP, 1983.

Boyd, Melba Joyce. *Discarded Legacy: Politics and Poetics in the Life of Frances E. W. Harper 1825–1911.* Detroit: Wayne State UP, 1994.

Brigance, William Norwood, ed. *A History and Criticism of American Public Address.* 3 vols. New York: Russell & Russell, 1960.

Brody, Jennifer DeVere. "*Impossible Purities: Blackness, Femininity, and Victorian Culture.* Durham: Duke UP, 1998.

Brooke, John L. "On the Edges of the Public Sphere." *William and Mary Quarterly* 62.1 (Jan. 2005): 93–98.

Broughton, Virginia. *Twenty Year's Experience of a Missionary.* 1907. *Spiritual Narratives.* Ed. Susan Houchins. Schomburg Library of Nineteenth-Century Black Women Writers. New York: Oxford UP, 1988.

Brown, Annie E. *Religious Work and Travels.* Chester: Olin T. Pancoast, 1909.

Brown, Charlotte Hawkins. "Women's Interracial Conference. Memphis, Tennessee. Morning Session, October 8, 1920. Address by Mrs. Charlotte Hawkins Brown." *How Did Black and White Southern Women Campaign to End Lynching, 1890-1942?* in *Women and Social Movements in the United States, 1600-2000.* Alexandria: Alexander Street Press, 1997-2009. Document 6.

Brown, Hallie Quinn. *Homespun Heroines and Other Women of Distinction.* 1926. New York: Oxford UP, 1988.

Brown, Right Reverend John M. "Two questions have disturbed the public mind . . ." *AME Church Review* 1886: 354–61.

Bruce, Dickson D., Jr. *And They All Sang Hallelujah: Plain-Folk Camp-Meeting Religion, 1800–1845.* Knoxville: U of Tennessee P, 1974.

Brundage, W. Fitzhugh. "Introduction." Brundage, *Under Sentence of Death* 1–20.

———, ed. *Under Sentence of Death: Lynching in the South.* Chapel Hill: U of North Carolina P, 1997.

Butler, Judith. *Bodies that Matter: On the Discursive Limits of Sex.* New York: Routledge, 1994.

Campbell, Karlyn Kohrs. *Man Cannot Speak for Her: A Critical Study of Early Feminist Rhetoric.* 2 vols. Westport: Greenwood, 1989.

Carby, Hazel V. "Policing the Black Woman's Body in an Urban Context." *Critical Inquiry* 18 (1992): 738–55.

———. *Reconstructing Womanhood: The Emergence of the Afro-American Woman Novelist.* New York: Oxford UP, 1987.

Cash, Floris Barnett. "Associations for the Protection of Negro Women." *Black Women in America: An Historical Encyclopaedia.* Ed. Darlene Clark Hine, Elsa Barkley Brown, and Rosalyn Terborg-Penn. 3 vols. New York: Carlson, 1993. 1: 51–52.

———. "White Rose Mission, New York City." *Black Women in America: An Historical Encyclopaedia.* Ed. Darlene Clark Hine, Elsa Barkley Brown, and Rosalyn Terborg-Penn. 3 vols. New York: Carlson, 1993. 1258–59.

Castiglia, Christopher. *Interior States: Institutional Consciousness and the Inner Life of Democracy in the Antebellum United States.* Durham: Duke UP, 2008.

Castronovo, Russ. "Souls that Matter: Social Death and the Pedagogy of Democratic Citizenship." *Materializing Democracy: Toward a Revitalized Cultural Politics.* Ed. Russ Castronovo and Dana Nelson. Durham: Duke UP, 2002. 116–43.

Child, Lydia Maria. *Letters from New York.* New York: Charles S. Frances, 1843.

Clark, Anna. "The New Poor Law and the Breadwinner Wage: Contrasting Assumptions." *Journal of Social History* 34.2 (2000): 261–81.

————. *The Struggle for the Breeches: Gender and the Making of the British Working Class*. Berkeley: U of California P, 1995.

————. "Wild Workhouse Girls and the Liberal Imperial State in Mid-Nineteenth-Century Ireland." *Journal of Social History* 39.2 (2005): 389–410.

Coleman, Willi. "'Like Hot Lead to Pour on the Americans . . .': Sarah Parker Remond—From Slame, Mass., to the British Isles." *Woman's Rights and Transatlantic Antislavery in the Era of Emancipation*. Ed. Kathryn Kish Sklar and James Brewer Stewart. New Haven: Yale UP, 2007. 173–88.

Collins, Patricia Hill. *Black Feminist Thought: Knowledge, Consciousness, and the Politics of Empowerment*. New York: Routledge, 1991.

Conaway, Carol B. "Mary Ann Shadd Cary: A Visionary of the Black Press." *Black Women's Intellectual Traditions: Speaking Their Minds*. Ed. Kristin Waters and Carol B. Conaway. Burlington: U of Vermont P, 2007. 216–45.

Connor, Kimberly Rae. *Conversions and Visions in the Writings of African-American Women* Knoxville: U of Tennessee P, 1994.

Cooper, Anna Julia. "Has America a Race Problem? If So, How Can It Best Be Solved?" 1892. *The Voice of Anna Julia Cooper, Including* A Voice from the South *and Other Important Essays, Papers, and Letters*. Ed. Charles Lemert and Esme Bhan. Boston: Rowman & Littlefield, 1998. 121–33.

————. "Woman versus the Indian." 1891. *The Voice of Anna Julia Cooper, Including* A Voice from the South *and Other Important Essays, Papers, and Letters*. Ed. Charles Lemert and Esme Bhan. Boston: Rowman & Littlefield, 1998. 88–108.

Craft, William, and Ellen Craft. *Running a Thousand Miles for Freedom: The Escape of William and Ellen Craft from Slavery, by William Craft and Ellen Craft*. 1860. Ed. Barbara McCaskill. Athens: U of Georgia P, 1999.

Crossley, Nick, and John Michael Roberts. "Introduction." *After Habermas: New Perspectives on the Public Sphere*. Oxford: Blackwell, 2004. 1–27.

Culp, Daniel Wallace. *Twentieth-Century Negro Literature or a Cyclopedia of Thought*. Naperville: J. L. Nichols, 1902.

Curtis White, Katherine J. "Women in the Great Migration: Economic Activity of Black and White Southern-Born Female Migrants in 19120, 1940, and 1970." *Social Science History* 29.3 (2005): 413–55.

Dahlberg, Lincoln. "The Habermasian Public Sphere: Taking Difference Seriously?" *Theory and Society* 34 (2005): 111–36.

Daniel, Walter C. *Black Journals of the United States*. Westport: Greenwood, 1982.

Dann, Martin E., ed. *The Black Press, 1827–1890: The Quest for National Identity*. New York: G. P. Putnam, 1971.

Davis, Angela Y. *Blues Legacies and Black Feminism: Gertrude "Ma" Rainey, Bessie Smith, and Billie Holiday.* New York: Vintage, 1998.

——. *Women, Race and Class.* New York: Vintage, 1983.

Davis, Simone. "The 'Weak Race' and the Winchester: Political Voices in the Pamphlets of Ida B. Wells." *Legacy* 12.2 (1995): 77–97.

Dawson, Michael C. "A Black Counterpublic? Economic Earthquakes, Racial Agenda(s), and Black Politics." *The Black Public Sphere.* Ed. Black Public Sphere Collective. Chicago: U of Chicago P, 1995. 199–228.

Debo, Angie. *A History of the Indians of the United States.* Norman: U of Oklahoma P, 1970.

Deegan, Mary Jo. "Fannie Barrier Williams and Her Life as New Woman of Color in Chicago, 1893–1918." *The New Woman of Color: The Collected Writings of Fannie Barrier Williams, 1893–1918.* Ed. Mary Jo Deegan. DeKalb: Northern Illinois UP, 2002. xiii–lx.

Detweiler, Frederick G. *The Negro Press in the United States.* Chicago: U of Chicago P, 1922.

Devereux, Cecily. "'The Maiden Tribute' and the Rise of the White Slave in the Nineteenth Century: The Making of an Imperial Construct." *Victorian Review* 26.2 (2001): 1–23.

Dieter, Melvin Easterday. *The Holiness Revival of the Nineteenth Century.* Metuchen: Scarecrow, 1980.

Dodson, Jualynne. "Introduction." *An Autobiography: The Story of the Lord's Dealings with Mrs. Amanda Smith the Colored Evangelist.* 1893. New York: Oxford UP, 1988. xxvii–xlii.

——. "Nineteenth-Century A.M.E. Preaching Women." *Women in New Worlds.* Ed. Hilah F. Thomas and Rosemary Skinner Keller. Nashville: Abingdon, 1981. 276–89.

——. "Power and Surrogate Leadership: Black Women and Organized Religion." *Sage* 5.2 (1988): 37–42.

"Donation Party." *Voice of the Fugitive* 19 Nov. 1851.

Douglass, Sarah Mapps [Zillah]. "Extract from a letter written to a friend, Feb. 23d. 1832." *Liberator* 21 July 1832.

——. [Sophanisba]. "Family Worship." *The Liberator* 8 Sep. 1832.

——. [Zillah]. "Moonlight." *The Liberator* 7 Apr. 1832.

——. "Reply to Woodby." *The Liberator* 18 Aug. 1832.

Douglass-Chinn, Richard J. *Preacher Woman Sings the Blues: The Autobiographies of Nineteenth-Century African American Evangelists.* Columbia: U of Missouri P, 2001.

Dred Scott v. Sandford. 60 U.S. 393 (1856). *Enfacto.* <http://www.enfacto.com/case/U.S./60/393/>.

duCille, Ann. *The Coupling Convention: Sex, Text, and Tradition in Black Women's Fiction.* New York: Oxford UP, 1993.

Dunbar, Erica Armstrong. *A Fragile Freedom: African American Women and Emancipation in the Antebellum City.* New Haven: Yale UP, 2008.

Duster, Alfreda M., ed. *Crusade for Justice: The Autobiography of Ida B. Wells.* Chicago: U of Chicago P, 1970.

Early, Sarah J. W. "Editorial 'Following the Trail of the Fathers': Priscilla Baltimore." *AME Church Review* Apr.–June 1964: 3–5.

Elaw, Zilpha. *Memoirs of the Life, Religious Experience, Ministerial Travels and Labors of Mrs. Zilpha Elaw.* 1846. Andrews, *Sisters of the Spirit* 49–160.

Elizabeth. *Memoir of Old Elizabeth, a Coloured Woman.* 1863. *Six Women's Slave Narratives.* Ed. William L. Andrews. Schomburg Library of Nineteenth-Century Black Women Writers. New York: Oxford UP, 1988.

Engs, Robert F. "Red, Black, and White: A Study in Intellectual Inequality." *Religion, Race, and Reconstruction.* Ed. J. Morgan Kousser and James M. McPherson. New York: Oxford UP, 1982. 243–65.

Ernest, John. *Liberation Historiography: African American Writers and the Challenge of History, 1794–1861.* Chapel Hill: U of North Carolina P, 2004.

———. "Representing Chaos: William Crafts' *Running a Thousand Miles for Freedom.*" *PMLA* 121.2 (2006): 469–83.

———. "The Floating Icon and the Fluid Text: Rereading the *Narrative of Sojourner Truth.*" *American Literature* 78 (2006): 459–486.

Estlin, J. B., to Maria Chapman. 3 Apr. 1852, Bayswater. MS A.912, v. 26, no. 23. Weston Papers, Boston Public Library.

Estlin, Mary, to Anne Weston. 9 May 1851, Bristol. MS A.92, v. 25, no.87. Weston Papers, Boston Public Library.

Farrison, William. *William Wells Brown: Author and Reformer.* Chicago: U of Chicago P, 1969.

"Female Suffrage . . . Woman Demands Equality with the Negro." *New York World* 10 May 1867.

Fernheimer, Janice W. "Arguing from Difference: Cooper, Emerson, Guizot, and a More Harmonious America." *Black Women's Intellectual Traditions: Speaking Their Minds.* Ed. Kristin Waters and Carol B. Conaway. Burlington: U of Vermont P, 2007. 287–305.

Fine, Gary Alan, and Brooke Harrington. "Tiny Publics: Small Groups and Civil Society." *Sociological Theory* 22.3 (Sep. 2004): 341–56.

Fisch, Audrey. *American Slaves in Victorian England: Abolitionist Politics in Popular Literature and Culture.* Cambridge: Cambridge UP, 2000.

Fitch, Suzanne Pullon, and Roseann M. Mandziuk. *Sojourner Truth as Orator: Wit, Story, and Song.* Westport: Greenwood, 1997.

Fletcher, Alice C. "Our Duty to Dependent Races." *Transactions of the National Council of Women of the United States, Assembled in Washington, D.C. February 22 to 25, 1891.* Ed. Rachel Foster Avery. Philadelphia: Lippincott, 1891. 83–84.

Foner, Philip S., and Robert James Branham. "Introduction." *Lift Every Voice: African American Oratory, 1787–1900.* Ed. Philip S. Foner and Robert James Branham. Tuscaloosa: U of Alabama P, 1948.

Foote, Julia. *A Brand Plucked from the Fire: An Autobiographical Sketch by Mrs Julia A. Foote.* 1879. Andrews, *Sisters of the Spirit* 161–234.

Foreman, P. Gabrielle. "'Reading Aright': White Slavery, Black Referents, and the Strategy of Histotextuality in *Iola Leroy*." *Yale Journal of Criticism* 10.2 (1997): 327–54.

"For sale . . ." *The Liberator* 1.41 (8 Oct. 1831).

Foster, Frances Smith. "Gender, Genre, and Vulgar Secularism: The Case of Frances Ellen Watkins Harper and the AME Press." *Recovered Writers/Recovered Texts.* Ed. Dolan Hubbard. Knoxville: Tennessee Studies in Literature, 1997:46-59.

———. *Written by Herself: Literary Production by African American Women, 1746–1892.* Bloomington: Indiana UP, 1993.

———, ed, *A Brighter Coming Day: A Frances Ellen Watkins Harper Reader.* New York: Feminist, 1990.

Foster, R. F. *Modern Ireland 1600–1972.* London: Penguin, 1988.

Fowler, Henry. *The American Pulpit: Sketches, Biographical and Descriptive of Living American Preachers, and of the Religious Movements and Distinctive Ideas Which They Represent.* New York: J. M. Fairchild, 1856.

Fraser, Nancy. "Politics, Culture, and the Public Sphere: Toward a Postmodern Conception." *Social Postmodernism: Beyond Identity Politics.* Ed. Linda Nicholson and Steven Seidman. Cambridge: Cambridge UP, 1995. 287–312.

———. "Rethinking the Public Sphere: A Contribution to the Critique of Actually Existing Democracy." *Habermas and the Public Sphere.* Ed. Craig Calhoun. Cambridge: MIT, 1992. 109–42.

Frazier, E. Franklin, and C. Eric Lincoln. *The Negro Church in America.* New York: Schocken, 1974.

Fuchs, Sabrina. "Victoria Earle Smith." *Encyclopedia of African-American Culture and History.* 5 vols. Farmington Hills: Gale, 2001. <http://galenet. galegroup,com/servlet/HistRC/>.

"Fugitive Slaves at the Great Exhibition." Rpt. in *The Liberator* 18 July 1851.

Gage, Frances D. "Letter from Mrs Gage." *The Lily* (June 1852).

―――. "Reminiscences." *The History of Woman Suffrage.* Ed. Elizabeth Cady Stanton, Susan B. Anthony, and Matilda Joslyn Gage. 1882. 10 vols. New York: Arno, 1969. 1: 115–17.

Gardner, Eric, ed. *Jennie Carter: A Black Journalist of the Early West.* Jackson: UP of Mississippi, 2007.

Garrison, William Lloyd. "It is proper to state . . ." *The Liberator* 28 April 1832.

Gates, Henry Louis, Jr. *The Signifying Monkey: A Theory of African-American Literary Criticism.* New York: Oxford UP, 1988.

"The General Conference." *Christian Recorder* 29 May 1884.

George, Carol V. R. "Widening the Circle: The Black Church and the Abolitionist Crusade, 1830–1860." *African American Religion: Interpretive Essays in History and Culture.* Ed. Timothy E. Fulop and Albert J. Raboteau. New York: Routledge, 1996. 155–73.

Giddings, Paula. *When and Where I Enter: The Impact of Black Women on Race and Sex in America.* New York: Morrow, 1984.

Gilbert, Olive, and Frances Titus. *Narrative of Sojourner Truth; a Bondswoman of Olden Time, with a History of her Labors and Correspondence Draw from her "Book of Life."* 1878. Ed. Henry Louis Gates Jr. Schomburg Library of Nineteenth-Century Black Women Writers. New York: Oxford UP, 1991.

Gilkes, Cheryl Townsend. "The Politics of 'Silence': Dual-Sex Political Systems and Women's Traditions of Conflict in African-American Religion." *African American Christianity: Essays in History.* Ed. Paul E. Johnson. Berkeley: U of California P, 1994. 80–110.

Glaude, Eddie S., Jr. *Exodus! Religion, Race, and Nation in Early Nineteenth-Century Black America.* Chicago: U of Chicago P, 2000.

Goldsby, Jacqueline. "The High and Low Tech of It: The Meaning of Lynching and the Death of Emmett Till." *Yale Journal of Criticism* 9.2 (1996): 245–82.

Gosse, Van. "'As a Nation, the English Are Our Friends': The Emergence of African American Politics in the British Atlantic World, 1772–1861." *American Historical Review* 113.4 (2008): 1003–28.

Grammer, Elizabeth. *Some Wild Visions: Autobiographies by Female Itinerant Evangelists in Nineteenth-Century America.* New York: Oxford UP, 2003.

Greyser, Naomi. "Affective Geographies: Sojourner Truth's *Narrative,* Feminism, and the Ethical Bind of Sentimentalism." *American Literature* 79.2 (2007): 275-305.

Griffin, Larry J., Paula Clark, and Joanne C. Sandberg. "Narrative and Event: Lynching and Historical Sociology." Brundage, *Under Sentence of Death* 24–47.

Gunning, Sandra. *Race, Rape, and Lynching: The Red Record of American Literature, 1890–1912.* New York: Oxford UP, 1996.

Guy-Sheftall, Beverly. *Daughters of Sorrow: Attitudes Towards Black Women, 1880–1920.* Carlson, 1990.

Habermas, Jürgen. *The Structural Transformation of the Public Sphere: An Inquiry into a Category of Bourgeois Society.* Trans. Thomas Burger. Cambridge: MIT, 1989.

Hall, Jacquelyn Dowd. "Antilynching Movement." *Black Women in America: An Historical Encyclopedia.* Ed. Darlene Clark Hine, Elsa Barkley Brown, and Rosalyn Terborg-Penn. 3 vols. New York: Carlson, 1993. 1: 38–41.

Hall, Rosalind. "'A Poor Cotton Weyvwer': Poverty and the Cotton Famine in Clitheroe." *Social History* 28.2 (2003): 227-250.

"Hampton Institute." *Encyclopedia of North American Indians.* Houghton Mifflin. <http://college.hmco.com/history/readerscomp/naind/html/na_014000_hamptoninsti.htm>

Hanaford, Phebe. *Daughters of America; or, Women of the Century.* Augusta: True, 1882.

Handy, Rt. Rev. James A. *Scraps of African Methodist Episcopal History.* Philadelphia: A.M.E. Book Concern, 1902.

Harley, Sharon. "When your Work Is Not Who You Are: The Development of a Working-Class Consciousness among Afro-American Women." *Gender, Class, Race, and Reform in the Progressive Era.* Ed. Noralee Frankel and Nancy S. Dye. Lexington: UP of Kentucky, 1991. 42–55.

Harper, Frances Ellen Watkins. "Duty to Dependent Races." *Transactions of the National Council of Women of the United States, Assembled in Washington, D.C. February 22 to 25, 1891.* Ed. Rachel Foster Avery. Philadelphia: Lippincott, 1891.

———. "We Are All Bound Up Together." 1866. *A Brighter Coming Day: A Frances Ellen Watkins Harper Reader.* Ed. Frances Smith Foster. New York: Feminist Press, 1990.

Hartman, Saidiya V. *Scenes of Subjection: Terror, Slavery and Self-Making in Nineteenth-Century America.* New York: Oxford UP, 1997.

Hatton, Louise. "Biographical Sketch." Richardson, *Maria* 91–93.

Haywood, Chanta M. *Prophesying Daughters: Black Women Preachers and the Word, 1823–1913*. Columbia: U of Missouri P, 2003.

Hersch, Blanche Glassman. *The Slavery of Sex: Feminist-Abolitionists in America*. Urbana: U of Illinois P, 1978.

Higginbotham, Evelyn Brooks. *Righteous Discontent: The Women's Movement in the Black Baptist Church, 1890–1920*. Cambridge: Harvard UP, 1993.

Hill, Mike, and Warren Montag. "Introduction." *Masses, Classes and the Public Sphere*. Ed. Mike Hill and Warren Montag. London: Verso, 2000. 1–10.

Hirschfelder, Arlene, and Martha Kreipe de Montano. *The Native American Almanac: A Portrait of Native America Today*. New York: Macmillan, 1993.

The History of Woman Suffrage. Ed. Elizabeth Cady Stanton, Susan B. Anthony, and Matilda Joslyn Gage. 1882. 10 vols. New York: Arno P, 1969.

Holloway, Karla F. C. "The Body Politic." *Subjects and Citizens: Nation, Race, and Gender from* Oroonoko *to Anita Hill*. Ed. Michael Moon and Cathy N. Davidson. Durham: Duke UP, 1995. 482–95.

Holt, Thomas C. "Afterword: Mapping the Black Public Sphere." *The Black Public Sphere*. Ed. Black Public Sphere Collective. Chicago: U of Chicago P, 1995. 325–28.

hooks, bell. *Talking Back: Thinking Feminist, Thinking Black*. Boston: South End, 1989.

Hopkins, Pauline E. "Famous Women of the Negro Race. IV. Some Literary Workers." *The Colored American Magazine* 4 (Mar. 1902): 276–80.

Horton, James Oliver, and Lois E. Horton. *In Hope of Liberty: Culture, Community and Protest Among Northern Free Blacks, 1700–1860*. New York: Oxford UP, 1997.

Humez, Jean McMahon. "Female Preaching and the AME Church, 1820–1852." Humez, *Gifts of Power* 311–27.

———. "Introduction." *Gifts of Power: The Writings of Rebecca Jackson, Black Visionary, Shaker Eldress*. Ed. Jean McMahon Humez. U of Massachusetts P, 1981. 1–64.

Hunter, William R. "Do Not Be Conformed Unto This World: An Analysis of Religious Experience in the Nineteenth-Century African American Spiritual Narrative." *Nineteenth Century Studies* 8 (1994): 75–88.

Hunton, Addie. Employment of Colored Women in Chicago." *The Crisis* 1.3 (Jan. 1911): 24–25.

———. "Negro Womanhood Defended." *Voice of the Negro* 1.7 (July 1904): 280–82.

———. "Women's Clubs. Caring for Young Women." *The Crisis* 2.3 (July 1911): 121–22.

Hurston, Zora Neale. *Mules and Men*. 1935. New York: Harper and Row, 1990.

Hutchinson, George. *The Harlem Renaissance in Black and White*. Cambridge: Belknap, 1995.

Hutton, Frankie. *The Early Black Press in America, 1827–1860*. Westport: Greenwood, 1993.

"Ida B. Wells's Crusade." *New York Sun* 26 July 1894.

"Ida Wells Abroad." *Memphis Appeal-Avalanche* 23 May 1893: 4.

"Introductory." *Provincial Freeman* 24 Mar. 1853.

Jackson, Rebecca Cox. *Gifts of Power: The Writings of Rebecca Jackson, Black Visionary, Shaker Eldress*. 1830-1864. Ed. Jean McMahon Humez. U of Massachusetts P, 1981.

Johnson, Rev. James H. A. "Female Preachers." *AME Church Review* Oct. 1884: 102–5.

Johnston, James H. *Race Relations in Virginia and Miscegenation in the South, 1776–1860*. Amherst: U of Massachusetts P, 1970.

Jones, Beverly Washington, ed. *Quest for Equality: The Life and Writings of Mary Eliza Church Terrell, 1863–1954*. Brooklyn: Carlson, 1990.

Jones, Martha S. *All Bound Up Together: The Woman Question in African American Public Culture, 1830–1900*. Chapel Hill: U of North Carolina P, 2007.

"Just published . . ." *The Liberator* 2.11 (17 Mar. 1832).

Kelley, Robin D. G. *Race Rebels: Culture, Politics, and the Black Working Class*. New York: Free, 1994.

Kellor, Frances A. "Southern Girls in the North: The Problem of Their Protection." *Charities* 13.25 (18 Mar. 1905): 584–85.

Kinealy, Christine. "The Liberator Daniel O'Connell and Anti-Slavery." *History Today* 57.12: 51–57.

Knupfer, Anne Meis. *Toward a Tenderer Humanity and a Nobler Womanhood: African American Women's Clubs in Turn-of-the-Century Chicago*. New York: New York UP, 1996.

Landsman, Gail H. "The 'Other' as Political Symbol: Images of Indians in the Woman Suffrage Movement." *Ethnohistory* 39.3 (Summer 1992): 247–84.

Laqueur, Thomas. "Bodies, Details and the Humanitarian Narrative." *The New Cultural History*. Ed. Lynn Hunt. Berkeley: U of California P, 1989.

Lasser, Carol. "Century of Struggle, Decades of Revision: A Retrospective on Eleanor Flexner's Suffrage History." *Reviews in American History* 15.2 (June 1987): 344–54.

Lebsock, Suzanne. "Women and American Politics, 1880-1920." In *Women, Politics, and Change.* Eds. Louise A. Tilly and Patricia Gurin. New York: Russell Sage Foundation, 1990. 35-62.

"Lecture on American Slavery." a. *Clonmel Chronicle* 16 Apr. 1859: 2.

"Lecture on American Slavery." b. *Waterford Mail* 9 Apr. 1859: 2.

"Lecture on Slavery." *Waterford Mail* 12 Apr. 1859: 3.

Lee, Jarena. *The Life and Religious Experience of Jarena Lee.* 1836. Andrews, *Sisters of the Spirit* 25–48.

———. *Religious Experience and Journal of Mrs Jarena Lee, Giving an Account of Her Call to Preach the Gospel.* 1849. *Spiritual Narratives.* Ed. Susan Houchins. Schomburg Library of Nineteenth-Century Black Women Writers. New York: Oxford UP, 1988.

Lemert, Charles. "Anna Julia Cooper: The Colored Woman's Office." Lemert and Bhan, *Voice* 1-50.

Lemert, Charles and Esme Bhan, eds. *The Voice of Anna Julia Cooper, Including* A Voice from the South *and Other Important Essays, Papers, and Letters.* Boston: Rowman & Littlefield, 1998.

Lerner, Gerda. *Black Women in White America: A Documentary History.* New York: Vintage, 1972.

Levander, Caroline Field. "Bawdy Talk: The Politics of Women's Public Speech in *The Lectures* and *The Bostonians.*" *American Literature* 67.3 (1995): 467–85.

Levine, Lawrence W. *Black Culture and Black Consciousness: Afro-American Folk Thought from Slavery to Freedom.* New York: Oxford UP, 1977.

"Life of Edward Norris Kirk." *American Missionary* 32.2 (Feb. 1878). <http://cdl.library.cornell.edu/cgi-bin/moa/moa-cgi?notisid=ABK5794-0032-35>.

Limpton, Joseph, to Samuel May Jr. Letter. 3 Mar. 1851. Anti-slavery Manuscripts, MSB 1.6, v. 4, no.22. Boston Public Library.

Lincoln, Eric C., and Lawrence H. Mamiya. *The Black Church in the African American Experience.* Durham: Duke UP, 1990.

Linkugel, Wil A., and Martha Solomon. *Anna Howard Shaw: Suffrage Orator and Social Reformer.* Westport: Greenwood, 1991.

Lipscomb, Drema R. "Sojourner Truth: A Practical Public Discourse." *Reclaiming Rhetorica: Women in the Rhetorical Tradition.* Ed. Andrea Lunsford. Pittsburgh: U of Pittsburgh P, 1995. 227–45.

Logan, Shirley Wilson. *"We Are Coming": The Persuasive Discourse of Nineteenth-Century Black Women.* Carbondale: Southern Illinois UP, 1999.

———. "'What Are We Worth': Anna Julia Cooper Defines Black Women's Work at the Dawn of the Twentieth Century." *Black Women and Work.* Ed. Sharon

Harley and the Black Women and Work Collective. New Brunswick: Rutgers, 2002. 146-163.

Lowenberg, James, and Ruth Bogin, eds. *Black Women in Nineteenth-Century American Life: Their Words, Their Thoughts, Their Feelings.* Pennsylvania State UP, 1976.

Mabee, Carleton, with Susan Mabee Newhouse. *Sojourner Truth: Slave, Prophet, Legend.* New York: New York UP, 1993.

Maloney, Thomas N. "African American Migration to the North: New Evidence for the 1910s." *Economic Inquiry* 40.1 (Jan. 2002): 1–11.

Mathes, Valerie Sherer. "Nineteenth-Century Women and Reform: The Women's National Indian Association." *American Indian Quarterly* 14.1 (Winter 1990): 1–18.

Matthews, Victoria Earle. "Some of the Dangers Confronting Southern Girls in the North." *Hampton Negro Conference* 2 (July 1898): 62–69.

May, Samuel, to J. B. Estlin. 2 Feb. 1849. Anti-slavery Manuscripts. MSB 1.6. Boston Public Library.

Mayer, Henry. *All on Fire: William Lloyd Garrison and the Abolition of Slavery.* New York: St. Martin's, 1998.

McCaskill, Barbara. "Introduction: William and Ellen Craft in Transatlantic Literature and Life." *Running a Thousand Miles for Freedom: The Escape of William and Ellen Craft from Slavery, by William Craft and Ellen Craft.* Ed. Barbara McCaskill. Athens: U of Georgia P, 1999. vii–xxv.

———. "'Yours Very Truly': Ellen Craft—The Fugitive as Text and Artifact." *African American Review* 28.4 (1994): 509–29.

McDowell, Deborah. "Transferences—Black Feminist Discourse: The 'Practice' of 'Theory.'" *Feminism Beside Itself.* Ed. Diane Elam and Robyn Wiegman. New York: Routledge, 1995. 93–118.

McHenry, Elizabeth. *Forgotten Readers: Recovering the Lost History of African American Literary Societies.* Durham: Duke UP, 2002.

McKay, Nellie Y. "Nineteenth-Century Black Women's Spiritual Autobiographies: Religious Faith and Self-Empowerment." *Interpreting Women's Lives: Feminist Theory and Personal Narratives.* Ed. Joy Webster Barbre, Amt Farrell, Shirley Nelson Garner, Susan Geiger, Ruth Ellen Boetcher Joeres, Susan M. A. Lyons, Mary Jo Maynes, Pamela Mittlefehldt, Riv-Ellen Prell, and Virginia Steinhagen. Bloomington: Indiana UP, 1989. 139–54.

McMurray, Linda O. *To Keep the Waters Troubled: The Life of Ida B. Wells.* Oxford: Oxford UP, 1998.

Memoir of Mrs Chloe Spear, a Native of Africa, Who Was Enslaved in Childhood, and Died in Boston, January 3, 1815 . . . Aged 65 Years. By a Lady of Boston. Boston: James Loring, 1832.

Midgley, Clare. "British Abolition and Feminism in Transatlantic Perspective." *Woman's Rights and Transatlantic Antislavery in the Era of Emancipation.* Ed. Kathryn Kish Sklar and James Brewer Stewart. New Haven: Yale UP, 2007. 121–39.

———. *Women Against Slavery: The British Campaigns, 1780–1870.* London: Routledge, 1992.

Mindich, David T. Z. *Just the Facts: How "Objectivity" Came to Define American Journalism.* New York: New York UP, 1998.

"The Ministry of the A.M.E. Church." 2000. *A.M.E. Today.* 17 Dec. 2003. <http://www.ame-today.com/abcsofame/ministry.shtml>.

"Miss Ida B. Wells, a negro lady . . ." *Ladies' Pictorial* May1893. Box 8, Folder 10. Ida B. Wells Papers. Special Collections, University of Chicago.

"Miss Remand's [*sic*] Lectures." *Waterford Mail* 29 Mar. 1859: 1.

"Miss Remond's Anti-Slavery Lecture." *Freeman's Journal* 15 Mar. 1859: 3.

"Miss Remond's First Lecture in Dublin." *Anti-Slavery Advocate* 1 Apr. 1859: 221–24.

"Miss S. Remond." *Constitution; or, Cork Advertiser* 16 Apr. 1859: 2.

"Mob Convention in New York." *The History of Woman Suffrage.* Ed. Elizabeth Cady Stanton, Susan B. Anthony, and Matilda Joslyn Gage. 1882. 10 vols. New York: Arno, 1969. 1: 546–77.

Moody, Joycelyn. "On the Road with God: Travel and Quest in Early Nineteenth-Century African American Holy Women's Narratives." *Religion and Literature* 27.1 (1995): 35–51.

———. *Sentimental Confessions: Spiritual Narratives of Nineteenth-Century African American Women.* Athens: U of Georgia P, 2001.

Moses, Wilson Jeremiah. *Black Messiahs and Uncle Toms: Social and Literary Manipulations of a Religious Myth.* University Park: Pennsylvania State UP, 1982.

Mossell, Mrs N. F. [Gertrude]. "Our Woman's Department. Woman Suffrage." *New York Freeman* 26 Dec. 1885: 2.

———. *The Work of the Afro-American Woman.* 1894. New York: Oxford UP, 1988.

Mott, Frank Luther. *American Journalism, A History: 1690–1960.* 3rd ed. New York: Macmillan, 1962.

"MR. EDITOR." *Provincial Freeman* 22 Apr. 1854.

"MR. FREEMAN." *Provincial Freeman* 29 Apr. 1854.

Murphy, Angela F. "Daniel O'Connell and the 'American Eagle' in 1845: Slavery, Diplomacy, Nativism, and the Collapse of America's First Irish Nationalist Movement." *Journal of American Ethnic History* 26.2 (2007): 3–26.

Nelson, Bruce. "'Come Out of Such a Land, You Irishmen': Daniel O'Connell, American Slavery, and the Marking of the 'Irish Race.'" Éire-Ireland 42.1–2 (2007): 58–81.

Neswald, Elizabeth. "Science, Sociability and the Improvement of Ireland: The Galway Mechanics' Institute, 1826–51." *British Society for the History of Science* 39.4 (2006): 503–34.

Neverdon-Morton, Cynthia. *Afro-American Women of the South and the Advancement of the Race, 1895–1925*. Knoxville: U of Tennessee P, 1989.

"The Ninth Crusade." *The Crisis* (Mar. 1923): 213–17.

Norton, Mrs. [Caroline]. "One of Our Legal Fictions." Rpt. in *Provincial Freeman* 10 June 1854.

"Notice." *The Liberator* 3.37 (14 Sept. 1833).

Olund, Eric N. "Public Domesticity During the Indian Reform Era; or, Mrs. Jackson Is Induced to Go to Washington." *Gender Place & Culture: A Journal of Feminist Geography* 9.2 (June 2002): 153–66.

Omolade, Barbara. "Hearts of Darkness." *Powers of Desire: The Politics of Sexuality.* Ed. Ann Snitow et al. New York: Monthly Review, 1983.

"Our Boston Correspondence." *National Anti-Slavery Standard* 11 Sep. 1869.

Oxford English Dictionary. 2nd ed. Prep. J. A. Simpson and E. S. C. Weiner. 20 vols. Oxford: Clarendon, 1989.

Painter, Nell. "*Representing* Truth: Sojourner Truth's Knowing and Becoming Known." *Journal of American History* 81.2 (1994): 461-492.

————."Difference, Slavery, and Memory: Sojourner Truth in Feminist Abolitionism." *The Abolitionist Sisterhood: Women's Political Culture in Antebellum America.* Ed. Jean Fagan Yellin and John C. Van Horne. Ithaca: Cornell UP, 1995. 139–58.

————. *Sojourner Truth: A Life, a Symbol.* New York: Norton, 1996.

Palmer, Phyllis Marynick. "White Women/Black Women: The Dualism of Female Identity and Experience in the United States." *Feminist Studies* 9.1 (1983): 151–70.

Park, You-me, and Gayle Wald. "Native Daughters in the Promised Land: Gender, Race, and the Question of Separate Spheres." *Masses, Classes, and the Public Sphere.* Ed. Mike Hill and Warren Montag. 226–250.

Payne, Daniel A. *History of the African Methodist Episcopal Church.* 1891. Vol. 1. New York: Johnson Reprint, 1968.

Penn, I. Garland. *The Afro-American Press and Its Editors.* Springfield: Willey, 1891.

Peterson, Carla L. *"Doers of the Word": African-American Women Speakers and Writers in the North (1830–1880).* Oxford: Oxford UP, 1995.

Poovey, Mary. *Uneven Developments: The Ideological Work of Gender in Mid-Victorian England.* Chicago: U of Chicago P, 1988.

Potter, Vilma Raskin. *A Reference Guide to Afro-American Publications and Editors, 1827–1946.* Ames: Iowa State UP, 1993.

"The Power of Woman." *AME Church Magazine* 1.2 (1841): 53–59.

"The Power of the Newspaper Press—Slavery." *Provincial Freeman,* Extra, 31 July 1856.

Pride, Armistead S., and Clint C. Wilson II. *A History of the Black Press.* Washington, D.C.: Howard UP, 1997.

"Protection of Girlhood." *Philanthropist* 1 (Oct. 1886): 2. <http://womhist. binghamton.edu/aoc/doc5.htm>.

Quarles, Benjamin. *Black Abolitionists.* Oxford: Oxford UP, 1969.

Raboteau, Albert J. *Slave Religion: The "Invisible Institution" in the Antebellum South.* Oxford: Oxford UP, 1978.

Rael, Patrick. *Black Identity and Black Protest in the Antebellum North.* Chapel Hill: U of North Carolina P, 2002.

Reed, Harry. *Platform for Change: The Foundations of the Northern Free Black Community, 1775–1865.* East Lansing: Michigan State UP, 1994.

Rhodes, Jane. *Mary Ann Shadd Cary: The Black Press and Protest in the Nineteenth Century.* Bloomington: Indiana UP, 1998.

Rice, Alan. "The Cotton that Connects, the Cloth that Binds: Manchester's Civil War, Abe's Statue, and Lubaina Himid's Transnational Polemic." *Atlantic Studies* 4.2 (2007): 285–303.

Richardson, Marilyn. "Introduction." Richardson, *Maria* 1–27.

———. "Maria W. Stewart: America's First Black Woman Political Writer." *Black Women's Intellectual Traditions: Speaking Their Minds.* Ed. Kristin Waters and Carol B. Conaway. Burlington: U of Vermont P, 2007. 13–37.

———, ed. *Maria W. Stewart, America's First Black Woman Political Writer: Essays and Speeches.* Bloomington: Indiana UP, 1987.

———. "Preface." Richardson, *Maria* xiii–xvii.

———. "'What If I Am a Woman?' Maria W. Stewart's Defense of Black Women's Political Activism." *Courage and Conscience: Black and White Abolitionists in Boston.* Ed. Donald M. Jacobs. Bloomington: Indiana UP, 1993. 191–206.

Ripley, C. Peter. "Introduction." *The Black Abolitionist Papers.* Ed. C. Peter Ripley, Jeffery S. Rossbach, Roy E. Finkenbine, Fiona E. Spiers, and Debra Susie. Chapel Hill: U of North Carolina P, 1985. Vol. 1: 3–35.

Robbins, Bruce. "Introduction: The Public as Phantom." *The Phantom Public Sphere.* Ed. Bruce Robbins. Minneapolis: U of Minnesota P, 1993. vii–xxvi.

Robinson, Marius. "Women's Rights Convention. Sojourner Truth." *The Anti-Slavery Bugle* 21 June 1851.

Romero, Lora. *Home Fronts: Domesticity and Its Critics in the Antebellum United States.* Durham: Duke UP, 1997.

Royster, Jacqueline Jones. "To Call a Thing by Its True Name: The Rhetoric of Ida B. Wells." *Reclaiming Rhetorica: Women in the Rhetorical Tradition.* Ed. Andrea Lunsford. Pittsburgh: U of Pittsburgh P, 1995. 167–84.

———. *Traces of a Stream: Literacy and Social Change Among African American Women.* Pittsburgh: U of Pittsburgh P, 2000.

Ryan, Mary P. "Gender and Public Access: Women's Politics in Nineteenth-Century America." *Habermas and the Public Sphere.* Ed. Craig Calhoun. Cambridge: MIT, 1992. 259–89.

———. *Women in Public: Between Banners and Ballots, 1825–1880.* Baltimore: John Hopkins UP, 1990.

Salem, Dorothy. *To Better Our World: Black Women in Organized Reform, 1890–1920.* New York: Carlson, 1990.

Samuels, Ellen. "'A Complication of Complaints': Untangling Disability, Race, and Gender in William and Ellen Craft's *Running a Thousand Miles for Freedom.*" *MELUS* 31.3 (2006): 15–47.

Sanchez-Eppler, Karen. "Bodily Bonds: The Intersecting Rhetorics of Feminism and Abolition." *Representations* 24 (1988): 28–59.

Santamarina, Xiomara. *Belabored Professions: Narratives of African American Working Womanhood.* Chapel Hill: U of North Carolina P, 2005.

Sasson, Diane. *The Shaker Spiritual Narrative.* Knoxville: U of Tennessee P, 1993.

Scarry, Elaine. *The Body in Pain: The Making and Unmaking of the World.* New York: Oxford UP, 1985.

Schechter, Patricia A. *Ida B. Wells-Barnett and American Reform, 1880–1930.* Chapel Hill: U of North Carolina P, 2001.

Scott, Joan. "Fantasy Echo: History and the Construction of Identity." *Critical Inquiry* 27.2 (2001): 284–304.

———. "Universalism and the History of Feminism." *differences* 7.1 (1995): 1-14.

"Sentiment Against Lynching." *Parsons Weekly Blade* 24 May 1894.

Shadd Cary, Mary Ann. "Dear 'C.'" *Provincial Freeman* 21 Oct. 1854.

———. "Fugitive Slaves in Canada." *Provincial Freeman* 25 Mar. 1854.

———. "The Humbug of Reform." *Provincial Freeman* 27 May 1854.

———. "Meeting to Organize the Provincial Union." *Provincial Freeman* 19 Aug. 1854.

———. "Remarks." *Provincial Freeman* 26 Aug. 1854.

———. To Frederick Douglass. *North Star* 23 Mar. 1849.

———. "Trade for Our Boys." *New National Era* 21 Mar. 1872.

———. "Woman's Rights." *Provincial Freeman* 6 May 1854.

"Shame of America." *The Crisis* 25.4 (Feb. 1923): 167–69.

Shammas, Carole. "Re-Assessing the Married Women's Property Acts." *Journal of Women's History* 6.1 (Spring 1994): 9–30.

Shaw, Anna Howard. "Women vs Indians." *The History of Woman Suffrage.* Vol. 4, *1883–1900.* Ed. Susan B. Anthony and Ida Husted Harper. New York: Arno, 1969. 182–83.

Shaw, Stephanie J. "Black Club Women and the Creation of the National Association of Colored Women." *"We Specialize in the Wholly Impossible": A Reader in Black Women's History.* Ed. Darlene Clark Hine, Wilma King, and Linda Reed. New York: Carlson, 1995. 433–47.

———. *What a Woman Ought to Be and Do: Black Professional Women Workers during the Jim Crow Era.* Chicago: U of Chicago P, 1996.

Silone-Yates, Josephine. "Woman as a Factor in the Solution of Race Problems." *The Colored American Magazine* (Feb. 1907): 126–35.

Simien, Evelyn M. "Black Feminist Theory: Charting a Course for Black Women's Studies in Political Science." *Black Women's Intellectual Traditions: Speaking Their Minds.* Ed. Kristin Waters and Carol B. Conaway. Burlington: U of Vermont P, 2007. 419–32.

Sklar, Kathryn Kish. "'Women Who Speak for an Entire Nation': American and British Women Compared at the World Anti-Slavery Convention, London, 1840." *Pacific Historical Review* 59.4 (1990): 453–99.

Smith, Amanda Berry. *An Autobiography: The Story of the Lord's Dealings with Mrs. Amanda Smith the Colored Evangelist.* 1893. Ed. Jualynne E. Dodson. Schomburg Library of Nineteenth-Century Black Women Writers. New York: Oxford UP, 1988.

Smith, Charles Spencer. *A History of the African Methodist Episcopal Church.* 1922. New York: Johnson Reprint, 1968.

Smith, Lucy Wilmot. "Some Female Writers of the Negro Race." *Journalist* 7 (26 Jan. 1889): 4–6. Rpt. as "Women as Journalists." *Indianapolis Freeman* 23 Feb. 1889.

Smith, Sidonie. "Resisting the Gaze of Embodiment: Women's Autobiography in the Nineteenth Century." *American Women's Autobiography: Fea(s)ts of Memory.* Ed. Margo Culley. Madison: U of Wisconsin P, 1992. 75–110.

Smith, Valerie. "Black Feminist Theory and the Representation of the 'Other.'" *Changing Our Own Words.* Ed. Cheryl A. Wall. New Brunswick: Rutgers UP, 1989. 38–57.

Sobel, Mechal. *Trabelin' On: The Slave Journey to an Afro-Baptist Faith.* Princeton: Princeton UP, 1988.

"Sojourner Truth on the Press. To the Editor of the *World.*" *New York World* 13 May 1867.

"Southern Negro Women and Race Co-operation." 28–30 June 1921. Commission on Interracial Cooperation Papers. <http://womhist.binghamton.edu/aswpl/doc7.htm>.

"The *Southern Workman.* . . ." *Southern Workman* 33 (Sep. 1904): 466.

Spillers, Hortense J. "Interstices: A Small Drama of Words." *Pleasure and Danger: Exploring Female Sexuality.* Ed. Carole S. Vance. Boston: Routledge and Kegan Paul, 1984. 73–100.

———. "Mama's Baby, Papa's Maybe: An American Grammar Book." *diacritics* 17 (1987): 65–81.

Squires, Catherine R. "Rethinking the Black Public Sphere: An Alternative Vocabulary for Multiple Public Spheres." *Communication Theory* 12.4 (Nov. 2002): 446–68.

———. "The Black Press and the State: Attracting Unwanted (?) Attention." *Counterpublics and the State.* Eds. Robert Asen and Daniel C. Brouwer. Albany: SUNY P, 2001. 111-136.

Sterling, Dorothy, ed. *We Are Your Sisters: Black Women in the Nineteenth Century.* New York: Norton, 1984.

Stetson, Erlene, and Linda David. *Glorying in Tribulation: The Lifework of Sojourner Truth.* East Lansing: Michigan State UP, 1994.

Stewart, Maria W. "AN ADDRESS, Delivered at the African Masonic Hall in Boston, Feb. 27, 1833. By Mrs Maria W. Stewart." *The Liberator* 3.17 (27 Apr. 1833).

———. "AN ADDRESS, Delivered in the African Masonic Hall, in Boston, Feb. 27, 1833. By Mrs Mara W. Stewart. (Concluded.)" *The Liberator* 3.18 (4 May 1833).

———. "Cause for Encouragement." *The Liberator* 2.28 (14 July 1832).

———. "For the Liberator. AN ADDRESS, Delivered Before the Afric-American Female Intelligence Society of Boston. By Mrs. Maria W. Stewart." *The Liberator* 2.17 (28 Apr. 1832).

———. "LECTURE. Delivered at The Franklin Hall, Boston, September 21st, 1832. By Mrs Maria W. Stewart." *The Liberator* 2.46 (17 Nov. 1832).

———. "Mrs Steward's [*sic*] Essays." *The Liberator* 2.1 (7 Jan. 1832).

———. "Mrs. Stewart's Farewell Address to Her Friends in the City of Boston (1833)." Richardson, *Maria* 65–74.

———. *Religion and the Pure Principles of Morality, the Sure Foundation on Which We Must Build. Productions from the Pen of* MRS. MARIA W. STEWARD [*sic*]*, Widow of the Late James W. Steward, of Boston.* 1831. Richardson, *Maria* 28–42.

Still, William. "Miss M. A. Shadd." *Provincial Freeman* 24 Mar. 1855.

———. *The Underground Railroad.* 1872. New York, Arno, 1968.

Streitmatter, Rodger. "Maria W. Stewart: The First Female African-American Journalist." *Historical Journal of Massachusetts* 21.2 (1993): 44–59.

———. *Raising Her Voice: African-American Women Journalists Who Changed History.* Lexington: UP of Kentucky, 1994.

Strong, Douglas M. *They Walked in the Spirit: Personal Faith and Social Action in America.* Louisville: Westminster John Knox, 1997.

Tamarkin, Elisa. "Black Anglophilia; or, The Sociability of Antislavery." *American Literary History* 14.3 (2002): 444–78.

Tate, Gayle T. *Unknown Tongues: Black Women's Political Activism in the Antebellum Era, 1830–1860.* East Lansing: Michigan State UP, 2003.

Terborg-Penn, Rosalyn. *African American Women in the Struggle for the Vote, 1850–1920.* Bloomington: Indiana UP, 1998.

Terrell, Mary Church. "The Duty of the National Association of Colored Women." *AME Church Review* 16.3 (Jan. 1900). Rpt. in *Can I Get a Witness: Prophetic Religious Voices of African American Women, an Anthology.* Ed. Marcia Riggs. New York: Orbis, 1997. 68–78.

———. "The International Congress of Women Recently Held in Berlin, Germany." *Voice of the Negro* Oct. 1904: 454–61.

———. "Lynching from a Negro's Point of View." *North American Review* 178 (1904): 853–68.

Terry, Esther. "Sojourner Truth: The Person Behind the Libyan Sibyl." *Massachusetts Review* 26.2-3(1985): 425-444.

Thompson, Mildred I. *Ida B. Wells-Barnett: An Exploratory Study of an American Black Woman, 1893–1930.* Brooklyn: Carlson, 1990.

Tickner, Lisa. *The Spectacle of Women: Imagery of the Suffrage Campaign 1907–14.* Chicago: U of Chicago P, 1988.

Tillman, Katherine Davis. "Lines to Ida B. Wells." *Christian Recorder* 5 July 1894: 1.

Tolnay, Stewart E. "The African American 'Great Migration' and Beyond." *Annual Review of Sociology* 29 (2003): 209–32.

Toole, Janet. "Workers and Slaves: Class Relations in South Lancashire in the Time of the Cotton Famine." *Labour History Review* 63.2 (1998): 160–81.

Townes, Emilie M. "Black Women: From Slavery to Womanist Liberation." *In Our Own Voices: Four Centuries of American Women's Religious Writing.* Ed. Rosemary Skinner Keller and Rosemary Radford Ruether. San Francisco: HarperCollins, 1995. 155–205.

Tucker, David. M. "Miss Ida B. Wells and Memphis Lynching." *Phylon* 32.2 (1971): 112–22.

Turner, Victor. *From Ritual to Theatre: The Human Seriousness of Play.* New York: Performing Arts Journal, 1982.

Utley, Ebony A. "Woman Made of Words: The Rhetorical Invention of Maria W. Stewart." *Black Women's Intellectual Traditions: Speaking Their Minds.* Ed. Kristin Waters and Carol B. Conaway. Burlington: U of Vermont P, 2007. 55–71.

Vale, Gilbert. *Fanaticism: Its Source and Influence, Illustrated by the Simple Narrative of Isabella, in the Case of Matthias, Mr and Mrs B. Folger, Mr Pierson, Mr Mills, Catherine, Isabella, &c. &c. A Reply to W. L. Stone with Descriptive Portraits of all the Parties, While at Sing-Sing and at Third Street—Containing the Whole Truth—and Nothing but the Truth.* New York: G. Vale, 1835.

"Views of American Slavery." *Aberdeen Journal* 12 Feb. 1851.

Wade-Gayles, Gloria. "Black Women Journalists in the South, 1880-1905: An Approach to the Study of Black Women's History." *Callaloo* 4.11–13 (1981): 138–52.

Walkowitz, Judith R. *City of Dreadful Delight: Narratives of Sexual Danger in Late-Victorian London.* Chicago: U of Chicago P, 1992.

Waller, Rev. Owen Meredith. *The Episcopal Church and the Colored People: A Statement of Facts.* Washington, D.C.: Emmett C. Jones, 1898.

Ware, Vron. *Beyond the Pale: White Women, Racism and History.* London: Verso, 1992.

Warner, Michael. "The Mass Public and the Mass Subject." *The Phantom Public Sphere.* Ed. Bruce Robbins. Minneapolis: U of Minnesota P, 1993. 234–56.

———. *Publics and Counterpublics.* New York: Zone Books, 2002.

Washington, Mary Helen. "Introduction." *A Voice from the South, by a Black Woman of the South.* Oxford: Oxford UP, 1988.

Waters, Kristin and Carol B. Conaway, eds. *Black Women's Intellectual Traditions: Speaking Their Minds.* Burlington: U of Vermont P, 2007.

Wayman, Alexander W. *Cyclopaedia of African Methodism.* Baltimore: Methodist Episcopal Book Depository, 1882.

Weinauer, Ellen M. "'A Most Respectable Looking Gentleman': Passing, Possession, and Transgression in *Running a Thousand Miles for Freedom.*" *Passing and the Fictions of Identity.* Ed. Elaine K. Ginsberg. Durham: Duke UP, 1996. 37–56.

Wells, Ida B. "Ida B. Wells Abroad. Her Reply to Governor Northen and Others." *Daily Inter-Ocean* [Chicago] 7 July 1894: 13. Box 11, Folder 4. Ida B. Wells Papers. Special Collections, University of Chicago.

———. "Ida B. Wells Abroad. Lectures in Bristol, England, on American Lynch Law." *Daily Inter-Ocean* [Chicago] 19 May 1894: 16. Box 11, Folder 4. Ida B. Wells Papers. Special Collections, University of Chicago.

———. "Ida B. Wells Abroad. Talking in Liverpool Against Lynchers of Negroes." *Daily Inter-Ocean* [Chicago] 9 Apr. 1894. Box 10, Folder 4. Ida B. Wells Papers. Special Collections, University of Chicago.

———. "Ida B. Wells Abroad. The Bishop of Manchester on American Lynching." *Daily Inter-Ocean* [Chicago] 28 Apr. 1894. Box 1, Ida B. Wells-Barnett File. Miscellaneous American Letters and Papers. Schomburg Center, New York Public Library.

———. "Ida B. Wells Abroad. The Nemesis of Southern Lynchers Again in England." *Daily Inter-Ocean* [Chicago] 2 Apr. 1894. Rpt. in Duster 127–31.

———. "Lynching: Our National Crime." 1909. Rpt. in Thompson 261–65.

———. "Lynch Law in All Its Phases." *Our Day* 11.65 (May 1893): 333–47.

———. *Lynch Law in Georgia. By Ida B. Wells-Barnett; A Six Weeks' Record in the Center of Southern Civilization, as Faithfully Chronicled by the "Atlanta Journal" and the "Atlanta Constitution." Also the Full Report of Louis P. Le Vin, the Chicago Detective Sent to Investigate the Burning of Samuel Hose, the Torture and Hanging of Elijah Strickland, the Colored Preacher, and the Lynching of Nine Men for Alleged Arson.* Chicago: Ida B. Wells-Barnett, 1899.

———. "Lynch Law in the United States." *Birmingham Daily Post* 14 May 1894. Box 8, Folder 10. Ida B. Wells Papers. Special Collections, University of Chicago.

———. "The Negro's Case in Equity." *Independent* 26 Apr. 1900: 1010–11.

———. *A Red Record: Tabulated Statistics and Alleged Causes of Lynching in the United States, 1892–1893–1894.* 1895. Rpt. in *Selected Works of Ida B. Wells-Barnett.* Ed. Trudier Harris. New York: Oxford UP, 1991. 138–252.

———. *Southern Horrors: Lynch Law in All Its Phases.* 1892. Rpt. in *Selected Works of Ida B. Wells-Barnett.* Ed. Trudier Harris. New York: Oxford UP, 1991. 14–45.

Wiegman, Robyn. *American Anatomies: Theorizing Race and Gender.* Durham: Duke UP, 1995.

"William and Ellen Craft." *The Liberator* 26 Sep. 1851.

Williams, Fannie Barrier. "The Awakening of Women." *AME Church Review* Apr. 1897: 392–398.

———. "Great Britain's Compliment to American Colored Women." *The Woman's Era* 1.5 (Aug. 1894): 1.

———. "The Intellectual Progress of the Colored Women of the United States Since the Emancipation Proclamation." 1893. *Lift Every Voice: African American Oratory, 1787–1900.* Ed. Philip S. Foner and Robert James Branham. Tuscaloosa: U of Alabama P, 1998. 761–71.

———. "Social Bonds in the 'Black Belt' of Chicago." *Charities* 15.1(7 Oct. 1905): 40–44.

———. "The Need for Social Settlement Work for the City Negro." *Southern Workman* 33 (Sep. 1904): 501–506.

Wolcott, Victoria W. *Remaking Respectability: African American Women in Interwar Detroit* Chapel Hill: U of North Carolina P, 2001.

Wolseley, Roland E. *The Black Press, U.S.A.* 2nd ed. Ames: Iowa State UP, 1990.

"Woman's Convention." *The Liberator* 13 June 1851.

"Woman's Rights Convention Meeting at the Broadway Tabernacle." *New York Daily Times* 8 Sep. 1853.

"Woman Suffrage: Proceedings of the Equal Rights Convention." *New York World* 11 May 1867.

Wood, Marcus. *Blind Memory: Visual Representations of Slavery in England and America, 1780–1865.* Manchester: Manchester UP, 2000.

Wright, Richard R., Jr. *Centennial Encyclopaedia of the African Methodist Episcopal Church.* Philadelphia: Book Concern of the AME Church, 1916.

Yee, Shirley J. *Black Women Abolitionists: A Study in Activism, 1828–1860.* Knoxville: U of Tennessee P, 1992.

Yellin, Jean Fagan. *Women and Sisters: The Antislavery Feminists in American Culture.* New Haven: Yale UP, 1989.

Young, Iris Marion. "Impartiality and the Civic Public: Some Implications of Feminist Critiques of Moral and Political Theory." *Feminism as Critique: On the Politics of Gender in Late Capitalist Societies.* Ed. Seyla Benhabib and Drucilla Cornell. London: Polity, 1987. 57–76.

———. *Justice and the Politics of Difference.* Princeton: Princeton UP, 1990.

Zackodnik, Teresa C. *The Mulatta and the Politics of Race.* Jackson: U of Mississippi P, 2004.

Index

Numbers in *italics* indicate portraits.

Press, Platform, Pulpit was designed and typeset on a Macintosh OS 10.5 computer system using InDesign software. The body text is set in 10.5/13.5 Adobe Garamond Pro and display type is set in Aspire. This book was designed and typeset by Stephanie Thompson and manufactured by Thomson-Shore, Inc.